Contents

KT-524-660

Introduction to

Cyprus

Birthplace of Aphrodite, Cyprus has seduced and inspired generations of travellers. From Mycenean Greeks and invading Persians to sunburnt Crusaders, Ottoman pashas and, latterly, British and Russian expats, each has left their mark. Yet as well as a complex, multilayered past, the word "Cyprus" also conjures up images of dazzling beaches, shimmering blue seas, endless summers and tables groaning under platters of meze and bottles of sweet chilled wine.

And it is to this touristic idyll that thousands return each year. **British visitors** in particular warm to not just the climate but the familiar traces of home: cars driving on the left, red pillar boxes and even the comforting sight of Marks & Spencer amid the palms and searing heat – a legacy of decades of colonial rule. Another aspect of the island's reputation, either enticing or off-putting depending on your interests, is as a hedonistic, lager-fuelled heaven/hell. A heady mix of cheap flights, cheaper drinks and bored squaddies from Britain's two military bases on the island has inevitably led to some frankly grim scenes at many resorts. Yet, determined action by the local authorities in places like Agia Napa, combined with clubbers inevitably moving on to the next big thing, has led recently to a much more sedate ambience.

Venture beyond the resort restaurants knocking out fish and chips, pizza and, more recently, Russian borscht, and it's not hard to find another Cyprus. Traces of the exotic and Levantine are never far away from elegantly ruined Lusignan and Venetian **castles** and teetering **Islamic minarets** to cool **mountain villages** hiding sacred icons from the very first days of Christianity. The other key attraction is the Cypriots themselves, who, whether Greek or Turkish in ancestry seem to have a shared DNA programmed to **welcome visitors**, particularly those with youngsters in tow – if eating out with your kids, don't expect the tutting and disapproving glances you may be used to at home. And if you are travelling alone, be prepared to answer countless questions about your family, occupation, even your salary. Cypriots have few inhibitions about satisfying their curiosity,

ABOVE GIRNE (KYRENIA) HARBOUR

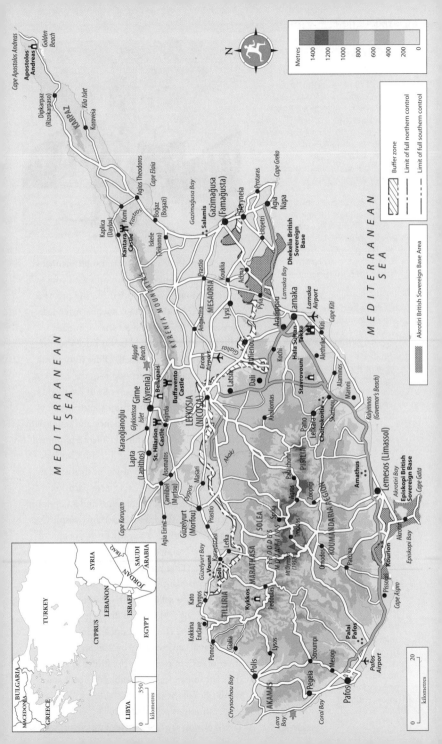

FACT FILE

• Cyprus, with a land area of 9251 square kilometres, is the third largest island in the Mediterranean. Its nearest neighbours are Turkey (75km) and Syria (105km) respectively. The capital, Lefkosia or Nicosia is over 900km from Athens and only 250km from Beirut. The island's highest point, at 1952m, is Mount Olympus.

• The official population (of the whole island) stands at just under 900,000, of which 75.4 percent are Greek Cypriot (and therefore Orthodox Christian), ten percent Turkish Cypriot (and therefore Muslim) and 14.6 percent expats.

• The government of the Republic of Cyprus (and therefore de jure of the whole island) is a democracy which, since 2004, has been a member of the EU. North Cyprus, occupied by Turkey since 1974, has declared itself to be the "Turkish Republic of North Cyprus", but is recognized internationally only by Turkey. Since 2003 the number of crossing points on the dividing (and UN-administered) Green Line has increased to seven. Attempts to reunite the island are on-going.

• Over 1 million Britons visit Cyprus each year (42 percent of total arrivals). The fastest growing group of visitors are Russians (over 470,000 in 2012).

• Famous people of Cypriot origin include singers George Michael, Yusuf Islam (Cat Stevens), Peter Andre and Tulisa Contostavlos (N-Dubz), actress Angela Bowie (ex-wife of David), sportspersons Marco Baghdatis (tennis) and Muzzy Izzet (Premiership football), celebrity chef George Calombaris (Masterchef Australia), businessmen Stelios Haji-Ioannou (founder of easyJet) and Asil Nadir (of Polly Peck fame) and artist Tracey Emin.

and it is almost certain that your mild-mannered interrogator will have a connection with your own country – cousins who work there, siblings who are at university there, or even whole extended parts of the family who have settled abroad.

Beyond the smiles there is also a deep-rooted attachment to the land itself. Older readers will have memories of the period, from the 1950s to the 1970s, when Cyprus was one of the world's major trouble spots. First came the struggle by Greek Cypriots for **independence** and **union with Greece**, then intercommunal violence prompted by fears among the minority Turkish Cypriots, and finally the **Turkish invasion** of the island in 1974 which resulted in its de facto partition between a Turkish Cypriot north and a Greek Cypriot south. Bitterness caused by the split lives on. Yet, while this is a tragedy for the people of Cyprus, the easing of tensions and the **opening up of the Green Line** between north and south during the early years of the twenty-first century gives the island a unique selling point – it is now possible to include both sides of the divide in any planned holiday. Where else, for example, can you visit two "capital" cities simply by walking down a street or take in two distinct cultures in a single day? For some ideas on combining north and south sides of the islands see p.20; for practicalities see p.28 and p.200.

ABOVE AGIOS LAZARUS, LARNAKA **OPPOSITE** VIEW FROM BUFFAVENTO CASTLE, KYRENIA MOUNTAINS

THE ROUGH GUIDE TO

Cyprus

written and researched by

Jos Simon

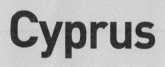

roughguides.com

Where to go

One of the great advantages of Cyprus as a holiday destination is that it's a relatively small island offering a huge variety of attractions, scenery and activities linked together by an **excellent road system**. Wherever you stay, you can get to pretty much anywhere else with a minimum of fuss.

The vast majority of tourists begin their trip on the narrow coastal strip in the south, which hosts the main towns of **Larnaka**, **Lemesos** and **Pafos**, each with a historic old town, promenade and popular beaches. Beyond them, to the north, foothills rise to the island's main mountain range, the **Troodos Massif**, dotted with villages, churches and monasteries. To the west of the island is a plateau covered in **vineyards**, the great wilderness forest of **Tiliria** and the stark empty beauty of the **Akamas Peninsula**. North of the Troodos (and lying within Turkish-occupied north Cyprus), lie the more impressive but less lofty mountains of the **Kyrenia Range**. Beyond here is the even narrower northern coastal strip on which Girne/Kyrenia is by far the most important and most beautiful town. To the east is the broad and largely flat **Mesaorian Plain** on which stands the island's divided capital **Nicosia**, known today as Lefkosia (south) or Lefkoşa (north); further east is the crumbling port city of **Famagusta/Gazimağusa**, with its range of pretty and not-so-pretty ruins, and the long, tapering **Karpaz Peninsula**, home to wild donkeys and far-flung villages.

ABOVE CAPE GREKO

Author picks

Our intrepid author has visited every corner of Cyprus, north and south, to bring you some unique travelling experiences. These are some of his personal favourites.

Spectacular ruins On headlands high above the azure Mediterranean, the Palace of Vouni in the north (p.230) and Ancient Kourion in the south (p.99) take some beating.

Unexpected pleasures Pafos Zoo (p.132) is a delight even if you don't normally like zoos, as are the naive sculptures and paintings of Costas Argyrou in the village of Mazotos (p.72). Don't miss, also, the quirky folk museums housed in many Cypriot villages: two of the best are to be found in Agia Varvara, south of Lefkosia (p.193), and Steni, south of Polis (p.141).

Waterfall walk The Kaledonia Trail in the lofty Troodos Mountains (see box, p.151) takes you to the highest waterfall on the island – a welcome escape from the heat.

Castle heaven Though it lacks the sheer wow factor (and crowds) of St Hilarion (p.220), little-visited Buffavento Castle (p.223) can't be beaten for atmosphere.

Marvellous marinas Small boat harbours, often hosting a colourful collection of fishing vessels and lined with seafood restaurants are one of the highlights of the island. Try low-key Lakki (p.138) or picturesque Potamos Liopetriou (p.61).

People-watching Cyprus is a great place for sipping a frappe (iced coffee) and watching the world go by. Try Gazimağusa's central square (p.234), Lemesos's newly remodelled town centre (p.82), the cafés around stunning Bellapais Abbey (p.224), or Lefkosa's renovated Buyuk Han (p.205).

Sweet treats Cypriots have a notoriously sweet tooth – try the local version of Turkish Delight, *loukoumia*, on sale in Geroskipou (see box, p.125), unbeatable ice cream at McKenzie Beach in Larnaka (p.53) or heavenly baklava at *Petek* in Gazimağusa (p.238).

> Our author recommendations don't end here. We've flagged up our favourite places – a perfectly sited hotel, an atmospheric café, a special restaurant – throughout the guide, highlighted with the ★ symbol.

FROM TOP ANCIENT KOURION; LOUKOUMIA "CYPRUS DELIGHT"

For traditional sun, sea and sand holidays, you have an extensive choice – in the south, **Protaras** and **Agia Napa** east of Larnaka, the beaches either side of Lemesos, Pafos and its satellite **Coral Bay** are packed with **resorts** offering a range of activities; in the north, the coast either side of Girne and north of Gazimağusa offers more of the same. For smaller hotels with a more individual character, try the north coast around **Polis** and the Akamas Peninsula, or the **hill villages** of the Troodos Mountains which offer traditional homes converted into guesthouses.

For a taste of Cyprus's newly developed **restaurant scene** head to Lemesos, the island's gastronomic capital. South Lefkosia also boasts several cool cafés and Cyprus's best **shopping**, while the northern towns of Girne and Gazimağusa provide relaxed harbourside dining. If your particular interest is in **history**, you'll find that virtually every region has its Roman (or earlier) ruin, its Byzantine church, a Crusader castle or Ottoman mosque, plus some grand British colonial architecture. If you're a hiker, make for the Troodos or Kyrenia mountains; golfers will enjoy the fine courses in Pafos and Girne. Wherever you are based, look out for the colourful religious and village **festivals** that take place across the island in spring, summer and autumn.

In terms of what to avoid, be aware that certain southern resorts (especially parts of Lemesos) can be quite sleazy, (dominated, it's said, by the Russian mafia), with dubious "gentlemen's clubs" and working girls operating openly in the streets. North Cyprus has also developed a reputation for vice and more obviously gambling; its dozens of **casinos** attract not only Turks from the mainland but also, perhaps surprisingly, hedonists from the south.

ABOVE LOFOU, TROODOS MOUNTAINS

When to go

The **tourist season** in Cyprus lasts from April to October. During this time there should be no trouble getting flights and hotels, all the attractions, restaurants and so on will be open, and there should be numerous activities and festivals to keep you occupied. The downside is, of course, overcrowding and inflated prices. Given a choice, try to avoid the fierce **August heat** (remember, Cyprus is just off the coast of the Middle East). If school holidays oblige you to visit the island in late July/August, make sure you're in an air-conditioned hotel and are driving an air-conditioned car. The **autumn**, too, can be remarkably hot and humid, so don't bank on cool, pleasant weather in September or even October. Pick of the times to visit Cyprus has got to be the **spring**, when skies are blue, the air is warm and balmy, the uplands are a luxuriant green, the streams and reservoirs are full of water, and there are wild flowers everywhere. To further refine your choice, try if possible to be in Cyprus during the **Greek Easter** – it's a major celebration in the Orthodox calendar, and there are interesting and picturesque events going on in towns and villages across the island. Much of this advice applies to the **north** as well as the south, though festivals will in general be Muslim rather than Christian, and the north coast can be cooler than the rest of the island thanks to mountain breezes from the Kyrenia Range.

During **winter** your experience of Cypriot life is likely to be far more authentic and less touristy, but a lot of places will be shut, and the weather will be more unsettled and even quite cold – a plus if you're there to avail yourself of the island's limited skiing opportunities, but a bit of a pain otherwise.

AVERAGE MONTHLY MAXIMUM TEMPERATURES

	Jan	Feb	March	April	May	June	July	Aug	Sept	Oct	Nov	Dec
COASTAL (LEMESOS)												
Max °C	17	17	19	22	25	29	31	31	29	27	22	18
Max °F	63	62	66	80	77	84	88	88	84	81	72	65
INLAND (LEFKOSIA)												
Max °C	15	16	19	24	29	34	37	37	33	29	22	17
Max °F	60	60	66	75	85	94	99	98	92	84	72	63
HILLY AREAS (AGROS)												
Max °C	10	11	14	19	24	29	32	32	28	24	17	12
Max °F	51	51	58	66	75	84	89	89	83	75	63	54

things not to miss

It's not possible to see everything that Cyprus has to offer in one trip – and we don't suggest you try. What follows is a selective and subjective taste of the island's highlights: superb ancient and religious sites, unforgettable scenery and energetic activities. All highlights have a page reference to take you straight into the Guide, where you can find out more. Coloured numbers refer to chapters in the Guide section.

1

1 TURTLE-WATCHING
Page 220

Beaches in both the south and the north represent some of the last Mediterranean nesting places of green and loggerhead turtles.

2 THE AKAMAS PENINSULA
Page 133

With no main roads, few people and a spectacular coastline, this area is a pleasant contrast to the more developed and crowded parts of the island.

3 BELLAPAIS
Page 224

Made famous by Lawrence Durrell, who once lived here, Bellapais is beautifully set around its medieval monastery.

4 EASTER
Page 32

Easter is the most important festival in the Greek Orthodox calendar, and it is celebrated across the republic, often with lavish processions.

5 GIRNE (KYRENIA)
Page 211

Undoubtedly the most picturesque port on the island, with a perfect harbour backed by the majestic Kyrenia Mountains.

6 HIKING
Page 33
Cyprus has some top-quality hiking trails, particularly in the Troodos Massif – even in high summer, the altitude makes for a pleasant walking climate.

7 LEMESOS RESTAURANTS
Page 94
The south's great multicultural port is developing a reputation as the gourmet capital of the island.

8 BUYUK HAN
Page 205
This beautifully renovated "Great Inn" at the heart of Lefkosa's old town is a great place to shop or simply unwind.

9 PAINTED CHURCHES OF THE TROODOS MOUNTAINS
Page 156
These beautifully painted wooden churches have been granted UNESCO World Heritage status.

10 WINE TASTING
Page 92
Follow one of six wine-tasting routes, drop into the Cypriot Wine Museum or throw yourself into the bacchanal of the Lemesos Wine Festival.

11 ST HILARION
Page 220
A fantastical castle, said to have been the inspiration for Walt Disney's Magic Kingdom.

12 KYKKOS MONASTERY
Page 157
Of the dozens of monasteries in Cyprus, Kykkos is the most captivating.

14

15

16

17

21

18 HALA SULTAN TEKKE
Page 53
A perfectly proportioned mosque, sitting among elegant palm trees on the edge of Larnaka's blinding-white salt lake.

19 CAFÉ CULTURE
Pages 30 & 188
From small village *kafenions* occupied by old men sipping strong coffee to smart Nicosia establishments packed with the young and stylish, café culture flourishes across the island.

20 PAFOS MOSAICS
Page 116
These stunningly vivid mosaics give an insight into the life of the Roman elite on the island.

21 GAZIMAĞUSA (FAMAGUSTA)
Page 231
One of Cyprus's great cities, where modern life takes place among ruins generated by the Ottoman siege of the city over four centuries ago.

22 NORTH COAST BEACHES
Page 246
Cyprus has hundreds of beaches, though arguably the finest – such as Golden Sands – are strung along the north coast and Karpaz Peninsula.

22

Itineraries

Given its relatively compact size, Cyprus rewards those with a sense of wanderlust. Within an hour or so's drive you can leave the beach and find yourself exploring a cool mountain monastery or wandering the streets of an ancient Roman city. The following itineraries can all be done within a fortnight, giving you a taste of both sides of the island.

THE GRAND TOUR

Two weeks in Cyprus and not sure where to start? Our Grand Tour puts you on the right track.

❶ **Larnaka** Home to the island's biggest airport, Larnaka is the inevitable start point for many visitors to Cyprus. However, its elegant promenade, beautiful Agios Lazaros cathedral, ancient ruins, and a vibrant resort are reason to linger. **See p.47**

❷ **Lemesos** Cyprus's second city, with a reputation for great restaurants, has transformed itself recently through sympathetic city-centre development into the definition of laidback Mediterranean living. **See p.82**

❸ **The Troodos Mountains** Small villages, lovely monasteries and churches, cool mountain air, the Troodos Massif offers a startling contrast to the more hectic coast. **See p.146**

❹ **Pafos** Known for its family-friendly resorts, Pafos has, among the hotels, shops and restaurants, a pretty harbour, some world-class historical monuments and a fascinating hinterland of small villages.
See p.110

❺ **Girne (Kyrenia)** The most beautiful harbour town on the island, and a good introduction to life in north Cyprus, Girne has a stunning castle, a relaxed atmosphere and offers wonderful days out to St Hilarion Castle and Bellapais Abbey. **See p.211**

❻ **Nicosia (Lefkosia/Lefkoşa)** Cyprus's capital, with a wealth of monuments, museums and good shopping and eating, can, for the first time since 1974, be treated as a single city: visit either from Girne or from Larnaka. You can cross from one side to the other in a matter of minutes. **See p.170 & p.198**

❼ **Gazimağusa (Famagusta)** An ancient port city defined by its elegantly ruined old town, pounded by the Ottomans in 1571. Nearby are the magnificent ruins of Ancient Salamis and also the unsettling sight of Varosha, derelict since 1974. **See p.231**

EAST CYPRUS

East Cyprus, particularly Larnaka district, boasts some of the island's finest beaches, the party town of Agia Napa and several crossing points to the north.

❶ **Agia Napa** Once the archetypal 18–30 resort, Agia Napa has morphed into a more sophisticated desination with a surprising smattering of museums and other attractions. **See p.58**

❷ **Larnaka** Worth a day or two for its promenade, town centre beach and marina, and also its old fort, Pierides museum and Agios Lazaros Church. **See p.47**

ABOVE COAST ROAD, KARPAZ PENINSULA

❸ Nicosia Take a walking tour of both north and south sides of the city, then drive across the Green Line and north to Girne, stopping off at St Hilarion Castle on the way. **See p.176**

❹ The Karpaz Peninsula Explore the villages and small-scale sights of the Karpaz Peninsula. Look out for its wild donkeys, and press on to lonely Apostolos Andreas monastery, both the easternmost and the northernmost point on the island. **See p.244**

❺ Salamis You could spend an entire day exploring the ancient city of Salamis, the nearby Royal Tombs, Monastery of St Barnabas and the ruins of Enkomi-Alasia – all within a couple of kilometres of each other. **See p.238**

❻ Gazimağusa (Famagusta) A modern city with an old town at its heart, a place for strolling, sitting in cafés, and admiring the historical ruins. **See p.231**

❼ Derynia Cross back into the republic at Agios Nikolaos, drive around the Kokkinochoria (red villages), and drop into the Cultural Centre of Occupied Famagusta to take a look at Varosha from the other side. **See p.69**

WEST CYPRUS

The west side of the island presents untouched wilderness, lively resorts and some of the island's most important archeological sites.

❶ Pafos With an airport second in importance only to Larnaka, Pafos is the best place to start a tour of the west. Don't miss the town's spectacular UNESCO-listed Roman mosaics, important early Christian remains, eerie Tombs of the Kings or, just to the southeast, the ruins of Palaipafos and pretty Petra tou Romiou, birthplace of Aphrodite. **See p.110**

❷ Polis Driving from Pafos to Polis, take time to look at the Monastery of Agios Neofytos, Pafos Zoo, and the numerous villages, known for their traditions and their wine, in between. Polis is also the gateway to the Akamas Peninsula. **See p.136**

❸ Kato Pyrgos Having driven northeast around Chrysochou Bay, through the villages of Pomos and Pachyammos, stay for a while in quiet Kato Pyrgos, exploring from here the forests of Tiliria. **See p.140**

❹ Vouni and Soloi Cross the Green Line into north Cyprus at Limnitis/Yesilirmak, and take time to look first at the remains of the Palace of Vouni, then of Soloi. Continue to Güzelyurt, an unpretentious market town with an interesting museum. **See p.228 & p.230**

❺ The northern Troodos After Güzelyurt, cross back into the south at Zodeia/Astromeritis and head up into the northern Troodos regions of Marathasa and Solea, staying perhaps in Kakopetria. Head south to the coastal motorway, then west to Pafos Airport and your flight home. **See p.154 & p.159**

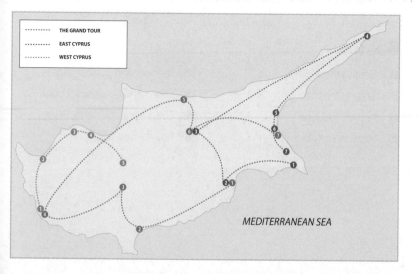

··········	THE GRAND TOUR
··········	EAST CYPRUS
··········	WEST CYPRUS

MEDITERRANEAN SEA

GOATS CROSSING, TROODOS FOOTHILLS

Basics

Getting there

Although the bulk of foreign visitors to Cyprus arrive on a package tour, you can also find competitive deals by arranging your own flights and accommodation. The republic has two international airports (Larnaka and Pafos), and there are frequent direct flights to both from London, Manchester and numerous regional airports in the UK. Other major hubs for Cyprus include Athens, Amsterdam and Brussels. Turkish-occupied north Cyprus (the "TRNC") has one international airport at Ercan to which there are no direct flights other than from Turkey. A ferry service also links Turkey with north Cyprus.

Since Cyprus is a smallish island, and has an excellent motorway system joining all the main towns and holiday areas, price can be as much of a factor as transfer times in choosing your airport. However, Larnaka is the biggest and busiest, and therefore offers the widest choice of flights and arrival times and links with the rest of the island.

There are no direct flights to Cyprus from the US, Canada, South Africa, Australia or New Zealand, so journeys involve at least one change of plane, often in London, Athens or Dubai.

Flights from the UK and Ireland

Many British airports offer flights either to Larnaka, Pafos or both, though some are restricted to the summer months. Flight times to Cyprus from London are usually around 4hr 30min. Flights from Ireland require at least one, and often two, stops, and therefore take the best part of a day. Add another 40min for flights to Ercan in north Cyprus which must touch down in Turkey first. Costs can vary enormously, coming in as low as £150 return during low season, but soaring in summer to £300 or more, though with an average of £250–300. Fares can also jump during the Greek Orthodox Easter (not always the same as the Western European

Easter) as expats flood home for this most important of festivals. Of course many of the bargain rates from budget carriers become increasingly less so once you've paid extra for your hold luggage, meals, your choice of seat and so on.

TO LARNACA AND PAFOS

British Airways Ⓦ ba.com. London Heathrow and Manchester to Larnaka (and Pafos in the summer).

Cyprus Airways Ⓦ cyprUSir.com. Larnaka and Pafos from London Heathrow and Manchester.

easyJet Ⓦ easyjet.com. Larnaka from London Gatwick and Pafos from London Gatwick, Luton, Manchester, Bristol and Edinburgh.

First Choice Airways Ⓦ firstchoice.co.uk. Pafos from Gatwick, Manchester, Birmingham, Glasgow, Doncaster (all year). Larnaka from Bristol, Gatwick, Manchester, Newcastle (April–Oct).

Jet2 Ⓦ jet2.com. Flights to Larnaka (from Leeds and Manchester) and Pafos (East Midlands, Manchester, Leeds, Newcastle, Glasgow).

Monarch Airlines Ⓦ monarch.co.uk. Larnaka (from Birmingham, Manchester, Luton, Gatwick) and Pafos (from Birmingham, Manchester, Gatwick).

Ryanair Ⓦ ryanair.com. Pafos from Stansted.

Thomas Cook Airlines Ⓦ thomascook.com. Larnaka and Pafos from London Gatwick and most regional airports: Aberdeen, Belfast, Birmingham, Bristol, Cardiff, East Midlands, Glasgow, Leeds/Bradford, Manchester and Newcastle.

Thomson Ⓦ thomson.co.uk. To Larnaca and Pafos from London Gatwick and Stansted plus many UK regional airports: Aberdeen, Belfast, Birmingham, Bristol, Cardiff, East Midlands, Exeter, Glasgow, Leeds/Bradford, Manchester and Newcastle. Also from Dublin.

TO ERCAN (NORTH CYPRUS)

Atlasjet Ⓦ atlasjet.com. Stansted to Ercan via Istanbul.

Pegasus Ⓦ flypgs.com. Stansted to Ercan via Istanbul or Antalya.

Turkish Airlines Ⓦ turkishairlines.com. Ercan via Istanbul from London Gatwick and Heathrow plus Manchester and Birmingham.

Flights from the US and Canada

There are no direct flights from the US and Canada to Cyprus. North American visitors must therefore travel via London, Athens, or other European hub airports. Numerous airlines offer one- or two-stop flights, and round-trip costs can vary between US$1300 and US$2000 from New York and US$2200 to US$3100

TRAVEL TO NORTH CYPRUS

The Cypriot government issues dire warnings about using the north's Ercan airport in terms both of safety and of legal consequences, pointing out that the flights from Turkey breach UN Security Council resolutions. This, however, seems not to worry the increasing number of visitors who travel there. Since the relaxation of controls regarding crossing the Green Line from south to north (see p.28), Larnaka has become a good base from which to drop into the north. The north is also accessible by sea from the Turkish mainland, with routes to Girne and Gazimağusa.

A BETTER KIND OF TRAVEL

At Rough Guides we are passionately committed to travel. We believe it helps us understand the world we live in and the people we share it with – and of course tourism is vital to many developing economies. But the scale of modern tourism has also damaged some places irreparably, and climate change is accelerated by most forms of transport, especially flying. All Rough Guides' flights are carbon-offset, and every year we donate money to a variety of environmental charities.

from Los Angeles, though the cheapest fares tend to be from the smaller airports – Newark, New Jersey, for example, has fares that start at around US$840. Flights from Toronto, Montreal and Vancouver start at under Can$1000. The best deals from North America to Cyprus seem to be from American Airlines (Ⓦ americanairlines.co.uk), Delta (Ⓦ delta.com), Air Canada (Ⓦ aircanada.com), Lufthansa (Ⓦ lufthansa .com) and British Airways (Ⓦ ba.com).

Flights from Australia, New Zealand and South Africa

Travelling from Australia, New Zealand or South Africa to Cyprus involves at least one stopover, usually via a Middle Eastern hub such as Dubai. One-stop flights from Australia start at around AUS$2000; from New Zealand NZ$2500. The cheapest route from South Africa is Johannesburg via Dubai with prices starting at R7000. Emirates (Ⓦ emirates), code-sharing with BA and Qantas, appear to offer the most competitive deals.

Ferries

Since concerns about international terrorism closed its ferry ports back in 2001, the only viable way of visiting the south, unless you have access to an ocean-going yacht, is by air. However, there are several sea routes between the Turkish mainland and north Cyprus, with passenger-only ferries being a lot quicker than car ferries: Mersin–Gazimağusa (Mon, Wed & Fri, with return trips on Tues, Thurs & Sun); Tasucu –Girne (daily); Alanya–Girne (Mon & Thurs).

Agents and operators

FLIGHT AGENTS

North South Travel Ⓦ northsouthtravel.co.uk. Friendly,

competitive travel agency, offering discounted fares worldwide. Profits are used to support projects in the developing world, especially the promotion of sustainable tourism.

STA Travel Ⓦ statravel.co.uk. Worldwide specialists in independent travel; also student IDs, travel insurance, car rental, rail passes, and more. Good discounts for students and under-26s.

Trailfinders Ⓦ trailfinders.com. One of the best-informed and most efficient agents for independent travellers.

Travel CUTS Ⓦ travelcuts.com. Canadian youth and student travel firm.

USIT Ireland Ⓦ usit.ie. Ireland's main student and youth travel specialists.

CYPRUS SPECIALISTS

Anatolian Sky Holidays Ⓦ anatolianskyholidays.co.uk. North Cyprus specialist with a choice of hotels in Girne and Gazimağusa, with flights to Larnaka Airport.

Amathus Holidays Ⓦ amathusholidays.co.uk. Hotel packages for all the main resorts, including Lakki, Polis and Pissouri.

Cyplon Holidays Ⓦ cyplon.co.uk. Wide choice of resort packages across the south, with useful online "Holiday Finder" facility.

Cyprus Active Ⓦ cyprUSctive.com. Range of activities – walking, cycling, horseriding, paragliding, scuba diving, cooking.

Cyprus Direct Ⓦ cyprusdirectholidays.com. North Cyprus specialist offering flights to Ercan and hotels mainly but not exclusively in the Girne area.

Cyprus Villages Ⓦ cyprusvillages.com.cy. Offers not only traditional accommodation, but also activity-based holidays: cycling, walking and yoga.

Sun Island Tours Ⓦ sunislandtours.com.au. Australian-based company specializing in Middle Eastern and Med holidays including packages to the most popular Cypriot holiday areas.

Sunvil Ⓦ sunvil.co.uk. The premier tour operator for Cyprus, offering mainly self-catering villa and agrotourism holidays. Look out for their brochure "Real Cyprus".

THE NORTH/SOUTH DIVIDE AND THE "TRNC"

After its occupation by the Turkish army, the north declared itself to be the "Turkish Federated State of Cyprus" before unilaterally declaring independence in 1983 as the "Turkish Republic of North Cyprus". This title has no international validity, and is strongly resented by the Republic of Cyprus, the only legitimate government of the whole island. For ease of reference we have largely referred to the TRNC as "the north" and the rest of the island, that controlled by the republic government, as "the south". Where the title TRNC is used it is for convenience, and implies no endorsement of the Turkish occupation.

Getting around

The bulk of visitors to Cyprus rely on tour-company coaches to get around. Independent travellers have a choice of renting vehicles (cars/motorbikes/ scooters/quad bikes), catching buses, or taking taxis. For the more intrepid, walking and cycling are also options. The transport system in the north is nowhere near as well-developed as that of the south, and your best bet here is to rent a car or book a tour.

By bus

Following reorganization in 2010, the south now has a good urban and **intercity bus system**. Buses are modern, usually on time, and although run by different companies in each district (Zinonas in Larnaka, OSEA in the Agia Napa/Protaras area – sometimes called "free Famagusta", EMEL in Lemesos, OSYPA in Pafos, and OSEL in Nicosia) fares are standard and simple: single journey €1, daily ticket €2, weekly ticket €10, monthly ticket €30, daily intercity €10). Each company has its own contact number and website: Lefkosia (☎77777755, ⓦosel.com.cy), Lemesos (☎77778121, ⓦlemesos buses.com), Larnaka (☎80007744, ⓦzinonasbuses .com), Pafos (☎80005588, ⓦpafosbuses.com), Famagusta (☎23819090, ⓦosea.com.cy). You can also access information about Intercity Buses and airport shuttles on ☎80007789, ⓦintercity-buses .com. A very useful combined website at ⓦcyprus bybus.com pulls all the information together. **Rural**

buses, especially in the Troodos Mountains, are less frequent and less reliable.

Bus services in **the north** are unreliable, don't seem to follow a timetable, will often wait until the bus is full before setting off, and are little used by visitors. Indeed, native Turkish Cypriots rarely use them either, so you're likely to find yourself sitting next to Turkish mainland settlers or Turkish army personnel. If you decide to brave this rather chaotic system, note that fares fall into the €1–3 range.

By car and motorcycle

The best and most efficient way of getting around Cyprus is to **rent a car** or, if you're not put off by their poor safety record, motorcycles, quad bikes, scooters or beach buggies. Car rental starts at around €34 per day in summer, €20 per day in winter – the longer the rental period, the lower the rate – but it's worth prebooking and shopping around. And if you intend exploring the remoter parts of the island, it is well worth splashing out on a **4WD**, especially as normal rental agreements often exclude driving on dirt roads. Petrol costs around €1.30 and diesel just over €1 per litre, and there are plenty of filling stations. Bear in mind, though, that many are closed in August, so it pays to keep your tank as full as you can.

Motorways (prefix "A") and main roads (prefix "B") are of good quality but side roads, especially in the mountains, might be unsurfaced. Visitors from the UK will feel particularly at home because driving is on the left, cars are right-hand drive, and there's a

SOUTH CYPRUS DISTANCE CHART (KM)

	Lefkosia						
Lemesos	86	Lemesos					
Pafos	149	68	Pafos				
Larnaka	45	71	139	Larnaka	Troodos		
Troodos Resort	71	45	113	111	Resort	Agia	
Agia Napa	80	106	175	41	152	Napa	
Polis	176	98	35	165	148	197	Polis
Paralimni (Protaras)	83	110	179	45	156	9	201

NORTH CYPRUS DISTANCE CHART (KM)

	Lefkoşa			
Girne	26	Girne		
Gazimağusa	61	73	Gazimağusa	
Güzelyurt	40	48	94	Güzelyurt
Dipkarpaz	123	133	80	158

whole host of familiar street furniture, from Belisha beacons to zebra crossings. **Speed limits** (strictly enforced) are as follows: motorways max 100km/h, min 65km/h. Unless otherwise indicated main roads have a limit of 80km/h; built-up areas 50km/h.

Parking is free in many villages, while town-centre car parks charge €1.70 to €3 for half a day. On-street parking in major towns is meter controlled, falling in the range €0.80–2 during office hours. Parking is free on Saturday afternoons, Sundays and public holidays.

Driving in the north is similar to driving in the south: cars keep to the left, signs are international, there are plenty of petrol stations, road signs are usually in kilometres, though sometimes in miles. Because development has been patchy, you might well come across bottlenecks where good new roads disgorge traffic onto narrow unimproved ones.

Driving tips

Contrary to popular belief, Cypriots are usually courteous drivers. However, some drive very fast, while others, especially in rural areas, drive insanely slowly, accustomed, seemingly, to the speed of a donkey. While the fatality rate on Cyprus's roads is higher than the UK's (particularly low) figure, it still compares well with, for example, Greece and the US.

• Alcohol limits are low – 50mg of alcohol per 100ml of blood (compared with 80mg per 100 ml in the UK) – and punishment for exceeding them severe. The only way to be sure of not falling foul of the law is not to drink at all if you're driving.

• Children must use restraints appropriate to their height and weight. In taxis, they can use rear seat adult seatbelts if that's all that's available. Rear-facing baby seats must not be used in front seats protected by air bags, unless the air bags have been deactivated.

• Jaywalking in towns seems to be endemic, often because the pavement is obstructed by telegraph poles, restaurant tables and chairs, eccentrically parked vehicles and so on.

• You'll often see several people crammed onto a single moped – treat them with caution.

• Donkeys (often heavily laden) and goats can be a hazard on country roads.

• Don't cross double lines to overtake.

• Don't acknowledge courtesy by holding out your hand palm outwards. This is, in Cyprus as in Greece, a very rude gesture.

• For roadside assistance call the Cyprus Automobile Association (☎ 22313233, ⓦ caa.com.cy. In case of accidents, call 112.

CAR RENTAL IN THE SOUTH

Main towns and cities are well served by **rental agencies**, both local and international. Those in holiday areas like Pafos and Agia Napa offer a range of vehicles in addition to cars – scooters, motorcycles, quad bikes and buggies.

Drivers under 25 who have been driving for less than three years must inform the rental agency so that special under-age insurance can be provided.

If you rent a car in the south, most companies will allow you to cross to the north, but you'll need

---

FIVE GREAT DRIVES

For such a small island, Cyprus offers a remarkable variety of exhilarating drives, from the ups and downs of the Troodos Massif to the off-road excitement of the Akamas Peninsula.

Lemesos to Pafos Take the old road B6 west from Lemesos, first through the Home Counties tidiness of the British Akrotiri base, then past the castle at Kolissi and the ancient sites at Kurion and the Sanctuary of Apollon Ylatis, to the beautiful coast at Petra tou Romiou.

Pafos to Pano Panagia A steep climb up from Pafos, along the E606, brings you to rolling upland vineyards, pretty villages and monasteries, and the birthplace of Archbishop Makarios III.

The Akamas Peninsula The empty wilderness of the Akamas Peninsula can be explored by car (though only a 4WD will do), from the Avagas Gorge in the south to Lara Bay in the middle and the Baths of Aphrodite in the north.

Güzelyurt to Kykkos Monastery Experience both sides of the Green Line by driving through the orange groves of Güzelyurt, along the pretty north coast past the ancient sites of Soli and Vouni, across to Kato Pyrgos then south through the dense forests of Tilliria via beautiful Cedar Valley to lofty Kykkos, Cyprus's most famous monastery.

Lefkoşa to Girne This north Cyprus loop takes you north from the capital through the Kyrenia Mountains to the coast and west to Girne. Diversions off this route allow you to take in Buffavento and St Hilarion castles and the superb Belapais Abbey.

to arrange your own insurance at the crossing point – there will be a booth where you can do this. Petsas Rent a Car (see below) will arrange this on your behalf.

Alamo Ⓦ alamo.com (Larnaka and Pafos airports)

Auto Europe Ⓦ autoeurope.com (All main towns)

Avis Ⓦ avis.com (All main towns)

Budget Ⓦ budget.com. Larnaka and Pafos airports.

Carhire3000 Ⓦ carhire3000.com. All main towns.

DriveCyprus Ⓦ drivecyprus.com. Online broker which can arrange car hire in any of the republic's main towns.

Europcar Ⓦ europcar.com. All main towns.

Hertz Ⓦ hertz.com. All main towns.

Holiday Autos Ⓦ holidayautos.co.uk. All main towns.

National Ⓦ nationalcar.com. Larnaka and Pafos airports.

Petsas Rent a Car Ⓦ petsas.com.cy. Larnaka, Pafos and Ercan airports, and will also arrange insurance for north Cyprus.

Rental Car Group Ⓦ rentalcargroup.com. All main towns.

Skycars Ⓦ skycars.com. All main towns.

SIXT Ⓦ sixt.com. All main towns.

CAR RENTAL IN THE NORTH

Since none of the big international car rental companies cover **north Cyprus**, you're limited to local firms. However, most will deliver and pick up from your hotel, or from Ercan Airport, and some now include that service for Larnaka. Note that to rent a car in north Cyprus you must be at least 25 years old.

The TRNC Rent a Car Association produces a booklet annually with advice on renting cars in the north, and the phone numbers of about forty rental companies. Otherwise, try: North Cyprus Car Hire Services (Ⓦ cyprus-car.net) or Sun Rent a Car (Ⓦ sunrentacar.com).

Taxis

In the south taxis are numerous in larger towns and cities and can either be hailed from the street or picked up at ranks. All **urban taxis** should have meters and fares are controlled by the government. In rural areas taxis do not have meters, so it's as well to agree a fare before setting off. The fare structure for urban taxis is complicated: it is divided into day (6.01am–8.30pm) and night tariffs, with an initial charge (day €3.42, night €4.36) and a fare per km (day €0.73, night €0.85). There are also charges for waiting (per hour), for luggage (per item) and during public holidays. In **the north**, taxis (marked by a "Taksi" sign on the roof) do not have meters, so you should agree a price before getting in. Taxis are not allowed to cruise, and operate from official ranks which are closed at night. In both the south

and the north you can also use **shared taxis**, which carry between four and eight passengers, between main towns. In the south (where they are also called Transurban Taxis) these operate on a fixed half-hourly timetable from 6am to 6pm (Sundays 7am to 5pm); in the north (where they are known as dolmuses), they usually wait until they are full.

By bike

Cyprus's mild climate is ideal for cyclists, though during midsummer the obvious precautions – helmet, sun cream, plenty of drinking water – should be taken. Most towns in the south have **bike rental** companies, and mountain and road bikes are readily available, with charges usually being around €50 for three days, €100 for a week. A new cycle track has recently been established in the Troodos Mountains, with nearly 60km of well-signposted surfaced and unsurfaced track. For information on cycling in Cyprus, contact the Cyprus Cycling Federation, 21, Amphipoleos Street, Nicosia ☎ 22449870, Ⓦ cypruscycling.com. The renting of bikes in the north is less developed than in the south, but a number of hotels will be able to help arrange this.

Accommodation

Cyprus, north and south, has a huge range of hotels, hotel-apartments and villas, ranging from the palatial to the cheap-and-cheerful. There is also a growing number of "agrotourism" options – village houses, barns, small public buildings adapted and renovated to provide modern comforts and facilities. However, unlike in Greece for example, the renting of rooms in the homes of local people does not feature strongly.

The south

All tourist accommodation in the republic is registered with, and classified by, the Cyprus Tourist Organization, listed in their annual "Guide to hotels and other tourist establishments" (available at Ⓦ visitcyprus.com). Although attempts by the CTO to standardise accommodation have been largely successful, there is still a big gap between the best and the worst – it's always worth checking your proposed accommodation on websites such as Trip

ACCOMMODATION PRICES

Accommodation prices given in this guide are for the cheapest double room in high season (ie July and August). This is the "rack" rate and does not take into account discounts or "web only" deals. An up-to-date list of maximum prices agreed by the CTO is available on its website ⓦvisitcyprus.com. Rates include service charges and VAT, and usually breakfast – if breakfast is not included, this is stated in the review. For ease of comparison, hotel prices in north Cyprus are given in euros.

Advisor. The CTO also, surprisingly, includes a list of hotels in the two main tourist areas of north Cyprus (Gazimağusa/Famagusta and Girne/Kyrenia), though with warnings given about land ownership issues.

In all establishments **rates** are approved by the CTO, and guaranteed for the range of dates specified. Rates should be displayed in the room or apartment, and include overnight stay, breakfast, VAT and ten-percent local taxes. Air conditioning is compulsory in three- to five-star hotels and "category A" apartments and villas in the big resorts

on the coast, though not in the Troodos Mountains. There are reduced rates for single occupancy, children sleeping in parents' rooms, and for additional guests in apartments.

The north

Partly because of the isolation of the north since 1974, and partly because of the lack of investment caused by this, **north Cypriot hotels** can often seem old-fashioned and down-at-heel, particularly outside the main tourist areas of Girne and Gazimağusa. Staff, though often friendly enough, can appear poorly trained and may speak only Turkish. However, it must be taken into account that many such hotels are aimed primarily at Turkish businessmen or gamblers while some operate as thinly disguised brothels. Therefore, families or solo female travellers can find themselves feeling uncomfortable. On the other hand, rates are generally lower than in the south.

Bear in mind also that **land ownership** in the north is still extremely controversial. Many of the north's hotels and villas, once owned by Greek Cypriots, are regarded in the south as stolen property. The Cypriot Ministry of Foreign Affairs publish a list giving the ownership status of every hotel in the occupied north – only sixteen are

CROSSING THE GREEN LINE

With seven crossing points now open across the **Green Line** – the de facto border separating the northern and southern sectors of Cyprus – visitors can stay in the south and cross to the north as often as they like. It's not yet quite as straightforward the other way around (cars rented in the north, for example, are not allowed to cross to the south), but things appear to become more relaxed each year. Visitors accustomed to heavily signposted checkpoints elsewhere in the world will be surprised at how anonymous these Cypriot ones are – on both sides of the Green Line. If you're not careful, you can find yourself stumped as to how to get back so be sure to take a note of landmarks and directions and take a map (preferably two, owing to the different place names used either side of the line). The crossing points (west to east) are:

Limnitis/Yesilirmak The most recent (and prettiest), crossing, in the hills above Kato Pyrgos. This represents the westernmost part of the TRNC (apart from the militarized Kokkina Enclave). The best crossing for visiting the Palace of Vouni and Soli from the west.

Astromeritis/Zodhia The best crossing for Morphou/Güzelyurt from the main Lefkosia–Troodos road. Cars only.

Agios Dometios/Metehan The closest vehicle crossing point to Lefkosia, ideal for Kerynia and the north coast.

Ledra Palace, Lefkosia Pedestrians only, just outside the Venetian walls on the western side of the city.

Ledra Street, Lefkosia Pedestrians only. At the top of south Nicosia's main shopping street, and therefore the best for exploring north Nicosia.

Pyla/Beyarmudu Best place to cross into the north from Larnaka.

Strovilia The easternmost crossing point, and the most convenient for visiting Gazimağusa (Famagusta) from Agia Napa, Paralimni and Deryneia.

considered legitimate, since they were owned by Turkish Cypriots before 1974, or are built on land owned by Turkish Cypriots (Ⓦmfa.gov.cy/occupiedarea-properties). While this is extremely unlikely to affect the casual visitor, it is worth bearing in mind for those considering buying or leasing property in the north.

Tourist accommodation in the north is listed in the "North Cyprus Hotel Guide", available at tourist offices and Ⓦnorthcyprus.net. Though the guide offers no guarantees regarding standards or prices (it is produced by the hotel owners themselves, after all), it is a useful summary and provides helpful lists of travel agencies, taxi and car rental firms, restaurants, festivals and museums.

Hotels and apartments

The bulk of the island's accommodation is dominated by big full-service **resort hotels** and holiday villages, concentrated in Agia Napa, Protaras, Larnaka, Lemesos and Pafos in the south and Girne and Gazimağusa in the north. Most include a choice of rooms, apartments and villas, restaurants, bars and shops, spas, sports facilities and kids, clubs, with access to private beaches. These are supplemented by apart-hotels where services are limited (though some do have swimming pools and café/restaurants) and kitchen facilities. Far less common are the smaller town-centre hotels and **guesthouses** which should appeal to those who like to be in the thick of things, but they can be very noisy, are less well-organized than the big establishments and, in the north especially, quality can't be assumed. In the Troodos Mountains, small hotels might be the only option. A range of private apartment rentals can also be found at Ⓦairbnb.

Self-catering villas

An increasingly popular accommodation type across the island is the **self-catering villa**, either purpose-built for the tourist trade or privately owned (often by Brits) who wish to offset part of the cost of their place in the sun by letting it out. Lettings are usually for one or two weeks, and are often part of a package which includes flights, the services of a courier and, in some cases, the use of a car. On average, you could expect to pay €900 (1 week) to €1400 (2 weeks) per person with flights and car hire included, varying according to season and how many people are in the party. Sunvil Holidays (see p.24), offers perhaps the widest choice of villas on the island.

Agrotourism

A similar sort of self-catering experience can be obtained by taking advantage of the burgeoning **agrotourism** industry, where traditional houses are modernized, often to a very high standard, and rented out. These are frequently in rural villages, and so are ideal for people who want something a bit different – peace and quiet and an insight into traditional Cypriot life. In some, guests might even be allowed to help with the harvest, or with milking the odd goat. For the full range of properties check out the excellent *Guide to Traditional Holiday Homes* published by the Cyprus Agrotourism Company (☎22340071, Ⓦagrotourism.com.cy). (For more on agrotourism, see box, p.74).

Hostels and campsites

Finally, there are hostels and campsites, though their numbers are severely limited. There are official CTO-approved **campsites** at Governors Beach,

---

SPECIAL PLACES TO STAY

Aunt Maria's, Lefkara A good example of the type of renovated traditional building being increasingly provided by the agrotourism industry, in this case in one of Cyprus's most famous villages. See p.79

Library Hotel, Kalavassos Luxurious facilities contained in a nineteenth-century building. And yes, it does have its own library. See p.79

Kiniras Hotel, Ktima Pafos Bright modern accommodation in a Venetian mansion. See p.122

Hostel, Stavros tis Psokas You can't get further away from it all than the hostel in the forest station at Stavros tis Psokas in the Tillirian forest. See p.141

Linos Inn, Kakopetria Accommodation in restored village homes in the old part of one of the Troodos Massif's most interesting villages. See p.161

Nostalgia, Girne Old-fashioned (the clue's in the name) and quirky hotel in the centre of Cyprus's most beautiful town. See p.218

Gardens of Irini, Bellapais Tiny guesthouse run by artistic expats. See p.226.

Geroskipou, Coral Bay and Polis, with two more in the Troodos Mountains, plus four **HI hostels** (ⓦ hihostels.com) at Girne, Pafos, Larnaka and Protaras. However, the only hostel that can be unreservedly recommended is the forest station hostel at Stavros tis Psokas deep in the Tillirian forests. Wild camping, while not specifically illegal (except on picnic grounds), is viewed with suspicion in both north and south.

Food and drink

Greek Cypriot food and drink is largely identical to Greek food. However, Cypriots themselves consider their cuisine to be far superior and point out differences, both in quality and sometimes in ingredients. So, for example, the Cypriot *koupepia* (stuffed vine leaves) contain minced meat as well as rice, whereas the Greek equivalent (dolmades) don't. That said, all the old Greek favourites will be found in most restaurants on the island – moussaka, souvlakia, stifado, kleftiko, sheftalia, keftedes, goubes, godopoulo (see p.267) and above all meze, together with dips such as tzatziki, taramasalata and hummus. If you're after traditional Greek food, look out for the presence of a large domed oven at the back of the restaurant, and/or a charcoal grill or "souvla". Fish is often of good quality and freshly caught – you might well be invited into the kitchen to choose from that day's catch.

The cuisine of north Cyprus is very similar to that of the south – after all, both communities had a shared history before 1974. The only gastronomic effect of the Turkish invasion of 1974 seems to be that international fast-food chains have been replaced by Turkish ones (the absence of McDonald's, Starbucks and their ilk is particularly noticeable). International wines and beers have been replaced by local or Turkish equivalents, and Greek brands have been replaced by Turkish ones. Ordering food in restaurants and buying it in supermarkets are getting easier as the practice of labelling in English as well as Turkish spreads.

Cypriot specialities

One of the most famous Cypriot products is **halloumi**, goat-or ewe's-milk cheese soaked in brine. Rubbery when raw, but lovely when fried or

> ### SIESTA TIME
> Most Cypriots still follow the practice of taking a long lunch/siesta break in the middle of the day, then working well into the evening, though there are signs that the Western European/American regime of a shorter break and an earlier finish is creeping in. Summer visitors would be well advised to follow the traditional practice – divide the day into morning and evening, and have a nap during the searing heat of the afternoon.

grilled, it has found its way into many Middle Eastern and Mediterranean dishes. Meat products to look out for include *lountza*, beautifully lean pork fillet, and *loukanika*, a spicy and very fatty smoked sausage; loukanika is something of an acquired taste – if you cook it in your apartment, you'll be able to smell it for days.

For street food, you could do worse than *tiropittes* (flaky pastry cheese pies) *spanakopittes* (similar, but with spinach), souvlakia wrapped in pitta bread, or corn on the cob.

For those with a **sweet tooth** there's *daktyla* (almond fried pastry), *lokmades* (fried pastry balls in syrup), *loukoumi*, known to the rest of the world (to the disgust of Greeks) as Turkish Delight, and so-called spoon sweets such as preserved quince, walnut or orange. **Soutzioukos** made of grape juice and almonds or walnuts, is supposed to be good for the libido. Cake and ice cream are also very popular – people often go out in the late evening, Italian style, just to visit *sacharoplasteia* for a wide choice of cakes, or gelato/cafés for ice cream.

Cypriots love their **fruit** (fresh, dried and preserved), olives and nuts – you'll find a bewildering variety on sale in any market or greengrocers. Indeed, for visitors in self-catering accommodation, shopping in Cypriot supermarkets, specialist shops and open-air markets is a highlight of their trip.

Breakfast and lunch

In days gone by Cypriots would usually help themselves to leftovers from the previous night before setting off to work. Today, **breakfasts** differ little from those favoured by the rest of Europe. Most hotels will offer the ubiquitous "continental breakfast" of croissants, bread and preserves, often supplemented with eggs, cheese and cold meats.

Most will also put on a traditional "full English", though any similarities between Cypriot and English bacon are coincidental. Lunch is served in most restaurants between noon and 2.30pm, and can vary from a light snack to a full meal.

Restaurants and eating out

Except for Sundays, when lunch can last most of the afternoon, Cypriots prefer to take their main meal in the evening, when temperatures have fallen to a pleasanter level. And because of the practice of having a siesta, they tend to **eat late**: restaurants rarely open much before 7pm, and most customers will arrive at any time from 8 or 9pm onwards. Restaurants can get very busy in high season, especially at weekends, so it's a good idea to make a reservation. Prices vary enormously, but allow for perhaps €40 for meze for two, with a bottle of wine, €50 for a three-course meal with a bottle of wine.

The variety of restaurants in Cyprus has increased exponentially during the last decade or two. Most popular are still the traditional **tavernas** (still the only option in many rural areas), or the slightly more formal *estiadoria*. But these have been joined by a host of restaurants offering cuisine from around the world: Italian, French, Chinese, Indian, Japanese, Thai, Lebanese, Arabic, Mexican, Russian and Armenian restaurants can all be found across the island. Fast food and "international cuisine" is ubiquitous, served up not only by the likes of Pizza Hut, McDonald's and KFC, but by local equivalents – Goody's, for example – and by the hundreds of restaurants aimed squarely at tourists (often recognizable by the photographs of the food outside). Though Cypriot restaurants are usually locally owned, a recent change has been that serving staff now often hail from Eastern Europe.

Drink

Cyprus has a long history of **winemaking** thanks mainly to its period under Lusignan (originally French Crusaders) rule. The bulk of its wine is produced in Lemesos and Pafos districts by four large wineries (ETKO, KEO, LOEL and SODAP). By far the most famous variety is the sweet dessert wine Commandaria, but a whole range of reds, whites and rosés, varying from very dry to very sweet, can be experienced on the six wine routes assembled by the tourist board (see p.104). Most wineries have tastings, and you can learn all you need to know about Cypriot wine at the Lemesos Wine Museum (see p.99).

For those looking for something a little stronger, the famous anise-flavoured **ouzo**, produced by distilling grape juice, is a popular aperitif, drunk neat and ice cold, or with water and/or ice (which makes the clear liquid turn milky). Stronger still is *zivania*, distilled from grape skins and local wines (tip: if mosquito bites are keeping you awake, alternately dab zivania on the bites and take a swallow – you'll be asleep in no time). Cyprus has long been renowned for its inexpensive **sherry** (many British drinkers of a certain age will have cut their teeth on Cyprus sherry from the local off-licence) and its brandy.

The needs of **beer** drinkers are met by locally brewed Carlsberg and Keo, though a wide range of imported beers are available in many bars. Fruit juices in Cyprus are good value, as is the local **coffee** (call it Turkish at your peril) – it is served in tiny cups which are half-full of grounds, and you must specify the degree of sweetness when you order (*glyco* – sweet, *metrio* – medium, *sketo* – unsweetened): sugar cannot be added once it's made. Ordinary instant coffee is also widely available (called "Nes" after "Nescafé"), and a

---

SIX GREAT RESTAURANTS

Militzis, Larnaka Cypriot food, knowledgeable Greek Cypriot waiters, and a setting beside the sea. See p.56

Aliada, Lemesos Mixture of traditional and international food served in an atmospheric old mansion in the Old Town. See p.94

Mylos Restaurant, Kakopetria Wide-ranging menu in imposing mill building overlooking one of the prettiest villages in the Troodos. See p.161

Yiannakos, Fikardou Greek Cypriot dining as it used to be in a picture-perfect restored mountain village. See p.167

Fanous, Lefkosia Hotel restaurant tucked away in one of the city's narrow lanes, with Lebanese food, hookah's and belly dancing. See p.188

Tree of Idleness, Bellapais Atmosphere in abundance. Turkish Cypriot food on the main square, opposite floodlit Bellapais Abbey. See p.225.

refreshing variant on a hot day is frappé, or iced coffee (check out ⓦcyprus.com/how-to-make-the-perfect-frappe.html for the lowdown on making your own).

Festivals and public holidays

In both north and south Cyprus there are two types of festivals and public holidays – those associated with religion or politics and local festivals. The former are covered below while a list of local festivals will be found in relevant chapters.

The south

Inevitably, given the importance of Easter in the Greek Orthodox Church (much more important, for example, than Christmas), a lot of the festivals relate to Easter – the run up to it, the day itself, and its aftermath. This is why Easter flights to Cyprus can be so expensive – there'll be competition from Cypriots wanting to go home for the holiday, and it's a great time to visit the island, with weather that's not too hot and lots of spring flowers.

The main festivals that are celebrated across the republic are as follows.

WINTER

Christmas (Dec 25). Although never as important as Easter in the Greek Orthodox Church, Christmas is increasingly celebrated as in the rest of Europe with church services and feasting. Children go from door to door, singing the traditional "Kalanda" Christmas songs in return for small sums of money, and special Christmas sweets (such as *kourabiedes* and *melomakarona*) are eaten.

New Year's Day (Jan 1) The feast day of Agios Vassilos, New Year's Day is celebrated by the eating of a special cake called "vassilopitta" baked the previous evening, and containing a coin which confers good luck on the person who finds it in their share.

Epiphany (Phota) (Jan) Together with Easter, one of the biggest religious festivals in the Greek Orthodox calendar. Epiphany celebrates the baptism of Christ, and the festivities culminate on Jan 6 with the "blessing of the water" – a religious procession walks through the streets to the sea or nearest lake, a cross is ceremonially baptized by being thrown into the water, then young men dive to try to retrieve it. The one who succeeds has his family blessed for the rest of that year.

Green Monday (Feb/March). Green Monday (also known as "clean Monday" or "pure Monday") marks the beginning of Lent, and is celebrated across the island with outdoor music, dancing, vegetarian food and kite flying. In Lemesos the period is celebrated by a full carnival

lasting a fortnight, with parades and fancy-dress parties, and much drinking and eating – meat during the first week, cheese during the second.

SPRING AND SUMMER

Easter (April/May). The biggest event in the Greek Orthodox calendar. There are processions on the evening of Good Friday, midnight Mass on Easter Saturday, and lots of eating and drinking and games on Easter Sunday and Monday.

Anthestiria (First Sunday in May). Probably with pagan roots going back to Ancient Greece, Anthestiria celebrates the arrival of Spring with parades of floats where the emphasis is on fresh flowers.

EU Accession Day (May 1). Public holiday marking the republic's accession to the European Union in 2004.

The Flood festival (Kataklysmos) (June). A day of celebration of the Holy Spirit which takes place 50 days after the Greek Easter, Kataklysmos has a complicated relationship with the New Testament, the Old Testament (in particular the Flood, hence the name) and even Greek mythology's Aphrodite and Adonis. As with many Cypriot festivals, it is strongly related to the sea, with religious ceremonies on the coast, concerts, boat races, swimming galas and water-throwing activities, all connected with Pentecost and the purification of both body and soul.

August Village Festivals (Aug) Look out for village festivals throughout the region – live music, traditional Greek dancing and lots of food and wine.

The north

North Cyprus uses the same Gregorian calendar as the rest of Europe, but its main religious festivals, shared with the rest of Islam, change by approximately eleven days each year owing to the lunar Muslim calendar. A number of secular celebrations coincide with important dates in Turkish history.

WINTER AND SPRING

Christmas Day (Dec 25). Not formally recognized, but increasingly celebrated, especially in tourist areas.

New Year's Day (Yilbasi) A one-day holiday similar to that in most countries.

Mevlud (Muhammad's Birthday) (February/March). A one-day break to celebrate the birth of the Prophet.

National Sovereignty and Children's Day (April 23). A celebration of the opening of the Grand National Assembly of Turkey in Ankara in 1920, an event which marked the establishment of the modern Turkish state. Shared with Turkey.

Labour Day (May 1) Youth and Sports Day (May 19). A commemoration of Ataturk's landing in Samsun, triggering the liberation movement in Turkey. Shared with Turkey.

SUMMER

Peace and Freedom Day (July 20). Marks the Turkish invasion of Cyprus, which was launched on July 20, 1974.

TMT Day (Aug 1). The TMT was a Turkish Cypriot paramilitary movement established in 1958. Its activities are remembered with folklore festivals in the bigger towns.

Victory Day (Aug 30). A commemoration of the battle which ended the Turkish War of Independence in 1922. Shared with Turkey.

Seker Bayrami (September). End of Ramadan (widely celebrated in Muslim countries as "Eid") marked by a three-day holiday, with exchange of presents, distribution of sweets (it is sometimes known as the sugar festival) and a funfair in north Nicosia. Most Turkish Cypriots will make some efforts to mark Ramadan by forsaking alcohol, not eating during daylight hours and praying more often. Nevertheless, disruption is minimal.

AUTUMN

Turkish National Day (October 29). Marks the proclamation of the Turkish republic in 1923. Actually starts at 1pm on the day before. Shared with Turkey.

Independence Day (November 15). Festival celebrating the declaration of the Turkish Republic of North Cyprus on this day in 1983.

Kurban Bayrami (November). Four-day celebration to mark Abraham's willingness to sacrifice his son. Families sacrifice a sheep or chicken according to means (though this practice is beginning to die out among Turkish Cypriots).

Sports and outdoor activities

As in Greece and Turkey, much of the male population of the island is obsessed with football. Otherwise, the most popular activities relate to the island's geography and climate, from paragliding and climbing to sailing and scuba diving or even, for a few weeks in the year, skiing on the snowcapped Troodos Mountains.

Air sports

With its excellent weather and varied terrain and coast, Cyprus is ideal for a range of air sports. For general information contact the Cyprus Airsports Federation (☎ 22339771, ✆ caf.org.cy). For parachuting get in touch with Stavros Kypragoras (☎ 99643068), for hang-gliding Sotos Christoforou (☎ 99606211), for paragliding Demetris Antoniou (☎ 99406507).

Birdwatching

Cypriots have the reputation for preferring to eat rather than watch songbirds, but the former is now illegal in the south. Those interested in birdwatching in Cyprus should contact BirdLife Cyprus (☎ 22455072, ✆ birdlifecyprus.org). For more on birdlife, see p.261.

Climbing and hiking

Popular sites for rock climbing/bouldering include Eagle Rock and the Chassamboulia rock in Pafos

---

TOP 5 NATIONAL PARKS

Cyprus has numerous national parks and nature reserves, which can range from fairly small semi-urban parks with picnic areas, children's playgrounds and a few paths, to large areas of countryside with extensive marked trails.

Troodos National Forest Park Covering 9147 hectares of the Troodos Mountains this is Cyprus's most visited national park, with four separate nature reserves, nine picnic sites, three campsites and ten nature trails covering over 57km.

Akamas Peninsula In Cyprus's northwest corner, the Akamas Peninsula is one of the island's most remote areas which can be accessed only on foot or via mountain bike, trail bike or 4WD. Once dominated by a British Army firing range it is now something of a haven for wildlife.

Petra tou Romiou National Forest Park Home to one of Cyprus's most photogenic beaches, said to be the birthplace of Aphrodite, the Petra tou Romiou National Forest Park covers 350 hectares of woodland and coast 10km outside Pafos.

Macheras National Forest Park This is the Troodos Park's little brother, covering 4523 hectares at the eastern end of the Troodos range, and notable for being empty, unspoilt and heavily forested.

Karpaz Peninsula North Cyprus has just one national park: the Karpaz Peninsula, the long tapering strip of land that heads northeast towards Asia Minor. Around 80km long but just 20km wide at the base, it has a very low population density (though its roads are manageable), and is famously home to feral donkeys.

District and Cave Greko near Agia Napa. For detailed information on climbing, contact the Cyprus Mountaineering and Sport Climbing Federation (☎ 97770067, ⓦ komoaa.com).

For hikers there are numerous marked trails in the Troodos Mountains (see p.151). A section of the European Long Distance Path E4 travels for 539km the length of the island, and there is 322km of good walking divided into 72 nature trails. An excellent booklet on the E4 Long Distance Path and the nature trails is available in CTO offices in Cyprus and abroad. The best general walking in the north is in the Kyrenia range.

Cycling

Cycling is a year-round activity in Cyprus, but conditions are best in spring and autumn. Mountain and road bikes can be rented in all main towns and holiday areas (guide rental €10–20 per day). For further information contact the Cyprus Cycling Federation (see p.27).

Fishing

Fishing, both sea-and freshwater (the latter primarily in reservoirs), are popular in Cyprus. The main source of information regarding angling in the south is the Department of Fisheries and Marine Research (☎ 22807862, ⓦ moa.gov.cy/dfmr), who publish a booklet on the subject. In the north look out for sea-fishing trips from the most popular harbours (for example, ⓦ fishingnorthcyprus.com, from Keryneia). It is possible to get permission to fish in reservoirs, but is probably not worth the effort.

Football

Football (soccer) is strongly supported across the island. The Cyprus Football Association runs a full league of four divisions with fourteen clubs in each, and there are three cup tournaments. Admission prices are a fraction of what UK league teams charge, and tickets can be bought at the ground, on the day. Despite being relative minnows, Cypriot clubs have reached the group stage of the Champions League three times in recent years, and in 2012 Lefkosia's Apoel became the first to reach the quarter finals.

Golf

There are four main golf courses in southern Cyprus, three in Pafos District, and one in Lemesos, with several others planned. For a summary see ⓦ cyprus -golf-courses.co.uk In north Cyprus, there are two. See the relevant chapters for details of each course.

Horseriding

There are numerous horseriding stables in Cyprus, and many offer holiday packages – look out for literature in the CTO office or your hotel. Two of the best are Ride in Cyprus (ⓦ rideincyprus.com), based just outside Pafos, and Drapia Farm in Kalavasos (book through ⓦ cyprusvillages.com).

Skiing

Though it might seem unlikely, from January to March there's usually enough snow on Cyprus's highest peak, Mount Olympus, to allow skiing. The Cyprus Ski Club operates a ski centre on the mountain with four ski lifts serving three slopes: a chairlift on Zeus slope, and T-bar lifts on Hera, Aphrodite and Hermes slopes. For further information, contact the Cyprus Ski Club (☎ 22449837, ⓦ cyprusski.com).

Tennis

There are hundreds of tennis courts across Cyprus run by the municipalities as well as many hotel courts. Most have all-weather surfaces and are floodlit. There are numerous local tennis and beach tennis tournaments, and, during the winter, the Cyprus Masters Cup and Aldiana Seniors Open tournament. Cyprus also plays in the Davis Cup. For further information contact the Cyprus Tennis Federation (☎ 22449860, ⓦ cyprustennis.com).

Watersports and diving

The main coastal holiday areas, in both north and south, all offer the full range of watersports, either through centres on or near the beach, or through the big hotels. Dive schools in both the south and the north offer accredited courses. Among the numerous recognized dive sites are the wrecks of the Vera K and the Achilleas off Pafos and the wrecks of HMS Cricket, a British army helicopter and, most famously, the Zenobia (see p.57) off Larnaka. For scuba diving, contact the Cyprus Federation of Underwater Activities (☎ 22754647, ⓦ cfua.org). Sailing is widely catered for, either within the island or visiting – there are many ports, marinas and fishing shelters from which to choose. For charters, try Sail Fascination

Shipping Ltd (☎25364200) in Lemesos, Armata (☎24665408) in Larnaka or Cyprus Yacht Charters (☎80000011) in Pafos.

Culture and etiquette

While Greek Cypriot and Turkish Cypriot communities shared a long history up to 1974, they are divided by culture, language and above all religion. Since 1974 and the de facto division of the island, these differences have become more entrenched, with both sides embittered by the island's history between the 1950s and 1970s, and more generally with the south looking back to the heritage of the ancient Greeks and the north to that of Turkey and the Ottoman Empire. Politics aside, a few generalizations can be made about the culture and etiquette that you'll experience across the island.

Cypriot society revolves around **family life**, and it is still common for families to eat together, either at home or in a restaurant, especially on Sundays. It is quite common, at the beach or at picnic areas, to see several cars disgorge extended families, including the elderly, teenagers and children, who proceed to set up barbecues, play music on portable CD players, and settle in for the day.

There is widespread respect for the elderly, consideration for pregnant women, and indulgence towards children. Pregnant women are particularly well looked after (partly because of an old wives' tale that if they don't get what they fancy to eat, the child will be birth-marked in an appropriate way). When Cypriots ask about your children or grandchildren, they're not just being polite, they really want to know, so tell them, and ask back.

It is quite common for Cypriots who have only just met strangers to invite them into their homes for a drink (always accompanied by a little something to eat) or even for a full meal. Sometimes this hospitality and genuine interest in others can seem a trifle intrusive to outsiders – expect to be cross-examined about your family relationships, your profession, even the details of your income. Cypriots are also lively conversationalists. What may to an outsider sound like a furious argument might well be a perfectly amicable conversation.

Despite the tribulations of the fight for independence in the 1950s and the perceived involvement of the UK and the US in the events of 1974, Cypriots seem to bear no ill-will towards British or American visitors. Many seem to have a high regard for them and have close friends or family in the UK and the US. However, the 1974 invasion and the whole gamut of problems it has caused are best avoided as a topic of conversation unless raised by Cypriots themselves.

Though young people in Cyprus party as hard as those of any other country, older Cypriots still tend to be socially conservative. Topless sunbathing is frowned upon on any but designated naturist areas, and you are expected to cover up when you come off the beach. In particular, dress codes in churches and monasteries are strictly enforced – long trousers and no bare chests for men, covered legs and shoulders for women.

In the south, the **Greek Orthodox Church**, its buildings and its clergy, are widely revered, and the church in general and local priests in particular wield considerable political and social clout. Church attendance is high, and Sunday visits to churches and monasteries are a popular day out. In the north, although the population is Muslim, the level of observance is not high – you'll rarely hear a call to prayer, the Western Saturday/Sunday weekend is followed rather than the more usual Friday/Saturday, and there are no problems in getting hold of alcohol.

Although things are changing in the towns, attitudes towards gender in rural villages can still seem relatively unenlightened, with women taking the traditional home-making, child-rearing role and men going to work or sitting in the *kafenion*, drinking coffee, reading the papers or playing *tavli*.

Attitudes to **gay people**, too, can display prejudice. Gay clubs do exist in large towns such as Lefkosia, Larnaka, Agia Napa, Lemesos and Pafos, and these are tolerated, but openly gay public behaviour might attract disapproving frowns and the clicking of tongues. Racial stereotyping and racist behaviour, except between Greeks and Turks, have not until recently been a problem, though the huge influx of outsiders, particularly non-EU workers who tend to do unskilled domestic and agricultural labour, has led to anti-immigration rhetoric from far-right groups and isolated outbreaks of violence.

After its accession to the EU, Cypriot **standards of living** in the south shot up. At the same time, north Cyprus had the air of a land left behind, compounded after the turn of the millennium by economic problems imported from mainland Turkey. Since the 2008 crash, as in much of the western world, attitudes in the south to the future have become distinctly gloomy, with a pessimism boosted by dire economic forecasts, lack of progress on the "Cyprus Problem" and the disastrous 2011 explosion on the south coast.

Travel essentials

Addresses

Addresses in the south use the same basic pattern as you'll find in the UK: after the name of the person or business, there's a street number and name (usually in that order but, if in Greek, sometimes reversed). This is followed by a four-digit post code and a region. The first digit of the post code tells you the region – 1 or 2: Lefkosia District; 3 or 4: Lemesos District; 5: Ammochostos District (also sometimes called "Free Famagusta" and included in this book with Larnaka District); 6 or 7: Larnaka District; 8: Pafos District and 9: Keryneia District.

Addresses in the north are often given in English as well as Turkish, and therefore are easy to understand. As they are sometimes given only in Turkish, it's useful to know some of the more common words you're likely to come across – Avenue: Caddesi (abbr. Cad); Cul-de-Sac: Cikmazi (abbr. Cik); Boulevard: Bulvan (abbr. Bul); Square: Meydani (abbr. Meyd) and Street: Sokak (abbr. Sok)

Costs

Many visitors to Cyprus have prepaid for almost everything before they arrive – flights, accommodation, car hire, trips, even, in many cases, meals. For independent travellers, it should be possible to get by on €65 per day (though €100 is more realistic) during high season, less in the winter. It does, of course, depend on what activities you take part in, and how you travel around. Typical costs might include breakfast (continental) €3.50–6; fixed-menu lunch €10–13.50; dinner (meze, inc drink) €20; single bus ticket €1; glass of beer €3.50–5; cinema ticket €7; theatre/concert ticket €20–35.

VAT and local taxes are included though non-EU residents can have VAT refunded on certain goods.

> ### TIPPING
> In most situations, a service charge of ten percent is already added to the bill, and all that is required is that when paying you round up to the nearest euro. If there is no service charge, than add ten percent yourself.

In the north costs are lower for goods imported from Turkey, higher for goods imported from the rest of the world.

Crime and personal safety

Despite a recent spike in the crime rate, Cyprus is still a relatively safe place for visitors. There's not much in the way of burglary or theft, and you're unlikely to see violence on the streets (except, perhaps, that caused by drunken visitors in places like Agia Napa). However, organized crime, especially from Russia in the south and Turkey in the north, has made inroads, and there is now a considerable amount of vice and prostitution. This is confined to bars, clubs and "cabarets" in clearly defined parts of the larger towns, particularly Lemesos, and as long as these areas are avoided there should be no problem. Women on their own can find themselves the subject of unwanted male attention, but Cypriot males are far less persistent than those in some other Mediterranean countries.

A brush with the law rather than criminals is a far more likely scenario. Speed limits are strictly enforced and driving with above the (low) permitted levels of alcohol in blood or breath carries severe penalties. Be cautious around military areas (particularly in the north). Where access is denied to civilians, stay away and take "No Photography" signs seriously.

Electricity

Electricity supply across the island is 230 volts supplied through 13 amp, three-square-pin plugs. Brits therefore need no adaptors, and can use equipment that they use at home. Others will need adaptors, and though they're readily available, it makes sense to bring your own.

Entry requirements

All that is needed by most foreign nationals to enter north or south Cyprus is a valid passport.

There are no restrictions on length of stay for EU nationals in the south; in the north they can stay for up to three months. Nationals of the US, Canada, Australia, New Zealand and Singapore can stay in the south or north for up to three months without a visa. The main complication likely to face visitors is if they want to cross into or out of Turkish-occupied north Cyprus. The republic's position is still that anybody **entering the north** through what they consider illegal ports or airports, or staying in hotels in the north that were owned by Greek Cypriots, might face legal sanctions, though the reality is that this has become increasingly unlikely. Visitors can cross from south to north Cyprus at any of the (currently seven) official crossing points (see box, p.28) – if travelling to the north, a visa is issued at the border, stamped on a separate slip of paper rather than your passport. If using a car rented in the south, a separate insurance policy will be needed for the north (see p.27).

Health

The main medical inconveniences are likely to be from sunstroke, insect bites, and the odd sting from a jellyfish. All General Hospitals (found in most major towns), and some private ones, have Accident and Emergency Departments which provide free emergency treatment to all. More routine treatment may have to be paid for so travel insurance is highly recommended. That said, EU citizens may be able to receive free or reduced-cost treatment in the republic on presentation of a European Health Insurance Card. In the north, all visitors are entitled to free emergency medical treatment, but beyond that it must be paid for, so, again, private insurance is strongly recommended. Pharmacies can help with common minor complaints and ailments. A good source of information, whether you're from an EU country or not, is ⓦ dh.gov.uk/travellers. Tap water in Cyprus is safe to drink, and doesn't have any noticeable chemical taste.

Insurance

Travel insurance, covering medical expenses, personal property, third-party liability, cancellation and so on is recommended. If you intend to try any of what might be considered dangerous or extreme sports, you should check to see whether they're covered, and if not, extend the cover accordingly. Bear in mind that some credit cards carry complimentary insurance. If you have anything stolen, report it to the police in order to get a crime or ID number for inclusion in your claim.

Internet

In the south, internet access is getting more widespread by the day. Most hotels now offer guests at the very least a dedicated machine, more commonly wi-fi in a restricted part of the hotel (bar or foyer), and increasingly wi-fi throughout. Some cafés, restaurants and bars also offer free wi-fi. If you can't find a wi-fi signal you may need to visit an internet café, found in most major towns (and usually packed with teenagers). Though lagging behind the south, wi-fi is becoming more common in tourist areas in north Cyprus.

Laundry

Most large hotels offer laundry services, or are happy to arrange them through reception. Dry cleaners will be found in town centres, with normal turnaround being two days – ask for a fast premium service if that's too long. There are also launderettes (laundromats) in the main towns.

Mail

The Cypriot postal system is relatively reliable, at least in areas controlled by the republic. Postcards sent home do arrive, though it can take a week or more. Stamps can be bought at newsagents, which is fine if it's for a standard item like a postcard, but anything more complicated should be paid for at a post office. In the south post offices are open Mon–Fri 7.30am–1.30pm & 3–5.30pm. Some offices which deal only with parcel post have the same morning hours, but are closed in the afternoons except Wednesday. In the north post offices are open Mon–Fri 7.30am–2pm & 4–6pm, Sat 8.30am–12.30pm, with later opening and earlier closing in winter. When writing to north Cyprus the destination, significantly, is "Mersin 10 Turkey" not "North Cyprus" – this is to circumvent an international postal union boycott.

Maps

The CTO produces a range of excellent free maps – one of the whole island ("A Visitor's Map of Cyprus") and separate ones for Agia Napa, Larnaka, Lemesos, Pafos, the Troodos Mountains and Lefkosia which include useful area and town centre maps. There are also special interest maps such as the *Rother Walking Guide Cyprus – South and North*, and *Cyprus:*

Car Tours and Walks in the Landscapes series. In the north, the Tourism Promotion and Marketing Department produce a good general tourist map on which are marked bathing beaches, watersports, sailing, petrol stations and a lot more, plus street maps for all the main towns.

Measurements

The Republic of Cyprus uses the **metric system**. Distances are in kilometres, areas in square kilometres or hectares, petrol is sold by the litre, weights are in grams and kilos, speed is in kilometres per hour (kp/h). In the north the situation is more complicated, with some distance markers in miles and survivals from Ottoman times such as the "okke" (just over a kilo) often used for selling fruit and vegetables.

Money

In the south, the currency is the **euro** (€), and it is very easy to access your money – there are numerous banks and ATMs, so much so that travellers' cheques are an endangered species. Credit cards are widely accepted. Banking hours are May–Sept Mon–Fri 8.15am–1.30pm; Oct–April Mon–Fri 8.30am–1.30pm. There are 24-hour exchange facilities at Larnaka and Pafos airports, and in Lemesos port. In the north, the **Turkish Lira** (TL) is the official currency, though euros, pounds sterling and US dollars are often accepted. Prices for north

---

PLACE NAMES IN CYPRUS

Although Cyprus's history of successive occupations by foreign powers and complicated recent political history gives the island a variety of interest and depth of cultural identity, one of the less useful results has been a total confusion as to **place names**. Lusignans, Venetians, Ottomans and British all modified the original Greek names as well as imposing their own, while in the north, the 1974 Turkish occupation was followed by the wholesale replacement of Greek place names by Turkish ones. As a result, if you are visiting the north from the south, you really do need maps which show the post-1974 place names. For this practical reason, in this guide the post-1974 names are used – it does not imply any endorsement of the Turkish occupation or of the new names. Furthermore, the original names are widely used by Turkish Cypriots themselves in the north, and in these cases the original name will be included in brackets when first used, and when referring to pre-1974 events.

As if this isn't complicated enough, in 1994 the south introduced its own changes, with the replacement of place names considered to have been imposed by imperialist rulers with names deemed to have a purer, more Greek ancestry. In some cases completely new names were introduced ("Lefkosia" for Nicosia, "Lemesos" for Limassol), or spellings were modified ("Larnaca" becoming Larnaka, "Paphos" becoming Pafos). These changes were not without controversy, and many Greek Cypriots in the south persist in using the old names – they even continue to be widely used on road signs. In this guide, the new names (as they appear on official CTO maps) are used, but with the old name in brackets on first use, or when referring to historical events.

Cyprus in this book are given in euros for accommodation and Turkish Lira for restaurants, museum admission and other fees.

Museums, archeological sites and places of worship

Most regional **museums** in the south are open every weekday morning from 8am, with closing times varying from 2.30pm to 5pm. At weekends, many museums are closed, though some open on Saturdays from 9am (usually to 3pm). The most important variation is the Cyprus Museum in Lefkosia, which is open on Sundays from 10am to 1pm, but closed on Mondays. Museum opening times in the north are similar, though sometimes with additional afternoon hours on Thursdays.

Archeological sites usually open daily at 8am, with closing hours varying according to season, from 5pm in winter to 7.30pm in summer. There is an almost universal admission charge for museums and archeological sites of €1.70 (though the Cyprus Museum is double this). In the north, the charge is usually around 5TL, though more for the more famous sites such as Girne Castle, Bellapais Abbey or Salamis.

Churches and mosques tend to be kept locked, with those who wish to visit needing to find the keyholder. However, the more heavily visited sites will often have a custodian hovering around. There are no fixed entrance charges, though all welcome donations. In both churches and mosques, modest dress is insisted upon for both men and women.

Newspapers

Most of the major UK and US **newspapers** can be bought in Cypriot newsagents, at the foreign sale cover price, though a day late. The emphasis tends to be on UK tabloids and the *Daily Mail* and *Express*. There are two Cypriot newspapers published in

English in the south: the *Cyprus Weekly* (Fri; ⓦincyprus.com.cy) and the excellent *Cyprus Mail* (daily except Mon; ⓦcyprus-mail.com), while in the north *Hurriyet Daily News* (ⓦhurriyetdailynews.com) and *Cyprus Today* ⓦcyprustoday.net) are in English.

Opening hours and public holidays

In the south, shop opening hours vary depending on season, type of shop and location. However, the broad rule of thumb is that shops are open for the whole day on Mondays, Tuesdays, Thursdays and Fridays, have earlier closing on Wednesdays and Saturdays, and are closed on Sundays. Closing times are quite late – often 7.30pm or 8pm. During the holiday season, and in holiday areas, the types of shops that tourists are most likely to use can be open for enormously long hours. The main public holidays, when banks and shops are usually closed, are as listed in "Festivals" (see p.32). In north Cyprus opening hours are continuous from 8am–5pm in winter, but in summer shops close during the heat of the day, and so are open 8am–2pm and 4–6pm.

Phones

There are two types of **public phones** – coin operated, and card operated. Cards for the latter are available from banks, post offices, kiosks and some shops. To phone within Cyprus, simply dial the eight-digit number used throughout this guide. In the north public phones are not common, but can usually be found in or around the local post office; all are card operated, with cards on sale from the post office or some kiosks.

If intending to use your **mobile/cell**, consult with your provider as to roaming arrangements and costs. It is often cheaper to buy a local SIM card if planning to make calls within Cyprus (though you may need to get your phone "unlocked" at a

CALLING HOME FROM ABROAD

Note that the initial zero is omitted from the area code when dialling the UK, Ireland, Australia and New Zealand from abroad.

Australia international access code + 61
New Zealand international access code + 64
UK international access code + 44
US and Canada international access code + 1
Ireland international access code + 353
South Africa international access code + 27

To call the Republic of Cyprus dial 00357 followed by the 6-digit number; for north Cyprus 0090, followed by 392 and the 7-digit local number.

specialist phone shop – a widely available service in the south, but confined to Girne and Lefkoşa in the north).

Photography

Photography is prohibited within **military areas** in both the south and the north, and this is strictly enforced. Many monasteries, churches and museums also ban photography, partly because of the intrusive nature of flash, but also because it can harm delicate paintings, artefacts and fabrics.

Shopping

Serious shopping for Cypriots is dominated by the malls and boutiques of **Lefkosia** (South Nicosia; see p.190), which far outrank anything on offer in Larnaka, Lemesos and Pafos. Nevertheless, you'll find the usual souvenirs – leather goods, especially bags, belts and shoes, ceramics, copper, silver and gold jewellery, woven basketwork, embroidery and lace – in resorts across the island. Wines and spirits, *loukoumi* (aka Turkish delight), various Cypriot sweets, nuts and olives, also make good-value **gifts**. Non-EU residents can claim VAT back on items carried home in their hand luggage as long as the overall value is €50 or more – shop where there's a **tax-free shopping** sign and ask for a tax-free receipt and get this stamped by customs officials as you leave Cyprus. When crossing the Green Line north to south you are restricted to 200 cigarettes, 1 litre of alcoholic beverage and no more than €100 worth of other goods. And take this restriction seriously – border staff often do spot checks on cars passing through the crossing points.

Cyprus has good open-air and covered markets which are worth visiting for both atmosphere and purchases, and large towns also have American-style shopping malls.

Haggling isn't really a part of the Cypriot culture (north or south), and you will usually be expected to pay the marked price. However, it might be worth trying to get the price down when chancing on a hotel off the street, or when renting a car. Souvenirs, too, might be subject to haggling if prices are not marked. Even then, reductions are likely to be relatively modest.

Time

Cyprus is two hours ahead of GMT, seven hours ahead of EST. Daylight Saving Time starts at 1am GMT on the last Sunday of March, when clocks go forward by 1 hour (ie GMT +3), and ends with a return to Standard Time at 1am GMT on the last Sunday in October. Cyprus is, therefore, usually two hours ahead of the UK.

Tourist information

The major source of information about the Republic of Cyprus is the **Cyprus Tourism Organisation** (CTO; Ⓦ visitcyprus.com). Click on "about us" at the bottom of the home page for a list of offices in Cyprus and abroad. The CTO produce a variety of extremely useful maps and pamphlets. It's also worth checking out the regional tourist board websites including: Ⓦ lemesostourism.com, Ⓦ larnakaregion.com, Ⓦ visitpafos.org.cy and Ⓦ agianapa.org.cy.

For northern Cyprus, three publications are particularly useful: *The North Cyprus Tourist Guide*, available from tourist offices and online at Ⓦ cyprus touristguide.com, the *North Cyprus Hotel Guide* produced by the North Cyprus Hoteliers Assocation KITOB, and the *Restaurant Guide of Northern Cyprus* produced by the Cyprus Turkish Restaurateurs Association (Ⓦ resbir.com). All are well-produced and informative, if rather dominated by adverts and sponsorship. Other useful websites include Ⓦ north cyprus.net, Ⓦ turkishcyprus.com, Ⓦ northerncyprus .com and Ⓦ welcometonorthcyprus.co.uk.

Travelling with children

Cyprus is a great destination for families, as Cypriot culture is so child-friendly. You'll find your own children smiled at, tickled under the chin and otherwise bathed in approval. You'll even get Cypriot teenagers making a fuss of babies – not something you see every day in Anglo-Saxon cultures.

All the paraphernalia of baby care – baby food, nappies/diapers, creams, powders and medication – are available in pharmacies and supermarkets, in international as well as local brands. Discreet breast-feeding is accepted. High chairs and books/toys in restaurants are increasingly available. Large hotels usually have a wide range of child-friendly services – kids' clubs, amusement arcades, playgrounds and so on – as well as baby-sitting services.

Travellers with disabilities

Provision for **disabled visitors** in Cyprus is patchy, though it's better in the south than in the north. The old towns of many resorts have

TOP 5 CHILDREN'S ATTRACTIONS

Waterworld Waterpark, Agia Napa One of Europe's biggest water parks, with delightfully tongue-in-cheek, Ancient Greek themes. See p.60

Fig Tree Bay, Protaras With beautiful sand, safe bathing, shops, showers, cafés, watersports and everything else that Cypriots deem necessary for a day at the beach, you can't beat Fig Tree Bay. See p.67.

Santa Marina Retreat, Lemesos District Lots of outdoor activities, with a particular emphasis on equestrian activities, plus a small museum and zoo. See p.98.

Aphrodite Water Park, Pafos Not as much fun as the water park in Agia Napa, but still worth a day out with the kids. See p.121.

Pafos Zoo Clean, well laid out, with clear explanations, Pafos Zoo is particularly strong on birds and reptiles, though does also have a range of the bigger beasts. See p.132.

winding, cobbled streets to negotiate and lots of steps. Some ancient sites are also difficult – check the Department of Antiquities website (🔘mcw .gov.cy) which gives detailed accessibility information for all monuments, sites and museums. Otherwise check out expat site 🔘cyprus .angloinfo.com which has a useful section for people with disabilities.

TV and radio

The two main radio stations with English-language programmes are CyBC Radio 2 (🔘cybc.com.cy, on 91.1FM) in the south and Bayrak (🔘brtk.net, on 87.8 and 105FM) in the north, together with numerous commercial stations, all on FM. English-language speakers might also try British Forces Broadcasting Services in Lefkosia (89.7FM) west Cyprus (92.1FM) east Cyprus (99.6FM), the BBC World Service (1323AM), and Voice of America (0100-0130kHz). CyBC also run the principal TV stations in the south (1 and 2), and in the north provision is by Kibris TV and BRT2. In the south people also tune in to Greek TV, as in the north they do to Turkish TV. Most hotels and many apartments and villas have major US and UK digital channels.

Larnaka and around

FIG TREE BAY

1

Larnaka and around

Of Cyprus's six districts, the one centred on Larnaka is probably perceived as the least glamorous. Yet it offers one of the best combinations of attractions, beaches, hotels and restaurants. An ideal mix of working town and holiday resort, Larnaka itself has enough day-to-day reality to provide insights into Cypriot life yet enough sights and activities to keep boredom at bay, including an impressive cathedral, a medieval fort and the wonderful Hala Sultan Tekke mosque. It also boasts the island's largest airport and a flourishing marina and therefore attracts a cosmopolitan bunch of expats, entrepreneurs and yachting folk as well as soldiers and diplomats working at the nearby British base at Dhekelia.

To the east of Larnaka is the peninsula upon which stand **Agia Napa**, **Protaras** and **Paralimni**, journey's end for thousands of visitors. Long derided as the haunt of lager louts and marauding squaddies, these settlements have left behind their growing pains and are now largely well-maintained and prosperous towns, devoted to the holiday industry it's true, but none the worst for that. They have plenty of places to stay and to eat, some fine museums, a string of blue-flag beaches and pretty boat-thronged harbours, plus a scattering of small villages (the **Kokkinochoria**) dotted with the sails of wind pumps.

To the west of Larnaka is an unspoilt rural hinterland of hill villages and small harbours where the pace of life is blissfully slow – driving west from Larnaka on local roads, you'll notice the difference as soon as you pass the airport. This area includes two important **Neolithic sites** at Tenta and Choirokoitia, the world-famous lace-making village of **Pano Lefkara**, and the impressively sited monastery at **Stavrovouni**. It is also where, in 2011, a catastrophic **explosion** ripped apart the Evangelos Florakis naval base. The damage is being repaired with commendable speed, but the political fallout rumbles on.

Brief history

The earliest traces of civilization in the Larnaka region are the remains of two Neolithic villages at Tenta and Choirokoitia (see p.75), which date from around 7000 BC. The history of the town itself stretches over 3000 years, having been founded in the late Bronze Age as **Kittim** (aka Cittium). Very early on, it was settled by the **Myceneans**, as part of their great outward expansion from mainland Greece. In the tenth century BC it became a ruin, probably as a result of earthquake followed by invasion but, from about 850 BC the town (now Kition) was developed as a copper-exporting port by the **Phoenicians**. The period of the wars between Greece and Persia was another difficult one for Larnaka – the city initially did very well by supporting the Persians, and in 450 BC successfully held out against the army of the famous general **Kimon**, who had arrived to try to add Cyprus to the Athenian empire. Kimon died during the siege of

STAVROVOUNI MONASTERY

Highlights

❶ Foinikoudes Larnaka's splendid palm-fringed promenade is a perfect spot to grab an iced coffee or something stronger. **See p.47**

❷ Potamos Liopetriou Two tavernas, a small beach, plus dozens of bobbing boats make for an idyllic combination. **See p.61**

❸ Fig Tree Bay Despite the crowds, clutter and noisy jet-skis, this is still an exquisite beach. See p.67

❹ Cultural Centre of Occupied Famagusta, Deryneia Food for thought on the division of the island, with views across to the ghost town of Varosha in north Cyprus. **See p.69**

❺ Mazotos Camel Park A classic family day out, plus a great restaurant. **See p.72**

❻ Costas Argyrou Museum Lovely naive artwork with a subtle sense of humour, in a crumbling building designed by the artist. See p.72

❼ Choirokoitia Ruins of a hillside village from nine thousand years ago, brought to life by imaginative reconstructions. **See p.75**

❽ Stavrovouni Monastery Traditional Cypriot monastery which, at almost 700m, offers wonderful views (though it's off limits to women). **See p.78**

HIGHLIGHTS ARE MARKED ON THE MAP ON P.46

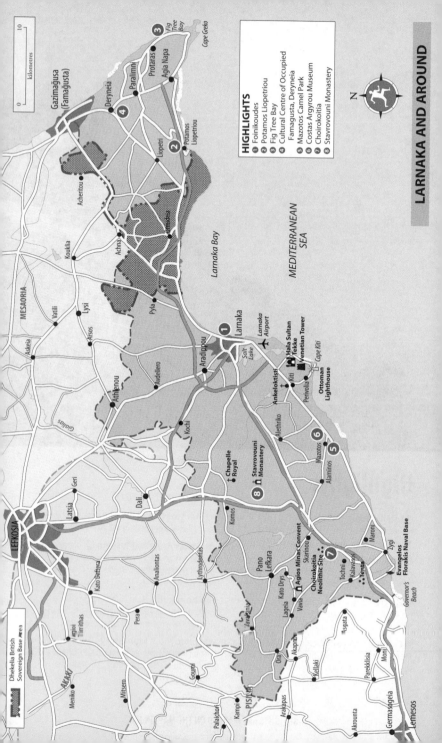

LARNAKA AND AROUND

HIGHLIGHTS
1. Foinikoudes
2. Potamos Liopetriou
3. Fig Tree Bay
4. Cultural Centre of Occupied Famagusta, Deryneia
5. Mazotos Camel Park
6. Costas Argyrou Museum
7. Choirokoitia
8. Stavrovouni Monastery

Larnaka – his marble bust stands on the promenade in the town – but the Greeks finally defeated Persia during the time of **Alexander the Great**, and conquered Cyprus in 323 BC.

During the following 350-plus years' rule by first **Greece** then **Rome** (during which it became Christian under the first Bishop of Kition, Lazaros), Larnaka became little more than a minor provincial town. This humble status continued under **Byzantine rule**. The last Byzantine king of Cyprus – Komnemos – was defeated in 1191 AD at the Battle of Choirokoitia by Richard the Lionheart initiating, in the following year, the period of Frankish Lusignan rule across the island. From 1489 it was part of the **Venetian empire**, and suffered from the preference given by the new rulers to Famagusta and Lemesos. Kition was now called Salina (after the salt lake). From 1571 to 1878 the **Ottomans** ruled Cyprus, and at least one village in the region did very well – Lefkara. Another name-change – the final one – occurred during this time: the town became Larnaka, after the graves ("larnax" is a sarcophagus) that were found outside the town, having accumulated over its long history. Larnaka flourished during the late Ottoman period with the town, now the main port on the island, attracting foreign consuls and merchants and their families (many of whom are buried at Agios Lazaros). Under the **British** (1878 to 1960), Larnaka's importance continued until it started to be eclipsed after World War II by Famagusta and Lemesos. Following the Turkish invasion in 1974, however, Larnaka became of primary importance thanks to its airport, which became the main point of entrance for visitors to the island after the closure of Nicosia International.

Larnaka

For many visitors to Cyprus, all they see of **LARNAKA** (the old spelling "Larnaca" is still commonly used) is its blinding white salt lake, visible as you come in to land at the airport, or whatever can be glimpsed from the windows of a coach speeding off to the resorts to the east and west. This is a pity, because the city has a unique character and atmosphere worth sampling for a couple of days. It also makes an excellent base from which to explore the rest of the island, connected as it is by motorway to Pafos and Lemesos in the west, Lefkosia in the north, and Protaras and Agia Napa in the east.

Larnaka is easy to get to know. The road that follows the beach between the marina in the north and the fort in the south – **Leoforos Athinon** – has a host of hotels and restaurants along the landward side and a sunbed-and-parasol-packed beach to the seaward, lined by the stately palm trees that give the pedestrianized seashore its name – **Foinikoudes (Palm Tree) Promenade**. Many of the main sights, including the **Municipal Cultural Centre,** the ancient church of of **Agios Lazaros** and the old **fort** are a few steps away from this axis. Further west are the town's **archeological** and **natural history museums**, the site of **Ancient Kition**, the **Municipal Theatre** and the impressive old **Kamares Turkish aqueduct**. South of the fort, along **Piyale Pasa** which continues to skirt the sea, are **Skala**, the old Turkish area now dominated by craft shops, the distinct holiday area of **McKenzie Beach**, and the huge **salt lake** with its haunting, palm-shaded **Hala Sultan Tekke**.

Foinikoudes (Palm Tree) promenade

Lined with hotels, cafés, restaurants and its titular palm trees, **Foinikoudes** probably shouldn't work, yet it does. Worthy of a French Riviera resort (albeit one dotted with *KFCs* and *McDonald's*) it radiates relaxation for both residents and holiday-makers. Try it on a Sunday evening, when it is thronged with Cypriots of all ages – family groups, children chasing after each other, flirting teenagers, old folk taking the air, as well as a fair contingent of visitors.

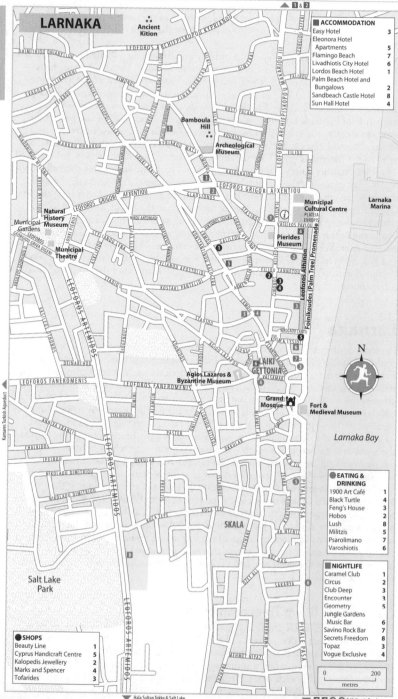

LARNAKA

Ancient Kition

Bamboula Hill

Archeological Museum

Natural History Museum

Municipal Gardens

Municipal Theatre

Municipal Cultural Centre

Pierides Museum

Larnaka Marina

Agios Lazaros & Byzantine Museum

Grand Mosque

Fort & Medieval Museum

Larnaka Bay

Kamares Turkish Aqueduct

LAIKI GEITONIA

SKALA

Salt Lake Park

Hala Sultan Tekke & Salt Lake

▼ 7, 8, 7, 8 & McKenzie Beach

N

0   200
metres

■ ACCOMMODATION

Easy Hotel	3
Eleonora Hotel Apartments	5
Flamingo Beach	7
Livadhiotis City Hotel	6
Lordos Beach Hotel	1
Palm Beach Hotel and Bungalows	2
Sandbeach Castle Hotel	8
Sun Hall Hotel	4

● EATING & DRINKING

1900 Art Café	1
Black Turtle	4
Feng's House	3
Hobos	2
Lush	8
Militzis	5
Psarolimano	7
Varoshiotis	6

■ NIGHTLIFE

Caramel Club	1
Circus	2
Club Deep	3
Encounter	3
Geometry	5
Jungle Gardens Music Bar	6
Savino Rock Bar	7
Secrets Freedom	8
Topaz	3
Vogue Exclusive	4

● SHOPS

Beauty Line	1
Cyprus Handicraft Centre	5
Kalopedis Jewellery	2
Marks and Spencer	4
Tofarides	3

LARNAKA ACTIVITIES

Despite being less overtly touristy than other island resorts there are a fair number of things to do dotted around Larnaka, many involving the sea. For divers it has one major advantage: the wreck of the *Zenobia*, one of the finest in the Mediterranean (see box p.57). **Dive-In** (☎ 24627469, ⓦ dive-In.com.cy) and **Alpha Divers Dive Centre** (☎ 99866383, ⓦ alpha-divers .com) both arrange dives to the Zenobia as do **Larnaca Napa Sea Cruises** (☎ 24656949, ⓦ zenobiadive.com) who also put on a range of cruises and fishing trips. For beach-based activities try **Central Water Sports** (☎ 99465855, ⓦ centralwatersports.com), in the hotel complex north of town on the Larnaka–Dhekelia Road, which offers the full range of parasailing, windsurfing, waterskiing, wakeboarding, speedboat/pedalo/canoe and dinghy rental, as well as banana boat rides. For a land-based adrenaline rush try **Quad Bike Safari** (☎ 24647729, ⓦ quadbikingsafari.com) on Dekelia road. Otherwise there's ten-pin bowling at **K-Max Bowling Centre** (Mon–Thurs 2pm –midnight, Sat 11am–1am, Sun 11am–midnight; ☎ 77778373, ⓦ kmaxbowling.com) in the same complex as the K Cineplex (see p.57), or, not very far away, on the opposite side of the aqueduct (but best approached from the airport road), the **Karting Center** (daily 10am–midnight; ☎ 70007677, ⓦ kartingcenter.com.cy).

Larnaka Marina

At the northern end of the promenade is **Larnaka Marina**, the largest on the island and an official port of entry to Cyprus with berths for 450 yachts. It is popular with sailors not least because of the huge choice of cafés and restaurants on its doorstep. Though the hoi polloi are not allowed in, you can still get a glimpse of how the other half live from the gates or the nearby beach. As boats come and go you'll hear languages from across the world – a whole mobile community who are spared the crowded airports that the rest of us have to endure. And the oft-repeated statement that Cyprus stands at the crossroads of three continents – Europe, Asia and Africa – comes alive here: Larnaka is a mere 110 nautical miles from Beirut, 145 from Tel Aviv and 230 from Port Said.

Right next to the marina entrance is the **Armenian Monument** which commemorates the landing of Armenian refugees in Larnaka in 1915, fleeing the genocide being perpetrated by the Ottomans during World War I. Larnaka is of course no stranger to refugees – the last influx followed the Turkish invasion of the island in 1974.

The Municipal Cultural Centre

Plateia Evropis • Tues–Fri 9am–2pm, Sat 9am–noon, Oct–April also Sun 9am–noon • Free • ☎ 24658848

In a row of five handsome British-era buildings – the old Customs Houses – that line the western edge of Pateia Evropis (Europe Square) just south of the marina, the **Municipal Cultural Centre** consists of an **art gallery** and the **Pierides Municipal Museum of Paleontology** (known locally as "Tornaritis", same hours as the centre). The gallery is devoted largely to Cypriot art, though it does have numerous visiting exhibitions; the museum to fossilized remains from all over the island. The building also houses the **Municipal Archives** (Mon–Fri 9am–1pm; free; ☎ 24657745), which, although likely to appeal more to local residents than visitors, does include a range of fascinating photographs of old Larnaka.

The Pierides Museum

4 Zenonos Kiteos • Mon–Thurs 9am–4pm, Fri & Sat 9am–1pm • €1.70 • ☎ 24814555

The **Pierides Museum** (or to give it its full, post-sponsorship title "The Pierides Museum Marfin Laiki Bank Cultural Centre") occupies the home of the eponymous Pierides family, about five minutes' walk from the Municipal Cultural Centre. Built

1

up over five generations, the collection started with the efforts of Demetrios Pierides (1811–95) to prevent the export to Europe and America of priceless Cypriot antiquities. With its shuttered windows, veranda and upstairs gallery, flagpole, elegant columns and balustrades, it looks like a Mississippi riverboat sailing down Zenonos Kiteos. Inside its shady interior, with its high ceilings, polished wood and tile floors and stately staircase (upstairs, incidentally, is out of bounds), is a wonderful collection of treasures from all over Cyprus. As you enter, the **Medieval room** on the right is succeeded by a room full of **Roman glass** and then a collection of **ancient maps** of Cyprus. Taking up the whole of the left-hand side of the building, a long room covers **Greek antiquities** from Neolithic to Classical times – statues, busts, bowls, vases. So used does one become to seeing copies in tourist shops that it's hard to realize that what you can see here are the genuine article. Look out particularly for the famous "**howling man**", an amusing figure sitting on a stool, elbows on knees, head thrown back and mouth wide open – water poured into his mouth would come out of the truncated appendage between his legs. Schoolboy humour perhaps, but over 7000 years old and exquisitely executed.

The Archeological Museum

Plateia Kalograion • Tues, Thurs & Fri 8am–3pm, Wed 8am–5pm, Sat 9am–3pm • €1.70 • ☎ 24304169

Despite some key pieces being nabbed by Lefkosia's Cyprus Museum, Larnaka's **Archeological Museum** makes a fair fist of outlining the history (and prehistory) of the district through its four galleries of well-displayed, comprehensively labelled artefacts.

The **entrance hall** includes two large limestone sarcophagi with carved male and female lids, and copies of important items which have now fetched up abroad – the stele (gravestone) of Sargon II (the original now in Berlin) and the statue of Artemis (now in Vienna). Among the highlights in the galleries are pieces taken from Choirokoitia and Tenta including a rebuilt Neolithic tomb, numerous pieces of Mycenean pottery, archaic terracotta figures (of a horse and rider, for example, and a man and woman in a chariot), a ceramic torch and foot warmer, and a variety of plaques and figurines from Ancient Kition (see p.50).

In the yard behind the museum is a collection of large **monumental sculptures** and stellae (a favourite basking place for lizards), a fascinating reconstructed olive press from the second century BC (they were still using the same design in the twentieth century), and useful information boards about the excavations of Kition – particularly exciting have been recent finds relating to the Phoenician harbour and boat sheds dating from the fifth century BC, and the Sanctuary of Astarte from a hundred years later.

Ancient Kition

Area II excavation Mon–Fri 9am–2.30pm and, from Sept–June, also Thurs 3–5pm • €1.70 • ☎ 24304115

The excavation of **Ancient Kition,** as Larnaka was once known, has thrown much light on the history of the town. A great deal of the remains lie beneath the modern town, and therefore cannot be explored by archeologists. However, the acropolis (Bamboula Hill) lies immediately behind the archeological museum, and has been excavated, as have two further sites (Areas I and III) which lie just north near the church of Panagia Chrysopolitissa.

The best place to see part of Ancient Kition, though, is the **Area II excavation** just off Leontiou Machaira, about fifteen minutes' walk north of the archeological museum. Though to the untutored eye the site is just a jumble of stones, comprehensive information boards explain what you're looking at, and wooden walkways give access to the site itself, including five consecutive temples (culminating in the Phoenician

ZENO AND THE BIRTH OF STOICISM

Just outside the Municipal Gardens stands a bust of the philosopher **Zeno**. Born in Larnaka around 336 BC, he became hooked on philosophy on a visit to Athens where he listened to the locals debating in the colonnaded arcade (the stoa) surrounding the market (agora). He stayed, studied and eventually taught, founding the Stoic (from stoa) school, which taught that the virtuous life should be lived in accordance with nature, conferring goodness and peace of mind, and that the best indication of a person's virtue was not what he said but how he lived. Stoicism's biggest cheerleaders were not Greek but Roman, in particular the emperor Marcus Aurelius and the historian Seneca who perhaps summed up the approach with "the happy life is to have a mind that is free, lofty, fearless and steadfast – a mind that is placed beyond the reach of fear, beyond the reach of desire". Zeno died in around 264 BC allegedly by the novel method of holding his breath.

Sanctuary of Astarte) and copper-smelting works perhaps connected to the four earlier temples, dating from the thirteenth to the eleventh centuries BC.

The Natural History Museum

Leoforos Grigoriou Afxentiou • June–Sept Tues–Sun 10am–1pm & 4–6pm, Oct–May 10am–1pm & 3–5pm • €1.70 • ☎ 24652569

Due west of the northern end of the promenade lie Larnaka's **Municipal Gardens**, well worth a detour not for the gardens themselves, though they're pleasant enough, but for the **Natural History Museum**. Small scale and understated, it nevertheless offers a good introduction to the flora and fauna of the region, with displays of stuffed animals and birds, and collections of insects, fossils, plants and minerals. Outside cages of live peacocks, geese and chickens provide a good distraction for kids. Elsewhere in the park are the **Municipal Library** and **Theatre**, several small statues (look out for the bust of Zeno – see box above – just outside the gardens), and a comprehensive children's playground.

The fort

Leoforos Athinon • June–Aug Mon–Fri 9am–7.30pm; Sept–May Mon–Fri 9am–5pm • €1.70 • ☎ 24304576

Once little more than a tumbledown ruin, Larnaka's **fort**, at the southern end of the promenade and separating it from Piyale Pasa and the old Turkish quarter, now provides a fine ending to the long promenade and beach. The fort was built during the reign of the Lusignan King of Cyprus, James I (1382–98 AD); it then fell into disrepair, was rebuilt by the Ottomans in the early seventeenth century, and was used as a prison by the British. Once through the Ottoman two-storey building which blocks off the end of the promenade, and past a row of medieval canons, you'll see to the immediate right a wooden staircase leading to the fort **museum**. Though it's all a bit jumbled, broadly Room I contains displays of early Christian artefacts, Room II photographs relating to the Byzantine period, and Room III an excellent collection of fourteenth- to sixteenth-century Byzantine and Islamic glazed pottery – the greens and browns of the sgraffito ware are truly stunning. There's also a reconstructed "divan room" – the sort of place where you'd lie around puffing dubious substances in your hookah. When you go back downstairs, you'll find that the lush **gardens** (which host summer evening concerts) are worth lingering in.

For a taste of the darker side of the fort's history, take a look in the room on the left of the main gate as you leave. Here is a massive wooden beam with a pit beneath it, discovered during renovation work – the gallows used by the British for executions. Relatives of the condemned were allowed to watch from the gardens, from where they wouldn't be able to hear the thump of the trapdoor opening. The last execution was carried out in 1945, shortly after which the police station was

1

transferred to its current, rather charming (for a police station) building at the north end of the promenade.

Grand Mosque (Buyuk Camii)

Larnaka's **Grand Mosque** stands next to the fort. Built in the sixteenth century and much restored since, both during the nineteenth century and in the last few years, it's a handsome building which serves the few Muslims left in the area. Though visitors are not admitted during prayers, you might be able to get in at other times, and even climb the minaret. The grave of Seyit Elhac Mehmet Aga, who restored the mosque in 1835, lies behind the building, and those of a number of other officials are at the front.

Agios Lazaros

Agiou Lazarou • **Church** daily April–Aug 8am–12.30pm & 2.30–6.30pm; Sept–March 8am–12.30pm & 2.30–5pm • donations requested. **Museum** Mon & Tues, Thurs & Fri 8.15am–12.30pm & 3–5.30pm, Wed & Sat 8.15am–12.30pm • Free • ☎ 24652498

Larnaka's cathedral, **Agios Lazaros** is just around the corner from the Grand Mosque – between them they marked the border between the Greek and Turkish Cypriot parts of town. Lazaros was one of the earliest Christians, having, famously, died and been brought back to life by Christ (see box below). Dating from the ninth-century AD when it was built to house the remains of the saint, the church has been through many changes. The southern portico was added in the eighteenth century, as was much of the internal woodwork – the iconostasis, the altar and the bishop's throne. Finally, in 1857 the belfry completed the building as it now stands.

The inside of the church has the usual Greek Orthodox sumptuousness, all carvings and gold leaf and brass, if a little muted by a fire in the 1970s. Look out in particular for the twelfth-century icon of St Lazaros, and, down some steps to the right after you've entered, the (empty) coffin of the saint himself.

In the arcade to the left of the church are a religious bookshop, an icon gallery and a small **Byzantine Museum**. To the right is a fascinating, and rather poignant, small **cemetery** where British and Dutch colonial administrators, merchants, missionaries and their families are buried – among them are Mary Palmer, the wife of Levant Company employee Samuel, buried with her infant daughter in 1720, and Helena Augusta Jane, daughter of the British Consul Niven Kerr, who died shortly before her first birthday in 1847. You'll also find the grave of Lorenzo Warriner Pease, an American missionary who lasted less than five years, and died at the age of 30 in 1839

LAZAROS: A MUCH-TRAVELLED CORPSE

Lazaros (or Lazarus in the Latinized form) was an early Christian in the Holy Land, who died, was buried (at Bethany), and, according to the Bible, was brought back to life by Christ. Orthodox tradition then suggests he fled to Cyprus (in fear of his life), where he became the first Bishop of Kition (Larnaka). Despite his holiness, Lazaros had a reputation as being something of a curmudgeon – it's said that, after his resurrection, he never smiled, the result presumably of the horrors he'd seen during his four days in the underworld. Local tradition also has it that he was responsible for creating Larnaka's salt lake, having cursed a local vineyard owner for not providing him with water. Lazaros is said to have lived for another thirty years after Christ's resurrection before dying (this time for good). Centuries later, in 890 AD, his sarcophagus was found, marked "Lazaros the four day dead and friend of Christ". The Byzantine Emperor, Leo VI, had the holy remains transported to Constantinople, and in return had a splendid church built on the spot where they were found (now Agios Lazaros cathedral). From Constantinople, the Crusaders took the remains to Marseilles where they promptly disappeared, never to be seen again.

– the diaries he kept between 1834 and 1839 provide a vivid picture of Cyprus and the Middle East at that time (see p.263).

Skala

The winding alleys and lanes of **Skala**, the old Turkish part of Larnaka, lie south of the fort and west of Piyale Pasa, the road (named for the Ottoman admiral who landed his army here during the invasion of 1570) that follows the shore southwards. The area retains its Turkish architecture and street names, though of course the Turkish Cypriot residents moved out in 1974, to be replaced by Greek Cypriot refugees from Famagusta and the Karpaz Peninsula.

McKenzie Beach

South of Skala, still following the coast, you come to an area which has a distinctive character – **McKenzie Beach**. Dotted with restaurants serving traditional Cypriot food, several apartment blocks and a couple of hotels, it is also the ice-cream capital of the region, with numerous *gelato* establishments which attract hoards of locals. A particularly agreeable section is the short stretch which starts at the Fishing Shelter, and runs along a serpentine wooden walkway past the *Psarolimano Restaurant* to the lifeguard tower and the golden, Blue Flag beach. A short distance beyond this a spur, left off Piyale Pasa, runs right up to the perimeter fence of the airport: close enough to smell the kerosene vapour and the tang of tortured rubber from the landing wheels.

Larnaka's salt lake

If you come in to land at Larnaka Airport during daylight hours you can't help but be aware of the huge **salt lake** around which the town is built. Consisting of extremely brackish water during the winter and blinding white dry salt during the summer, it is actually a complex of three interconnected lakes. Until quite recently salt was harvested here by donkey during the summer months, but today the lake is valued more as a habitat for around 85 species of bird, including its famous flamingos. Tradition has it that the salt lake was created in a fit of pique by St Lazaros (see box opposite).

Hala Sultan Tekke Mosque

May–Sept 7.30am–sunset; Oct–April 9am–sunset • donations requested

On the shore at the far end of the salt lake from Larnaka is one of the most important Muslim sites on the island, the **Hala Sultan Tekke Mosque**. With its elegant domes and minaret peeping out from a grove of palm and cypress trees on the shimmering edge of the lake (if you're lucky the lake will be full of pink clouds of flamingos) the mosque is extremely atmospheric (hence its frequent appearance on tourist literature), only slightly marred by the distracting wind turbines waving to you from the hillside behind.

The reason for the mosque's veneration is the presence of the tomb of **Umm Haram**, variously described as the friend or wet nurse of Mohammed. One of the earliest followers of the Prophet, the story goes that she accompanied an invading Arab force in 649 AD, was immediately thrown by her mule and was killed. A mosque was built on the site of her burial beneath, legend has it, stones from a prehistoric dolmen that stood on the spot.

There's a public footpath (the Kyprida Afroditi) along the edge of the lake to the mosque, with periodic benches (you'll need them if it's a hot day). Entry to the mosque's environs is through a couple of elegant gateways, and past a sign directing

1

you to recently discovered prehistoric remains. A hexagonal kiosk (*sadirvan*) outside the mosque's entrance allows the faithful to wash their feet before prayer – non-believers simply have to remove their shoes.

Inside, the mosque is attractively human in scale, the floor lined with decorative prayer mats. In an alcove lie two tombs – one of Umm Haram, the other (introduced in 1930) of the grandmother of King Hussein of Jordan. Yet another legend attached to the mosque is that the three stones of the dolmen that stands over the graves flew here from Mecca on the day of Umm Haram's death, and that the fifteen-tonne crosspiece were once suspended in midair, before coming to rest on the pillars. Incidentally, the current mosque is not particularly ancient, having been built in the early nineteenth century. But the whole scenic set piece reminds you that Cyprus lies on the very border of Western Europe and the Middle East.

Getting here can be a bit confusing – if **approaching from Larnaka**, as you get to the airport keep straight on at the first roundabout, and when you get to the next (signposted "Control Tower"), instead of going "through the roundabout" as the sign tells you to, double back as if returning to Larnaka. The turn-off to Hala Sultan Tekke is on the left, clearly signposted.

Kamares Aqueduct

At the opposite end of the salt lake from the airport, and best approached from the main Larnaka to Lemesos road (you can also get to it on a dirt road from the Hala Sultan Tekke mosque), is the remarkable **Kamares Aqueduct**. Built in 1745 by Abu Bekir Pasa, the then Ottoman governor of Cyprus, and designed to bring water into the town from 10km away, it was only replaced by modern pipes just before World War II. Nowadays its sinuous route across a shallow valley makes an impressive site, especially when lit up at night.

ARRIVAL AND DEPARTURE   LARNAKA

By air Larnaka Airport (☎ 24643576; 8.15am–11pm), through which the majority of visitors to Cyprus pass, is well organized and has all that new arrivals are likely to need for their onward journey – ATMs, car rental booths, a tourist information point, taxi stands and bus stops. There are frequent buses from the airport into Larnaka (€1; 30min) and also shuttles to Lefkosia and Lemesos. A number of routes link the airport to the town – 417/418/419/440 during the day, 446/456 at night. A taxi into Larnaka should cost around €10.

By bus The main intercity bus stop is at Finikoudes promenade just south of Plateia Evropis. **Destinations**: Agia Napa/Paralimni (Mon–Fri 10 daily, Sat & Sun 8 daily; 1hr); Lefkosia (Mon–Fri 12 daily, Sat & Sun 8 daily; 1hr); Lemesos (Mon–Fri 10 daily, Sat & Sun 8 daily; 1hr 30min). For timetables visit ⓦ intercity-buses.com.

GETTING AROUND

By bus Bus transport in Larnaka is efficient, provided by the blue buses of Zinonas Buses Ltd (☎ 80007744). Their own website (ⓦ zinonasbuses.com) isn't up to much – far better is ⓦ cyprusbybus.com. There is no central bus station, with most routes using one of three main stops – ask for details at the tourist office, where their excellent free map has the main stops and which routes they serve marked on it.

By taxi Taxis are plentiful and uniformly metered. Within the town centre, though, it's probably wise to consider walking rather than taking a cab – the one-way system is so labyrinthine that you could end up travelling several times further than the direct route.

INFORMATION AND TOURS

Tourist office The main office is at the British Colonial building on Plateia Vasileos Pavlou, backing onto the Municipal Cultural Centre. (Mon & Tues 8.15am–2.30pm, 3–6.15pm, Wed 8.15am–2.30pm, Thurs & Fri 8.15am–2.30pm, 3–6.30pm, Sat 8.15am–1.30pm; ☎ 24654322, ⓦ larnakaregion.com.

Sightseeing buses A useful way of getting your bearings once in Larnaka is the open-topped sightseeing bus. Love Buses offer tours that start and end on the promenade – or the police station if, as sometimes happens, the prom is closed. All the main sights mentioned above are included in the tour, which takes about an hour (11am, 3pm and 5.30pm; adults €10, children €5; ☎ 97761761). Otherwise try one of the **City**

Cruisers (☎ 70005960), a kind of space-age two-seater rickshaw, ridden by a professional guide. There's a choice of three routes (city centre, historical and arts and culture); they take 45–50min, and cost €12 per person.

ACCOMMODATION

Larnaka's big resort hotels are grouped up the coast to the northeast of the town, beyond the Nautical Club and the oil refineries. Within Larnaka itself are numerous smaller hotels and self-catering apartments. McKenzie Beach makes for a tempting alternative, though it is subject to aircraft noise from the airport.

TOWN CENTRE

Easy Hotel 1 Kimonos ☎ 24102703, ⓦ easyhotel.com. Centrally located a few yards from the Archeological Museum, *Easy Hotel* has the same ethos as that scion of a Cypriot family Stelios's other concerns – pared-back service, rock-bottom prices. So if the rooms seem a little Spartan (though quite tasteful), just look at your bill and smile. €34

★ **Eleonora Hotel Apartments** 55 Ermou ☎ 24624400, ⓦ eleonorahotelapts.com. Right in the centre, overlooking Ermou (Hermes) Square and its flamingo fountain, these recently renovated apartments are clean, functional and fully equipped, providing an ideal, low-cost base for exploring the town. €55

Livadhiotis City Hotel 50 Nikolaou Rossou ☎ 24626222, ⓦ livadhiotis.com. For those who wish to be at the heart of things, there couldn't be a better choice than the *Livadhiotis*. On a corner a few yards from Agios Lazaros church, and just around the corner from the promenade and Larnaka's main pub and restaurant area, it has 58 simple, recently refurbished rooms, all the in-room facilities you're likely to need, and a stylish café (*Café Blu*) and bar. €85

Sun Hall Hotel 6 Leoforos Athinon ☎ 24653341, ⓦ aquasolhotels.com. Wonderfully located on the promenade right next to the Municipal Cultural Centre, the *Sun Hall* combines the benefits of a town-centre business hotel with those of a holiday resort. It's just across the promenade from the beach, it has a swimming pool, gym, sauna, fitness room, restaurant and cocktail bar, and 24hr service. Rooms are tastefully smart after refurbishment (all have a fridge to keep drinks and snacks chilled). It is sometimes listed as offering apartments, but it doesn't. €148

BEACH HOTELS

Flamingo Beach Hotel 152 Pyiale Pasa ☎ 24646022, ⓦ flamingobeachcyprus.com. The *Flamingo* benefits from its location at the heart of McKenzie Beach. It has modern rooms (renovated 2007), a new patio area overlooking the beach, excellent wi-fi, regular buffet dinners and Greek music and dancing displays that are popular with residents and non-residents alike. €95

Lordos Beach Hotel Larnaka–Dekeleia Road, Pyla ☎ 24647444, ⓦ lordosbeach.com. Not quite as large as the Palm Beach (see below), and with a slightly less contemporary feel, the *Lordos Beach* offers a similar experience, though with a more limited range of facilities. It's always busy though, so they're doing something right. As with many establishments in Cyprus they seem to be making a big play for the Russian market. €100

★ **Palm Beach Hotel and Bungalows** Larnaka–Dekeleia Road, Pyla ☎ 24846600, ⓦ palmbeachhotel .com. The hotel has everything you need, which is just as well since it's a fair way out of the town. In fact, with its two restaurants, tavern, coffee shop, four bars, three swimming pools, watersports centre, tennis and squash courts, and for the children paddling pool, playground and kids' club, why would you want to go anywhere else? If you do, though, note that there's a bus stop and taxi rank just outside, and plenty of parking. Accommodation is comfortable and well-proportioned, with a wide choice of rooms, suites and bungalows. €136

LARNAKA FESTIVALS

As with towns and villages across Cyprus, Larnaka loves its festivals, and the major religious festivals (see p.55) are celebrated in the town with unrivalled enthusiasm. In addition, there are several celebrations that are unique to the town.

Procession of St Lazaros (April) Celebration of the feast day of the town's patron saint, which involves a procession through the streets headed by the icon of the saint normally kept in the church.

Anthestiria (May) With pagan roots going back to ancient Greece, Anthestiria celebrates the arrival of spring with parades of floats where the emphasis is on fresh flowers, which are carried down to the seafront.

Larnaka Summer Festival (July) A great celebration of the arts – drama, music, dance, film and poetry – at venues across the town.

August Village Festivals (August) Look out for village festivals throughout the region – live music, traditional Greek dancing and lots of food and wine.

1

Sandbeach Castle Hotel McKenzie Beach ☎24655437, ⊚castlehotel.com.cy. Well placed in popular McKenzie Beach, the *Sandbeach Castle* is a good basic hotel which is not only distinctive architecturally (it was built to look like a castle by the British District Commissioner, whose residence it was), but also one of the few which gives direct access to its own private sands. A terrace overlooks the beach, there's a comfortable, oddly homely bar, and waiting staff that speak good English – all seemingly Greek Cypriots from North London. **€75**

EATING AND DRINKING

Larnaka offers a good range of places to eat. There are some fine Greek Cypriot tavernas and fish restaurants strung along beside the sea on Piyale Pasa and McKenzie Beach. There's also particular concentration of bars and restaurants in the Laiki Geitonia district, clearly signposted off the promenade down near the fort.

★ **1900 Art Café** 6 Stasinou ☎24653027. By now something of an institution in Larnaka, the atmospheric *1900 Art Café* – all paintings on the walls, wooden floors and fires in winter in a mansion built in – yes – 1900 – offers good Cypriot food in convivial surroundings. Main courses include *stifado*, meatballs, stuffed vegetables and various chicken dishes, from around €9. If you get the chance, sit out on the balcony. Daily 6pm–1am

Black Turtle 11 Mehmet Ali ☎24650661. One of, if not the, oldest tavernas in Larnaka, the *Black Turtle* is a one off. Taking up the first floor of a distinctive old building just around the corner from Agios Lazaros, it serves both meze and à la carte meals. There's live Greek music and dancing on Friday and Saturday nights, starting at 10pm, and on these evenings there's a set menu at €16 per person not including drinks. Tues–Sat 5pm–1.30am

Feng's House 104 Leoforos Athinon ☎24657176. Well placed for people-watching on the promenade at the entrance to Laiki Geitonia district, and fronted by a cheery Buddha figure, *Feng's House* offers good quality Chinese food at reasonable prices, with main courses starting at around €8. Reservations recommended. Daily 12.30pm–midnight

★ **Hobos** 14 Leoforos Athinon ☎24815795. A popular café/restaurant providing a wide range of notparticularly Cypriot snacks – burgers at €6 to €9, or Italian dishes from €5.50 to €8.20, as well as cocktails around the €5 mark. It's a good choice for breakfast, and to bring kids – there's a small funfair on the pavement right next door. The steak house upstairs offers a range of quality beef and lamb dishes (€6–26), as well as a more varied menu (stuffed chicken breast, for example) Café: daily 9am–midnight; steak house Mon–Sat 4pm–midnight, Sun 11am–midnight.

Lush McKenzie Beach ☎70008089. The latest of a scrum of establishments on the sand at the far end of McKenzie Beach, *Lush* is a kind of one-stop-shop: beach café, swanky restaurant, cocktail bar, night club. International cuisine with good meat and pasta dishes, fancy cocktails, night-time dancing to DJs. And if you need further entertainment, take your airline spotting book – you get a good view of the planes landing at Larnaka Airport right next door. Daily 10am–midnight.

★ **Militzis** 42 Piyale Pasa ☎24655867. A hugely popular (with Cypriots as well as visitors) traditional Greek Cypriot restaurant just beyond the fort on busy sea-lapped Piyale Pasa, *Militzis* is hard to miss – there's a big wind-pump wreathed in climbing plants at the front, and an industrial-scale clay oven at the back. Its roasted and grilled meats are out of this world, the service is excellent, and the prices are very reasonable. Arrive early if you want to sit out on the terrace. Daily 12.30pm–midnight (kitchen closes 11.30pm).

Psarolimano 118 Piyale Pasa ☎24655408. You couldn't ask for a better-sited fish restaurant – it's on the dock at Larnaka's fishing harbour. Surrounded by potted greenery, it sticks largely to what it does best – fresh fish. Main dishes start at €12 though a lot of the prices are by weight (such as sea bass, €32 per kilo). Highly recommended. Daily noon–midnight

Varoshiotis 7 Piyale Pasa ☎70003536. Established in Larnaka by Vasos Varoshiotis when he and his family were forced to flee from their existing home and restaurant in Famagusta in 1974, *Varoshiotis* is now one of the town's leading fish restaurants, offering a range of delicious seafood meze and à la carte meals in tiled and ceiling-fanned splendour. Reservations recommended. Main courses between €10 and €25. Daily noon–midnight

NIGHTLIFE

For a relatively small town without the reputation for nightlife of an Agia Napa or Lemesos, Larnaka in fact does very well. It's sometimes difficult to differentiate between bars, pubs, restaurants and clubs – indeed, what is a café/bar during the day can become a lively venue during the evening and a nightclub into the small hours. For bar hopping the best bet is the small Laiki Geitonia area off the promenade down towards the fort.

BARS

Jungle Gardens Music Bar 101 Palaias Agoras ☎99409145 The *Jungle Gardens Music Bar* specializes in exotic cocktails and varied musical tastes and appeals to a younger crowd. Daily 4pm–late.

★ **Savino Rock Bar** 9 Watkins ☎24620861. Bar with

THE SINKING OF THE ZENOBIA

1

The wreck of the **Zenobia** lies in 43m of water some 1.5km off Larnaka. The story of its sinking remains something of a mystery. A brand new roll-on/roll-off ferry, launched in Sweden in 1979, the Zenobia embarked on its maiden voyage to Syria in 1980, sailing from Malmö and through the Straits of Gibraltar. As it approached Greece, steering problems started to develop, and the ship began listing to port. It became clear that a computer malfunction was causing excess water to be pumped into the ballast tanks. The problem apparently solved, the ship continued to Cyprus. While in Larnaka harbour, however, the listing recurred and got worse. Eventually the captain was ordered to take her out of the harbour, in case she sank and became a hazard to other ships. Anchored offshore, the situation got worse, so much so that the captain ordered the crew to abandon ship. In the early hours of 7 June, 1980 she turned turtle and sank. Compared to the usual shipwreck, the whole drama was played out relatively slowly, and as a result there was no loss of life (though several divers have been drowned in the wreck since). Apart from the catastrophic failure of a state-of-the-art ferry, the mystery is that despite her intrinsic value and the €200 million cargo she carried (including over 100 lorries), no investigation was ever carried out, and the owners never tried to collect the insurance. It's an ill wind, though – the wreck of the Zenobia is now considered to be one of the best dive sites in the world.

loud music, a wide range of beers, ciders and cocktails and the odd game of pool. Daily 7pm–late.

CLUBS

Caramel Club Agiou Spyridonos ⓦ caramel-disco.com. With its mirror balls, three bars and comfortable sofas, the *Caramel Club* has interestingly expanded its playlist to include Russian and Bulgarian hits as well as British, Greek and European ones – a sign of the times. 11pm till late.

Circus 17 Grigori Afxentiou ⓣ 99659498. *Circus* often has r'n'b nights with Greek and Cypriot DJs, and has a roof bar open during the summer. Fri & Sat midnight–4.30am.

Encounter 73 Leoforos Athinon. *Encounter* is a double-decker club consisting of *Club Deep* (ⓣ 24658230), offering a wide range of garage, old school, r'n'b and house, together with Greek hits; and downstairs in the basement

Topaz (ⓣ 24625272), which provides mainstream funky and deep house. Fri & Sat midnight–4am.

Geometry Karaoli & Demetriou ⓣ 99676134. Offers contemporary dance, and earns its name from the hundreds of crystals in its ceiling. Fri & Sat midnight–4am.

Secrets Freedom 67 Leoforos Artemidos ⓣ 99557433, ⓦ secrets-freedom-club. *Secrets Freedom* is a little out of the centre, on the main dual carriageway out to the airport (on the left just after Elomas Supermarket). One of the biggest and best of Cyprus's gay clubs, it welcomes straight as well as gay customers and puts on a wide range of special events and parties. 11pm–late.

Vogue Exclusive 19 Plateia Demetriou (4th floor) ⓣ 99344180. Commercial hits from Greece and beyond, a generous-sized dancefloor and a well-dressed, more mature clientele. Fri & Sat midnight–late.

ENTERTAINMENT

Casino Royal 33 Ithakis Court ⓣ 24664945. The usual range of gaming opportunities together with a free bar and buffet. Daily 24 hours.

Cinema ⓣ 24362167. The six-screen K Cineplex is at the intersection of Potamou Indou and Peloponisou west of the town centre near the Kamares Aqueduct.

Theatres Larnaca is justly proud of the range and quality of the dance, drama and music that it manages to provide.

Its four venues – the Municipal Theatre in the Municipal Gardens (ⓣ 24665794), the Pattichion Amphitheatre at the northern end of the Salt Lake (ⓣ 24629300), the Theatro Skala at 15 Kyriakou Matsi (ⓣ 24637952) and Antidoto Theatre on Agias Elenis (ⓣ 24822677) – together with the gardens in the old fort, mount a series of plays, concerts and performances of dance, especially during the summer months.

SHOPPING

Given fast motorway links with the capital, most locals head to Lefkosia for serious shopping. That said, Larnaka offers a fair range of shops, especially ones that are likely to appeal to visitors. The main shopping streets are Zinonos Kitieos, which runs parallel to the promenade one block west, Ermou which strikes northwest from Zinonos Kitieos's southern end, and the streets and alleys in between.

Beauty Line 51 Ermou ⓣ 24650181. One of a Cypriot chain of shops selling top-end beauty products and

perfume. April–Oct Mon, Tues & Thurs 9am–7pm, Wed 9am–2pm, Sat 9am–3pm; Nov–March Mon,

1

Tues & Thurs 9am–6pm, Wed 9am–2pm, Sat 9am–3pm.

Cyprus Handicraft Centre 6 Kosma Lysioti ☎ 24304327. One of a chain set up by the government (there's one in Lefkosia, Lemesos and Paphos as well) to ensure the survival of traditional crafts. Mon, Tues, Thurs & Fri 7.30am–5.30pm, Wed 7.30am–1pm, Sat 9am–1pm.

Dodici 173 Ermou ☎ 24823950. Classy men's and women's shoes from Greece. April–Oct Mon, Tues & Thurs 9am–7pm, Wed 9am–2pm, Sat 9am–3pm; Nov–March Mon, Tues & Thurs 9am–6pm, Wed 9am–2pm, Sat 9am–3pm.

Kalopedis Jewellery 38 Zinonos Kitieos ☎ 24655501, ⓦ kalopedis.com. A long-established family firm where the jewellery – much of it with a Greek theme – is designed

and made on the premises. Look out for worry beads, evil eye and Greek key pattern jewellery for example, and a wide range of both ancient and modern designs. Mon–Fri 9am–7pm, Sat 9am–2pm.

Marks & Spencer 57 Zinonos Kitieos ☎ 24654795. The well-loved British store, a shot of nostalgia for expats. Mon, Tues & Thurs 8am–8pm, Wed 8am–2pm, Fri 8am–7.30pm, Sat 8am–6pm.

Tofarides 45–47 Zinonos Kitieos ☎ 24654912. A newsagent, stationers and bookshop selling English language as well as Greek titles. April–Oct Mon, Tues & Thurs 9am–7pm, Wed 9am–2pm, Sat 9am–3pm; Nov–March Mon, Tues & Thurs 9am–6pm, Wed 9am–2pm, Sat 9am–3pm.

Agia Napa

AGIA NAPA (often transposed as Ayia Napa), 35km east of Larnaka, is not everybody's cup of tea. If you want peace and quiet, or to commune with nature, or to get to grips with traditional Cypriot life, go somewhere else. But if you're young and want the company of people of your own age and lots of stuff to do, or if you're a family with teenagers who are easily bored, this is one of the best holiday areas in Europe. The area is certainly overdeveloped, but no more so than any other typical Mediterranean package-holiday destination.

Though much of the resort's appeal is down to its nightlife, there's now a lot more to it than that. Its remarkably compact centre sits behind a surprisingly charming small harbour (Limanaki) with some fine stretches of sand, notably **Nissi beach**, running west from here. Look out too for **Agia Napa Monastery** and the excellent **Thalassa Museum**, the fine **amusement park** in the centre of town, and the colossal **Waterworld Waterpark** to the west.

Agia Napa Monastery

Plateia Seferi • Daily 9am–6pm • Free

Amid the bars and traffic of Agia Napa, it's something of a shock to find a beautifully renovated **monastery** (originally a convent) – looking like a stern elderly relative from a bygone age frowning at all the nonsense going on around her. As with many religious sites in Cyprus, it comes with a complicated and confused story. A hunter, out with his dog, discovered a cave and spring in the woods. Not only did his mangy dog develop a new healthy-looking coat after bathing in the spring water, but the hunter also found an icon of the Virgin Mary in the cave, hidden there during iconoclastic attacks on such pictures in the eighth or ninth centuries. This story led to widespread belief in the miraculous powers of the water and the icon. In around 1500, a convent was built on the site as a refuge for a Venetian noblewoman whose father had refused her permission

---

GUNS, GANGS AND GARAGE

Much of Agia Napa's toxic reputation stems from the early 2000s when turf wars between different UK garage "crews" broke out during which several people (including a young Dizzee Rascal) were stabbed. This violence was thought to be a thing of the past, though the mafia-style shooting of three Cypriots and two Romanians on the streets of the town in June 2012 and the murder of a young British soldier in a bar-room brawl in November 2012 show that there's no room for complacency, and that the improvement In Agia Napa's image is still very fragile.

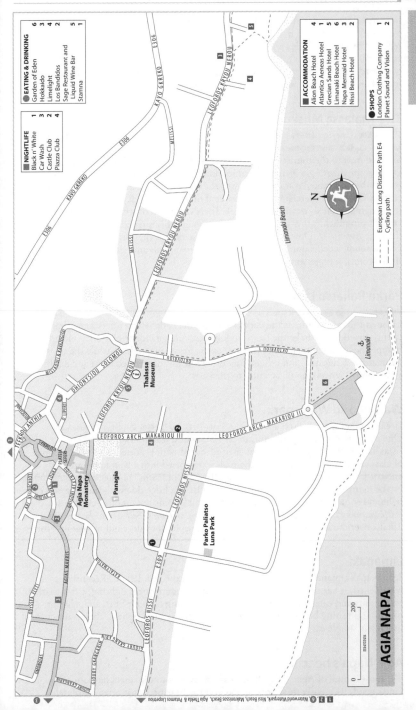

NIGHTLIFE	
Black n' White	1
Car Wash	3
Castle Club	2
Piazza Club	4

● EATING & DRINKING	
Garden of Eden	6
Hokkaido	3
Limelight	4
Los Bandidos	2
Sage Restaurant and Liquid Wine Bar	5
Stamna	1

■ ACCOMMODATION	
Alion Beach Hotel	4
Atlantica Aeneas Hotel	1
Grecian Sands Hotel	5
Limanaki Beach Hotel	6
Napa Mermaid Hotel	3
Nissi Beach Hotel	2

● SHOPS	
London Clothing Company	1
Planet Sound and Vision	2

AGIA NAPA

1

to marry a commoner. After the Ottoman conquest of 1571 the Roman Catholic Venetians were replaced by Greek Orthodox nuns, and in 1668 they in turn were replaced by monks. Today an Ecumenical Conference Centre, its courtyard and octagonal fountain are a haven of tranquillity at the heart of Agia Napa's frenzy. The courtyard and church (partly underground – this was the cave in which the icon was found) are open to the public, though there seems to be no sign of the icon.

The Thalassa Museum

14 Krynou Nerou • June–Sept Mon 9am–1pm & 6–10pm, Tues–Sat 9am–5pm, Sun 9am–1pm Oct–May Mon 9am–1pm, Tues–Sat 9am–5pm • €3 • ☎ 23816366, ⓦ museum.agianapa.org.cy.

Situated next to the tourist office, the **Thalassa Museum** ("Sea Museum") opened in 2006, emphasizes Agia Napa's determination to be known for more than drunken revels. The undoubted star of the show is the **Kyrenia II**, an exact replica of a fourth-century BC Greek merchant ship discovered off the coast of Kyrenia in the mid 1980s (the original is on show in Girne castle). There's also a reconstruction of a **papyrus vessel** from much earlier times (9200 BC), though this is based on far less evidence than the *Kyrenia II*. Downstairs in the semi-basement is the **Tornaritis-Pierides Marine Life Museum**, a collection of stuffed birds, fish, mammals and sea turtles together with shells, corals, sponges and lobsters.

Parko Paliatso Luna Park

Off Leoforos Nissi • Daily 6pm–late • Cost of rides varies, paid for by token

Close to the town centre is the **Parko Paliatso Luna Park**, which offers more than twenty-five rides, from gentle to white-knuckle. A large indoor play area (including bumper boats, teacups and trampolines) caters for small children, while the fearsome "Blizzard", "Slingshot" and others ring to the screams of terrified teens and adults. The sedate Ferris Wheel, for all, is a nod to the past.

Waterworld Waterpark

18 Agia Thekla • 10am–6pm • under-2s free, 3–12-year-olds €19, over-13s €33 • ☎ 23724444, ⓦ waterworldwaterpark.com

One of the largest waterparks in Europe **Waterworld Waterpark** is a cracker. Establishing its ethos as soon as you arrive (the car park is dotted with plaster copies of classical statues and buildings) the park is organized into a wonderful array of ancient-Greek-themed attractions – from the "Fall of Icarus" (a huge open slide topped by the figure of the sun) to the "Drop to Atlantis" (a huge ride with three-person cars, light and sound effects). The theme is carried on into its restaurants and shops – *Minotaur's Pizza, Homer's Burger Palace, Dionysos Temple Self-service Restaurant*. Totally over the top, but who knows, it might inspire the odd child to take up Homer.

Limanaki

Agia Napa's **Limanaki** or "little harbour" is an unexpected delight. Recently remodelled, it has convenient paved walkways, modern street lighting, a fish market, restaurants and cafés, all set around a vibrant jostling harbour of leisure, charter, tourist and fishing boats (guided into port by little conical lights). There's also a small beach and ample car parking.

Agia Napa's beaches

The most central of Agia Napa's **beaches** is right next to Limanaki harbour. Though the sand's good, it's a fairly thin strip, and as you might expect, it is often absolutely heaving. You're usually better off heading west to **Nissi Beach**, notable particularly for the small island ("Nissi" is the Greek for "island") in the bay to which you can swim or even wade. The sand here is particularly fine, there are plenty of watersports on offer, and the water, compared to the deep blue depths beyond the island, is a pale, shimmering ultramarine. Further west still, **Makronissos Beach** offers the usual mix of beach facilities, plus a bit of archeological interest. Three kilometres past here is **Agia Thekla**, a series of tiny bays dominated by a rather fine modern church of that name. What makes it special is the impromptu market that springs up around the church on Saturdays, flogging everything from fresh fruit to jewellery, toys and DVDs, all to the accompaniment of loud recorded Greek music.

Makronissos archeological site
Dawn–dusk • Free

Beyond Markonissos beach, and well signposted at the end of a paved road, is the **Makronissos archeological site**, a collection of nineteen rock-cut tombs that date from the years straddling the birth of Christ. It's like an underground village, with flights of steps, running down to tombs where bodies were placed in sarcophagi (one is on show at the Thalassa Museum).

The cave church at Agia Thekla

At Agia Thekla look out for the tiny **cave church** or tomb (nobody's quite sure which), let into a small rock face below the modern church – there are concrete steps down to it. The little church, marked by a cross on the rock above the entrance has a number of icons on the rock walls, and a table bearing offerings of oil and candles. Legend has it that this is where Pyiele Pasa landed during the Ottoman invasion of Cyprus in 1571.

Potamos Liopetriou

Three kilometres west of Agia Thekla (and a minute off the motorway – it's clearly signposted) is **Potamos Liopetriou**, a long sinuous estuary of a small river, lined on both sides with traditional Cypriot fishing boats. Two tavernas overlook the river – the *Potamos* about halfway down the crowded river bank, the *Demetrion* next to where the river disgorges into the bay beside a small sandy beach. Heavily featured in tourist-board literature, Potamos is a rare treat – there's nothing quite like it anywhere else on the island. Incidentally, the French poet Rimbaud worked here in the late 1870s as a quarry foreman, before having to return to France with suspected typhoid.

ARRIVAL AND INFORMATION   **AGIA NAPA**

By bus Agia Napa's main bus station is on Leoforos Arch. Makariou III, just north of the harbour. **Destinations** Larnaka (Mon–Fri 10 daily, Sat & Sun 5 daily; 1hr) Paralimni (Mon–Fri 10 daily, Sat & Sun 5 daily; 1hr)

Tourist office The main office is at Leoforos Kryou Nerou (Mon, Tues & Thurs, Fri 8.15am–2.30pm & 3–6.30pm; Wed & Sat 8.15am–2.30pm; ☎ 23721796), next to the Thalassa Museum. Be sure to pick up free copies of the two excellent maps of the area Agia Napa and Paralimni/Protaras.

Travel agents There are numerous travel agencies in Agia Napa which offer fixed coach trips, jeep safaris, boat cruises and the like (for example, Eman Travel and Tours, 32 Arch. Makariou III, ☎ 23721321).

GETTING AROUND

By bus Buses in the Agia Napa region are run by OSEA (☎ 23819090 ⓦ osea.com.cy). The most popular routes include the 101 and 102 to Paralimni, Protaras, Cape Greco and the Waterpark, the 201 and 301 circular routes around the Agia Napa area, and the 501 and 502 to Deryneia. Intercity buses to Larnaka and Lefkosia run every one to two hours (less frequently at weekends). The area also has tourist buses which are a good way of finding your bearings (Red Bus Tour ☎ 96423602).

By taxi As you'd expect in an area famous for its nightlife, the Agia Napa/Protaras/Paralimni area has numerous taxi companies, many of which publish a fixed price list for

1

popular journeys (try East Coast Taxis for example ☎ 23724343). Consider also the shared taxi service (see p.27).

By car and motorbike All the major car hire agents are represented with prices starting from €18 per day. One of the most popular ways of getting around the area is to rent a motorbike, buggy or quad bike. Prices can be quite steep – anything between €20 and €35 per day (often with a two-day minimum) for a small motorbike to between €300 and £400 a week for a large buggy (have a look, for example, at Easy Riders, based in Agia Napa's main square (☎ 23722438, ⓦ easyriders.com.cy)

ACTIVITIES

Boat trips Numerous boat trips run from Limanaki harbour. Try the glass-bottomed Yellow Submarine (☎ 99658280), which employs divers to attract fish to the viewing window, or the Dolphin Boat Safari (☎ 99607181), which runs trips to Famagusta and snorkelling trips. Fares start at around €10 and rise to €45 for a full day's fishing

Bungee jumping Bungee Downunder (☎ 99605248 May–Oct 3pm–1am) operate a scarily high crane at Nissi Beach. There's usually a barbecue and loud music as well.

Karting The best of several Karting tracks is EMW Go Cars next to Water World (☎ 23723111 6min €12, 10min; €16).

Watersports Your best bet is Nissi Beach which offers everything from banana boat rides to jet-skis, wakeboarding, water skiing and paragliding. For scuba diving try Sunfish Divers at 26 Arch. Makariou III (☎ 23721300, ⓦ sunfishdivers.com).

ACCOMMODATION

Agia Napa's main hotel areas are along Kryou Nerou, the road in from the east, and Leoforos Nissi (Nissi Avenue), the road that comes in from the west. For a degree of peace and quiet, go for the east; for busy beaches with lots of watersports, go for the west. There are also a few options in the heart of town close to the action.

★ **Alion Beach Hotel** Kryou Nerou ☎ 23722900, ⓦ alion.com. Set amid lush gardens on a sweeping beach, rooms have unfussy decor, there's a choice of five restaurant/bars, a health spa and fitness centre, indoor, outdoor and kids' pools, a range of entertainment and sports activities, though with more emphasis on adults than children. Open all year. **€200**

Atlantica Aeneas Hotel 100 Leoforos Nissi ☎ 23724000, ⓦ aeneas.com.cy. Notable for its position a short walk from popular Nissi Beach and its huge labyrinthine swimming pool with bridges, fountains, whirlpools, and three bars dotted among the foliage, the *Aeneas* is one of Agia Napa's flagship hotels. The range of facilities includes all you'd expect (spa, health club, hairdressing salon, souvenir shop, kids' club and lots more), and the service is effortlessly smooth and efficient. **€150**

Grecian Sands Hotel 44 Kryou Nero ☎ 23721616, ⓦ greciansands.com. Built after the Turkish invasion of 1974 during the first moves to re-establish Cyprus as a tourist destination, the *Grecian Sands* is in some ways rather old-fashioned. However, a rolling programme of refurbishment, a management that is on the ball (making a big play, for example, for the growing wedding trade) and an enviable position on a bay east of the town centre keep it competitive. **€100**

Limanaki Beach Hotel Limanaki ☎ 23721600, ⓦ agianapahotels.net. Right in the heart of things, virtually on the bustling harbour, the *Limanaki Beach* can't offer the range of facilities that the big resort hotels offer – why should it? But it manages a pool, sauna (extra charge), fitness room, bars and restaurant and a café. And all the other things that Agia Napa has to offer are on your doorstep. **€85**

★ **Napa Mermaid Hotel** 45 Kryou Nerou ☎ 23721606, ⓦ napamermaidhotel.com.cy. Elegant and immaculate, the *Napa Mermaid* is a triumph of style, comfort and cleanliness. There are two restaurants offering everything from snacks to fine dining, two bars, and facilities include the full range of swimming pools, health and fitness equipment, beauty treatments and sports, and thoughtful service. If the hotel has a downside it is the lack of beachfront. **€184**

Nissi Beach Hotel Leoforos Nissi ☎ 23721021, ⓦ nissi-beach.com. The unique selling point here is the hotel's position on one of the most popular beaches in Cyprus. With a range of restaurants and bars, health and beauty facilities, entertainment and sports opportunities, the *Nissi Beach* is ideal for adults, while its kids' club (with everything from face painting to mini discos), children's pool and two playgrounds keep the little ones happy. **€180**

EATING AND DRINKING

Garden of Eden 144 Leoforos Nissi ☎ 23724810, ⓦ thegardenofedencyprus.com. Good range of Greek and international dishes (you'll find shepherd's pie under "exotic and ethnic"), efficient and friendly service, with

main courses from around €6. Good indoor and alfresco dining, with children's playground to keep the kids occupied. April–Oct lunch and dinner.

Hokkaido 35 Agias Mavris ☎ 23721505, ⓦ hokkaidocy .com. Fine Japanese restaurant with accomplished cooks offering what amounts to a floor show, with food thrown in: sashimi and sushi, with most items on the menu between €4.80 and €13.50. Daily 5.30–11pm.

★ **Limelight** Dimetri Liperti ☎ 23721650, ⓦ wlimelighttaverna.com. Greek Cypriot taverna offering massive choice and portions of traditional food, for example, charcoal-grilled steak, lobster, suckling pig and much more, with prices mostly in the €9.40 – €16 range. The *keftedes* and *koupepia* are delicious. Mon–Sat noon–midnight.

Los Bandidos 2 Ari Velouchioti ☎ 23723528, ⓦ losbandidosmexican.com. Near the main square, *Los Bandidos* is claimed by some to be the best Mexican restaurant in Cyprus (though how many there are is

another question). The food is good, though service can be slow, especially at busy times. "Not just a restaurant, it's an experience" is its tagline – and the experience includes wearing sombreros or six-guns at the table. Main courses from €6.85, though you'll pay more for something exotic – €23 for a crocodile fajita, for example. Daily 5.30–11pm.

Sage Restaurant and Liquid Wine Bar 10 Kryou Nero ☎ 23816110, ⓦ sagerest.com. Modern Mediterranean-type menu of well-cooked food in a restaurant with stylish ambience, friendly (or, if you're a curmudgeon, intrusive) service, extensive opening hours and prices that range from €11 to €40. Daily 9am–2am.

Stamna Dimokratias ☎ 23721386, ⓦ stamnatavern .com. Family taverna in what it claims is Agia Napa's oldest house. Authentic Greek Cypriot food, together with more international dishes, at affordable prices (from around €6). Mid-April to mid-Oct 11am–1pm & 5pm–late.

NIGHTLIFE

While the wilder extremes of partying that gave Agia Napa an unenviable reputation throughout Europe have now been reined in, there is still a very lively scene. Clubs come and go, but some have become fixtures, in many cases by reinventing themselves every year or two. Most of the action centres on the main square in the town centre and roads leading off, with the scene really getting going in the small hours.

★ **Black n'White** 6 Louka Louka ☎ 2373340, ⓦ napasound.com. Established way back in 1985, the small and underground *Club Black n'White* is right in the centre of Agia Napa. With a mix of hip-hop, r'n'b and old-skool garage, it also maintains links with Choice FM, BBC 1XTRA and Kiss100. And when you're knackered, enjoy the chill-out lounge. March–Oct daily 1.30–4am, Nov–Feb Fri & Sat 1.30–4am.

Car Wash Agias Mavris ☎ 23723029, ⓦ facebook.com /carwashdiscoagianapa. Another stayer (established 1996). Emphasis on 1970s and 1980s disco, with unparalleled

sound system and lighting. Daily 1am–4.30am.

Castle Club Grigori Afxentiou ☎ 97775550, ⓦ thecastleclub.com. Large venue with three main rooms, 14 bars, VIP and chill-out lounges, and updated TV, sound and light systems, the *Castle Club* (yes, the building looks like a castle) offers a mixture of r'n'b, house, trance, chart and disco. Daily 1am–4.30am.

Piazza Club Arch. Makariou III ☎ 99388555, ⓦ clubpiazza.com. A relative newcomer (2005), Club Piazza sees itself as a cut above, with its flash decor and emphasis on Greek music. Fri & Sat 11pm–4am.

FESTIVALS AND ENTERTAINMENT

Agia Napa Festival (September). Held annually since 1985, the town's main festival is a feast of music, drama and dance, taking place largely in the town square and monastery.

Cultural Winter (November to April). Concerts and recitals put on by the municipality in the town (☎ 23816307

for details).

Folk singing and dancing (April to October). Every Sunday in Seferis Square.

Youth Festival (August). Free three-day event held in the square next to Limanaki harbour, with music of all sorts but mainly rock and metal.

SHOPPING

Most shops focus on the usual souvenirs – embroidered cloth, ceramics, copper, brass, woodcarving, jewellery, clothes, leather goods – but you can also find some designer bargains.

London Clothing Company 12 Leoforos Nissi ☎ 23723566. Crammed with locals as well as visitors looking for Versace, French Connection and so on. Mon–Sat 9am–11pm Sun 11am–7pm.

Planet Sound and Vision 27 Arch. Makariou III ☎ 23724010. Stocks not only a big range of CDs, DVDs and games, but also Napa compilations to remind you of your holiday, as well as tickets for gigs. Daily 9.30am–10pm.

SUN, SAND AND BARBED WIRE

The area around Agia Napa is one of the regions of the south most affected by the Turkish invasion of 1974 – in much of it you cannot but be aware of the Green Line, of the UN troops manning it, and of Turkish-occupied north Cyprus in many places within clear view beyond. The area, too, has a continued UK presence in the British base at Dekelia. If you stay within Agia Napa itself, then the only indication you're likely to have of this is the possible presence of British soldiers (though the town is supposedly out of bounds to them). But the short trip to Deryneia will give you a good view of ruined Varosha, left high and dry by the invasion (see box, p.237), and you can visit Gazimağusa (Famagusta) in the north by using either of the crossing points in the area (see box, p.231).

Around Agia Napa

A few kilometres northeast of Agia Napa are the fine beaches of **Protaras**, as well as rugged **Cape Greko**, perfect for exploring on foot or racing around in a dune buggy. Inland are the so-called "red villages" or **Kokkinochorio**, set among fields of red soil (hence the name) dotted with wind pumps and within spitting distance of the Turkish-occupied north. **Pyla**, in the Buffer Zone and the only combined Greek/Turkish Cypriot village remaining on the island, has one of the few points where you can cross into north Cyprus. **Deryneia**, on a north slope facing Famagusta and with views across the modern part of that city, flourished until 1974, and is now a derelict ghost town.

This easternmost part of south Cyprus is easily accessible – the national motorway links it to the rest of the island, while other excellent main roads (the E306, 307 and 327) make moving around within it a doddle. It also boasts a good bus service and even well-marked footpaths. Incidentally, the Agia Napa/Protaras area is technically part of Famagusta District, but since a large chunk of that is now occupied by the Turkish Army (and covered in Chapter 6), it has been included in this chapter.

Cape Greko

Separating the beaches of Agia Napa and Protaras, **Cape Greko** is a bare rocky headland dotted with sea caves. Though protected as a nature reserve, it gets busy with locals hurtling around on motorbikes and dune buggies. The road to the actual cape is cut off by a fence and a stout gate – it's a British military installation, and access is denied. However, a left turn before the gate will bring you to a natural rock bridge (much photographed, but you're not allowed to actually walk across it) and, a bit further on, the church of Agii Anargyrii. There's often an ice-cream van in the car park, and beyond the church there are steps down to a "sacred" sea cave and a signpost to others some 4km away. Along this stretch of the coast you are likely to come across cruise boats anchored offshore for people to have a swim, and youngsters testing their mettle by jumping or diving off the cliffs. If you're tempted yourself, be careful – there are dangerous currents.

Protaras

Beyond Cape Greko, and facing east, **PROTARAS** is a family-friendly version of its big brother, Agia Napa, along the coast. A long, linear strip from Agia Trias in the north to Fig Tree Bay in the south, Protaras largely fills in the space between the E306 Paralimni to Agia Napa road and the sea. In particular, it spreads along a one-way main street that loops down then rejoins the E306, with spurs heading east to the beaches. Its attractions are particularly human in scale and child-orientated – the **Ocean Aquarium**, the **Magical Dancing Waters**, the small **Water Park**, the **mini-golf courses** and amusement arcades. Like Agia Napa, Protaras also has its share of intimate Blue Flag **beaches**.

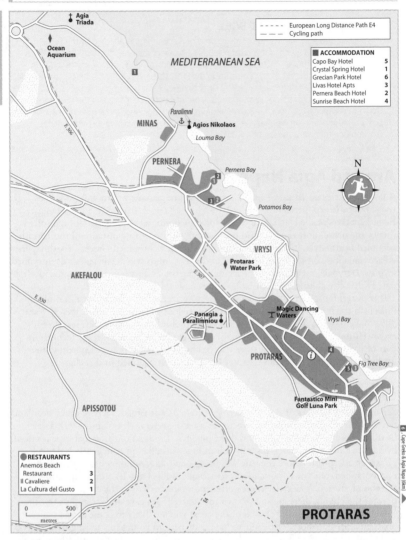

Ocean Aquarium

April–Oct 10am–6pm; Nov–March 9am–4pm • €12 • ☎ 23741111, ⓦ protarasaquarium.com

Housed in a purpose-built yellow structure on the main road from Protaras to Paralimni, the **Ocean Aquarium** is an eclectic mix of penguins, crocodiles, exotic birds, coral reefs and over 400 species of fish and turtles, few actually native to the region. It's expensive and does not compare well with aquariums elsewhere in the world. If you're stuck for something to do for an hour, though, and have very small children, it might just be worth it.

Magic Dancing Waters

9pm–10pm • €17 adults, €9 children, family of four €48 • ☎ 99623143, ⓦ magicdancing.szm.com

On the main street in the centre of Protaras, next to *McDonald's*, you'll find the **Magic Dancing Waters**. Imagine first of all a curtain of pulsing, churning water tinted by coloured lights, throbbing to highly amplified music. Progressively throw in a flashing laser show, and end with a crescendo of simulated volcanic eruptions, fire spilling out of the crater and smoke billowing everywhere, all to the sound of Europe's "The Final Countdown". This all happens in front of a terrace upon which the customers sit at tables, eating or drinking or both, it takes about an hour, and you'll either love it or hate it. What is indisputable is that it's not cheap.

Protaras Water Park

Off the Pernera road, next to the *Paschalia Hotel* • 10am–6pm • €17 (2 –10-year-olds €10, under-2s free) • ☎ 23833888

Though much smaller than the one in Agia Napa, the **Protaras Water Park** is ideal for families with children. With a pool with three big slides, two large intertwined tubes and smaller slides into the shallow end, plus games area, there's enough to keep the kids and adolescents happy, while the poolside bar, shop and restaurant allow adults to relax as they keep an eye on their offspring. The entry fees can seem a little steep, so you'd need to make sure you've time for a decent session, but prices often drop when business is slow.

Fantastico Mini Golf Luna Park

449 Protaras–Kavo Greko Avenue • 10am–10pm • €3–7 • ☎ 23833193

The best of several mini-golf courses in Protaras, this one's imaginative, well laid out and in really good condition (not always the case with this sort of attraction), with coin-op rides, bumper cars and a miniature train, and with a convenient restaurant offering reasonably priced meals, snacks and drinks.

Protaras beaches

Protaras more than outdoes Agia Napa in the range and quality of its **beaches**. At the far north of the town there's the fishing shelter of **Agia Triada** (just past the aquarium), there's bonny little harbour with a modern church, locals fishing off the rocks, and the ever-present *Helen Snacks* van providing sustenance. Just a couple of kilometres south, at **Paralimni**, a paved terrace overlooks a harbour full of fishing boats. There's a taverna (with no name) with a terrace offering fine views of the harbour, and the photogenic church of **Agios Nikolaos** on the end of the promontory to the right. Beyond the church, palm trees sweep down to the sandy beach of **Louma Bay** and its clutch of hotels. Further south a number of other beaches have equally good sand and numerous hotels and restaurants – **Pernera Bay**, **Potamos Bay**, **Vrissi Bay** and, the jewel in Protaras's crown, **Fig Tree Bay**, known for its beauty across the island. In some ways Fig Tree Bay (also known as Protaras Bay) is a victim of its own celebrity – the natural allure of its pellucid water, fine sand and, yes, even a few fig trees, has been tempered by wooden boardwalks, concrete steps, showers, and the roar of speedboats and jet-skis (try ⓦfigtreebaywatersports.com or ⓦstavroswatersports.com for watersports) – but its setting is still hard to beat.

ARRIVAL AND INFORMATION   PROTARAS

By bus There is no main bus station in Protaras, since the town is on the main Agia Napa to Paralimni route but there are regular stops along the two main roads. For bus routes from Agia Napa and Larnaka, see p.61.

Tourist office Cavo Greko, off Lefkolla Square (Mon, Tues & Thurs, Fri 8.15am–2.30pm & 3–6.30pm; Wed & Sat 8.15am–2.30pm, ☎ 23832865).

TOURS AND ACTIVITIES

A variety of cruises up the coast (most with swimming stops and barbecues), fishing trips and scuba-diving expeditions are on offer in the boat harbours around Protaras. Prices range from €10 to €45. For diving try Taba Diving School (☎ 23832680, ⓦ tabadivingcyprus.com) which is based in the *Pernera Beach Hotel*.

ACCOMMODATION

Capo Bay Hotel 2 Iasonos ☎ 23831101, ⓦ capobay .com. An attractively designed and luxurious hotel in

prime position on the beach in the centre of town, with a terrific range of rooms and suites, classy restaurants and bars, a large pool, gym, spa, diving centre, and sports facilities, and a kids' club. April–Oct. **€160**

Crystal Springs Beach Hotel 95 Vrysoudion ☎23826900, ⓦcrystalspringsbeachhotel.com. The elegant and luxurious *Crystal Springs* offers access to a sandy beach, its own scuba-diving centre, and a wide range of sporting and entertainment activities. If the hotel has a drawback it's the location, well away from the town centre, so to get anywhere else you need to drive, get a cab, or catch the bus outside the hotel. This might explain, of course, the wide range of in-house activities and also what is, for this grade of hotel, a very reasonable tariff. April–Oct. **€90**

Grecian Park Hotel 81 Konnos ☎23844000, ⓦgrecianpark.com. As regards location, it doesn't get any better than the *Grecian Park*, perched on its cliff above Konnos Bay, with views across to Cape Greko. From the same stable as the *Grecian Sands* in Agia Napa, the hotel boasts a cool elegance of design, a health club, spa and wellness centre, top-class restaurants (and its own nightclub and sushi bar) and in its *Cliff Bar* one of the best views on the island. There's a nature trail down onto Konnos Beach, and a kiosk there for drinks and snacks. April–Nov. **€220**

Livas Hotel Apartments 1 Thaleias ☎23831756, ⓦlivashotelapts.com. At rates below what you'll pay at the big hotels, the *Livas* offers clean rooms with kitchenette (useful for saving a few pennies if you don't wish to eat at the hotel's restaurant), two pools (one for kids), tennis court, pool table and video games. The studios and apartments are fairly Spartan, but then you'd not expect to be spending much time indoors. With friendly staff, a nearby beach and lots going on in the vicinity, it's a good budget choice. April–Oct. **€90**

Pernera Beach Hotel Pernera ☎23831011, ⓦpernera.com.cy. Terrific location right on Pernera Bay, with wrap around restaurant overlooking the beach. The hotel has a full entertainment package for kids and friendly, committed staff. It's also the base for the excellent Taba Diving School which operates right off the beach. **€65**

★ **Sunrise Beach Hotel** Vrissi Bay ☎23831501, ⓦsunrise.com.cy. Near the centre of Protaras on Vrissi Bay, a very popular beach with tourists and Cypriots alike, the *Sunrise Beach* has a beachside pool (with whirlpool), three restaurants, four bars, scuba-diving school, health club, a fitness centre and courts for tennis and squash. It is also a good choice for families – there's a kids' club, children's pool and playground, and children's menus and high chairs in the restaurants. April–Oct. **€146**

EATING AND DRINKING

Anemos Beach 7 Lasonos ☎23831488. Offers wide selection of meals (though its specialism is fish) and a large terrace with terrific views across Fig Tree Bay upon which to enjoy them. Main courses from €6.30. April–Oct 9am–11pm.

Il Cavaliere 6 Pernera ☎23831022. Fairly standard Italian restaurant – pasta, pizza – but with regional dishes as well, and particularly welcoming if you've got kids: children's menu and play area. Main courses from around €10. Daily 6–11pm.

★ **La Cultura del Gusto** 9 Ifestou (on way down to Pernera beach) ☎23833860. Excellent choice of modern Italian and Mediterranean staples as well as game and suckling pig. Main courses from around €9. Daily 5–11.30pm.

Paralimni

PARALIMNI, which took over the role of regional capital when Famagusta was cut off by the Turkish invasion of 1974, is easier-on-the-eye than a lot of guidebooks give it credit for. Though not exactly worth a special trip, it can be a welcome respite from the frenetic coastal strip. A big open town square boasts no fewer than **three churches**, all in a row – the big, brash new Agios Georgios, the mellow arcaded old Agios Georgios, and the appealing Panagia. Also around the square are a statue and **memorial** to local EOKA leader and regional commander-in-chief Tasos Markou (who disappeared during the 1974 invasion); a wind pump typical of those that dot this region's landscape; and a rather good **children's playground**. Around the corner from the square is an open-air theatre, and the town hall, frequently the happy scene of local weddings. Paralimni has become a fair shopping destination (it even has a Marks & Spencer), and also has numerous bars, cafés and restaurants.

The Kokkinochoria

The area around Paralimni is dotted with villages known collectively as the **KOKKINOCHORIA** (singular *Kokkinohorio*), or "red villages", which get their name from the rich red soil which surrounds them. This is market gardening country and is sprinkled with plastic greenhouses and the tall shapes of wind pumps which traditionally raised water from underground to irrigate the fields. There's not an awful lot to see, though you'll come across the odd museum – the **Avgorou Ethnographical Museum** (Mon–Fri 8.30am–1.30pm, Wed & Thurs also 4–6pm, Sat 9am–1pm; €1.70; ☎ 23923340) for example, well signposted from the A3 motorway, which offers an interesting if patchy picture of the past life of the village. Other notable villages in the area include Sotira, Frenaros and Xilofagou, all pleasant enough but lacking the present-day political intrerest of Deryneia and Pyla.

Deryneia

A few kilometres north of Paralimni, **DERYNEIA** has a dinky square containing the usual war memorial, a small church, and a *kafenio*. There's also a small **Folk Art Museum** – just off the main drag at 2 Demetris Lipertis and well signposted (Mon–Sat 9am–1pm, 4–6pm; €1.70). So far so typical of many Cypriot villages. The unique thing about Deryneia, though, is its position on a hillside overlooking the Green Line, which offers impressive views over Gazimağusa in north Cyprus (the town is still defiantly known as Famagusta here). Nowhere are the effects of the 1974 invasion clearer or more affecting. At the bottom of the slope the Turkish flags, military buildings and barbed wire begin, and beyond them stretches the suburb of Varosha, once a vibrant coastal resort, now a sorry expanse of empty and increasingly dilapidated buildings (see p.236).

The Cultural Centre of Occupied Famagusta

Mon–Fri 7.30am–4.30pm, Sat 9.30am–4.30pm • Free

The best place from which to view Varosha is the **Cultural Centre of Occupied Famagusta**, clearly signposted from the centre of the village. There's a short video to watch, a diorama of Famagusta, and you can borrow binoculars or a telescope (free of charge) and climb up to the rooftop viewing area. The highly committed curator is happy to answer any questions, and will pick you up on your terminology if you refer to "the border" – borders are between countries, and north Cyprus is an occupied zone, not a country. He'll also tell you about the murders of two Greek Cypriot young men

---

DEATH ON THE GREEN LINE

Ever since the Turkish invasion in 1974, incidents have flared up along the Green Line. Two of the worst happened in 1996. That year was the 22nd anniversary of the Turkish invasion of Cyprus and to mark the occasion over two hundred bikers left Berlin to ride to Lefkosia in order to demonstrate against the occupation. Under pressure from the UN the bikers were persuaded not to cross into north Cyprus. However, on August 11, a group of Greek Cypriot demonstrators ignored this and entered the Buffer Zone near Deryneia. Facing them were several hundred members of the Grey Wolves, a Turkish far-right group, as well as military personnel armed with batons. During the confusion, a young Greek Cypriot called Tassos Isaac was surrounded by a mob and beaten to death. Three days later, on August 14, during further demonstrations sparked by Isaac's funeral, Solomos Solomou, a relative of Isaac, climbed a flagpole in the Buffer Zone to pull down a Turkish flag. He was shot three times and died at the scene.

The two murders had several consequences. They represented a spectacular public relations own goal for Turkey and the north, having occurred in front of a scrum of journalists and photographers there to cover the demonstrations. The killers of both young Greek Cypriots were easily identified from numerous photographs and videos taken at the scene: Isaac was killed by a combination of Turkish settlers and Turkish Cypriots, Solomou by none other than the minister of agriculture of north Cyprus. Isaac and Solomou have since became martyrs to both Greek Cypriots and to citizens of Greece, and the whole tragedy drew further attention to the bitter division of the island.

1

PYLA: GATEWAY TO THE NORTH

PYLA is worth visiting for two reasons. One is that it is the only mixed Greek/Turkish village remaining on the island. It lies in the Buffer Zone between the Turkish Occupied Zone, the Cypriot Republic and the British Sovereign Base of Dhekelia, and has a population whose Greek Cypriot/Turkish Cypriot breakdown is roughly 2:1. Superficially at least, they seem to rub along fairly successfully, though schools and even cafés are segregated, and it may be that it's only the presence of a UN watchtower that keeps the peace.

The other reason is that it lies on one of the six crossing points into north Cyprus. This one's for vehicles, and it takes just a matter of minutes to get through the two checkpoints (though if you don't have motor insurance valid in the north, you'll need to take a policy out at the border – there's a kiosk). Make sure that you've got a good map – neither side goes out of its way to signpost the crossing – and that, if you're renting a car, you've cleared it with the rental company.

---

in 1996, during demonstrations against the Turkish occupation (see box, p.69). This makes for a sad, thought-provoking visit which emphasizes just what a disaster the events of 1974 were for both Greek and Turkish Cypriot communities on the island.

Achna Animal Park

Achna Dam • summer Mon, Wed, Fri, winter Tues • €69 adults, €38 children, inc. pick-up and return, €40/€20 if you make your own way there • ☎ 25586333, ⓦ argonaftis.com

Overlooking the Achna Dam about 15km west of Deryneia (and just below the Attila Line – Achna village itself is on the Turkish-occupied side) is the **Achna Animal Park**, a donkey sanctuary where the animals actually work for their keep. There's a small children's playground and a mini-menagerie of pigs, horses, sheep, goats, turtles, squirrels, guinea pigs, partridges, doves, finches and quail. But it's the "donkey safari" that's the star of the show, a ride along local paths to a fourteenth-century church and back. Tours begin at 11am, last for five hours and must be pre-booked.

West of Larnaka

The area to the west of Larnaka is an almost polar opposite to the in-your-face tourism and the ever-present political division to the east. Instead you'll find a rural hinterland of farmland and small villages, but with a host of diverting things to see and do. It has impressive **Venetian towers** at Kiti and Alaminos, venerable **churches** (Kiti, Pyrga), **monasteries** (Stavrovouni) and **convents** (Agia Minas), little **ports** like Zygi and **Troodos foothill villages** like Kato Drys. You can visit a **dam** at Kalavassos, **Neolithic settlements** at Tenta and Choirokoitia, the eccentric **museum** of naive artist **Costas Argyrou** at Mazotos, a **camel park** in the same village, a **donkey park** and a **wax museum** in Skarinou, and a **museum of embroidery and silver** (and lots and lots of lace and silverware shops) in Lefkara.

Kiti and Pervolia

West of Larnaka, just beyond the airport, is the odd, slightly windblown area around the villages of **Kiti** and **Pervolia**. Though increasingly dominated by the spread of apartment blocks and villas, it has several sights which offer a vivid introduction to different aspects of Cyprus's history. Principal among these is the famous church of Angeloktisti ("built by angels") in Kiti village – it's well signposted, and lies just off the main road into the village from Larnaka. Incidentally, be aware that there's another

CHOIROKOITIA (P.75) >

1

church right in the centre of the village at the intersection of several streets. It's attractive, but it's not the one.

Angeloktisti
Kiti • Mon–Sat 8am–noon & 2–4pm, Sun 9.30am–noon & 2–4pm

Built in the eleventh century on the ruins of a much earlier church, the exquisite church of **Angeloktisti** is famous partly for its architecture, but mainly for a very early (probably sixth century) **mosaic** which decorates the apse on the right after you've entered. Considered to be one of the, if not *the*, best mosaic in Cyprus, it is of the Virgin Mary and the baby Jesus, flanked by two archangels with peacock wings. Although damaged, this survivor from one and a half thousand years ago still has beauty enough to take your breath away. Outside is a massive terebinth tree with benches around its base, a small café and a children's playground.

The Venetian Tower
Just outside Perivolia (signposted "Pyrgos Rigenas") stands an immaculate (though much restored) **Venetian Tower**, built in the years before 1500 as part of an early-warning system to try to prevent an Ottoman invasion of the island. It might even have worked for a while – Venetian rule struggled on till 1571. Some six metres square at the base, there is no way to get into it (the door is about 3m off the ground), but despite its slightly forlorn air (it sits in scrub surrounded by a chain-link fence, though the gate is open) it's certainly atmospheric.

The Ottoman Lighthouse
Beyond the Venetian Tower, on Cape Kiti itself, a small holiday area of villas and hotels has grown up around the dinky little **lighthouse** built to warn shipping of the danger represented by the cape. It dates from 1864, during the dying years of the Ottoman occupation, and has a nine-metre octagonal tower and is attached to the lighthouse-keeper's cottage.

Mazotos Camel Park
Mazotos • Daily 9am–6pm • €3 (camel ride and additional €6) • ☎ 24991243, ⓦ camel-park.com

Some 10km west of Kiti, by the sleepy village of **Mazotos**, and well signposted (look out for little silhouettes of camels), is the **Mazotos Camel Park**, a sure-fire hit with families. In addition to its dozens of haughty, lugubrious camels (rides last 15min) there are ponies, donkeys, goats, ostriches, loads of amusements (a flight simulator, table tennis, mini-motor-bikes, bumper cars, trampoline, bouncy castle) and, oddly, reconstructions of a Cypriot farmhouse and a Bedouin tent. There's also a souvenir shop, an ice-cream kiosk, a swimming pool, and a surprisingly good restaurant.

The Costas Argyrou Museum
Mazotos • Tues–Fri 9am–noon & 2–4pm, Sat & Sun 9am–noon • Free • ☎ 24433335

Just before Mazotos village (if you end up on a dirt track, you've gone too far), is the excellent **Costas Argyrou Museum**. Costas Argyrou was a local man, born in 1917. During his fifties he visited Larnaka's archeological museum, which inspired him to devote the rest of his life to art. Untrained and working in the naive tradition, he started producing the range of paintings, sculptures, mosaics and woodcarvings now on show here. The themes are religion, mythology and the history of Cyprus, all created with an understated sense of humour and an eclectic use of materials. Next to the museum is a small **church** in which the artist had wanted to be buried along with his wife (he died in 2001). The authorities refused permission and he was buried in the local cemetery, so now two empty tombs take up the central floor space. There's a final footnote to this remarkable story. Argyrou designed the museum building himself, but, being as untrained in architecture as he was in art, it now has all sorts of structural problems which are plaguing the museum's administrators. Clearly naive architecture (like naive brain surgery) doesn't work.

Dipotamos Donkey Farm

Skarinou • €30 for activities plus food • ☎ 99620736, ⓦ cyprusdonkeyfarm.com

Beyond Mazotos, through the villages of Alaminos, with its Venetian tower, and Kofinou, known for the Skoutari pottery workshop, lies the village of Skarinou, home to the **Dipotamos Donkey Farm**. The farm has around 35 donkeys, plus ostriches, pigs and goats. There are also displays on *zivania*, the popular spirit, and wine production. Packages on offer include donkey-riding followed by an evening meal accompanied with displays of Cypriot dancing. Touristy, a bit naff, but fun.

Fatsa Wax Museum

April–Sept 9am–6.30pm; Oct–March 9am–5.30pm • €5 • ☎ 24621048, ⓦ cyprus-museum.com

Also in the village of Skarinou, 100m from the Skarinou-Lefkara exit on the motorway, is the **Fatsa Wax Museum**, recently relocated from nearby Lefkara. Created apparently by Russian wax-modellers, it offers scenes from traditional Cypriot life – raising water from a well, drinking in the *kafenio*, etc – as well as historical subjects including the Turkish and British occupations and the struggle for independence. Several of the latter are particularly graphic and some people could find them upsetting – particularly those showing the deaths of Solomos Solomou and Tassos Isaac. There's a rather perfunctory souvenir shop, a little café, and of course the workshop where the models are made.

Zygi

ZYGI is a small fishing port about halfway between Larnaka and Lemesos. Though somewhat lacking in atmosphere (it's harbour being so obviously new and raw), Zygi's pleasant position and good seafood restaurants have made it a popular day-trip and a location for second homes. Developed originally as a point of export for carob (sometimes known as locust) beans and boasting some attractive old carob warehouses, the village went into a brief decline as demand fell, but then received a population boost as refugees flooded in from the north after 1974. In July 2011 the massive explosion at the Evangelos Florakis Naval Base, just along the coast, caused widespread

---

THE BIG BANG: JANUARY 11, 2011

In the early hours of January 11, 2011, thousands of people in Larnaka district were awoken by a huge explosion at the **Evangelos Florakis naval base** just outside Zygi. A hundred containers of gunpowder and other explosives being stored at the base (confiscated from a Cyprus-registered ship taking them from Iran to the Gaza Strip in 2009) had ignited, either spontaneously or by the spread of a bush fire. Thirteen people died in the blast, among them the commander-in-chief of the navy, and damage was caused throughout the area. Cars on the Lemesos to Larnaka motorway were showered with debris, almost all the windows in Zygi were smashed, schools in both British Sovereign Bases had to be closed and the BBC transmitters broadcasting to the Middle East went off the air. Most seriously in the long term, the power station at nearby Vassilikou, which produced around half of the country's electricity, was destroyed. As a result, a rolling programme of power cuts had to be introduced, and generators brought in from Greece and Israel. Disputes as to who was to blame started immediately and continue to this day.

AGROTOURISM

Faced with the challenge of rural depopulation, Cypriots on both sides of the Green Line have come to the conclusion that one way of safeguarding their tradional lifestyles is to encourage the growth of **agrotourism**. This involves renovating attractive old buildings and farms to create atmospheric apartments, villas and small hotels, reviving rural crafts, and promoting local festivals. For more inforamtion check out the following organizations:

SOUTH CYPRUS

Cyprus Agrotourism Company
☎ 22340071, ⓦ agrotourism.com.cy. Supported by the Cyprus Tourism Organisation, the Cyprus Agrotourism Company handles properties across the island including a number of villages described in this chapter: Choirokoitia, Deryneia, Kalavasos, Kato Drys, Larnaka, Lefkara, Scarinou, Tochni and Vavla.
Cyprus Villages ☎ 24332998, ⓦ cyprusvillages.com.cy. Established by a Greek Cypriot in 1987, Cyprus Villages offers apartments and villas in Tochni and the

nearby villages of Kalavasos and Psematismenos.
The Laona Foundation Lemesos ☎ 25358632. The Laona Foundation promotes and supports agrotourism projects and rents villas through Sunvil Holidays to do that.
Skarinou Agrotourism 7731 Skarinou, Larnaka ☎ 24322089, ⓦ agrotourismincyprus .com. A small company which deals exclusively with five properties in the village of Skarinou, conveniently located close to the Larnaka–Lemesos motorway.

NORTH CYPRUS

Though the potential benefits of agrotourism are beginning to be recognized in the north, little headway has yet been made into actual provision. For a glimpse of things to come, take a look at ⓦ ecotourismcyprus.org, a local association trying to develop the village of Büyükkonuk in the Kyrenia Mountains.

damage (see box, p.73) in the village. In case you're wondering, the tall antennae to the west belong to the British East Mediterranean Relay Station.

Kalavasos

The village of **KALAVASOS** lies about 4km inland from Zygi, on the other side of the A1 motorway. It is nicely sited astride the valley of the Vasilikos River, and has a growing reputation as a centre for walking in the surrounding hills, and for horseriding and mountain biking from nearby Drapia Farm (☎ 24332998, ⓦ drapiahorseriding.com). It is also well worth the drive up the good quality road to the **Kalavasos Dam**. The surrounding countryside is a "nature conservation zone" where hunting is not allowed, and which therefore is a haven for wildlife. You can drive right along the top of the spillway and the dam itself from where there are sweeping views. The area around Kalavasos was once the centre of a flourishing copper and gypsum mining industry, the output of which flowed down a narrow-gauge railway to the port of Vasiliko for export. The industry is now defunct, but you can still see traces of the railway line – indeed, there's a surviving locomotive and wagons on a bridge over the river near the village, kept as a memorial and lit up at night. Since it lost its livelihood, the village has become a major agrotourism village, with many of its houses renovated and let to visitors.

Tochni

In the next valley east from Kalavasos is **TOCHNI**, a peaceful village with a quaint if slightly dishevelled look. Climbing up the steep sides of a ravine, with steep walls and houses perched above substantial drops, you'll often see local people sitting out on tiny balconies or small terraces to catch the breeze and enjoy the view. Legend has it that St Helena (mother of the Emperor Constantine and famous religious relic hunter – see box, p.77), on arrival in Cyprus from Jerusalem in 325, built a bridge in Tochni bearing a church in which to deposit a fragment of the true cross. That church was destroyed by fire, but a new one was built in the nineteenth century, also straddling a bridge. The combination of bridge, cloister and church tower make a picturesque group at the heart of the village. The history of Tochni has, alas, in more recent times been stained with blood. In 1974 an EOKA-B contingent massacred all 85 Turkish Cypriot male inhabitants of the village.

Neolithic settlements

The three valleys that run north from the main Larnaka–Lemesos roads (to Kalavasos, Tochni and Choirokoitia), contain two extremely important **Neolothic sites**, both well signposted from both the A1 and the B1.

Tenta

April–Oct 9.30am–5pm; Nov–March 8.30am–4pm • €1.70 • ⓦ tinyurl.com/tentasite

You can't miss the **Tenta** site – it's protected by a sort of modern wigwam, erected in 1995, that can be seen for miles around (including from the A1 motorway). Discovered in 1947 and further excavated between 1976 and 1984, the site was probably originally settled about 9000 years ago. It consists of the remains of clusters of circular huts made of limestone, sun-dried mud bricks and probably timber. Around 150 Neolithic people lived here, with their sheep, goats and pigs (but not cattle, for some reason). The dead were buried under the floor or just outside the huts; there were no grave goods but numerous utensils and ornaments (now in museums in Lefkosia and Larnaka) were found. The site was shut at the time of writing – the wigwam, which not only protects the site but which bears the viewing platform that circumscribes it, had been badly damaged by the explosion at the nearby Evangelos Florakis Naval Base, and no visitors will be allowed until it has been made safe.

Choirokoitia

June–Aug daily 8am–7.30pm; April, May, Sept & Oct 8am–6pm; Nov–March 8am–5pm • €1.70 • ☎ 24322710, ⓦ tinyurl.com /choirokoitia

The **Choirokoitia archeological site** is of similar age and type to the Tenta one, but is much more extensive, and contains modern reconstructions of what the circular huts might have looked like. Discovered in 1934, and excavated from 1936 to 1946, with additional work having been done since 1976, Choirokotia became a UNESCO World Heritage Site in 1998. It's now easily accessible from a comprehensive system of wooden steps and walkways, and has excellent information boards.

Uniquely, this Neolithic village had a massive **defensive wall** (of which a stretch of around nearly 200m still stands to a height of 4m or more on the side not protected by the river, and there's a vast entrance structure consisting of three flights of steps designed not only to allow those entering the village to climb up from the lower, external level, but also to act as a first line of defence against enemies. The huts vary in size, though are usually around 10m external diameter, 5m internally, and as at Tenta are built of stone and sun-dried mud bricks, with a probable timber superstructure. Interestingly, huts are clustered together around common courtyards, presumably according to function or family size, with this open area being used for activities such as grinding corn. The **reconstructed huts** at the bottom of the actual site were made as far as possible using only materials, techniques and skills available to the people of that time. So the mud bricks were made without moulds, and only pine timber was used. After the exertions of the site, especially if you've climbed right to the top, you could do worse than stop for drinks and a snack at the *Chrismarie Bakery* at the entrance to the car park.

1

Choirokoitia village

Beyond the Neolithic site on the F112, at the top of a long hill, stands **CHOIROKOITIA** itself, a village that occupies a long ridge with splendid views. It is reputedly the site of two influential medieval battles. The first was between **Richard the Lionheart** and **Isaac Komnenos** (see p.85) the then ruler of Cyprus, in 1191 – it is said that the final capture of Comnenos took place at Choirokoitia. The other battle took place in 1426 during the latter part of Lusignan rule. **King Janus of Cyprus** lost to a Mamluk/Egyptian army (partly because he couldn't give his troops the wine they wanted before battle), was captured, and spent ten months being humiliated before he was ransomed and returned to Cyprus. There's not much left to see of this "Battle of Choirokoitia" – just a small church where Janus was captured, and the remains of a Knights Templar tower where the crucial lack of wine became apparent. They're up a dirt track west of the village.

Vavla

The next hill village after Choirikoitia is **VAVLA**, at 500m fresh and cool even during the summer. Suffering severely from depopulation yet with lots of gorgeous traditional architecture, it has become a good illustration of the benefits of agrotourism – renovated houses provide accommodation for visitors who want to enjoy peaceful countryside dotted with carob, olive and almond trees, fields of cereal, herbs and wild flowers.

Agios Minas Convent

May–Sept 9am–noon & 3–6pm; Oct–April 9am–noon & 2–6pm, closed Sun

Between Vavla and Lefkara stands the **convent of Agios Minas**. Once through the entrance arch you pass a series of vivid modern mosaic/icons – the first is of Agios Minas himself – on the right before arriving at the convent itself. The buildings originate from the fifteenth century, though they were extensively renovated in around 1740. With its high buttressed walls and shuttered windows it looks a little forbidding, though once through the entrance you walk out into a lovely shady courtyard decorated with a riot of potted plants. The nuns make a living by painting and selling icons and producing and selling honey.

Kato Drys

Further invigorating hill driving brings you to **KATO DRYS**, which is tightly packed with atmospheric old houses. Though the village has traditionally survived by livestock farming and beekeeping, recent attempts have been made to establish vineyards in the area and a winery is planned. Remarkably for such a small place, Kato Drys is the birthplace of two famous Cypriots. **St Neophytos** founder of a famous monastery in the Pafos district and Reo Stakis, founder of the Stakis chain of hotels. The village also boasts not one but two museums: the Bee Museum (summer 10am–1pm, 4–7pm, winter Mon–Wed and Fri–Sun 10am–4pm; €2; ☎99892677) on the right as you enter the village, lies at the end of a path through a lush garden, and the **Rural Museum** (daily 9am–3pm, though can vary; ☎24342648) which is in a mellow old house full of agricultural equipment and odds and ends.

Pano Lefkara

The best known hill village in this region is **PANO (UPPER) LEFKARA** (there's also Kato – Lower – Lefkara just down the hill, but there's not a lot there), which stands at almost 700m above sea level, at the end of the excellent E105 that climbs up to it from the Larnaka to Lemesos road. (Parking is not allowed on the streets – they're too narrow – but there's a new two-storey car park at the top of the village, near the post office.)

Though pretty enough, Pano Lefkara's main claim to fame, attracting numerous tour coaches to the village, is its **lace, embroidery** and **silverware**. A local, probably apocryphal, legend suggests that **Leonardo da Vinci** was so impressed with the lace that he bought some for the altar cloth for Milan Cathedral. Today the village exports all over the world. Women in the village (seen patiently working their needles outside) are said to pass on their skills to their daughters when they get to the age of ten, while the men ply their trade making silver ornaments and jewellery. It is difficult to fathom how true this is today, and a lot of the stuff you'll see on sale is manufactured elsewhere, but there is still a good proportion of top-quality lace and embroidery for sale here. Be prepared, however, for ferociously hard sells and cunning subterfuges to get you into shops. Try D & A Lefkara Handicraft centre (☎24342686) on the left before you enter the village, or Harry and Maria Loizou (☎24342204).

The Patsalos Museum

Mon–Thurs 9.30am–4pm, Fri & Sat 10am–4pm • €1.70 • ☎24342326

Clearly signposted in the village centre, the **Patsalos Museum of Traditional Embroidery and Silversmithwork** (to give it its full, rather long-winded title) is located in a magnificent old house with blue doors and shutters (it belonged to one of the riches families in the village). A visit to the museum gives you a feel for what real Lefkara lace and embroidery looks like, and also displays furniture, textiles and pottery in series of elegant, high-ceilinged rooms.

Kornos

If Lefkara is famous for its lace, **KORNOS**, some 16km to the northeast along an excellent mountain road (and just west of the A1 Lemesos to Lefkosia motorway) is known for its **pottery**. As you approach the area you can see why – you will be surrounded by a strange moonscape of granite hills whose weathering has bequeathed the area with a layer of good-quality clay. In the past the village specialized in the huge geometrically decorated jars known as "pitharia" used for transporting water, wine, olive oil and even grain (and these days much used by householders to decorated their entrances or gardens) but the village's potters, adapting to circumstances, now produce items – jars, jugs, ceramics – more likely to appeal to visitors at the mercy of airline weight restrictions. The village is also trying to diversify into tobacco production.

ST HELENA, RELIC-FINDER GENERAL

Saint Helena (Agia Eleni) is a figure shrouded in mystery. The mother of the Emperor Constantine, nobody's sure where or when she was born, where she spent her early years, or even whether she was married to Constantine's father Constinius or was just his mistress. However, she burst into history when her son, by then emperor, asked her to visit the Holy Land to find and recover Judeo-Christian relics. Her trip occupied the years 326 AD to 328 AD – by which time she was in her seventies. While there, she investigated the scenes of Christ's birth, crucifixion and ascension, and had built the **Church of the Nativity** in Bethlehem and the Church of the Mount of Olives over the first and last of these. During the excavations, she is said to have discovered parts of Christ's tunic, ropes and nails used to bind him to the cross, the cross of the penitent thief and the **True Cross** itself (identified by its power to cure the sick). On her way back to Rome, the story goes, she came to Cyprus and built more churches leaving relics in Tochni (see p.74) and Stavrovouni (see p.78). She died around 330, and her tomb can today be seen in the Italian capital.

1

The Chapelle Royal

Just east of the main B1 Lemesos to Lefkosia road (signposted "Medieval Chapel"), on the right just as you come into the village of Pyrga, is the **Chapelle Royal**, a building whose fame is on first view hard to credit – a tiny (7m by 4m) oblong structure squashed between a much larger modern church and a children's playground. The reason so much is made of it is that it is the only complete survival from the last of the Lusignan rulers of Cyprus, King Janus. At the time of writing, the chapel was completely encased in scaffolding, but when the renovation is complete it should reveal a religious building of great interest. It was built in 1421 by King Janus as the chapel of a royal manor (since destroyed), and is decorated internally with **frescoes** in a mish-mash of Byzantine and Italian styles, but with **inscriptions** in Medieval French. Since the French seems to have been written phonetically, it is thought that the frescoes may have been the work of a native Greek Cypriot. In a crucifixion scene, two figures kneeling at the foot of the cross are thought to be those of the king and his (second) wife Charlotte de Bourbon. Their piety, alas, did them little good. Within five years she was dead and he was riding backwards on a donkey in Cairo, being jeered at by the populace.

Stavrovouni Monastery

April–Aug 8am–noon & 3–6pm; Sept–March 7–11am & 2–5pm • Free • ☎ 22533630

South of Pyrga, and accessible from the old Lemesos to Lefkosia road (the B1), the **monastery of Stavrovouni** ("Hill of the Cross") – the oldest in Cyprus – tops an impressive 690m hill that rises steeply from the surrounding plain. According to legend the original monastery was established by **St Helena** in 327 AD to house some of the numerous **relics** she brought back from Jerusalem – a piece of the true cross, the whole of that of the penitent thief, and pieces of rope and nails used in the crucifixion. The monastery buildings were destroyed in 1426 after the battle of Choirokoitia again in 1570 during the Ottoman conquest, and yet again by fire in 1888 – so the current buildings date from the late nineteenth century.

With strong historical links with the monasteries of **Mount Athos** in northeastern Greece, the monks follow a similar regimen, setting aside a third of their day for prayer, a third for physical labour, and a third for rest. For the same reason Stavrovouni is the only Cypriot monastery that follows the Mount Athos practice of **banning females** – even baby girls are not allowed within its precinct. Ironic, really, given that the monastery was allegedly established by a woman. Photography is also banned (the whole mountain sits in the middle of a military zone). So men who visit the monastery must leave their cameras and their female companions at the gift shop/bookshop entrance. Women are allowed into the church at the opposite side of the car park, though this may be scant recompense.

Once through the entrance building, steep steps and a paved path lead up onto the summit, where the monastery buildings surround a courtyard. Visitors are allowed to enter the **church**, but not the area beyond the courtyard, which is reserved for monks. The church is small, and the only thing of note is a silver-encased wooden cross to the right of the iconostasis, perhaps representing St Helena's penitent thief's cross, and sometimes though not always present, a gilt reliquary containing, it's claimed, a few splinters of the true cross.

GETTING AROUND

WEST OF LARNAKA

By bus By far the best way of exploring the area to the west of Larnaka is to hire a car, though it is also relatively well-served by buses. Routes 401 to 410 all serve one or more of the villages described above: the 401, for example, links Larnaka to Kalavasos, Tochni, Choirokoitia and Kofinou. There are usually three buses a day (two on

Sundays). The 417, which runs to Kiti and Perivolia, is more frequent (12 per day, 9 at weekends), and there are also night buses (routes 448, 452 and 455).

By car Access to the area west of Larnaka is easiest on local roads beyond the airport for the nearer villages, otherwise via the A5/A1 motorway.

ACCOMMODATION

Unlike Larnaka itself and the tourist hotspots of Agia Napa and Protaras, there are not many big resorts in the area to the west. However, the coast is seeing hotels and villas popping up, and agrotourism is making headway, especially in the Troodos foothills.

Aunt Maria's Lefkara ☎ 99356652. Typical of the best of agrotourist accommodation, *Aunt Maria's* offers three one-bedroom and one three-bedroom self-catering apartments on the hillside near the village square, with a full range of facilities. Rooms are clean and simple. The house was renovated using traditional materials in 2008 and stands in well-designed gardens. **€120**

e-hotel Pervolia ☎ 24747000, ⊛ hotel-e.com. New hotel perched on the tip of Cape Kiti, right behind the lighthouse, with bang up-to-the-minute spa, gym, luxuriously appointed rooms, studios, suites and villas, excellent restaurant, two bars (a beach bar and one on the roof) and two pools – one indoor, one out (small, but surrounded by four-poster beds). Take its claim that it overlooks pristine white sands with a pinch of salt, though – the beach isn't up to much. **€154**

Lefkara Village Hotel Lefkara ☎ 24342154, ⊛ lefkarahotels.com. Ten comfortable en-suite rooms and a charming restaurant housed in an arcaded building which, at different times in its past, has been a pilgrims' hostel, a coffee shop and even a cinema. Despite its age, the hotel has a good array of mod cons, with satellite TV, a/c, heating and wi-fi in all rooms and is, of course, in one of the prettiest villages of the region. **€60**

Library Hotel Kalavassos ☎ 24817071, ⊛ libraryhotelcyprus.com. Nineteenth-century stone building housing eight rooms and three suites opening onto a courtyard. True to its name it has a lounge which is also a library; what you might not expect is that it also has an air of pampered luxury with a wellness suite, fine restaurant and outdoor Jacuzzi. Adults only. **€130**

EATING AND DRINKING

The region west of Larnaka has a wealth of restaurants which Cypriots are prepared to drive considerable distances to reach. Thus the clientele at tavernas and restaurants is a good mix of locals and discerning types from Lemesos and Lefkosia.

Archontiko Papadopoulo 67 Arch. Makarios III Avenue, Kornos ☎ 24531000; ⊛ archontiko papadopoulou.com.cy. An elegant old balconied house – all stone floors and gorgeous high ceilings – knocking out delicious Greek Cypriot food and drink at surprisingly reasonable prices: main courses around €14–25. You can eat inside, in the courtyard or on a balcony. Look out for the village's trademark product – the large clay jars or *pitharia*. Tues–Sun 9.30am–3pm, 6–11.30pm.

Camel Park Tavern Mazotos ☎ 24991243. If you're visiting the camel park, you could do a lot worse than eat at the park's restaurant. Pasta dishes come in at €7–10, grilled meats at €9.50–13, and there's a big range of snacks, pizzas, sandwiches to suit all ages. You can eat outside, in the shade of a colonnaded veranda, or inside. The horse-drawn cart on the roof makes the restaurant hard to miss. Daily 9am–6pm.

★ **Captain's Table** 48 Grigoris Afxentiou, Zygi ☎ 24333737. One of the best of Zygi's numerous fish restaurants, the *Captain's Table* is in an unbeatable location right on the new boat-crowded harbour. On two floors, it offers main courses that start at €22 (try the love plate at €87

for two) and is known for its lobster dishes (priced per kilo, so it's difficult to judge the value). It also provides a choice of "Meat Dishes for the Non Fish Lover" at from €18 to €32. Not a cheap night out, but wonderful food in a dockside setting. The loos are impressive too. Daily noon–11pm.

Platanos Taverna Kato Drys ☎ 24342160. Just outside Kato Drys, the *Platanos* is a typical Cypriot taverna with tables and chairs spread out beneath a large plane tree. Main courses start at €7, with meze at €15 per person. 9am–late, closed Mon.

Santa Elena 4 Apostolou Varnava, Zygi ☎ 24332203. Another of Zygi's numerous fish restaurants, *Santa Elena* is housed in an old Turkish carob warehouse opposite the church, and has clean lines and cheerful tablecloths. Healthy portions at reasonable prices – main courses €8–20. Daily 11am–midnight.

★ **Tochni Taverna** Tochni ☎ 24332998. Run by Cyprus Villages (their office reception is in the same building), the *Tochni Taverna* specializes in traditional Cypriot food – souvlakia, *stifado*, *koupepia* et al – even the humble *fasolia* (bean stew). Nice views across the village. Daily 7.30am–11pm (closed 7 March–7 April).

Lemesos and around

OMODOS MONASTERY

Lemesos and around

Lemesos (Limassol) is the republic's second city and premier port, with a reputation for fast living, frenetic (and occasionally sleazy) nightlife, fine hotels and sophisticated restaurants. The rest of the region boasts numerous traditional villages, the outstanding archeological sites of Amathus and Kourion, two of the greatest Crusader castles in Lemesos and Kolossi, and, in the Troodos foothills, a wealth of pretty hill villages and vineyards, the latter linked by well-marked wine routes.

The coast east and west of Lemesos has its fair share of vast hotel complexes attached to mediocre beaches, though there are enough amusement parks (including the island's largest water park) to keep children and youg adults entertained. If you're seeking something quieter head south towards the the British Sovereign Base at **Akrotiri**, which has blocked development in those directions. With good motorway links with Pafos, Nicosia, Larnaka and Ayia Napa, and good links by ordinary road with the Troodos Mountains, Lemesos is one of the most convenient places to stay on the island.

Lemesos

LEMESOS (still widely known as "Limassol") is a teeming multicultural city of 200,000 which grew substantially after 1974, when Greek Cypriots flooded in from the north. Since then, it's welcomed migrants from Lebanon, Iraq and other Middle Eastern trouble spots. Russians, too, are very much in evidence – you'll see Cyrillic script in menus and shop signs across town.

The city centre is remarkably compact. It stretches about 1km from the castle and old harbour to the Municipal Gardens in the west. Near the castle are a cathedral and mosque as well as the cool cafés, bars and restaurants of the redeveloped **Carob Mill complex**. Inland is the old **Turkish quarter**, ideal for aimless wanderings. Along the seafront a 16km pedestrian and cycle path links the old town with sandy beaches further east.

At the time of writing city-centre development projects were producing a lot of dust and disruption but the parts which have been completed bode well for the future, especially the new marina which should provide a classy focus point.

Brief history

Once a nondescript fishing village overshadowed by its eminent neighbours Kourion to the west and Amathus to the east, Lemesos became a little more high profile when its competitors were destroyed in seventh-century Saracen raids. However, it was Richard the Lionheart who really put it on the map when he landed to rescue his sister Joan and his fiancé Berengaria from the ruler of Cyprus Isaac Komnonos (see box, p.85).

Richard the Lionheart p.85
Black Gold: the carob Tree p.88
Lemesos Wine Festival p.89
Lemesos Festivals p.96

George H. McFadden p.101
Wildlife in the Akrotiri p.102
The Wine Routes p.104
The Linovamvakoi p.106

CAROB MILL COMPLEX, LEMESOS

Highlights

❶ Carob Mill Complex, Lemesos A lively area of museums, bars and restaurants in Lemesos old town, particularly vibrant at night when everything's lit up. **See p.88**

❷ Lemesos Wine Festival Whether you're an earnest oenophile or a jolly boozer, the Lemesos Wine Festival offers good value and the chance to try wine from all over Cyprus in convivial surroundings. **See p.89**

❸ Santa Marina Retreat An unexpected haven of tranquillity in the hills above Lemesos, combining horseriding with adventure activities on the site of an old copper mine. **See p.98**

❹ Kolossi Castle Literally a massive reminder of Cyprus's links with the world of medieval knights. **See p.99**

❺ Cyprus Wine Museum All you need to know about Cypriot wine and its place in the island's history, nicely packaged in a traditional house. **See p.99**

❻ Ancient Kourion Perched on a promontory high above the Mediterranean, Kourion is one of the island's most spectacular ancient sites. **See p.99**

❼ Omodos A village rightly proud of both its history and its wine, with cobbled square, monastery, winery and lots of stalls and shops. **See p.105**

HIGHLIGHTS ARE MARKED ON THE MAP ON P.84

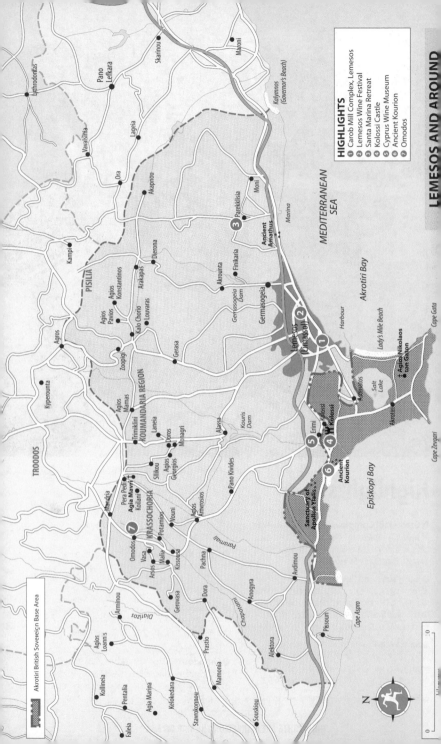

HIGHLIGHTS

1. Carob Mill Complex, Lemesos
2. Lemesos Wine Festival
3. Santa Marina Retreat
4. Kolossi Castle
5. Cyprus Wine Museum
6. Ancient Kourion
7. Omodos

LEMESOS AND AROUND

MEDITERRANEAN SEA

TROODOS

PISILIA

KOUMANDARIA REGION

KRASSOCHORIA

Akrotiri British Sovereign Base Area

Akrotiri Bay

Episkopi Bay

Sanctuary of Apollion Ylatis

Ancient Kourion

Ancient Amathus

Lemesos (Limassol)

Cape Gata

Cape Zevgari

Cape Aspro

N

RICHARD THE LIONHEART

In April 1191 Richard the Lionheart of England was sailing from Messina to Acre on the Third Crusade when his fleet was dispersed by a storm. A number of ships were wrecked on the Cypriot coast, one carrying treasure destined to finance the campaign, another his sister Joan and his fiancé Berengaria. At the start of May Richard landed in Lemesos and demanded that the ruler of Cyprus, one Isaac Komnenos, return the two women and the treasure (which loomed largest in his mind it is difficult to say). Komnenos, who had a reputation as a violent bully, refused, so Richard promptly sacked the city and went on to conquer the rest of the island. This was done under the leadership of Guy de Lusignan, one of Richard's crusader generals and at the time nominal king of the crusader state of Jerusalem. Komnenos was captured and put in silver chains (since, so the story goes, he'd been promised that he would never be put in irons). While this was going on, Richard and Berengaria were married in Lemesos, he becoming king of Cyprus, she becoming queen of both Cyprus and England. Richard then proceeded to pick up the reins of his main priority – the Crusade. To raise money for this expensive endeavour, he sold Cyprus to the Knights Templar who, when they found it more bother than it was worth, passed it on to Guy de Lusignan, who became first in a long line of Lusignan rulers of the island.

The city received another boost to its fortunes a century later when, with the fall of Acre, the two great Crusader organizations, the Knights Templar and the Knights Hospitallers, fell back to Cyprus and made Lemesos their headquarters. When the Templars were purged and outlawed in 1307, the Hospitallers adopted their lands and their influence. Lemesos's story during the following two centuries was one of prosperity interspersed with earthquakes and attacks from the sea. During the Ottoman occupation from the sixteenth century onwards, it settled back into obscurity, stymied by a swingeing harbour duty designed to concentrate trade in Larnaka. This trend was partially reversed under British rule, with road building and harbour improvements, and in particular by the huge growth in British Empire demand for the region's wine. By the end of the nineteenth century Lemesos was established as a major port. Its importance has since been enhanced by the Turkish invasion, which not only denied the republic access to the port of Famagusta, but created an influx of refugees from the north which more than tripled its population.

The castle

Mon–Sat 9am–5pm, Sun 10am–1pm • €3.40 • ☎ 25305419

Built by the Lusignans in the fourteenth century on the site of an earlier Byzantine fortification (supposedly the venue for Richard the Lionheart's marriage to Berengaria in 1191), **Lemesos Castle** has been destroyed numerous times. A Genoese assault in 1373 was followed by a partial collapse during an earthquake of 1525. The castle was demolished and rebuilt only to be destroyed again by the the Venetians towards the end of the 1560s. After the Turkish conquest it was rebuilt once more, later becoming a military HQ and jail under the British. Further restored in the 1950s the building is in good order, and, since 1987 has contained the **Cyprus Medieval Museum** (hours and contact details as for the castle).

Seemingly under siege by the restaurants and bars of the old town, the building itself, which is entered up steps in the north wall, is an impressively vast maze of rooms, staircases and vaulted ceilings, but its numerous restorations rob it of any claim to classic Medieval military architecture. The contents of the **museum** are also something of a hotch potch, with pistols, rifles and canons from various eras, a fine-looking suit of armour (a copy, alas), helmets, stirrups, pottery, coins, silver plate, tankards, candlesticks and lamps all jostling for attention. There are tombstones rescued from an Augustinian establishment in Lefkosia, an interesting photo display illustrating the development of Byzantine ecclesiastical architecture, some classic sgraffito pottery, a

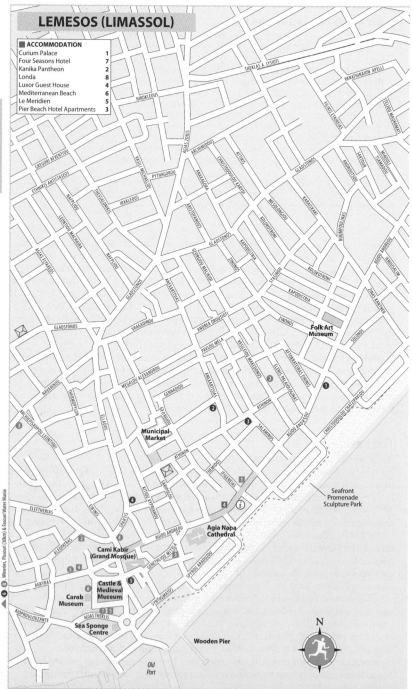

LEMESOS (LIMASSOL)

ACCOMMODATION

Curium Palace	1
Four Seasons Hotel	7
Kanika Pantheon	2
Londa	8
Luxor Guest House	4
Mediterranean Beach	6
Le Meridien	5
Pier Beach Hotel Apartments	3

Folk Art Museum

Seafront Promenade Sculpture Park

Municipal Market

Agia Napa Cathedral

Cami Kabir (Grand Mosque)

Castle & Medieval Museum

Carob Museum

Sea Sponge Centre

Wooden Pier

Old Port

Wineries, Pissouri (30km) & Faourt Water Mania

N

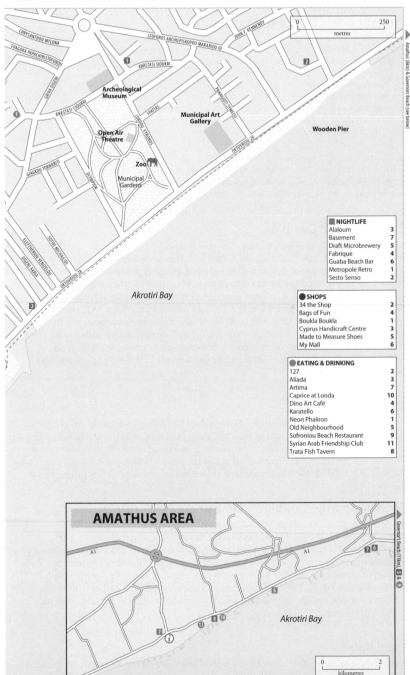

Amathus (6km) & Governor's Beach (see below)

Archeological Museum

Municipal Art Gallery

Wooden Pier

Open Air Theatre

Zoo

Municipal Gardens

Akrotiri Bay

■ NIGHTLIFE	
Alaloum	3
Basement	7
Draft Microbrewery	5
Fabrique	4
Guaba Beach Bar	6
Metropole Retro	1
Sesto Senso	2

● SHOPS	
34 the Shop	2
Bags of Fun	4
Boukla Boukla	1
Cyprus Handicraft Centre	3
Made to Measure Shoes	5
My Mall	6

● EATING & DRINKING	
127	2
Aliada	3
Artima	7
Caprice at Londa	10
Dino Art Café	4
Karatello	6
Neon Phaliron	1
Old Neighbourhood	5
Sofroniou Beach Restaurant	9
Syrian Arab Friendship Club	11
Trata Fish Tavern	8

AMATHUS AREA

Governor's Beach (11km)

A1

Akrotiri Bay

BLACK GOLD: THE CAROB TREE

Found across the Mediterranean region, the carob tree (Ceratonia Siliqua) grows up to ten metres tall, and produces broad-bean-like pods which, when ripe, turn black and fall to the ground. The pods are then eaten by animals and birds (or become stuck to the soles of your shoes) which helps to distribute the seeds far and wide.

Carob production has a long history in Cyprus. It was an important source of sugar before cane and beet (carob syrup was known as "black gold"). It is still widely used as a substitute for chocolate in baking and in health foods, and has been an ingredient in the production of everything from film to medicine. You'll see carob warehouses in many of the island's coastal towns (see also Zygi, p.73 and Lakki, p.139).

---

seventh-century bronze lamp from Amathus, and the relief tombstone of a priest dating from 1558, looking stark and strangely modern. Perhaps the best thing about a visit here are the views from the castle battlements.

The Carob Mill Complex

Vasilissis Street • Open daily though times vary according to season • Free • ☏ 25342123

Immediately behind the castle lies the Carob Mill Complex, a great example of a tasteful urban regeneration project. This L-shaped group of pristine early twentieth-century industrial buildings in mellow yellow stone consists of the **Carob Museum** and cultural centre, and to the southwest a string of hip modern restaurants and bars (among them the *Artima Bistro* and the *Draught Microbrewery*, see p.94). The museum houses some impressively large and complete carob-crushing equipment, still in use up to the 1970s, together with displays centring on this important local industry (see box above). The exhibition area hosts a variety of events, many concerned with food – Greek cooking, for example, or molecular cuisine; others involve musical recitals, concerts and lectures.

The Old Port

Lemesos is renovating its previously down-at-heel **Old Port** waterfront in a €24 million development partly funded by the EU. The plans include a brand-new nautical museum, a marina, and a number of residential and commercial developments. At the time of writing, therefore, there was no access for visitors. However, it should considerably enhance the area – at least if the artist's impressions are anything to go by.

The Sea Sponge Exhibition Centre

Mon–Fri 9am–7pm, Sat 9am–3pm • Free • ☏ 25871656, ⊕ apacy.com

Behind the castle, **The Sea Sponge Exhibition Centre** is unashamedly kitsch but nevertheless great fun. A shop that sells sponges and loofahs of all shapes and sizes, it's diversified into other products such as natural soaps, olive oil and spa products. Displays are interspersed with jolly nautical artefacts such as a diver's helmet, ship's wheels, lifebuoys, even a life-sized model of Jacques Cousteau, together with shells, fish, and hundreds of sponges and loofahs: a good source of small portable gifts for people back home.

Cami Kabir

East of the castle on Genethliou Mitela is the **Cami Kabir (Grand Mosque)**. Surrounded by a medieval tangle of alleys and snickets, coming across it is always a surprise. If the gate's open, have a look, though avoid prayer times. The only part of the building visible as you approach is the rather stumpy minaret, standing above the surrounding roofs. A haven of peace, the mosque is fronted by a small courtyard containing fountains used by the faithful to wash their feet before entering. The sixteenth-century building itself, with its striking alternating courses of yellow and ochre brickwork, is more interesting as a working mosque than for any historical importance, though recent excavations have uncovered the remains of its tenth-century precursor.

The cathedral

The **Cathedral of Agia Napa** on Agiou Andreou Street, a couple of minutes' walk from the mosque, was built towards the end of the nineteenth century and lacks the atmospheric setting or architecture of its Islamic rival. The interior does, however, provide a classic example of Greek Orthodox (over) decoration.

The Municipal Market

Georgiou Gennadiou • Mon–Sat 6am–3pm

Housed in a spacious and airy building off Saripolou dating from 1917, the **Municipal Fruit and Vegetable Market** is worth a quick visit. Entering through its imposing arch-topped doorway, you're soon enveloped by a bustling atmosphere with stalls lit by large fanlights and rows of small windows. On sale are a wide selection of foodstuffs – fruit, vegetables, nuts, honey, nougat and much else, together with attractive basketwork and ornamental gourds. The building has been nicely renovated, as has the square on which it stands, which has shops and restaurants around the edge. It's a great meeting place for locals and visitors.

The promenade

Lemesos **promenade**, made up of a paved walkway interspersed with boardwalks, runs 16km east along the coast from the Old Port to the hotel complex at Amathus. It passes through a lovely **sculpture park** dating from the start of the millennium, and offers views of the shipping lanes that lead into Lemesos harbour – the ships stand on the horizon like blocks of flats. Watch out, though, for earnest joggers and speeding cyclists. Beside the walkway runs a passable beach, dotted with loungers and sun umbrellas, and with the occasional café and restaurant.

The Municipal Gardens and Zoo

Oktovriou 28 • **Gardens** Summer 7am–8.30pm, winter 7am–7.30pm • €5 **Zoo** • Summer 9am–7pm; winter 9am–4pm; ☎ 25588345

About 1.5km east from the Old Port, facing the coast road, the **Municipal Gardens** mark the edge of Lemesos's extended city centre. Wooded with pine, palm and eucalyptus trees, the gardens, though relatively small, are a good place to wander

---

LEMESOS WINE FESTIVAL

Over two weekends in the middle of September the Municipal Gardens are transformed into a tent city as the **Lemesos Wine Festival** (⊕ limassolmunicipal.com.cy/wine) hits town. The festival offers, in the words of the organizers "a revival of ancient festive manifestations of worship of Dionysus and Aphrodite" or, to the more cynical, a chance to get very drunk. Dozens of Cypriot wine producers offer tastings and talks there's plenty of information on the island's wine routes. It's an inclusive, fun affair – giant figures dressed in traditional Cypriot costume wander around the park holding bunches of grapes in one hand and wine bottles in the other. Free buses run to the festival from all over Cyprus, and entry fees (adults €6, children 13–18 €5, children up to 12 €4) are modest.

around, have picnics and let the children loose. Note, however, the formidable list of prohibitions posted at entrances to the park: no dogs, scooters, bikes, cars, ball games, roller skates, roller blades.

Within the park are three attractions: the newly renovated **Zoo**, which specializes in smaller animals and birds (pony rides also available), a small, rather forgettable **Museum of Natural History**, and an **Open Air Theatre** which puts on regular summer concerts (look out for details at the tourist office). The gardens also play host to the greatest **wine festival** on the island (see box, p.89), well worth timing your visit for.

The Folk Art Museum

253 St Andrews Street • Daily 8.30am–2.30pm • €2 • ☎ 25362303, ⓦ tinyurl.com/lemesosfolkart

A few hundred yards southwest of the Municipal Gardens stands the city's **Folk Art Museum**. Most of the items in the collection originate from the late nineteenth and early twentieth centuries – jewellery, lace, costume both urban and rural, domestic equipment, furniture, agricultural tools, examples of woodcarving, a loom with all its associated equipment. Don't neglect, either, to look down at your feet – the museum has a variety of handsome tiled floors.

The Municipal Art Gallery

Oktovriou 28 • Mon–Fri 8.30am–1.30pm, 3–5.30pm • Free • ☎ 25586212, ⓦ tinyurl.com/lemesosgallery

On the seafront just east of the Municipal Gardens, the **Municipal Art Gallery** offers the chance to cast an eye over the work of noted Cypriot artists from the city's permanent collection, as well as enjoying works from further afield in a series of temporary exhibitions. The paintings illustrate the fact that Cypriot art is clearly part of the European mainstream, with a mixture of naturalistic figurative and abstract art, expressed through painting, sculpture and ceramics, as well as some mixed-media work. A further reason to visit the museum is the building itself, classic Art Deco architecture dating from just before World War II.

The Archeological Museum

Vyronos/Siokri Street • Tues, Thurs & Fri 8am–3pm, Wed 8am–5pm, Sat 9am–3pm • €1.70 • ☎ 25305157

Just north of the Municipal Gardens is the town's now rather dated-looking **Archeological Museum** which was opened in 1975, an impressive achievement considering that this was immediately after the Turkish invasion of 1974.

Organized into **prehistoric** (8000–1050 BC) and **historic** (1050 BC–400 AD) eras, exhibits are well-displayed and labelled in English as well as Greek (though the information is a little basic). As in most archeological museums, there are hundreds of pots (clay is one of the great survivors), including some very large urns, much of it from Sotira and Erini, and other domestic items which really bring the past alive, such as mirrors, spoons, tweezers, glassware and items in ivory. In addition there are numerous **Greek and Roman statues**, many, it has now been discovered, carved in workshops at Fasoula, 9km north of the city. Look out particularly for the statue of the Egyptian God Bes, from second/third century AD Amathus. It consists of a torso and head, below which, on a separate fragment, are his feet. But it's the face that draws the eye – it is notable for its extreme pug-ugliness. Even more affecting is the fragment of a statue, also from Amathus and dating from 324–150 BC, of the lower part of a man's anatomy, from the hem of his toga to just above the feet. Not much there to get excited about, you may think. But it's the pose that is so touching – the legs are crossed at the calf, as if he's leaning on a lamppost, waiting for a bus.

SANCTUARY OF APOLLON, ANCIENT KOURION (P.100) >

Fasouri Water Mania

May to Oct, daily 10am–6pm · adults €29, children 3–12 €16 · ☎ 25714235, ⓦ fasouri-watermania.com

Just west of the city centre, **Fasouri Water Mania** bills itself as the "No1 waterpark in Cyprus". It certainly has a wide range of slides, pools, paddle boats, swings, together with the usual fast-food joints and souvenir shops. Look out in particular for the giant mushroom-like "Wet Bubble" and the vertiginious "Kamikaze" slide which reaches speeds of 50kph. A shuttle bus runs to the park from all the main hotels along the seafront between *Le Meridien* and the *Pier Beach Hotel Apartments*. Not cheap but perfect on a hot day (arrive early to make the most of it).

Lemesos city wineries

ETKO Mon–Fri 8.30am–2.30pm · ☎ 25573391, ⓦ etkowines.com · **KEO** ☎ 25853100, ⓦ keogroup.com Mon–Fri from 10am · **SODAP** 18 Synergatismou · Mon–Thurs 8am–2pm, Fri 8am–1pm ☎ 25564605, ⓦ sodap.com.cy. All offer free tours and tastings

There are numerous **wineries** in Lemesos: three of the biggest, the unromantically named **ETKO**, **KEO** and **SODAP**, stretch out west of the Old Port and offer tours and tastings. Walk or take the #30 bus – you don't want to risk driving after the tasting. Unless you're with an organized tour for which you've paid, they're free. A word of warning: don't expect locals in traditional dress treading grapes or rustic equipment – wine production is these days highly industrialized and these spotless, stainless-steel factories could just as well be making widgets as wine. For a more bucolic vineyard experience follow one of the wine routes (see box, p.104).

ARRIVAL AND DEPARTURE   LEMESOS

By plane Lemesos is roughly equidistant between the republic's two main airports at Larnaka and Pafos and is linked to both by fast motorways. There's a shuttle bus between Larnaka Airport and Lemesos (Lemesos Airport Express ☎ 77777075, ⓦ pameaerodromio.eu). It costs €8 one-way, with the drop-off point on Christofi Ergatoudi, in front of Agios Georgios Havouzas Church northeast of the centre. From Pafos Airport you'll need to head into Pafos itself then take one of the Intercity Buses (☎ 24643493, ⓦ intercity-buses.com).

By bus Lemesos's links to other parts of Cyprus by bus are good. Buses can be caught at both the old and the new ports. They depart every one to two hours: Larnaka (1hr 30min) Nicosia (1hr 45min); Pafos (1hr).

GETTING AROUND

By bus Lemesos has a well-organized bus system covering all parts of the city centre, outlying suburbs, and villages throughout Lemesos District. All routes are run by EMEL (☎ 77778121, ⓦ lemesosbuses.com). The main bus station is on Leontiou, beyond its intersection with Gladstonos. The most useful route for tourists is the #30, which runs from the city centre along the seafront.

By taxi As in all Cyprus's main towns, taxis operate 24 hours, and all have compulsory meters (see p.27). If you have any issues regarding taxis or taxi drivers, contact the Road Transport Department (Korivou-Kampos Polemidion ☎ 25870453).

Car rental All the main international car rental companies have offices in Lemesos. There are also numerous local companies. Try Chris Car Hire 1178, Makariou III ☎ 25820100, ⓦ chriscarhire.com; or St Georges Car Hire 62 Makariou III ☎ 25562027.

INFORMATION AND TOURS

Tourist office Lemesos's tourist office (Mon–Fri 8.15am–2.30pm & 4–6.30pm, closed Wed pm, Sat 8.15am–1.30pm; ☎ 25362756) is at 142 Agiou Andreou, the pedestrianized street running parallel to the seafront, close to the intersection with Ifigeneias. There's also a branch office at Dasoudi, in the main tourist area east of the city (same opening hours). The office runs occasional guided walks around Lemesos (usually Mon 10am).

Recommended tour operators Argonaftis Tours (☎ 25586333, ⓦ argonaftis.com); Amathus Tours (☎ 25346464 ⓦ amathustravel.com; Louis Cruises (☎ 22588000, ⓦ louiscruises.com); Salamis Tours (☎ 25860000, ⓦ salamiscyprus.com); Sea Island Travel and Tours (☎ 25583728, ⓦ seaislandtravel.com. Louis Cruises and Salamis Tours run short cruises to the Holy Land, Egypt and Rhodes – they usually leave Lemesos harbour in late afternoon.

ACTIVITIES

There are no shortage of activities if lazing on beaches begins to pall. Most hotels and beaches offer watersports, while the main focus for splashing about is the Fasouri Water Mania park (see p.92).

Go-karting The Need 4 Speed, Erimi Village (☎ 99462269, ⓦ limassolcity.com/go-karts). Closed Mon.
Golf Vikla Golf and Country Club Vikla Village, Kellaki, northeast of Lemesos (☎ 99674218, ⓦ vikla4golf.com). Green fees July–Aug €20; club hire available.
Horseriding As well as the Santa Marina Retreat (see p.98), try Amathus Park Riding School, Parekklisia Village (☎ 99604109) or Curium Equestrian in Parekklisia Village (☎ 99564232).

Pool and snooker Century House of Billiards at 29 Gladstonos (☎ 25745547) offers snooker, billiards and American pool tables. Daily 10am–1am.
Tennis Most large hotels have their own tennis facilities for guests otherwise try the Lemesos Sporting Club at 4 Zachariadou (☎ 25564697).
Ten-pin bowling Space Bowling 1, Erakleous, Mouttagiaka Tourist area (☎ 25310000); Galaktika 53 Makariou III, (☎ 25750666).

ACCOMMODATION

Most accommodation in Lemesos is strung out along the coast road east from the city centre. In particular, there are two main concentrations – the big package holiday and resort hotels in the area around the Amathus archeological site, and smaller, more traditional and cheaper hotels dotted around the Municipal Gardens. In addition, a small resort area is developing in and around Pissouri Bay, west of the British Sovereign Base. In villages north of the city, an increasing number of traditional houses, vacated by depopulation, are being converted in agrotourism schemes (see box, p.74).

LEMESOS
Curium Palace 11 Vyronos ☎ 25891100, ⓦ curiumpalace.com. Well placed in the Municipal Gardens area of the city, the *Curium Palace* is likely to appeal to those who favour a more quirky, non-chain-hotel atmosphere. It's a little dated but it provides as much peace and quiet as you're likely to get in a Cypriot city centre establishment. March–Oct. **€108**
Kanika Pantheon 332 Oktovriou 28 ☎ 25591111, ⓦ kanikahotels.com. In a side street off the main coast road, just beyond the Municipal Gardens, the *Kanika Pantheon* is a good solid three-star, with rooms that are basic but clean, a small oblong pool, and friendly staff and services that ensure repeat bookings. There's a good choice of places to eat and drink nearby, and during high season the hotel puts on a lot of activities – trips to local wineries, strolls around Lemesos and along the front, dance lessons and so on. May–Oct. **€126**
★ **Londa** 72 Yeoryiou tou Protou ☎ 25865555, ⓦ londahotel.com. Approximately halfway along the coast road between the city centre and Amathus, the *Londa* bills itself as "Cyprus's first boutique hotel". Completely renovated in 2005, the rooms are stylishly designed with expensive-looking furniture and beautiful bed linen, while the restaurant and bar could be described as "futuristic minimalist". A classy pool area, spa and gym complete the picture, though the beach is nothing to write home about. Best for couples or those with babies. Feb–Oct. **€160**
Luxor Guest House 101 Agios Andreas Street ☎ 25362265, ⓦ luxorlimassol.com. Somewhere between a B&B and a hostel – its website sums things up honestly, stating "we are not about conventional luxury" – the *Luxor* offers good value and a convenient location close to the tourist office. Rooms are more cheap than cheerful, and vary considerably, so check before committing. **€35**
Pier Beach Hotel Apartments 261a Oktovriou 28 ☎ 25749000. On the coast road before you get to the Municipal Gardens (near St Catherine's Church), the *Pier Beach* is more like a hotel than an apartment block – with its own restaurant, roof-terrace and bar. Accommodation is clean and simple, staff are welcoming, there are fine sea views at the front and parking at the rear – an excellent, inexpensive alternative to the usual Lemesos accommodation, and within easy reach, by car, bus or on foot, of the city centre. Expect, though, a fair amount of traffic noise. Breakfast not included. **€85**

AMATHUS
★ **Four Seasons Hotel** ☎ 25858000, ⓦ fourseasons .com.cy. One of the best-known hotels on Cyprus, the *Four Seasons* is a large, popular five-star located on the beach in Amathus. Set in luxurious grounds with a great pool, the hotel has all the bells and whistles you might expect – a PADI dive centre, a wide range of room types, places to eat, drink and shop and the only Shiseido Spa on Cyprus – together with a nicely understated decor and helpful staff. It can get very crowded in high season, especially with conventions or weddings going on. Those without kids might want to look out for the adult-only pool: it's marginally more relaxing. More peaceful too are the sea-facing rooms: the others face a busy four-lane highway. **€350**

2

2

Mediterranean Beach ☎25311777, ⓦmedbeach .com. Close to the Amathus archeological site – and therefore about 9km from the city centre – the *Mediterranean Beach* is a four-star hotel which feels as if it deserves an extra star. Its pool is intricate and interesting, with attractive terraces and bars dotted throughout. There are five restaurants and numerous bars, lots to do – water and other sports, health spa and so on – with live music and folk nights. The accommodation itself, however, despite a cheerful Mediterranean colour scheme, feels rather regimented, organized in vast honeycomb blocks. March–Oct. €180

Le Meridien Lemesos Spa and Resort Old Nicosia–Lemesos Road ☎25862000, ⓦlemeridienLemesos .com. Located beyond Amathus, just after the marina, *Le Meridien* is even bigger than the *Four Seasons*, and a little cheaper. It boasts terrific facilities and a personal level of service which belies its size. With its own Blue Flag beach, a wide range of watersports, comprehensive children's activities and a state-of-the-art spa and health club, you'll never have to step outside the grounds. Which, given its considerable distance from the city centre, is probably just as well. €272

PISSOURI BAY

Columbia Beach Resort & Columbia Beach Hotel ☎25833000/25833333, ⓦcolumbia-hotels.com. Dominating the beach at Pissouri Bay, the *Columbia Beach Resort* and *Columbia Beach Hotel* (the latter a cheaper version of the former) have comprehensive facilities, including a vast pool, spa and health club, restaurants, bars and sports facilities. They even have their own rather luridly painted chapel. All year. Beach Resort €343, Beach Hotel €235

Hill View Hotel Apartments 60 Stadiou ☎25221972, ⓦhillview.com.cy. A cracking little hotel perched above Pissouri, the *Hill View* has enormous rooms and suites, a super bar and restaurant, a small swimming pool, terrific views across the town towards the sea or back towards the mountains, and staff who couldn't be more helpful, all at bargain prices. €55

EATING AND DRINKING

Lemesos is unquestionably the best place to eat out in Cyprus, with the widest range and quality of places to eat. This is partly because it is both a year-round city and a multiculural one with an eclectic range of cuisines on offer. As elsewhere in the world, restaurants come and go, and while those recommended below have demonstrated a certain staying power, this shouldn't deter you from seeking out exciting new ones.

LEMESOS

127 Eleni Paleologinas ☎25343990. Somewhere between a café, a bar and a restaurant, *127* offers a good selection of salads, sandwiches and light meals. Not easy to find down a side street in the old town. Decor and music are laidback, and there's a garden at the rear. Prices start at around €5. Mon–Thurs 10am–1am, Sat & Sun noon–1am.

Aliada 117 Eirinis ☎25340758, ⓦaliada.com.cy. The *Aliada* is best known for its sumptuous, table-groaning cold buffets of traditional Greek/Cypriot food. It's located in a period mansion set in the heart of the old town, with fine tiled floors and an atmospheric walled garden. There's a set menu at €26 consisting of a soup to start, followed by the cold buffet, a main course (the chicken kebabs and home-made burgers are recommended) and a choice of sweets from a trolley, often eaten to the accompaniment of a tinkling piano. Mon–Sat 8–11pm. Reservations essential Fri & Sat.

Artima Carob Mill Complex ☎25820466. One of the cluster of restaurants and bars in the atmospheric Carob Mill Complex behind the castle. Stylish Italian/Mediterranean food in spacious bistro surroundings, with additional tables outside and on an internal balcony. Try the Wagyu beef fillet, or any of the pasta dishes. Main courses €13–37. Daily 1–3pm, 7.30pm–11pm.

★ **Caprice at Londa** Londa Hotel, 72 Yeoryiou tou Protou ☎25865555, ⓦlondahotel.com. Fine-dining hotel restaurant with a choice of Italian-influenced à la carte or bistro menus. Main courses on the à la carte menu start at €17, with most falling between €21.50 and €34, while the bistro menu offers a range of snacks, sandwiches and salads (€8 to €19) and main courses from €12.50 (a cheeseburger) to €34 (Angus sirloin). Daily 12.30–3pm & 7.30–11pm.

★ **Dino Art Café** 62–66 Eirinis ☎25762030. Centrally located near the castle and the port, the welcoming *Dino Art Café* is more of an experience than just somewhere to eat. A range of colossal sandwiches, and inventive salads, sushi, savouries and deserts created by owner Dino Kosti start at around €7. There's free wi-fi, and often art and photographic exhibitions. Mon–Sat 10.30am–midnight, Sun 4pm–midnight.

★ **Draft Microbrewery** Carob Mill Complex ☎25820470, ⓦcarobmill-restaurants.com. Another highlight of the Carob Mill Complex, the *Draft Microbrewery* (Cyprus's first) has a stylish long bar backed by vast copper vats brewing its signature ale. Top-notch bar food (nachos, chicken wings and steaks from €8–12) soaks up the booze, while in the evening DJs take to the decks. Daily noon–2am.

Karatello Carob Mill Complex ☎25820464. Extensive

meze choices (you fill in a tick-box sheet and hand it to the waiter) or à la carte (the *kleftiko*'s good) in a cool well-lit room with bare brick walls. Outdoor seating at the base of the castle walls, live Cypriot music Fridays and Saturdays during autumn and winter. From around €10. Dinner only 7–11pm.

Neon Phaliron 135 Gladstonos ☎25365768, ⓦneonphaliron.com. Posh-nosh restaurant yet with large portions, plucking its recipes from Greece, Turkey, Italy, the Caribbean and elsewhere, with particular emphasis on seafood and steak. Cool brown and cream interior, extensive wine list (there's a separate "wine lounge" open daily 10am–midnight, closes 4pm on Sun). Main courses start at around €15. Daily 10am–4pm, Mon–Sat 6.30pm–midnight.

★ **Old Neighbourhood (Ta Psarakia tou Nikou)** 14 Angkyras ☎25376082. Noted for the freshness of its ingredients, the *Old Neighbourhood* looks a bit touristy yet attracts a lot of locals after good traditional Greek Cypriot food. It can get very busy, especially at weekends, when there is often live music. Mains from €18. Mon–Sat 6pm–midnight.

Trata Fish Tavern 4, Iakovou Tompazi ☎25586600. Located among the hotels east of Lemesos, this specialist fish restaurant is known for its seafood meze (from €20).

Simple, minimalist decor, very busy at weekends, popular with locals. Mon–Sat 6–11pm, Sun noon–4pm.

AMATHUS AND GOVERNOR'S BEACH

★ **Sofroniou Beach Restaurant** Governor's Beach ☎25632312. One of a number of tavernas along the cliffs at Governor's Beach, the *Sofroniou Beach* is a reliable option for Greek Cypriot food. You can eat inside or out, and the views across to what remains of the Evangelos Florakis naval base are quite attractive after dark – the chimneys and gantries are dotted with red lights. Food is traditional taverna fare, and is very reasonable – a mixed grill costs €6, kalamari €13. It's wise to book, especially at weekends. Mon–Sat noon–10pm & Sun lunch.

Syrian Arab Friendship Club 3 Iliados ☎25328838. Out towards the Amathus hotel complex (it's roughly opposite the *Apollonia Beach Hotel*), the *Syrian Arab Friendship Club* (and who needs friends more at the moment?) provides its customers with Middle Eastern food (all pulses, herbs, spices, grilled meats and sticky puddings) in distinctly Middle Eastern surroundings. Hubble-bubble pipes abound; you might even be entertained by belly dancers. Authenticity is attested to by the number of expat Arabs who use the place. Main courses from €10 (meze from €16). Daily noon–11pm.

NIGHTLIFE

Lemesos has a vibrant nightlife, fuelled not only by holiday-makers but also by young locals. As a rule of thumb, clubs in the Amathus/Agios Tychon/Germasogeia area east of the city tend to be mainly for tourists, while city centre clubs attract both locals and visitors. Like many other port cities it also has a seedy side with a range of "gentlemens clubs" with names like *Mirage Topless* and *Silk and Velvet* spread along the seafront.

LEMESOS

Alaloum 1 Loutron ☎25369726. Long-established gay club, housed in an old mansion in the city centre between the cathedral and the Old Harbour. Both Greek and international music in a heavily gay, but straight-friendly atmosphere. Daily 10pm–3am (4am Fri & Sat).

★ **Fabrique** 18 Agkyras ☎99549809. In the city centre just north of the castle, *Fabrique* occupies what was once a workshop – the clue is in the name. This gives it an interestingly industrial atmosphere. Greek and international music for a younger set. Daily 10pm till late.

Metropole Retro 6 Ifigeneias Street ☎25357676. It does exactly what it says on the tin – it's in the *Metropole Hotel* (just off the main coast road a short walk from the city centre), and it concentrates on retro music from the 1970s, 1980s and 1990s. A big club spreading over two floors, it has three bars and a large dancefloor. Fri & Sat 11pm till late.

Sesto Senso 45 Promachon Eleftherias ☎25879080. Greek and international music for a slightly older crowd, a

mixture of locals and tourists. Dress to impress or you might not get in – the Beatles might have had the clientele in mind when they sang, "How does it feel to be one of the beautiful people?" Daily 11pm–4am.

AMATHUS

Basement 91 Yeoryiou tou Protou ☎25325752, ⓦbasementclub.net. Small, often crowded club whose hefty sound system knocks out house, r'n'b, dance, with occasional progressive house and trance evenings. Over-18s only, with few customers into their thirties, and you'd better dress up. Daily 11pm–4am.

Guaba Beach Bar ☎96682865, ⓦguababeachbar .com. Next to the *Aquarius Hotel* out towards Amathus, the *Guaba Beach Bar* is right on the beach, and offers a diet of house, dance and electro to a young, energetic clientele fuelled by relatively cheap cocktails. Frequent guest DJs. Dress code is jeans and T-shirt at the formal end, barely covered at the more relaxed. Camouflage nets provide a modicum of shade during the day. May–Sept 9am–2am.

2

2

LEMESOS FESTIVALS

FEB & MARCH
Carnival (10 days before Lent – usually Feb/March). All the usual components of a carnival are held in various parts of the city: masque balls, parties, parades of floats, fancy dress, singing, dancing, eating and drinking.

MAY
Flower Festival (early May). Includes traditional singing and dancing, a craft market as well as the flower parade along the seafront. Held in the Potamos Yermasoyia district, 3km east of the old town.

JUNE
European Dance Festival (w rialto.com.cy). Performances by European and Cypriot dance groups in the Rialto Theatre.
Russian–Cypriot Festival (early June) A sign of the growing influence of Russia on Cyprus. Dance, music, clowns, fireworks and a lot of commercial displays.
Shakespeare Festival Plays by the bard

mounted in the spectacular ancient theatre at Kourion (€20 admission).

JULY
Amathusia Festival Performance by a variety of contemporary dance groups, music groups and choirs. Only of interest to those who want to get an insight into Cyprus's serious music scene, though the setting, in the ruins of Ancient Amathous, is wonderful.
Ethnic World Music Festival (w rialto.com.cy). World music performed at the Rialto Theatre.
Lemesos Beer Festival Free entrance, live music, and lots of local and imported beer. Held, like the wine festival, in the Municipal Gardens.

AUGUST, SEPT & OCT
Lemesos Wine Festival (see box, p.89).
International Documentary Festival (Aug; w filmfestival.co.cy) and **Short Film Festival of Cyprus** (Oct; w isffc.com.cy). Held at the Rialto Theatre, with workshops and lectures as well as the film screenings.

ENTERTAINMENT

K-Cineplex 8 Ariadnis w kcineplex.com. One of a chain with cinemas also in Nicosia and Larnaka, Lemesos's K-Cineplex is certainly the best, and certainly accessible in the tourist area east of the city. It shows up-to-the-minute English-language films on five screens, and there's a cafeteria, juice bar and air conditioning throughout.

Rialto Theatre 19 Andrea Drousioti w rialto.com.cy. A striking old theatre, recently renovated. As well as concerts, gigs and plays it hosts several festivals (see box above).

SHOPPING

Most of Lemesos's shops are concentrated broadly in the area between Leoforos Archiepiskopou Makariou III, which arches around the city centre to the north of the Old Town, and the main road along the seafront (called, as it travels east, Syntagmos, Spyrou Araouzou, Christodoulou Chatzipavlou and finally Oktovriou 28). Makariou III has numerous international stores selling all the top clothing labels, and other streets to look out for are Kolonakiou (sportswear, more clothes and household goods), and Anexartisias and Agiou Andreou (clothes, jewellery, shoes, leather goods), which cross just off the seafront road.

ANTIQUES, ARTS AND CRAFTS
Cyprus Handicraft Centre 25 Themidos. Guaranteed quality Cypriot gifts and souvenirs – handicrafts, jewellery, pottery, all made locally using traditional methods. May–Sept Mon, Tues, Thurs & Fri 8am–1pm, 4–7pm, Wed & Sat 8am–1pm; Oct–April Mon, Tues, Thurs & Fri 8am–1pm & 2.30–5.30pm, Wed & Sat 8am–1pm.

CLOTHES, SHOES AND ACCESSORIES
34 the Shop 34 Andrea Themistokleous w 34theshop.com. Smart clothes, shoes and accessories for children and adults. Branches also in Anexartisias Street and in Nicosia. Mon, Tues, Thurs & Fri 9am–7.30pm, Wed 9am–2pm, Sat 9am–6pm.

Bags of Fun 44 Ellados. Lots of bags, but also accessories and costume jewellery. May–Sept Mon, Tues, Thurs & Fri 9am–1pm, 2.30–6.30pm; Wed & Sat 9am–1pm. Oct–April Mon, Tues, Thurs & Fri 9am–1pm, 2.30–6pm, Wed & Sat 10am–1.30pm.

Boukla Boukla 252 Agiou Andreou. Boutique selling top-end women's fashion by Greek designers. Mon, Tues, Thurs & Fri 10am–1pm & 4–7pm; Wed & Sat 10am–2pm.

Made to Measure Shoes 14 Tzami (Jami) Street. Shoes, boots, sandals, and specialist riding, golf and orthopaedic shoes made to measure. Orders can be completed within two to three days so there's usually time to fly home with your purchase rather than ship it. Mon–Fri 8am–6pm.

DEPARTMENT STORES AND MALLS

My Mall 285 Franklin Roosevelt, Zakaki ☎ 25343777, ⓦ www.mymall.com.cy. The largest mall in Cyprus with a range of big-name shops including Apple, M&S, Lacoste, Monsoon, Ralph Lauren, Zara and many more, over three floors. There are fifteen restaurants and coffee shops, a bowling alley, ice rink, children's play area and video arcade. Ample parking. The mall is located southwest of the city centre off the Akrotiri road (#30 bus). Mall shops 9am–6pm; dining and entertainment 10am–midnight.

2

DIRECTORY

Banks and exchange There are numerous banks, most with ATMs, throughout Lemesos: Bank of Cyprus: main branch 1 Saripolou Street ☎ 25155000 (numerous other branches across the city, check ⓦ bankofcyprus.com.cy); Hellenic Bank Archbishop Makarios III branch ☎ 25502000 (check ⓦ hellenicbank.com for more branches); Marfin Laiki main branch ☎ 80002000, ⓦ marfinbank.com.cy; and hundreds more.

Hospital Lemesos General, Nikaias, Pano Polemidia ☎ 25801100.

Internet Many hotels and some restaurants have free wi-fi. Otherwise, try *Euronet Café* at 16 Gladstonos ☎ 25342262.

Medical Doctors on call ☎ 90901435.

Pharmacies Agathocles Kyriazis, 13 Andrea Themistokleous Street ☎ 25364451 Near the Municipal Market.

Police Lemesos Divisional HQ ☎ 25805050. North of the city on Leontiou, near where it intersects with Gladstonos.

Post Office The Central Post Office at the western end of Gladstonos is a fair distance from the centre. The most convenient is the branch at 2 Saripolou Street.

East of Lemesos

Between Lemesos and the border with Larnaka district, and equally accessible (and well-signposted) from the A1 motorway and B1 coast road, are one of Cyprus's best known beaches, **Governor's Beach**, one of its greatest archeological sites at **Amathus**, and an attraction which typifies Cypriot enterprise and entrepreneurial spirit–the **Santa Marina Retreat**.

Governor's Beach

A pretty group of coves notable for its dark sand and bright white cliffs, **Governor's Beach** lies just off the A1, and gets very busy, especially at weekends. It has all the facilities you need for a civilized day at the seaside – tavernas showers, beach umbrellas and loungers – with easy access via a clifftop path and a number of flights of steps down to the sand. The low chalk cliffs are topped by luxuriant vegetation, and contrast with the dark sand of the beaches, which are interspersed with further outcrops of chalk, one of which, much used by anglers, juts menacingly out of the sea like the shark in *Jaws*.

The eastward view from the beach, once merely unedifyingly industrial, now takes in the dramatic aftermath of the island's worst peacetime disaster, the Evangelos Florakis Naval Base explosion of January, 2011 (see box, p.73). The tattered remains of the Vasilikou power station squat next to the base's red and white chimneys, with the radio masts of the BBC relay station at Zygi in the background.

Ancient Amathus

June–Aug 8am–7.30pm; April–May & Sept–Oct 8am–6pm • Nov–March 8am–5pm • €1.70 • ⓦ tinyurl.com/amathus

Nine kilometres or so east of Lemesos centre and clearly visible right next to the B1 coast road, **Ancient Amathus (Amathous)** is of enormous significance in the history of Cyprus, with origins that can be traced back over three thousand years. Unfortunately,

2

its present-day remains don't quite live up to its historical importance, and despite perfectly adequate information boards on site, it's difficult to get, from the jumble of masonry, columns and drums, a mental picture of what the city must have been like during its heyday. It is, however, certainly accessible to thousands of holiday-makers: it's right next to one of the biggest hotel complexes on the island.

The city was probably first established by Greek islanders fleeing from the eastward spread of the Dorian invasion around 1000 BC, though myth has it that a pregnant Ariadne, eloping with Theseus from Minoan Crete, died in childbirth at Amathus and was buried nearby. By around 800 BC the city had been settled and developed by the Phoenicians, and a new harbour built. During this time **temples to Aphrodite** and Hercules were established (Amathus was one of Hercules's sons). The city supported the Persians during the Greco-Persian wars, and was subsequently ruled by the heirs of Alexander the Great and the Ptolemies. During the Roman occupation it became one of four prosperous regional capitals, but subsequently suffered Arab raids in the seventh century AD, and attack by Richard the Lionheart in 1191. History then passed it by, with much looting of treasures and stealing of stone, and it became largely forgotten until it was identified in the late nineteenth century by British archeologists A.H. Smith and J.L. Myers, and excavated from the 1970s on by the French School of Athens.

Today the broad areas of ancient Amathus can, with effort, be discerned, with the open agora, or market place backed by the acropolis hill behind. The outline of houses can be seen, together with sections of wall, the rills and pipes of a water distribution system, a temple and several later Byzantine basilicas. The remains of the famous harbour cannot be seen, since they now lie underwater immediately off the beach. Many of the finds from the site can be seen in Lemesos's Archeological Museum (see p.90) and Nicosia's Cyprus Museum (see p.179); others have been plundered during Cyprus's periods of occupation – a two-metre-high, fourteen-tonne stone jar is now in the Louvre in Paris, for example, while other treasures are lodged in the British Museum and New York's Metropolitan Museum of Art.

The Santa Marina Retreat

Spyrou Ahimastour Avenue, Parekklisia • Tues–Sun 9am–6pm • €3 (under-16s free), activities extra and prebooking is highly recommended • ☎ 99545454, 🌐 santamarinaretreat.com

Just outside the village of Pareklissia north of the A1's junction 21 lies the **Santa Marina Retreat**. Once a disused copper mine, it's now a popular and surprisingly peaceful mixture of stud farm and activity centre. It combines stables, paddocks, two race tracks, even a horse exercise pool, with a putting green, driving range, archery area, football pitches, adventure playground, climbing wall and a ten-metre-high "sky trail". For the less sporty there's a lake stocked with koi, a barn containing displays tracing the history of horses in Cyprus, a small petting zoo, a Venetian chapel and the Manghaleni copper mine, the original development on the site, with its own visitor centre. As well as the somewhat pricey organized activities (archery €8 for 15min, mountain-bike hire €12/hour), there are nature trails which can be explored on foot as well as on horseback or by bike. Once you're done riding/climbing/hiking, you can take refreshment at the very pleasant *Terrace Café*.

West of Lemesos

To the west of Lemesos are to be found three first-rate attractions: the greatest Greco-Roman site on the island at **Kourion**, the best-preserved Crusader castle at **Kolossi**, and a fine private **Wine Museum** at Erimi. All are a few minutes' drive from each other. Beyond them are some surprisingly uncrowded beaches.

Kolossi Castle

June–Aug 8am–7.30pm; April–May & Sept–Oct 8am–6pm; Nov–March 8am–5pm • €1.70 • 📞 25934907, 🌐 tinyurl.com/kolossi

Eleven kilometres west of Lemesos, at the southern edge of the village of the same name, is **Kolossi Castle** a great brutalist lump of Crusader military architecture, impressive in both its dimensions and its state of preservation. Originally built by the Knights Hospitaller in 1210 AD on land granted to them by the Lusignans, it became far more important after 1291 when, following their retreat from the Holy Land, the Hospitallers made Kolossi their military headquarters. It fell into the hands of their rivals the Knights Templar in 1306, but was returned to the Hospitallers six years later when the Templar order was dissolved. Although the Hospitallers subsequently moved their main operation to Rhodes, Kolossi Castle remained their command centre in Cyprus, controlling more than forty villages in the region (still called "the Koumandaria"). In 1426 the castle was destroyed in a Mameluke attack, then rebuilt in its present form by Louis de Magnac in around 1454 – his coat of arms can be seen, together with those of Jerusalem, Cyprus and Armenia, in a recessed cross on the eastern external wall of the castle.

The castle follows the classic medieval design of a square keep. The sides are 16m long on the outside, 13.5m on the inside, and 21m tall. Accommodation inside is on three floors, and the views from the crenelated roof are worth the climb up the steep spiral steps.

As interesting as the castle itself are the ruins in its grounds. The main building, which looks for all the world like a church, is actually a sugar factory, and although there is no access for visitors, the aqueduct which brought water to the cane-crushing mill can clearly be seen. The millstone is still in situ. In 1488 the sugar factory was transferred from the Hospitallers to the Venetians, following their takeover of the island, and production continued into the seventeenth century, when competition with the West Indies finally brought Cypriot sugar production to an end.

The Cyprus Wine Museum

42 Paphou Street, Erimi • Daily 9am–5pm • €5 inc wine tasting and nibbles, €4 entry only, under-12s free • 📞 25873808, 🌐 cypruswinemuseum.com

Based in a lovely traditional house in Erini, some 10km west of Lemesos centre, the excellent **Cyprus Wine Museum** provides the lowdown on over five thousand years of wine production on the island, as well as, of course, the opportunity to sample a few vintages. With almost divine appropriateness, shortly after the museum was opened in 2004 wine flasks were discovered close to Erini village and dated to around 3500 BC, among the earliest evidence of wine production in Europe. Divided broadly into the past (upstairs) and present (downstairs), you'll find lots of information on these discoveries and the evolution of the famous Commandaria sweet white wine under the Knights Templars. Good use is made of quotations from ancient writers and depictions in ancient mosaics, there are photographs and tableaux, an interesting audiovisual presentation and a useful pictorial wall map of the vineyards of Lemesos and Pafos districts.

Ancient Kourion

June–Aug 8am–7.30pm; April–May & Sept–Oct 8am–6pm; Nov–March 8am–5pm • €1.70 • 📞 25934250, 🌐 tinyurl.com/kourionsite

The **Kourion** complex of archeological sites (including the Sanctuary of Apollo) has what TV property shows would call "the wow factor". Sitting high on a hill overlooking the deep blue of the Mediterranean, its tumble of ochre columns and walls, its theatre set like a fossilized shell into the hillside, its paved roads and mosaic floors are both spectacular and well-preserved, offering a portal through which we can glimpse life as it was lived two thousand years ago. Settlement in the

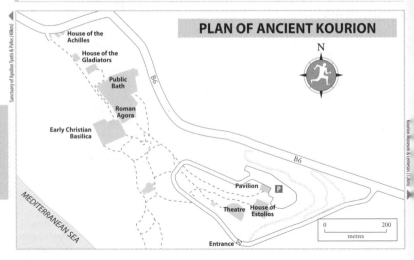

PLAN OF ANCIENT KOURION

N

House of the
Achilles

House of the
Gladiators

Public
Bath

Roman
Agora

Early Christian
Basilica

B6

B6

Pavilion

P

Theatre   House of
Estolios

MEDITERRANEAN SEA

0   200
metres

Entrance

Sanctuary of Apollon Yiatis & Pafos (40km)

Kourion Museum & Lemesos (12km)

2

area goes back to Neolithic times, with the city of Kourion itself being established during the Mycenean and Dorian invasions of Cyprus from about 1200 BC. Nearly all of what you can see today, though, is of Roman origin, revealed by excavations from the 1930s onwards by a series of American teams, and from 1964 by the Cypriot Department of Antiquities.

After passing through the main entrance, visit the pavilion area which houses a relief model of the whole site as well as a small cafeteria and toilets. Immediately in front of the pavilion are two of the gems of the site. The **House of Estolios**, sitting under its elegant timber protective roof, gives a good idea of the sort of luxury enjoyed by a rich Roman of the fourth or fifth century AD, with its numerous rooms, courtyards, bath complex and intricate mosaic floors of fish, birds, and one of a young woman holding a measuring rod, with the word "Ktisis' ("Creation') above it. Inscriptions tell us not only the house-owner's name, but also the fact that he was a Christian. One inscription, at the entrance, charmingly welcomes the visitor: "Enter to thy good fortune and may thy coming bless this house". Next to the house sits Kourion's famous **theatre**, first erected in the second century BC, but rebuilt by the Romans in the second-century AD. Seating 3500 spectators, it is still used today for cultural events.

A short walk to the northwest lies the **Roman Agora** (marketplace) and public baths, and beyond them the **House of the Gladiators**, a third-century AD structure so-called because of its vivid mosaics of gladiatorial combat, and the **House of Achilles**, a fourth-century AD Roman villa named, again, for a mosaic showing the revealing of Achilles' true identity by Odysseus in the court of the king Lycomedes at Skyros. These are the highlights of the site, though in amongst them are subsequent remains of early Christian origin.

The Sanctuary of Apollon Ylatis

June–Aug 8am–7.30pm • April–May & Sept–Oct 8am–6pm; Nov–March 8am–5pm • €1.70 • ⓦ tinyurl.com/kourionsite

Two kilometres west of the main Kourion site is the **Sanctuary of Apollon Ylatis**, originating from as early as the eighth-century BC, and dedicated to "Apollo of the Woods". Much modified over the twelve hundred years up to the fourth century AD, with most of what is now visible dating from the first century AD, it is as impressive and as enlightening as the remains of Kourion itself, and in some ways even easier to get your head around, the only drawback for the visitor being that some of the information boards are beginning to fade badly in the sun.

On entering the site, the first building of note is the **palaestra** or gymnasium, a succession of rooms lining the edges of an open space where athletes could be seen exercising or taking part in wrestling bouts. Across the entrance where once stood the **Kourion Gate** lie the remains of the **baths.** West of this cluster of buildings, the remains of a colonnade mark a large building along the south side of the sanctuary, presumed to have been **dormitories** for pilgrims. At its western end are the remains of the **Pafos Gate**, to the north of which is a further building whose function is not clear – perhaps a **display hall** for votive offerings. Directly east across from this, and next to the baths, is the **Priest's House**, probably incorporating the temple kitchens and treasury. Beside it is a **pit** into which votive offerings would be thrown.

Striking north from this cluster of buildings the paved "**Sacred Way**" climbs up past a circular structure, thought to have been a **sacred garden,** to the beating heart of the Sanctuary, the **Temple of Apollo** itself. Standing at the end of twelve steps, it is flanked by the remains of an ancient **altar**, at which votive offerings were perhaps dedicated to the god. Touching this altar was, according to ancient sources, a sacrilege which would earn the unfortunate culprit a plunge from nearby cliffs into the sea.

The Kourion Museum

Mon, Tues & Thurs, Fri 8am–3pm; Wed 8am–5pm • €1.70 • ☎ 25991049, ⬚ tinyurl.com/kourionsite

Best visited after the site itself, the **Kourion museum** is lodged in a colonial-style house (well signposted to the right off the main road to Kourion as you approach from Lemesos) which was built for George H. McFadden (see box below), the American archeologist who started excavations here in 1933. Bronze Age artefacts and tomb goods are displayed in the first room while the main exhibition hall features finds from Kourion and the Sanctuary of Apollon Ylatis. These include votive figures, a bronze strigil or body scraper, arrowheads, a miner's terracotta lamp, a good selection of different types of pottery and statues, among them a boy riding on a dolphin and a head of Aphrodite. One of the most affecting finds is a family group of male, female and child skeletons, victims of a major fourth-century earthquake, disovered in the remains of a Roman house.

Pissouri Bay

Along the coast beyond Erimi and the Kourion/Kolossi sites, several beaches remain relatively unspoiled, protected from development by the fact that they are within the boundaries of the British Sovereign Base. **Paramali** and **Evdimou** beaches, each with a taverna, are worth braving the dirt tracks to get to. Beyond them, the first village and beach outside British control – **PISSOURI** and **PISSOURI BAY** – are developing into a stylish holiday resort, which makes for a pleasant alternative to

---

GEORGE H. MCFADDEN

Something of a real-life Indiana Jones, George H. McFadden was a graduate of Princeton University (class of 1930) who became the leading light in the excavation of the Kourion archeological site. In charge of a University of Pennsylvania excavation team, he was working on the site off and on for nearly twenty years from 1933, wintering on site and returning to America for the summer. Work stopped when the US entered World War II in 1941 and resumed in 1948. Though some doubts have been cast on the rigour of his methodology, his work certainly drew attention to the importance of the site, and paved the way for further work by the Cypriot Department of Antiquities from 1964. McFadden is still revered in the area, and his death by drowning at the age of 46 in a sailing accident on April 19, 1953 is regarded as a great tragedy. As the framed eulogy in the Museum rather floridly put it, "It was fitting that he should find his end in the Greek and briny sea whence came the goddess of beauty herself to his beloved island – Cyprus".

both Lemesos and Pafos. Popular with families from the base, the village has a range of accommodation and places to eat, while the beach resort, some 3km south, has windsurfing facilities and is quiet and unhurried. The beach itself is long (2km) and scenic, sweeping up to Cape Aspro, named for its supposedly white cliffs (they're more a pale brown).

Anoyira

From Pissouri village, a short diversion inland brings you to **ANOYIRA**, a tangle of lanes and alleys and old houses perched on an escarpment. Unspoilt, the village is beginning to realize its tourist potential, not least by being the only place on the island where *pasteli*, a traditional sweet made from carob juice, is made. You can find out all about it at the **Pasteli Museum** (⊙25221500); the sweet itself is something of an acquired taste. Other attractions include the ruins of **Timios Stavros** monastery, slowly being renovated, **Oleastro** (daily 10am–7pm; €3; ⊙99565768, ⓌWoleastro.com.cy), an olive mill/museum/coffee shop, which does for olives what the Pasteli Museum does for carob juice, and **Nicolaidi's Winery** (⊙25221709).

The Akrotiri Peninsula

The **AKROTIRI PENINSULA** lies southwest of Lemesos, the bulk of it occupied by the British Sovereign Base, one of two retained by the UK when Cyprus became independent in 1960. Driving through it can be a disorienting experience, since it looks and feels like a chunk of suburban England, out of place in the climate of Cyprus's southernmost point. However much one feels that this remnant of Britain's imperial past is somehow inappropriate to the twenty-first century, it has had the collateral benefit of stopping the westward spread of Lemesos's unattractive sprawl.

There's not a lot to draw the visitor out onto the peninsula itself but three attractions are well worth the drive.

The Akrotiri Environmental Centre

4640 Akrotiri Village • Mon–Fri 8.30am–3pm • Free • ⊙ 25826562, ⓌW english.akrotirienvironment.com

The **Akrotiri Environmental Education and Information Centre**, to give it its full title, was set up in July 2004, and is financed partly by the British government. Though established mainly as a sort of outdoor classroom for schoolchildren from all over Cyprus, it's open to anybody who's interested. The centre is easy to find, being right on the main road that runs south past Akrotiri village – it looks like a shop, has a wooden canopy and a carving of what looks like a leprechaun next to the front door. Immediately inside is an exhibition and laboratory area, with microscopes, touch-screen computers and other hands-on stuff: "How many bird species occur at Akrotiri?"; "Guess the plant species from the smell and feel", and so on. On the roof is a observation kiosk with telescopes, binoculars and identification charts. A 2km trail

---

WILDLIFE IN THE AKROTIRI

The Akrotiri Peninsula is of great environmental significance, having been designated a wetland of international importance in 2003 under the Ramsar Convention. It is also interesting geologically, having once been a separate island now joined to the rest of Cyprus. At its centre is a salt lake similar to the one in Larnaka, which fills with water in winter and dries out in summer. The peninsula boasts 27 natural habitats hosting a wide diversity of plants, animals and birds – the famous greater flamingo, but also the glossy ibis, the demoiselle crane and a variety of other waders, ducks and gulls.

leads into the village where there's a basket-weaving shop using traditional methods as well as an interesting church.

Agios Nikolaos ton Gaton (St Nicholas of the Cats)

Akrotiri • Daily 8am–5pm • Donation expected • ☎ 25952621

Just after the environmental centre, a narrow road leads off the main highway, heading due east across the southern edge of the salt lake. After about 2.5km, a parking area on the right marks the entrance to the monastery of **Agios Nikolaos ton Gaton**. Originally established in 325 AD, the present buildings date from the thirteenth to the fifteenth centuries. Surrounded by citrus groves, and altogether rather unprepossessing, the monastery owes its celebrity to the presence of the **cats** that give it its name. They were introduced, it is said, by St Helena (see p.77), to keep the monastery clear of snakes or, as another racier version has it, to replace young boys as companions for the monks. The monastery was abandoned after the sixteenth-century Ottoman invasion, but has since been taken in hand by an order of nuns who are bringing it back to life (and who look at visitors rather as if they expect them to make off with the silver). There seems to be a cheerful acceptance of modern life – air conditioning, plastic patio furniture – as well as the retention of older things, not only the buildings themselves, but in the grounds, an old well and water trough. The practice of keeping cats around ecclesiastical buildings spread to other parts of Cyprus and beyond – indeed, today, you'll see far more cats in Larnaka's Hala Sultan Tekke than in St Nicholas of the Cats.

Lady's Mile Beach

After Agios Nikolaos ton Gaton the road deteriorates into a dirt track, and finally runs out onto a vast area of hard-packed sand crisscrossed with tyre tracks which ends with a series of short barriers against which there are usually cars parked. Beyond this is the 7km **Lady's Mile Beach**, which sounds nicer than it is. Dotted with several tavernas and lifeguard towers, the beach does have sand of good quality, but it's rather narrow and the views across the bay to the industrial port of Lemesos add little to its allure. The beach, incidentally, is not named after the Virgin Mary or even Aphrodite, as might seem likely in Cyprus, but after a horse called Lady whose polo-playing military owner used the beach for a gallop every morning. How quintessentially colonial.

The Troodos foothills

Spreading in an arc north of Lemesos, the **Troodos foothills** offer an opportunity to get away from the brashness and heat of the city and the coast. This is open countryside that rises in a series of ridges towards the heights of the Troodos massif, dotted with hill villages that have supported themselves over the centuries by cultivating citrus fruits, olives and above all **wine**. The southward-facing slopes provide the perfect terroir for growing grapes (particularly indigenous Mavro and Xynisteri and imported Grenache and Cabernet Sauvignon varieties) something they've been doing in this area for over five thousand years.

It's not easy to explore the foothills of Lemesos district in any systematic way. One approach would be to follow the **wine routes** organized by the Cyprus Tourism Organisation and contained in a useful free guidebook available from tourist centres and participating wineries.

Another approach might be to cluster the villages to be visited into geographical groups – the ones sometimes called the "**Krassochoria**" (Wine Villages) to the west, the group in the centre, once ruled by the Hospitallers in Kolossi and known collectively as the **Koumandaria**, and the villages to the east marketed, hopefully, by the tourist

2

> ### THE WINE ROUTES
>
> The Cyprus Tourist Organisation's excellent guide to **wine routes** in Pafos and Lemesos Districts is a must for any oenophiles visiting Cyprus. Six routes are described, three in Pafos District, three in Lemesos District. The routes are also clearly signposted on the ground with signs that are, appropriately, a Burgundy colour. Each route includes a summary of the climate, terrain, vineyards and grape varieties to be experienced, a detailed description of the roads to be travelled and the villages to be visited, and a list of wineries and tavernas to be found along the way, together with a lot of advice on the storage and drinking of wine. The Lemesos District is covered by Route 4 (the Krassochoria), Route 5 (Koumandaria) and Route 6 (Pitsilia).

authorities as "the Cypriot Tuscany". Or you can, of course, simply meander through the region, going where the spirit takes you. Do, though, stick to the main roads, even though this can mean a lot of doubling back – what on the map may look like a tempting short-cut between villages could turn out to be a rutted dirt road for which you'll need a 4WD.

The Krassochoria (wine villages)

The Krassochoria are best approached, appropriately enough, through **Erimi**, home of the Cyprus Wine Museum. Driving away from Lemesos through the village with the museum on your left, cross the bridge then turn right onto the E601. This is Wine Route 4, which visits a total of twenty villages, the best of which are covered below.

Vouni

After Agios Amvrosios, follow signs to the right for **VOUNI**, a delightful hill village built on a ridge at the confluence of two rivers. With its mountain architecture protected by law, its winding lanes, numerous balconied houses, lush gardens of fig, pomegranate, apricot, orange, lemon and almond trees, and views across the gorge, it gives some idea of what these hill villages must have been like during their heyday. Though now in something of a decline caused by rural depopulation – it once had 2500 residents, compared to its current hundred or so – there is still a lot of renovation going on, and families which have left often maintain the ancestral home as a summer residence. Sadly, the Vouni donkey sanctuary, once a highlight of the region, has now closed.

Koilani

Five kilometres along the winding and scenic road northeast of Vouni, **KOILANI** is very much a wine village, though it did make a brief appearance in Cypriot history when Richard the Lionheart destroyed a camp here set up by Isaac Komnenos. The village today has the usual narrow winding streets and alleys as well as great views of the surrounding mountains. Two wineries to look out for are **Vardalis** (✆25470261, ⊕vardaliswinery.com) and **Agia Mavri Ltd** (✆25470225), both of which run free tastings, have English-speaking guides and ample parking. The former also has a restaurant and runs vineyard tours. Elsewhere in the village, there's a small, free **ecclesiastical museum** (all year; free; ✆99302086) containing mainly icons, woodcarving and ornate metalwork covering seven hundred years of the village's history (star attraction: the skull of Agia Mavri, the village patron), and an even smaller **Museum of Viticulture** (✆25433031). About 1km east of the village is the pitched-roof church of **Agia Mavri**, striklingly set in a river gorge. The legend of the saint is that she was a virgin whose father was insisting that, for financial or dynastic reasons, she must marry a man she loathed. On the wedding night she fled, but was cornered by her father and her suitor at the stream where the church stands today. Calling on the Virgin Mary to save her, the cliff behind swallowed her up, and she was never seen again. The church was established to commemorate the event. If the story doesn't do it for you, note that there's a taverna across the road that might repay attention.

Malia

Return to the E601 and continue north and you'll come to three villages which lie off to the left (west). The first, **MALIA**, was notable until 1974 for its large Turkish Cypriot minority, attested to by the minaret which is still visible in the village. The main reason for visiting the village today is the large winery, **Malia (Keo) Ltd** (T 25942131, W keogroup.com/wines), which, though built in 1930, was fully modernized in 1996. Notable for being one of the few Cypriot wineries to produce Riesling, it has free tastings, a shop, ample parking, audiovisual presentations, a restaurant and vineyard tours.

2

Vasa

Just north, at the base of a steep hill with a severe hairpin bend at the bottom, **VASA** is yet another nice village, dotted with *pitharia*, the huge earthenware wine containers found in gardens, courtyards and inside houses themselves. Most villages have their fair share of these, a reminder that, in days gone by, each household made its own wine. At the northern edge of the village is the **Vasa Winery** (T 25945999, W vasawinery.com) which offers tastings, though not in English.

Arsos

A little further northwest is the village of **ARSOS**, one of the largest wine producers in the region. It boasts lots of renovation and the modern **Nikolettino Winery** (T 99437137, W nikolettino.com), which mounts the best range of services of any of the wineries in the area: audiovisual introduction, shop, restaurant, English-language vineyard tours and tastings (for which there is a charge).

Omodos

OMODOS is the epitome of the Troodos foothills wine village. That's why it attracts so many visitors and that's why it's lambasted for being too touristy. Don't listen to the critics – if you've only got time for one village, make it this one. Surrounded by vineyards, Omodos is laid out around a large pedestrianized cobbled square which slopes gently down to **Timiou Stavrou (Holy Cross) Monastery**. Outside the entrance a statue commemorates a past abbot, Dositheos, who was one of 486 Greek Cypriots beheaded or hanged in Nicosia by the Turkish authorities on July 10, 1821 during the Greek War of Independence. Inside, what was the monastery church now acts as the parish church, while several of the rooms and outbuildings have been colonized by the **Struggle Museum**, which has lots of memorabilia of the EOKA campaign against the British (see p.256). Other areas of the monastery host an **Icon Museum**, which not only includes icons, but also decorative woodcarving (look up at the ceiling for a wonderful example), and an **Ecclesiastical Museum**. All are free, and give a taste of how the village sees itself.

Around the square are a bunch of souvenir shops, together with a good range of taverna/café-bars: check out the *Village Inn*, for example. Look out too for the children's coin-operated rides just outside the monastery – not Thomas the Tank Engine or Bob the Builder, but disconcertingly realistic donkeys. The emphatic "Only for Children" notices seem to imply that they've had problems with adults, perhaps over-indulging with the local vino. There's a massive old wine press near the square, dating from the Lusignan period, while just outside the village is the **Linos Winery** (T 25422700, W linoswinery.com) which is geared up for large parties of visitors (English spoken, ample parking, and there's a shop). As well as wine,

2

THE LINOVAMVAKOI

The **Linovamvakoi** (singular Linovamvakos) were descendants of the Venetians and Greek Cypriots who, for pragmatic reasons, superficially converted to Islam while remaining Christian in belief (being a Muslim was initially safer, and later carried considerable benefits and tax breaks under the Ottomans). The first wave of converts tended to be Roman Catholic, later ones Greek Orthodox. The name comes from a type of two-ply cloth which was cotton on the outside, linen on the inside, that is "Muslim on the outside, Christian on the inside". When the British took over Cyprus, many Linovamakoi reverted to Christianity, but others remained Muslim, either because mixed marriages had muddied the waters (many were spurned by the local Orthodox communities), or because of rumours that Britain might hand Cyprus back to Turkish rule. It is also true that the British authorities did not make reversion easy. Many of those who remained Muslim became, in due course, integrated into what is today thought of as the Turkish Cypriot community.

Omodos also makes *zivania*, an explosive spirit, together with a number of sweets made from wine must.

The Koumandaria

The group of villages in the central foothills above Lemesos are collectively known as the **KOUMANDARIA**. While of great importance to those who know about wine – "Commandaria" is one of the oldest wines in the world – they lack the character of the villages to the west, though the pleasantly cool climate offers respite from the heat of the coast. The most direct route up to these villages is up the B8, from Junction 28 on the A1 as it curves around the north of Lemeso; for a more interesting return trip, use the E110.

The first group of villages of passing interest lie off to the west of the B8, starting with **MONAGRI**. The fact that it was once one of the Linovamvaki villages (see box above) is illustrated by the fact that, in the church of the **Archangelos monastery** in the village there's a mihrab, a semicircular niche in the wall, indicating the direction of Mecca. There's a Roman olive mill (the only one on the island) in the outbuildings. Beyond Monagri, the villages of **Agios Georgios** and **Silikou** are worth a brief stop and stroll. If you return to Monagri, a left turn brings you to **DOROS**, yet another vineyard-surrounded village, this time with a winery with visitor facilities. Next to the sixteenth-century church of Agios Epifanios, the **Karseras Winery** (☎99413238) provides ample parking and free tasting, and, if you phone to prearrange the visit, commentaries in English.

Back on the B8, a short detour north of Doros and east of the main road, takes you to the nicely preserved village of **LANEIA**, one of the prettiest in the Kommandaria. Spreading across several small hills, it offers a number of cafés, tavernas and shops, a supermarket and post office. It's also home to a lot of expats, many of them artists who sell their work here. For example visit Michael Owen Galleries (☎25432404, ⓦmichaelowengallery.com), or take a look at the work of Anne Pays (ⓦannepays.com).

Continuing north on the B8, a right turn onto the F812 after **TRIMIKLINI** brings you to the village of **Agios Mamas** and then, just east of the E110, the substantial village of **Kalo Chorio, Zoopigi** to the north, and beyond **Kalo Choirio**, **Agios Pavlos** and **Agios Constantinos**. The air here (at around 700m) is beautifully cool and fragrant with the scent of citrus orchards, while the villages have lots of colourful gardens to appreciate. In Kalo Chorio the **Co-operative Company of Viniculture** (☎25542266) offers free wine tastings.

The return to Lemesos down the E110 can, with diversions, take in the village of **Louvaras**, whose village centre is unspoilt, and whose painted chapel of Agios Mamas is well worth seeking out.

The eastern foothills

The villages of the **eastern foothills** of the Lemesos region have less of specific interest to the visitor than those of the centre and west. However, a drive through the empty countryside that rises steadily towards the mountains from the coast can be exhilarating, and helps to emphasize that, despite the overcrowding caused by the influx of migrants from the north in 1974, there are still empty parts of the island, even close to the main conurbations.

The best route to take is the F128, from Junction 24 on the A1. Within minutes the lake of **Germasogeia** appears on the right, often thronged with determined canoeists and rowers out practising, the shore dotted with their cars and those of supporters. For energetic visitors there's a nature trail (clearly signposted), and for hungry ones there's a café/snack bar in the nearby village of **FINIKARIA.**

From the reservoir, the road winds upwards above the Germasogeia river through the heart of the **Lemesos Forest**, a hilly wilderness of brush, cypress and olive trees. Despite the proximity of Lemesos, there's a real feeling of isolation here – between the dam and the sizeable settlement of **ARAKAPAS**, there's only one village: **DIERONA**, sprawling on its hillside. From Arakapas, the road west gives access to the Koumandaria villages.

2

Pafos and around

AKAMAS PENINSULA COAST

Pafos and around

Pafos district, which takes up the whole of the western end of Cyprus, is probably the single most varied and most attractive region on the island. Wild and remote in parts, it was long regarded in the rest of Cyprus as something of a rural backwater, its inhabitants frequently lampooned as clueless country bumpkins. This situation changed substantially in the 1980s with the opening of Pafos Airport and the development of motorway links with the rest of the island. Suddenly the Pafos area became a magnet for developers keen to exploit its natural riches.

3

For a start, it has the longest **coastline** of any district, swinging around from **Aphrodite's birthplace** in the south to **Aphrodite's Baths** in the north and beyond, with beaches facing south, west and north along its length. It has, in the **Akamas Peninsula** and the forests of **Tilliria**, two of the island's great wilderness areas, crisscrossed with trails and dotted with picnic sites. And inland stretch beautiful sunny uplands, carpeted in vineyards and dotted with wineries, monasteries and pretty villages. **Pafos town** itself might at first appear to be the archetypal beach-and-booze resort – no different, you might think, from hundreds of others across the Mediterranean. Yet look more closely and, laced through the maze of bars and restaurants and hotels are a number of fascinating historical remains, some of which have been granted UNESCO World Heritage status. And in **Polis** on the north coast, with its beach, little fishing port and hinterland villages and unspoilt stretch of coast, it has an away-from-it-all feel, ideal for those seeking relaxation.

Pafos

PAFOS (locals still often use the old spelling, "Paphos") comes in two parts, each with a distinct character. **Kato (Lower) Pafos** is the area around the harbour and castle, from which it also runs south along and behind a palm-studded promenade (Poseidonos). This is the main tourist area, packed with hotels, cafés, bars, restaurants, souvenir shops, amusement arcades, a couple of indifferent beaches, boat-cruise touts and all the other joys of the seaside. However, leavening this unrelenting holiday heaven/hell are some truly excellent historical and archeological sites which require no effort to see. As well as the **castle** there are the magnificent **Roman mosaics** immediately behind the harbour, a group of **Byzantine remains** linked with Saint Paul directly across the road, and the eerie **Tombs of the Kings** to the north.

Ktima Pafos (perhaps best translated as "the lands of Pafos") lies 3km north, on a steep hillside overlooking the lower town. Its narrow winding streets provide a contrast with Kato Pafos and there are several worthwhile sites including a medieval **mosque** and **hammam** as well as an **art gallery** and a couple of diverting **museums**. In general,

ROMAN MOSAICS, PAFOS

Highlights

❶ Roman Mosaics, Pafos Some of the most perfectly preserved Roman mosaics in the world. **See p.116**

❷ Shopping in Ktima Pafos All the fun of the bazaar, in a warren of roofed narrow streets in Pafos old town. **See p.119**

❸ Geroskipou Folk Art Museum One of the best folk museums on the island – a terrific glimpse into the past of ordinary Cypriots. See **p.124**

❹ Aphrodite's birthplace A fine beach, so photogenic it appears widely on tourist literature, which has a rich crop of mythical associations. **See p.125**

❺ Agios Neofytos Monastery Not only an excellent example of a Greek Orthodox monastery, but with a fascinating back story and a museum to boot. **See p.128**

❻ The Grivas Museum An illuminating if one-sided introduction to the EOKA leader and his campaign against the British. **See p.131**

❼ Akamas Peninsula Empty, unspoilt hills and beaches, coastal vistas and numerous marked hiking trails. **See p.133**

❽ Polis With its pretty fishing port, Lakki, Polis is a reminder of how Pafos district used to be, before the motorway and the airport arrived. See **p.136**

HIGHLIGHTS ARE MARKED ON THE MAP ON P.112

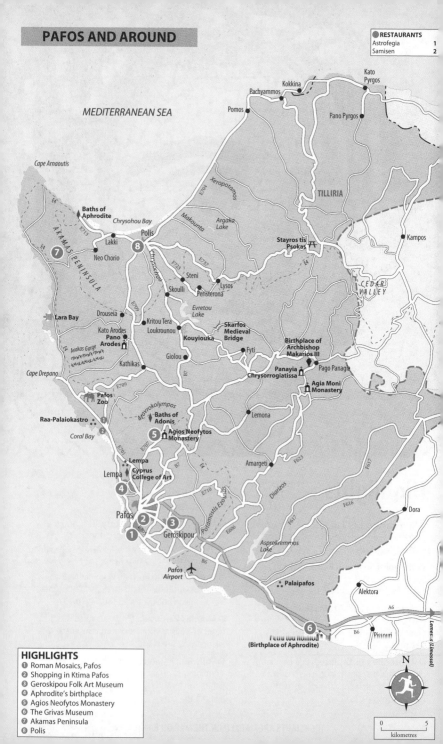

Ktima Pafos offers a less hurried experience than the rather brash lower town – it even seems cooler, though the 65m elevation is hardly enough to account for it.

Brief history

The original town, **Palaipafos**, lies some 22km to the southeast of the present one, on the edge of the modern village of Kouklia (see p.125). It was established during the late Hellenistic period, and was one of two city kingdoms in the west – the other being Marion, near modern-day Polis. When **Alexander the Great** died in 323 BC, the Pafiot king **Nicocles** was faced with the same dilemma as all the other towns in Cyprus – which of Alexander's warring successors to support. He chose the Egyptian **Ptolemy** dynasty, who indeed eventually won. This did Nicocles little good, however. Deciding to rule Cyprus directly rather than through a proxy, the Ptolemies used a false charge of treason to get rid of him (Nicocles avoided execution by committing suicide). The new rulers of Cyprus decided to move the administrative capital from Salamis in the east to the fine new city of **Nea Pafos** in the west: apart from being closer to their home base of Alexandria, it was convenient for patrolling the western approaches to the island, and, through the thick forests inland, able to meet the almost insatiable demand for timber of the Egyptian navy.

The transition to **Roman rule** in 58 BC did Pafos no harm at all, and it continued as the capital of the island. This period was the high point of Pafos's fortunes, and the origin of its wonderful Roman mosaics and plentiful early Christian ruins. The New Testament (Acts 13, verses 4 to 13) relates how **St Paul** visited Pafos and converted the Roman ruler of the island, Sergius Paulus, to the new faith, though not before the evangelist was tied to a post (the so-called St Paul's Pillar) and lashed "forty times less one" for spreading the gospel.

In 365 AD the city was destroyed by an **earthquake**, and in 653 AD by a Saracen raid. It never recovered. Most of the inhabitants moved away from the coast, onto the hill of what today is Ktima Pafos, and the status of capital was moved back to Salamis. The harbour silted up, the land around it became marshy, and for centuries visitors to what remained of Pafos had little good to say about it. In the fourteenth century the **Lusignans** built a castle to protect Christians in transit to the Holy Lands; in the sixteenth century the Ottomans built a fort on its remains. But Pafos continued as a quiet backwater until the building of the airport and the motorway in the late twentieth century brought about a surge in tourism.

Kato Pafos

The heart of Kato Pafos is the **harbour area**, a south-facing hooked finger that seems to beckon in boats from the sea. The harbour combines workaday buildings – the Customs House, Department of Fisheries and the Port Authority – with important historic sites including the **castle**, the wave-washed remains of an ancient breakwater, and the memorial to St Paul's visit during his first missionary journey. Close by is the entrance to the **archeological park** that contains the town's world-famous **mosaics**. Also jostling for your attention are dozens of cafés, restaurants, bars, souvenir shops and boat-trip touts who line the pedestrianized quayside.

The castle

June–Aug 8am–7.30pm; April–May & Sept–Oct 8am–6pm; Nov–March 8am–5pm • €1.70

Pafos Castle, sitting at the edge of the harbour and reflected in the water that surrounds it, presents a scene worthy of any romantic watercolourist. As with many Cypriot castles it has a complex back story: built by the Lusignans around 1391, it was destroyed by an earthquake towards the end of the fifteenth century, and what was left was levelled by the Venetians to prevent it falling into the hands of the Turks. Despite this, the castle was rebuilt and garrisoned by the Ottomans in 1592. After the British takeover of Cyprus, the castle was relegated to a salt store. The main attraction of a visit

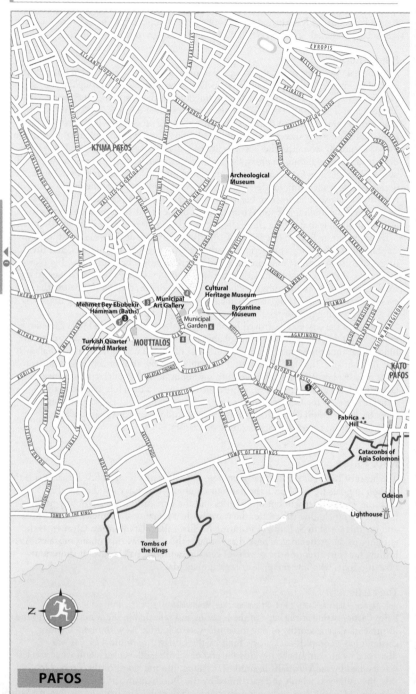

KTIMA PAFOS

Archeological Museum

Municipal Art Gallery

Cultural Heritage Museum

Mehmet Bey Ebubekir Hammam (Baths)

Byzantine Museum

Municipal Garden

Turkish Quarter Covered Market

MOUTTALOS

KATO PAFOS

Fabrica Hill

Tombs of the Kings

Catacombs of Agia Solomoni

Odeion

Lighthouse

Tombs of the Kings

N

PAFOS

MEDITERRANEAN SEA

Limnarka

Lusignan
Baths

Ottoman Baths

Chrysopolitissa
& St. Paul's Pillar

Saranta
Kolones

Agora

Roman
Mosaics

*Pafos
Harbour*

Pafos
Castle

3

■ NIGHTLIFE	
Cartel Fashion Club	1
Different	4
Level	3
Loft	2

● RESTAURANTS	
Cavallini	2
Fettas	4
Hondros	9
La Sardeena Pa Gino	8
Laona	5
Myrra	3
Ocean Basket	1
St. Paul's Pillar	7
Syrian Restaurant	6

● SHOPS	
Cyprus Handicrafts Centre	3
Municipal Market	2
Timi Car Boot Sale	1

■ ACCOMMODATION	
Agapinor Hotel	8
Alexander the Great	5
Almyra Hotel	7
Amathus Beach	2
Annabelle	9
Apollonia Holiday Apartments	4
Axiothea Hotel	6
Daphne Hotel APB	10
Kiniras	3
Pioneer Beach Hotel	1

0	500

metres

is to climb up to the battlements where once twelve cannons stood guard. The clear field of fire they required now offers excellent views across the harbour to the distant low hills to the north.

The Roman mosaics

June–Aug 8am–7.30pm; April–May & Sept–Oct 8am–6pm, Nov–March 8am–5pm • €3.40 • ☎ 26306217

Housed in an archeological park northwest of the harbour (you can't miss the large entrance gates just behind the quay), Pafos's **Roman mosaics** are one of the glories of Cyprus and simply unmissable. The mosaics were first revealed in 1942 when British soldiers digging trenches for air-raid shelters uncovered a representation of Hercules and the Lion. The ancient artwork was swiftly covered up to protect it from German bombs and its location, and even existence, in due course forgotten. In the 1960s, more mosaics were revealed during building work, and the Department of Antiquities stepped in to excavate the site. So far, four villas have been unearthed, each named after one of the more notable mosaics it contains.

3

Planning your visit

Set aside at least half a day to see the mosaics. Once through the rather incongrous modern entrance gates, you'll see the barn-like stone **visitor's centre** which provides a perfectly judged series of introductory information boards. It's also worth buying the excellent guide to the mosaics published by the Bank of Cyprus Foundation (€5.50). However, instead of following the order contained in it, and most guidebooks, visit the **Houses of Theseus, Aion** and **Orpheus** first, then take on the biggest and best, the **House of Dionysos**. This allows you to better appreciate the scale of the site.

Elsewhere in the archeological park are other structures – the remains of the **agora**, the reconstructed **odeion** in which concerts and plays are held during the summer, a pretty little **lighthouse**, and the jumbled remains of a Lusignan fortress, **Saranda Kolones** ("forty columns"). They're worth a quick look, perhaps, but only if you've already paid to get in to view the mosaics.

The Houses of Theseus, Aion and Orpheus

The first villa you come to, **The House of Theseus**, contains the mosaic discovered in 1941: *Theseus and the Minotaur*. A circular artwork, it positively glows in its uncovered setting of ochre floors and what remains of dried mud-brick walls. Note the maze-like geometric design that surrounds the central medallion – this represents the Labyrinth in which Theseus slew the Minotaur. The **House of Aion** is named after the pagan god Aion depicted inside (though only the his head survives). You can also make out Apollo

---

MOSAICS – A ROUGH GUIDE

Mosaics such as those found in Pafos were expensive to make, and therefore were confined to public buildings and the houses of the rich. Even in the great villas of important men, mosaics were installed only in the public rooms where they could be seen and admired (and envied) by visitors. In bedrooms floors were far more likely to be of simple pebbles set in mortar, while kitchens and workshops would have to manage with beaten earth floors. Most mosaic customers chose from a library of set patterns while the super-rich commissioned their own designs.

The artworks were painstakingly created by dozens of men using small cubes of pottery or glass called tesserae. First, relatively unskilled apprentices hacked out and levelled the ground before filling it with crushed stone, gravel and/or pottery shards mixed with lime mortar. After this a layer of fine plaster was laid, into which the tesserae were set. More skilled workmen creatied geometric patterns, while compositions involving figurative representation of humans and animals would be left to the master craftsman. Finally, marble dust, sand and lime were rubbed over the finished surface to fill in the joints and any cracks, and a drainage hole was created so that the mosaic could be periodically washed with water.

and Hermes amongst these fourth-century mosaics. The **House of Orpheus** further west features the god of music charming various animals with his lyre.

The House of Dionysos

There is no doubt, that the jewel in the crown of the Pafos mosaics is the **House of Dionysos**. This represents the central public area of a rich man's home, clustered around an atrium. The mosaics here are stunning and all the more remarkable considering that the complex suffered a direct hit during a Turkish air raid in 1974. While there isn't room in a general guidebook to cover them all or in detail, there are several that stand out. First, as you enter, is the **Scylla mosaic** in Room 1, which is rather drab and incomplete, but is the only one from the early Hellenic period (late fourth/early third century BC), making it by far the oldest mosaic on Cyprus. Found at a lower level, it was lifted and relaid here, and depicts the girl/monster Scylla (of Scylla and Charybdis fame), bewitched by Circe, who attacked all ships that ventured between Sicily and the Italian mainland. She is portrayed holding a trident in one hand and the mast of a ship in the other, and she has a body which ends in a serpent's tail and crab's claws. Beyond this, look out for the figure of Ganymede being carried off by Zeus in the form of an eagle (Room 8), and the hunting scenes in the porticos that surrounded the atrium: a leopard with the head of a donkey in its mouth, pouring blood and with the decapitated body lying nearby (Room 10), a hunter attacking a leopard with a spear (Room 11), a running tiger, a hunter attacking a bull and another attacking a lion (Room 12). A particularly graphic and interesting group of mosaics adorn the westernmost portico (Room 16). One, showing the story of **Icarios and the god Dionysos**, depicts a mythic booze-up. Icarios, the first maker of wine, is surrounded by inebriated shepherds intent on murdering him. Icarios's right hand points to the figures of Dionysos, the god of wine (who taught Icarios how to make it), and Akme, the personification of perfection. They too are drinking, but with decorum and restraint. Standing at the entrance to the "tablinum" or dining room, it appears to be a polite warning to guests not to overindulge.

Chrysopolitissa and St Paul's Pillar

On the other side of Leoforos Apostolou Paulou from the archeological park are **Chrysopolitissa** and **St Paul's Pillar**, the first of several survivals from the period after the end of the Roman Empire. Despite being just a few hundred metres from the busy road linking Kato Pafos to Ktima Pafos, and not far from the crowded promenade, the sense of peace and history is palpable. The ruins of the huge Christian basilica of **Panagia Chrysopolitissa** (the earliest parts of which date from the fourth century AD), with its seven aisles, surround the sixteenth-century church of **Agia Kyriaki**, the whole creating a harmonious and picturesque scene of jumbled columns, mosaic fragments (interesting, though not a patch on the ones across the road) and low stone walls. Here it was, tradition has it, that **St Paul** was chained to a column and scourged 39 times (one of five times he received this punishment from the Jews according to 2 Corinthians 11:24–29). The column is clearly labelled, though it looks a little like a modern concrete bollard. A further memorial is dedicated to **Eric Ejegod**, King of Denmark from 1095 to 1103, who died in Pafos on his way to the Holy Land. New walkways (being constructed at the time of writing) should provide improved access to the ruins.

The Ottoman and Lusignan baths

At the northern corner of the enclosure which contains Chrysopolitissa and Agia Kyriaki are the ramshackle remains of **Ottoman baths**, their characteristic domes dotted with circular thick glass windows, and substantial vaulting revealed by their derelict state. Further north is a better-preserved bathhouse, the sign in front of which identifies it as Ottoman but which is most likely **Lusignan** with later Ottoman modifications. With its stout walls, several glass-dotted domes and massive walls of dressed stone, it's well worth a look even though there's no access to the interior.

The catacombs of Agia Solomani

The **catacombs of Agia Solomani** – dank in atmosphere, obscure in origin – show the stubborn will of the early faithful to worship. Right next to busy Leoforou Apostolou Pavlou, about 800m north of the harbour, the well-signposted entrance is overlooked by a large terebinth tree covered in twists of cloth and paper – votive prayer offerings common on holy sites (both Christian and Muslim) throughout the Middle East. In its shade a flight of steps takes you down into hollowed out rock chambers. The first has several icons, a gate covered in more prayer offerings, the odd plastic bottle of oil and a sign asking you not to light candles. Further steps take you down into a flooded chamber, perhaps a holy well. It may be that the catacombs were once a pagan shrine which was later used as a synagogue in Roman times, before becoming a shrine dedicated to Agia Solomoni, the Jewish mother of the seven **Maccabee brothers**. On a practical note, a sturdy metal box on the surface above the catacombs invites your contributions.

Fabrica Hill

On the east side of Leoforos Apostolou Pavlou, where it intersects with Agion Anargyron, stands the rocky outcrop of **Fabrica Hill**, scored with excavations from a fourth-century AD stone quarry. In many places its tunnels and nooks were recycled as burial places. Some of the tombs, dotted with icons and votive offerings, can be seen from Agia Kyriakis, the side street which skirts the hill on its eastern side. Visible too are the remains of a recently excavated **classical theatre**, set like a fossil shell into the hillside and created, not by building, but by digging out the living rock. Archeological exploration continues on the northern face of the hill, much of which is now fenced off, though there's still access in places. Be careful if you do visit – the ground is very uneven and in places, columns of rock are left to hold the roof up.

The Tombs of the Kings

June–Aug 8am–7.30pm; April–May & Sept–Oct 8am–6pm; Nov–March 8am–5pm • €1.70 • ☏ 26306217

North of the main part of Kato Pafos, between the main coast road Tafon ton Vasileon and the sea, lies one of the strangest, most atmospheric ancient sites you're likely to come across – the so-called **Tombs of the Kings**. This is an extensive necropolis, a city of the dead, used from the third century BC to the fourth century AD for the burial, not of kings, but of high-up administrators, civil servants and their families. There is evidence that early Christians also used it to bury their dead, while in the Middle Ages people even lived in the tombs.

In the nineteenth century, the indefatigable **Luigi Palma di Cesnola** (see box below) plundered the tombs. More considered excavations continued in the early twentieth

---

TOMB RAIDER: LUIGI PALMA DI CESNOLA

In the literature surrounding a lot of Cypriot archeological sites, the name of **Luigi Palma di Cesnola** (1832–1904) has attracted a fair amount of infamy. An Italian soldier of fortune, he fought on the Union side in the American Civil War, eventually winning the Congressional Medal of Honor. When the war ended, he was rewarded with an appointment as US consul in Larnaka, where he served from 1865 to 1877. A keen amateur archeologist, he spent his twelve years in Cyprus cheerfully digging up antiquities all over the island – especially from Kition in Larnaka, Idalion in Lefkosia, Amathus and Kurion in Lemesos and the Tombs of the Kings in Pafos – discovering, so he claimed, 35,000 items. Most of these he sold abroad, in particular to the Metropolitan Museum of Art in New York (whose first director he became in 1879). Di Cesnola's methods were unorthodox to say the least – leaving the bulk of the work to assistants he often invented discovery locations, rarely photographed finds, and exaggerated their signficance. And the accusations didn't stop there – during his time at the Met he was accused of carrying out "deceptive restorations", and of being insufferable to his staff. He died in New York in 1904, and is buried in nearby Valhalla.

century, but systematic archeological exploration by the Cyprus Department of Antiquities didn't start until 1977. Since then, eight large tomb complexes have been identified. Each follows a similar plan, with an underground atrium surrounded by Doric columns and a portico, with the tombs dug into the walls behind – imagine a Greek temple, but built in a deep pit. The actual burial chambers and niches would have had plastered walls covered in frescoes, but apart from suggestions of colour here and there, these have now disappeared. Mind where you tread (especially if you have children in tow) – the unfenced drops into the tombs are sometimes quite considerable. The whole necropolis is scattered across an arid, rocky promontory with views of the sea and passing ships, and although sources of water are provided, take a hat, sunscreen and plenty of water (an ice-cream van is usually on site during the summer months).

Ktima Pafos

A short bus ride up from Kato Pafos stands **KTIMA PAFOS**, the more sedate administrative centre of the town. Its most atmospheric part is the old **Turkish Quarter**, or Mouttalos. This teeming area of narrow lanes has been turned into a covered market by the addition of glass and timber roofs. In these labyrinthine streets you can buy anything from souvenirs to slippers to sunglasses, bookmarks to belts, key rings to tablecloths. A snack bar sits in the depths of the market and, running along the edge that overlooks the main road and fine views down towards the harbour, a series of cafés and restaurants.

The Mehmet Bey Ebubekir Hammam

Located opposite the covered market, next to a large car park • Opening hours vary • Free

Built in 1592 by the Ottoman Governor of Pafos **Mehmet Bey Ebubekir** (who also built the nearby Cami Kebir, or Grand Mosque), and sporting the usual bottle-glass-dotted domes, this **hammam** served the Muslim community for three hundred years before being turned into a museum by the British. As you wander through the interconnected rooms, information boards explain the principal features of baths across the island – the tepid room, the hot room, the stoke pit, the changing room and so on. Some areas are fitted out as they would be in a working hammam, and in places transparent panels have been built into the floor so that you can see the hypocaust (underfloor heating system) below.

The Municipal Gardens

In the space between Gladstonos (the extension of Leoforos Apostolou Pavlou) and the east-bound Leoforos Georgiou Griva Digeni lie the extensive **Municipal Gardens**. Here you'll find the town hall, the Pafos Bishopric, the **Municipal Art Gallery** (daily 10am– 1pm & Mon–Fri 3–8pm; Nov–March closes 5pm; ☎26930653) and, in the streets just south of it, two museums worth visiting: the Byzantine Museum and the Cultural Heritage Museum. At the bottom of the gardens is **Kostis Palamas Square**, centred on a Neoclassical rotunda, and across from this a memorial to Kostis Palamas (1859–1943), the Greek poet who composed the words to the Olympic Hymn.

The Byzantine Museum

5 Andrea Ioannou • Mon–Fri 9am–3pm, Sat 9am–1pm • €1.70 • ☎ 06231393

In an imposing building next to, and run by, the Holy Bishopric of Pafos, the **Byzantine Museum** houses a wonderful collection of icons. Among them is one claimed to be the oldest in Cyprus – that of Saint Marina flanked by scenes from her martyrdom, which dates from the seventh or eighth century – together with many more from the twelfth to nineteenth centuries. Other rooms contain frescoes rescued from derelict churches, wood and metal artwork, vestments and other embroidered cloth, manuscripts and old printed books.

The Cultural Heritage Museum

1 Exo Vrisis · Mon–Sat 9.30am–5pm, Sun 10am–1pm ·€1.70 · ☎ 26932010

Generally called the "Ethnographical Museum" in tourist maps, but signposted as the **Cultural Heritage Museum**, this is a private collection of finds collected by George S. Eliades, a local secondary-school teacher and amateur archeologist. Laid out on two floors plus the garden at the rear, the museum's charm lies in the sheer variety of exhibits, though the labelling is a little patchy. Of particular interest are architectural details such as decorative lintels, and the tools associated with particular trades – spinning and weaving, winemaking, grinding corn, and so on. In the grounds are a wagon, traditional stone-built ovens, and even a pre-Christian tomb.

Pafos Archeological Museum

Leoforos Georgiou Griva Digeni ·Tues, Thurs & Fri 8am–2.30pm, Wed 8am–5pm · €1.70 · ☎ 26306215

About 1km east of the Municipal Gardens, **Pafos Archeological Museum** (also called the "District Museum") is a useful adjunct to visits to the sights of Kato Pafos. There are five rooms in all, housing, respectively, Chalcolithic remains (Room I), Archaic and Classical artefacts (Room II), objects from Hellenic and Romans times (Room III), and Roman and early Christian finds from Kato Pafos (Rooms IV and V). All are worthy of unhurried viewing, but if you're short of time, concentrate on the last two. Highlights include a second-century AD statue of Asklepios from the House of Theseus, an exquisite pair of gold earrings dating from the third century BC, a medieval sword and helmet, glazed pottery from the thirteenth century AD, and a series of glazed ceramic vessels shaped to different parts of the human anatomy – these were filled with hot or cold water to bring relief from injury or disease.

ARRIVAL AND DEPARTURE   PAFOS

By plane Pafos Airport is 16km east of the town, connected by both a main road (B6) and a motorway (A6). A new terminal was opened in 2008, and it now has all the facilities you'd expect in an international airport – bank and cash point, tourist information, car rental and taxi ranks (agree a fare before getting in). Two bus routes run from the airport into town: the #612 to the Harbour Bus Station in Kato Pafos (May–Oct hourly 7.30am–midnight; Nov–April 11.30am–2.30pm, & 5.30–8.30pm), and the #613 to the Karavella terminus in Ktima Pafos (8am–7pm).

By bus Intercity buses from throughout the republic arrive at the Karavella terminus in Ktima Pafos. **Destinations**: Lemesos (Mon–Fri 8 daily, Sat & Sun 4 daily); Larnaka (Mon–Fri 10 daily, Sat & Sun 6 daily); Lefkosia (Mon–Fri 5 daily, Sat & Sun 2 daily).

GETTING AROUND

The two halves of Pafos are small enough to be explored on foot. Getting from one to the other is a long walk (3km) so a bus is preferable.

By bus Local buses in Pafos are run by OSYPA (⊛ pafosbuses.com). There are two bus stations serving the two parts of the town: the Harbour Bus Station in Kato Pafos, and the Karavella Bus Station in Ktima Pafos, linked to each other by routes #606 and #610. For Coral Bay take the #615 from the harbour. From Karavella Bus Station, useful routes include Polis (#602, #605, #614) and Episkopi (#609), and Geroskipou (#601).

By taxi As in the other main towns you can either pre-book taxis or hail a taxi on the street. All taxis have metres and the charges are standard across Cyprus.

By car Pafos is fairly car friendly in that there are large free car parks (in Kato Pafos just behind the harbour, in Ktima Pafos south of the hammam). Elsewhere, there are numerous pay-and-display car parks, and particularly in Ktima Pafos, a fair amount of on-street parking.

INFORMATION

Tourist office The main tourist office is in the centre of Ktima Pafos, at the top of Gladstonos on the right (daily except Sun 8.15am–2pm & 3–6.15pm, Wed closed pm; ☎ 26932841, ⊛ visitpafos.org). Another office serves Kato Pafos at 63a Poseidonos (hours as for the Gladstonos office; ☎ 26930521) and at Pafos Airport (daily 9am–11pm; ☎ 26007368).

PAFOS REGION FESTIVALS

MAY
Anthestiria Flower Festival Celebrates the arrival of spring, with floats covered in flowers parading down the seafront.
Pafos Guitar Festival Classical guitar festival with concerts and master classes.

JUNE
Choir Festival International choir festival held in the ancient odeion.

JULY
Paradise Jazz Festival (ⓦparadise-jazz .com) Small but perfectly formed jazz festival held in Pomos (see p.121).
Koumandaria Festival Celebrations of the famous wine in a number of Koumandaria villages.
Memory Concert Musical performances in front of the castle.

Ancient Greek Drama (July and Aug) Part of an island-wide festival, with a performance in the Ancient Odeon on Fabrica Hill in Kato Pafos.

AUGUST
Arkadia Festival A village festival in Kallepeia, with food, drink and music.
Dionysia Festival Three-day wine festival with wide range of displays, food and dance, held in the village of Stroumbi.

SEPTEMBER
Aphrodite Festival (ⓦpafc.com.cy). An opera company is invited each year to mount a production in front of the castle.
Ierokipia Cultural Festival Music, dance and exhibitions in the main square at Geroskipou.

ACTIVITIES

Bowling Cosmic Ten Pin Bowling on Leoforos Apostolou Pavlou (☎26220033; €5.50 per game) has 18 lanes. For lawn/crown green bowls try the *Athena Beach Hotel* (☎26884300, ⓦathena-cbh.com; €8 or €5 for hotel guests) on Poseidonos.

Go karting Coral Bay Karting Centre (☎70001314; 20min €20) has one and two-seater karts. Daily noon–6pm.

Water slides Aphrodite Water Park off Poseidonos (☎26913638, ⓦaphroditewaterpark.com; €29) offers a wide range of water slides (including the white-knuckle "zero gravity"), plus one of the largest wave pools in Europe. May–June 10.30am–5.50pm, July–Aug 10am–6pm, Sept–Oct 10am–5pm; bus #11 or #15.

GOLF
Aphrodite Hills Golf Club Koulia ☎26828200. Affordable 18-hole courses from €49 per round.
Elea Golf Club Geroskipou ☎26202001, ⓦeleaestate .com. Designed by Nick Faldo, this is the newest and most exclusive of Cyprus's 18-hole courses, a 10min drive from Pafos and close to the airport. Green fees: €120 high season (Sept–Nov & Feb–May), low season €85.
Pafos Golf Driving Range On the E701 between Pafos and Coral Bay ☎26271555, ⓦpaphosgolfrange.com. For those who don't want to splash out on the big prestigious 18-hole courses, this might be the answer. 65 balls €5, 105 balls €8, club rental €5 per half set.

ACCOMMODATION

The bulk of the big resort hotels are clustered along the beach road (Poseidonos) that stretches to the southeast of Kato Pafos and along the coast road to the north (Tafon ton Vasileon) which runs past the Tombs of the Kings. For something smaller and with a little more atmosphere try staying in Ktima Pafos.

KATO PAFOS AND POSEIDONOS
Alexander the Great Poseidonos ☎26965000, ⓦkanikahotels.com. Recently refurbished and highly popular, the *Alexander the Great* is well placed within walking distance (about 600m) from the centre of Kato Pafos. Staff are friendly, and thought goes into removing perpetual irritants like nabbing a sunbed – you're allocated one for the whole of your stay. €182

Almyra 12 Poseidonos ☎26888700, ⓦalmyra.com. Just on the edge of Kato Pafos centre, the *Almyra* combines proximity to everything with an expansive site and facilities. Cool, clean look, elegant terrace overlooking the sea, spectacular pools indoor and out, plus a huge range of activities, including those for children. €250

★**Amathus Beach** Poseidonos ☎26883333, ⓦamathus-hotels.com/paphos. Top-end luxury holiday resort hotel at the far end of Poseidonos, about 4km from the centre of Kato Pafos. So, despite what the hotel says, not really within walking distance on a hot day. But, since it has every facility you can imagine, including a fabulous spa and pool area, as well as hugely attentive staff (iced face towels available on request, tea brought out to you on a silver platter) you might never want to go out. Minimum stay five nights. €277

3

Annabelle 10 Poseidonos 📞26885000, 🖥annabelle .com.cy. Luxurious, beachfront hotel with excellent facilities and staff. Its six acres of palm-fringed gardens are set around meandering free-form pools – almost over-the-top but not quite. Remarkably quiet for a hotel so close to the centre of Kato Pafos. Activities on offer include yoga tennis, scuba diving and kitesurfing. **€270**

★ **Apollonia Holiday Apartments** 20 Ikarou 📞26221787, 🖥appolloniacy.com. In the heart of Kato Pafos, near the post office, the *Apollonia* is a welcome contrast with the all-bells-and-whistles beach hotels, giving the greater freedom and lower prices that self-catering apartments offer. Good range of apartment types, swimming pool, a "trust the drinker" bar, free wi-fi throughout, and perfectly adequate furniture and fittings. Communal areas are fine, if florid. **€82**

★ **Daphne Hotel Apartments** 3 Alkminis 📞26933110, 🖥daphne-hotel.com. Good basic accommodation just behind the Kato Pafos seafront, with clean simple apartments, small pool, bar/restaurant on site. Not luxurious, but a place to lay your head. It's in the absolute epicentre of the pub and bar area of Pafos, so be prepared for bustle and noise. Breakfast extra. **€72**

Pioneer Beach Hotel Poseidonos 📞26945000, 🖥pioneer-cbh.com. At the furthest end of Poseidonos, and therefore 3km southeast of the centre of Kato Pafos, the *Pioneer Beach* is too far from the centre to walk in, but equally clear of the town-centre noise. Terrific setting, good beach, and close to public swimming pool, playing fields,

bowling green and the Aphrodite Water Park. Well-appointed rooms and full range of services as you'd expect (though wi-fi, surprisingly, is not free). Four-night mininum stay. **€166**

KTIMA PAFOS

Agapinor Hotel 24–30 Nikodimou Mylona 📞26933926, 🖥www.agapinorhotel.com.cy. Conveniently located in Ktima Pafos, the *Agapinor* is a good base for those who are more inclined towards shopping and sightseeing rather than lazing on the beach. It has a smallish pool and separate children's pool, café, bar and restaurant, but it is the location (and budget price) rather than facilities that is its USP. Minimum two-night stay. **€72**

Axiothea Hotel 2 Ivis Malioti 📞26932866, 🖥axiotheahotel.com. Budget hotel just south of the Municipal Gardens in Ktima Pafos, and therefore within easy reach of the museums and the shops of the Turkish quarter. Five storeys high and set on a hillside, the views are wonderful. Rooms are basic but clean, services limited, and the restaurant only serves breakfast, but you're in the heart of things so it doesn't matter. **€60**

Kiniras Hotel 91 Makarios 📞99436442, 🖥kiniras .cy.net. A boutique hotel in a fifteenth-century Venetian mansion in the centre of Ktima Pafos, the family-run *Kiniras* has bright colourful modern rooms, a gorgeous, plant-decked restaurant offering traditional Cypriot dishes and paintings by the owner throughout. Award-winning service and a relaxed atmosphere. **€60**

EATING AND DRINKING

KATO PAFOS AND POSEIDONOS

Cavallini 65 Poseidonos 📞26964164. Near the *Amathus Beach Hotel*, this quality Italian restaurant marries an excellent (child-friendly) atmosphere with authentic reasonably priced food. Some surprising choices – for example, quail in brandy. Main courses €12–20. Parking can be difficult in high season. Daily 6.30–10.30pm.

★ **Hondros** 96 Apostolos Pavlos 📞26934256. Claims to be the oldest traditional taverna in Pafos (established 1953). Excellent Greek Cypriot food, plenty of seating inside and out and a traditional wood-fired oven and charcoal grill outside. Main courses €10–20, meze from €18.50. Right on the main road, though, so there can be a lot of traffic noise. Booking recommended. Lunch and dinner.

La Sardegna da Gino 70 Apostolos Pavlos 📞26933399. About 200m past the Begonia Garden Centre crossroads, on the way to Ktima Pafos. Owned and run by a Sardinian, this place specializes in delicious wood-fired pizzas, with a huge variety of toppings. Prices (€10–15) seem steep until you see the size of the pizzas. Wed–Sun 6pm–11pm.

Ocean Basket Avanti Holiday Village Piazza 📞26961379. A couple of kilometres along Poseidonos in the Avanti Holiday Village (and therefore well placed for all

the hotels in that area), the *Ocean Basket* is one of a large South African chain of seafood restaurants. Fast-food ambience, good fresh fish, great value for money. Mains €8–16. Mon–Thurs noon–7.30pm, Fri noon–10.30pm, Sun noon–9.30pm.

Saint Paul's Pillar 7 St Paul's Pillar St 📞99450423. Endearingly ramshackle little restaurant on the approach to the ruins that include St Paul's Pillar – the clue's in the name and address. The menu is a mixture of Cypriot staples, English breakfasts, sandwiches and burgers, and a wide variety of specials. Good value and amazingly quiet considering it's next to a busy road. Snacks €4–7, selection of "village" dishes €10. Mon–Sat 9am–10pm.

★ **Syrian Restaurant** 14 Pafias Afroditis 📞26600278. Great spot for lunch, hidden away in the back streets north of Chryssopolitissa and St Paul's Pillar. The food is, as you'd expect, Middle Eastern, as is the atmosphere and background music. Good hummus and falafel, plus grilled meats. Mains €7–8, meze €16. Daily 11am–midnight.

KTIMA PAFOS

Fettas 33 Ioanni Agroti 📞26937822. Good-value Greek

food at a small taverna patronized mainly by Greek Cypriots. Copious meat meze, with a menu that varies with the seasons. Most main courses fall into the range €10–20. Gets busy – it's wise to book. Mon–Sat 6.30–11pm.

Laona 6 Votsis ☎26937121. In a back street near the covered market in Ktima Pafos, the *Laona* isn't easy to find – if lost, phone, and the owner will come to get you. A gem of an old-fashioned Greek restaurant which doesn't overdo the choices – the menu is on the blackboard, and staff will advise if you're not sure what to have. Mains €8–10, meze €13.50–17. Daily 8am–4pm.

Myrra 37 Neopoleos Street ☎26937822. At the corner with Lambrou Sepi in Ktima Pafos, the friendly, family-run *Myrra* occupies a slightly dishevelled house with occasionally naff decor. Good grills and meze, own-label wine, and organic, seasonal veg grown by the owners. Mains from €9. Reservations recommended at weekends. Mon–Sat 6–11pm.

CORAL BAY AND BEYOND

★ **Agios Georgios Restaurant and Fish Tavern** Agios Georgios ☎26621306. Overlooking the little harbour on Cape Drepano, this is a popular restaurant with locals. Great views, and the fish on offer is freshly caught. Expect to pay €12–15 for individual dishes, or €20 for fish meze. Daily summer 9am–10pm, winter 8.30am–6pm.

★ **Astrofegia** Coral Bay ☎26622500. Although it has a small seating area in a conservatory, *Astrofegia*'s great strength is as a takeaway. It offers a range of traditional Greek food, and not just the sort of kebabs you'd get back home – pick from a daily changing menu of stews and hot-plate dishes, plus a wide range of vegetarian mains featuring cracked wheat, ladies fingers, sweet potato, lentils. A godsend if you're staying in the Coral Bay area. Dishes of the day €4–9. Daily 9am–11pm.

Samisen 57 Coral Bay Avenue ☎26622243, ⓦsamisenjapanese.com. Highly rated Japanese restaurant in the centre of Coral Bay, where the culinary theatricals are as entertaining as the food itself. First-class cuisine – order a set menu if you don't know your way around Japanese food, or pick and mix if you do. Sushi €2.50–8 per item. Kids portions half size and half price. Daily 12.30–11pm.

NIGHTLIFE

Barrio del Mar Geroskipou. Vast (2000 capacity) beach club with six bars and a thumping sound system. Mainstream Greek and international music, resident DJs. Entry €12. May–Sept Mon–Sat 11pm–3.30am. Sun 3–9.30pm.

Cartel Fashion Club 31 Poseidonos. Rooftop venue with views of the castle and harbour. Resident and guest DJs, varied cocktails (expensive), older would-be sophisticated clientele. Wed–Sun 11pm onwards (every night in late July/early August).

Different Agias Napas. In the pedestrianized heart of Kato Pafos, just behind the seafront, *Different* prides itself on its wide range of musical tastes and on being LGBT-friendly. Sun–Thurs 9am–2pm, Fri & Sat 9pm–4am.

★ **Level** Apostolou Pavlou, Kato Pafos. About halfway between Kato and Ktima Pafos, the *Level Club* caters for a late-twenties upwards age group. Moving feast of special events Fridays, standard mainstream DJ sets Saturdays. Fri & Sat 11pm–4am.

Loft 1 Archemidous. On the east side of Kato Pafos centre. Outside dancing in summer to Greek, pop, r'n'b and electronica; inside in winter. All age clientele, dramatic special acts featuring flames. Mon–Sat 11pm till late.

ENTERTAINMENT

Cinemas Cine Oasis 35 Apostolou Pavlou (☎26951325) halfway between Kato and Ktima Pafos; Othellos Cinema 41 Evagora Pallikaridi, Ktima Pafos (☎26946256); Revekka Cinema 1 Vasili Michailidi, Geroskipou (☎26962984).

Theatres Summer productions are mounted at The Odion on Fabrica Hill and Castle Square.

SHOPPING

Cyprus Handicrafts Service 64 Leoforos Apostolou Pavlou, Kato Pafos ☎26306243. One of the government-run chains selling good-quality art copies and craft output. Summer: Mon, Tues, Thurs & Fri 7am–2pm & 4–7pm, Wed 7.30am–2pm, Sat 8am–1pm; winter: Mon, Tues, Thurs & Fri 7am–2pm, 2.30–5.30pm, Wed 7.30am–2pm, Sat 8am–1pm.

Pafos Municipal Market Agora Street old town. Buzzing fruit and veg market surrounded by covered-over pedestrianized streets. Mon–Sat 6am–1pm.

Timi Car Boot Sale Timi Village (near the airport). Worth a look for bargain hunters. Sun 7am–2pm.

DIRECTORY

Banks and exchange There are numerous banks throughout Kato and Ktima Pafos, most of which have ATMs. Bank of Cyprus has branches at 1 Poseidonos (☎26936151) and 1 Akamantidos (☎22128000) and Hellenic Banks at Kennedy Square (☎26505616) and Chloraka (☎26505242).

3

Internet Internet cafés come and go, but try *Maroushia Café* on Ioanni Agroti ☎ 26947240.

Medical Pafos General Hospital Anavargos, Ktima Pafos ☎ 26803145, Polis Hospital ☎ 26821800; private doctors available at weekends/holidays ☎ 90901436; pharmacies after hours ☎ 90901416.

Police Central Police Station, Griva Digeni and Gregori Afxentiou ☎ 26806060; Port and Marine Police ☎ 26811390, Traffic police ☎ 26806111.

Post office There are three post offices serving the main areas of the town – the Old Post Office on Nicodemou Milona (Ktima Pafos) and one on Ikarou (Kato Pafos).

Around Pafos

Pafos is blessed with numerous day-trip destinations. To the southeast is **Geroskipou** with its fine church and first-rate folk museum and, beyond it on the outskirts of the village of Kouklia, the remains of **Palaipafos** (the original town of Pafos) with, on the coast, the pretty cove of **Petra tou Romiou**, legendary **birthplace of Aphrodite**. Driving east and northeast involves a climb to a plateau dotted with villages and vineyards, the **Monastery of Agios Neofytos** and the large village of **Pano Panagia**, birthplace of Archbishop Makarios III. Driving along the coast road north from Pafos takes you through a resort area with good **beaches**, some interesting small museums and a well-run **zoo**.

Geroskipou

GEROSKIPOU, although a separate municipality southeast of Pafos, is now virtually a suburb of the larger town. Yet its handsome square, dominated by the large church of Agia Paraskevi and its fame as a centre of *loukoumia* production (see box opposite), give it a character all of its own. The name Geroskipou derives from the Greek for "Holy Garden", a reference to the nearby temple of Aphrodite in Palaipafos.

The Folk Art Museum

June–Aug Mon–Fri 8am –2pm, Sat 9am–5pm; Sept–May Mon–Wed & Fri 8am–2pm, Thurs 8am–2pm &3–6pm, Sat 9am–5pm • €1.70 • ☎ 26306216

Clearly signposted on the left as you enter Geroskipou on the old Lemesos road, just before you get to the main square, is the town's **Folk Art Museum**, one of the best on the island. Its location, the "House of Hadjismith", is a listed building once owned by one Andreas Zoumboulakis, the British Vice Consul from 1800 to 1864. In fact much of the enjoyment of this museum lies in its setting – shady paved courtyards, wooden shutters and balconies, flagged rooms and rustic stone walls. The eclectic collection features everything from complicated "wedding breads" and traditional waistcoats and scarves to musical instruments and even children's swimming floats made from gourds. Look out too for the "*tapatsia*", a basket which was slung from the ceiling on a rope to keep bread out of the reach of vermin. Everything is clearly labelled in Greek and English, with occasional sketches showing how things worked.

Agia Paraskevi

8am–1pm & 2–5pm (closes 4pm in winter) • Free

The church of **Agia Paraskevi**, overlooking the main square of the town (join the locals in pausing for a drink or something to eat), is an important and rare Byzantine structure originating in the ninth century AD. It has five domes over a nave and two aisles, with an additional small dome over an odd little annexe attached below the belfry, used as a reliquary. Inside is a range of frescoes, some "aniconic" (that is using crosses and abstract patterns rather than representations of human figures) dating from the period when the iconoclasts held sway in the Byzantine Empire. Later representational wall paintings date from the twelfth to fifteenth centuries.

LOUKOUMIA – CYPRIOT DELIGHT

Geroskipou is famous for its "**loukoumia**", or what the rest of the world calls Turkish Delight. Indeed, it has Protected Geographical Indication, like champagne or Cornish pasties. Many shops along the main road and in the square sell the sweet, and it's far more versatile than you might imagine. You can buy *loukoumia* flavoured with chocolate, nuts, vanilla, lemon, orange, mint or banana as well as the more traditional rose-petal flavour. Try Aphrodite Delights (ⓦwww.aphroditedelights.com), for example, which has a slick showroom, and visitor centre a couple of minutes walk from the main square.

Palaipafos

Daily 8am–4pm • €3.40 • ☎ 26432155

Sixteen kilometres southeast from Pafos, near the village of **KOUKLIA**, is the site of Nea Pafos's ancient predecessor, **Palaipafos**. It's a romantic spot with the distant Mediterranean looming behind. Among the ruins is a **Sanctuary to Aphrodite**, a range of Roman remains, as well as Lusignan buildings and the church of **Panagia Katholiki**. While the site is of inestimable archeological importance, having been continuously occupied from 2800 BC, it's difficult to grasp on the ground. For example the sanctuary itself amounts to little more than some massive blocks of dressed stone. Perhaps of more interest are the mosaics, part of a house built by a wealthy Roman. Information boards tell you all you need to know, and more, of the cult of Aphrodite (see box, p.126), though as you stand in the sun reading them, your thirst for knowledge might be trumped by your thirst for a drink.

The most visible structure on the site is the so-called Lusignan manor house of **La Cavocle**, actually built in the thirteenth century AD to administer local sugar production. It was adapted after the Ottoman Conquest to become the residence of a local Turkish *chiflik* (landowner). Now the **Kouklia Local Museum** (daily 7.30am–2.30pm), it contains a conical black stone thought to represent Aphrodite, and a massive bath carved out of chalk from around 1000 BC. The downstairs Gothic rib-vaulted banqueting room is often used for music recitals.

Before leaving, try to have a look at the fascinating remains of Palaipafos's **northeast gate** on the Marchellos Hill – it's about 700m through the village on the road (F612) to Archimandrita. This complicated and formidable fortification shows in detail the effects of the **Persian siege of 498 BC**. The Persians had thrown up a huge siege ramp against the city walls. In response the defenders laboriously dug four tunnels under the walls, eventually managing to set fire to the ramp with burning oil. One of the tunnels (Tunnel 1) is still intact, and the paraphernalia used by the diggers – oil lamps, water jugs and even the bronze cauldrons that carried the oil – have been recovered. Whether the ruse succeeded or not, it would only have caused a temporary setback, since we know that the Persians breached the gate and the city fell. During the century following the siege, the Paphians, while renovating the defences, found it easier to incorporate the remains of the ramp into the new defences rather than try to remove them.

Petra tou Romiou (The birthplace of Aphrodite)

An attractive pebble beach, 9km or so west of Kouklia (and technically in Lemesos district), **Petra tou Romiou**, is where, according to legend, Aphrodite rose from the sea and came ashore (which may explain the sanctuary nearby). The Greek name refers to a different myth: Digenes Akritas, also known as Romios (or, more disappointingly, Basil), was the Byzantine hero of an epic song who killed bears, lions and dragons with his bare hands, and leapt from Cyprus to Asia Minor, gaining purchase by grabbing the Five Finger Mountain near Kyrenia. He once vanquished some foes by throwing huge rocks at them, one of which is the biggest of those on the western tip of Petra tou Romiou. The beach is easy to access (the coast road sweeps past just above it).

3

THE CULT OF APHRODITE

You won't have been in Cyprus long before you become aware of the island's proud association with **Aphrodite**, whether it's the dozens of hotels and restaurants named in her honour or everything from tea towels to T-shirts bearing her image. A brief primer is therefore worthwhile.

In the beginning there were only two beings – **Ge**, goddess of earth, and **Uranus**, god of the sky. Their children became known as the **Titans**. **Cronus**, their leader, on his mother's orders cut off the genitals of his father, and threw them into the sea. From the resulting maelstrom of foam ("aphros"), the comely Aphrodite arose, and floated ashore on a scallop shell. She became the goddess of love – to be more specific, of beauty, pleasure and procreation – and created havoc with her power to bewitch both mortals and gods. The stories about her are copious. The most important in the Cypriot tradition involves **Kinyras**, king of Cyprus. He became Aphrodite's adoring acolyte and favourite but was tricked into sleeping with his daughter, Myrrha, by a jealous Aphrodite. Kinyras almost kills Myrrha before the gods intervene, turning her into a fragrant myrrh tree. From the trunk of this tree **Adonis**, the ideal male, was born. Aphrodite soon falls in love with him, as does Persephone, queen of the Underworld. The pair fight over him until he is killed by a wild boar, and dies in Aphrodite's arms.

The **cult of Aphrodite**, practiced at temple sites across the island, seems to have degenerated from a celebration of love and fertility to temple rites that included orgies and prostitution. Fifth-century BC Greek historian Herodotus describes how all women were expected to attend the temple and give themselves to any passing stranger. Attractive women, he comments wryly, could expect to complete their duty on the first night, while it might take ugly ones three or four years.

Aphrodite has, of course, been the subject of innumerable **sculptures and paintings**, from the demure Aphrodite of Cnidus and Botticelli's golden-haired Birth of Venus to various soft-porn representations by Victorian artists. A number of seashells are associated with her too – scallops, because that was what she rode ashore on – and the suggestively shaped cowrie, which is named Cypraeidae in her honour.

Lempa

The village of **LEMPA**, about 5km north from the centre of Pafos, has largely been swallowed up by suburbia. It does, however, have a quite separate history, being one of the oldest villages in Cyprus, dating from the Chalcolithic era. It was also, until 1974, almost entirely Turkish Cypriot. In their place came a tide of students: the Cyprus College of Art, forced to leave Famagusta during the conflict, has resettled here.

Prehistoric Lempa

Open access • Free

A Chalcolithic village dating from about 3500 to 2500 BC, **Prehistoric Lempa** consists of a cluster of round houses made of stone and mud similar to those at Tenta and Choirokoitia. There are several modern reconstructions, each with low circular mud-brick foundations, mud-and-straw walls and timber joists upon which is laid a stone and earth roof. One of the huts, much larger than the others, has walls which are decorated inside and out by patterns in ochre paint, and has a central hearth surrounded by massive tree-trunk pillars holding up the roof.

The Cyprus College of Art

6 Eleftherias Street • 24254042, artcyprus.org

The Cyprus College of Art was formed in 1969 by Cypriot artist Stass Paraskos (see box, p.128). Very much focused on art rather than academia, the college has the feel of a cooperative, reflecting its origins in the British art school ethos of the late 1960s. For the visitor, the main attraction is its famous, or infamous, "**Artistic Wall of Lempa**",

3

THE UNLIKELY BIRTH OF THE CYPRUS COLLEGE OF ART

The **Cyprus College of Art** has somewhat eccentric origins. Greek Cypriot Stass Paraskos (born 1933 near Larnaka) travelled to Leeds in 1953 to become a chef in his brother's restaurant. The restaurant was popular with local art students, and when Paraskos not only showed an interest but also considerable ability in art, they encouraged him to apply to enter Leeds College of Art. Despite a lack of formal qualifications, he was accepted and flourished, later going on to teach at the college. In 1966 some of Paraskos's paintings – nudes – were judged to be "lewd and obscene" by the authorities. He became something of a cause célèbre, garnering support from Roy Jenkins and Ian Dury, punk music giant and fellow artist, who became a friend. Paraskos lost his case however, and was fined £5. In 1969, during tutorials conducted in a local pub, it was suggested that Paraskos use his Cypriot connections to arrange summer art schools on the island. This he did, and as it became an annual event, interest was expressed by numerous other art colleges. These informal arrangements grew into the Cyprus College of Art, based at first in Famagusta, moving to Pafos after the 1974 invasion, and settling finally in Lempa. In 2007 a second branch of the college, now known as the Cornaro Institute, was opened in Larnaka.

made up of hundreds of pieces and contributions by its students. Variously hailed as inspirational or damned as an eyesore, it's difficult not to smile at its sheer, unadulterated exuberance.

Agios Neofytos Monastery

9am–1pm & 2–6pm • €1 (including admission to museum)

Such is the ubiquity and range of monasteries in Cyprus that visiting them can begin to feel like a chore, at least for the non-believer. Not so in the case of **Agios Neofytos**, about 17km north of the centre of Pafos (best accessed by climbing up through Emba and Tala). It boasts a fascinating back story (see box opposite), and a spectacular setting worth a visit in itself. For a full appreciation of the monastery, do buy the guidebook published by the church authorities (€5).

The monastery itself, through the main gate, past the gift shop and café consists of a residential block, church and cloisters surrounding a lush garden; beyond here there's a spacious terrace dotted with benches overlooking the valley. At the far end of the terrace, accessed by a stone bridge, is the reason for all the fuss – the **Enkleistra,** the caves dug out by St Neofytos himself.

The Enkleistera consists of three rooms – the first two are the nave and sanctuary of a chapel (the Church of the Holy Cross), the third is Neofytos's cell. The walls of the **nave** are covered in **frescoes**, the upper ones sixteenth-century, the lower ones earlier works which could possibly have been painted by the saint's own hand. In the **sanctuary** are more frescoes, this time twelfth-century. Look out in particular for the one at the western end of the roof of Neofytos (the bearded figure with wings) being escorted to the Day Of Judgement by two angels. The saint's pious expression seems to suggest that he's taking nothing for granted and the inscription reads "I fervently pray that this image should come to pass". Beyond the sanctuary, through a low doorway, is the saint's **cell**, also frescoed, and contining a bed, table, desk, chair, bookshelf, even a quill niche, all carved out of the rock. It also houses his tomb – he expressed a wish that when he died, his body be interred in it, and the cave sealed off. However, in 1756 the sarcophagus was opened and his bones transferred to the the **monastery church**, where, once your eyes have adjusted to the gloom, you can see (and if you wish, kiss) his silver-encased skull, and inspect his sarcophagus – it's on the left, under the pulpit.

Across from the church is a **museum** (summer: same hours as monastery, winter: 9am–4pm), housing the monastery's many treasures – crosses, chalices, censers, sacred texts, bibles, vestments, icons and much else. Some of these objects are unbelievably

AGIOS NEOFYTOS – THE HERMIT SAINT

Agios Neofytos (1134–1219) was born near the village of Lefkara. As a boy he had a strong yearning towards the spiritual life, especially when his family arranged a marriage for him to which he took exception. He fled to the monastery of Chrystomos, near Buffavento Castle in the north, became a monk, and finally occupied a cave north of Pafos which had been vacated by a previous ascetic. Neofytos expanded it, and settled into a life of quiet contemplation. God clearly had other plans. Neofytos's reputation for piety had spread, and acolytes from far and wide converged on the cave, bringing food and other gifts. So raucous did this informal encampment become that poor old Neofytos had to retreat further (in 1197) by moving into the cave above, accessible only by a ladder which he pulled up behind him. The new cave he called, with touching optimism, "New Zion". Here he wrote a variety of commentaries, meditations, hymns and prayers, as well as a chronicle about the catastrophe that was overcoming Cyprus at the time – conquest by Richard the Lionheart and the start of Lusignan rule of the island. Not bad considering that he only learnt to read aged 18. Neofytos communicated with his followers through a hole in the floor and the site became the basis of an official monastery, the forerunner of the current one, established in 1170 AD. Neofytos died in around 1219, aged over eighty.

3

exquisite: the 1560 Venetian bible, for example, and an illuminated manuscript from the late eleventh century.

The Baths of Adonis

Daily 9am–8pm • €9 • ☏ 96321335, ⓦ adonisbathswaterfalls.com

The waterfalls and pools of **The Baths of Adonis**, north of Pafos, are widely touted as one of the district's premier attractions. While their location on the Mavrokolympos River is undeniably appealing, be prepared for a heavy dose of tourist kitsch. The baths were promoted by self-styled actor Pambos Theodorou, who appears to have a penchant for comically bad statues of Greek gods and mythical creatures. These include a plaster figure of Aphrodite which, at 10m high, is claimed to be the world's largest, and one of Adonis where women who wish to become pregnant are enjoined to touch his "appendage". On the positive side, plunging into the pools is certainly refreshing – it is not unknown for bathers to strip off completely though the water can be very cold, even in summer. There's also a good on-site café and a fine family restaurant, the *Vatouthkia* (☏ 99459163) a couple of kilometres before you get to the baths. Another word of warning: signs which direct you from all nearby roads ("Adonis Baths Mavrokolympos. The road is good for all cars") are optimistic to say the least – the road is absolutely awful.

Amargeti

About 24km northeast of Pafos (8km on the A6 motorway and a further 16km up into the hills on the E606), **AMARGETI** is a village whose air of tranquillity belies its (possibly apocryphal) racy past as the centre of a druggy cult. A rudimentary mud-brick temple was unearthed here stuffed with clay and rough-hewn votive figures dedicated to "Melanthios Apollonas" – perhaps "Apollo of the opium poppy". It's not too big a leap to believe that there may have been a cult of Apollo in which smoking opium played a part. It would certainly explain why the temple and the votive offerings were so half-hearted. Today the centrepiece of the village is the church of **Zoodochos Pigi** ("Life-giving spring"), which has a handsome terrace on which are displayed some monumental pieces of rural equipment, including several presses and an olive mill; the views aren't half bad either. The village square has a couple of tavernas: the *Zoodochos Pigi* (☏ 26723212) and the *Apollon* (☏ 99632631) and a mini market. A little further down the main street is a recently created (2009) **Folk Art Museum**, based in what was, until 1974, the Turkish Cypriot school. Fifty metres beyond the museum (and continuing the village's dedication to mind-altering substances) is the **Kalamos Winery** (☎26723224) – it does wine tastings for groups, and English is spoken. Its *zivania* is particularly highly thought of.

The Monastery of Agia Moni

The monastery of **Agia Moni**, further up the E606 towards Pano Panagia, is worth a brief stop, both for the peacefulness of the monastery itself (visitors are welcome as long as they are dressed appropriately), and for the wonderful views across vineyards towards the sea in one direction and Kannaviou Reservoir in the other. Although dating originally from the sixth century AD and apparently built over a pagan temple dedicated to Hera (it might even have used some of the masonry from the temple building), the current monastery is largely seventeenth and eighteenth century.

The Monastery of Panagia Chrysorrogiatissa

May–Aug 9.30am–12.30pm & 1.30–6.30pm; Sept–April 10am–12.30pm & 1.30–4pm • Free • ☎ 26722457

The **Monastery of Panagia Chrysorrogiatissa**, just north of Agia Moni on the left of the main road, was established in 1152 (though the current buildings date from 1770) by a certain Ignatios who, it was said, found an icon near Pafos which had been thrown into the sea in Asia Minor during the iconoclastic period and miraculously found its way to Cyprus. Popular for its frescoes, icons and various treasures, in many ways its chief claim to fame is its peculiar name, translated as "Our Lady of the Golden Pomegranate". The monastery sells its own wine, and outside is a stall selling nuts and preserves. The huge tree near the monastery – a *Pinus Brutia* (or, whisper it, Turkish Pine) – is 130 years old.

Pano Panagia

One of Cyprus's more remote villages, **PANO PANAGIA** lies 800m up at the edge of civilization, with the wilds of Tilliria stretching to the north and the rugged mountains of the Troodos range to the east. It would probably attract little attention if it wasn't for its connection with one of Cyprus's greatest sons – **Archbishop Makarios III** (see box, p.160) – architect of independence and first president of the republic.

The Birthplace Of Archbishop Makarios III

As you enter Pano Panagia from the south, a sign points down a narrow lane to the left, identifying the **birthplace of the archbishop**. Born Michail Christodolou Mouskos, son of a shepherd, he was raised in the village and tended his father's sheep in the surrounding hills. The house in which he lived as a child has now been turned into a **museum**. A simple double door in a stone wall (with a number "4" above) opens into a small garden from where a paved path leads up to the single-storey dwelling. It is simple and affecting – whitewashed walls, ornaments on shelves, sparse wall hangings, a ladder up to a sleeping platform, a cast-iron bed.

The Makarios III Historical and Cultural Centre

9am–1pm, 2–4pm • €0.50 • ☎ 26722473

A few metres up the main street is a small plateia dominated by a statue of the distinctive figure of the archbishop, his hand raised in blessing. The low building behind is the **Makarios III Historical and Cultural Centre**. Any fears that this will be an earnest trawl through the career of Makarios are soon dispelled – the centre is choc-a-bloc with touchingly personal memorabilia: his books, desk ornaments, photographs of the great man alongside world leaders (Indira Ghandi, Nehru, Nasser), his religious vestments, even his fountain pen, fork and dressing gown. It all has the unmistakeable stamp of the pride of a family, and of a village, in the achievements of one of its own.

Fyti

Of the villages that dot the upland vineyards west and south of Pano Panagia, the one most worth visiting is **FYTI**. High on a hill (680m) and overlooking the neighbouring villages of Kritou Marottou, Milia and Lasa, it is cool even in summer. Indeed, surrounded by cornfields, vineyards and woodland it's hard to believe you're on the edge of the Middle East. In the central square is a small church, Agios Dimitris, which looks more like a barn with a bell tower attached than the usual domed Byzantine structure. Surrounding it are trees offering shade, a bust and memorial fountain to local dignitaries, and a couple of tavernas – in short a perfect place to while away an afternoon. A couple of sights are devoted to the local weaving industry – a **factory shop** houses exhibitions of "Fytiotika", the local tapestry, and the **Fyti Museum of Weaving and Folkloric Art** (daily 8am–1pm & 2–5pm) contains a chaotic array of spinning and weaving machinery, and a wealth of old photographs, labelled in Greek and English. You don't have to pay to go in, though it's polite to at least drop some loose change into a brass bowl pointedly labelled "Museum Spende" and "Donations".

The Grivas Museum and Monument

9am–6pm • Free

On the Chlorakas coast 4km north of Kato Pafos, clearly signposted from the main road, a monument and statue mark the spot where **General George Grivas** (see p.165) landed on November 10, 1954 to spark off the **EOKA uprising**. Next to the memorial is a small museum housing the caïque *Agios Georgios* which ran guns and EOKA fighters during the struggle for independence before being intercepted by the British. The boat was bought by order of Archbishop Makarios to become a symbol of the resistance. Other (inevitably nationalistic) exhibits include weapons, documents and photographs relating to the gun-running activities along this coast, plus a visitors' book which makes enlightening reading – somebody who'd served in the British Army in Cyprus, for example, commented that the museum was "biased", which makes one wonder what they expected.

Coral Bay

CORAL BAY is a relatively quiet but rather characterless extension of the Pafos resort area, 12km north of the harbour. Its raison d' être is its couple of good beaches in contiguous bays, separated by a peninsula, with free access and parking, clear water and convenient beach bars and hotels. There's also a campsite, a couple of decent supermarkets, and an excellent takeaway. What really sets it apart is the Bronze Age **Maa-Palaiokastro prehistoric site**, which occupies the peninsula between the two bays. If driving, park at the *Thalassa Hotel*.

Maa-Palaiokastro

Daily 8.30am–4pm • €1.70 (same ticket for site and museum), ⓦ tinyurl.com/paliokastro

Maa-Palaiokastro dates from the first wave of Greeks to colonize Cyprus. These were Myceneans from the Aegean who came to the island around 1200 BC, starting the process of Hellenization. Excavations here have revealed imposing protective walls and some public buildings whose features show their Aegean heritage. Also discovered were the remains of earlier Chalcolithic inhabitants who lived in caves covered with timber constructions. There's not much for the non-specialist to see, though you can still follow the course of the two walls and some of the buildings.

In 1996 a modern **museum** was built on the site. Designed by Italian Andrea Bruno, its architecture is certainly innovative: the building looks as if a flying saucer had landed heavily and buried itself in the ground. The museum, accessed down a flight of steps, contains no original artefacts, but rather a restrained collection of copies and explanatory photographs and notes relating to the Maa-Palaiokastro site.

Pafos Zoo

St George, Peyia • 9am–6pm • €15.50, children aged 2 to 12 €8.50 • ☎ 26813852, ⓦ pafoszoo.com • Bus #616 from Coral Bay (which is in turn on the #615 from Kato Pafo)

Educational and well-organized, **Pafos Zoo** is well worth a visit. The whole park is attractively set on a gently sloping site laid around a water feature, with none of the feeling of claustrophobic exploitation you get at some zoos. There's a fair range of larger animals – lions, tigers, elephants, giraffes, camels, zebras – but given its origins (it was until recently Pafos Bird Park) it is particularly strong on birds, with a good selection of hornbills, toucans, flamingos, owls, eagles, doves, cockatoos, parakeets, cranes, storks and much more. The snake and reptile house is also particularly good. Despite its relative isolation, 15km from Pafos and 6km north of Coral Bay, the zoo is well signposted and runs transfers from hotels. So if the kids want to visit, you have no excuse. For a large family, though, it can be quite expensive.

On some tourist maps "**Snake George's Reptile Park**", just before the turn-off for the zoo, is still marked, though don't bother looking for it. Something of a cause célèbre, its lease ran out in 2009 and the local authority refused to renew it. "Snake George" himself (one Hans-Jorg Wiedi) was famous in Cyprus for his work with local breeds of reptiles – he even rediscovered the Cyprus Grass Snake, previously thought to be extinct. Once the park was closed the snakes were released into the wild.

Cape Drepano

Driving north from Pafos through banana plantations, you finally get to **CAPE DREPANO**, which marks the end of the main Pafos resort area and of the E701, and the beginning of the wild Akamas Peninsula. The cape, long a destination for pilgrimages, is marked by the village of **Agios Georgios** where everything is named after the titular saint: including the modern church sitting in the midst of a large car park (which often hosts market stalls), and the small medieval chapel beyond. Futher on are the remains of a huge **sixth-century basilica complex** (8.30am–4pm; €1.70; ☎26812301) discovered in the 1950s. Here you can distinguish the ground plans of three separate basilicas, extensive mosaics, a necropolis and pilgrims lodgings, together with survivals from an earlier Roman settlement. Below the archeological site are some rock-cut tombs in the cliff which can be approached from the top but are most clearly visible from the beach below.

But it's not just for the past that Agios Georgios is worth visiting – a splendidly sited **fish restaurant** (named *Agios Georgios* – see p.123) overlooks the flat-topped offshore **island of Geronisos** (upon which, incidentally, further archeological remains have been found) and a small modern harbour with a beach next to it, useable when it's not knee-deep in seaweed. There has been a long history of boats using this tiny haven, as it was directly on the route from Alexandria to Constantinople, and it is still thronged with fishing vessels.

The Akamas Peninsula

The **AKAMAS PENINSULA** makes up the northwest tip of Cyprus and is one of the least inhabited places on the island. It is an area of great beauty – especially the rugged coast – and attracts **walkers**, **mountain bikers** and **off-road drivers** (there are no main roads – just dirt tracks and footpaths). As with most peninsulas, where it begins is debatable. For the purposes of this book, it is broadly defined as the area north of Pegeia and west of Polis.

Once used as a **firing range** by the British Army – which kept away even the most determined hotel developers – the peninsula has an extraordinary range of **wildlife**, and contains virtually every type of habitat to be found on the island, from the dense forests of the south to arid pine scrub at the tip. Among the flora and fauna are 39 of Cyprus's endemic plants, 160 or more varieties of bird, twelve types of mammal, twenty reptile species and sixteen types of butterfly. Top billing, however, goes to the **sea turtles** (both green and loggerhead) which lay their eggs on the peninsula's beaches. Though not a national park, the peninsula does have some measure of **protection** – the Pegeia and Akamas Forests are the responsibility of the government, and other bits are controlled in various ways – but there seems to be no overarching plan to protect it. This is a worry, as powerful forces (not only the usual developers, but even the church) are keen to exploit the glorious beaches out here.

Driving on the Akamas means either **renting a 4WD** or signing up for a **jeep safari** and only experienced walkers, properly dressed and equipped, should attempt it on foot. Given its past role, if you find anything that looks like a live shell or other **ordnance**, leave well alone. For the faint of heart, the best way to see the peninsula is from the comfort of a boat – excursions run from Pafos and Lakki.

Akamas from the south

Around 19km from Pafos, just before getting to Agios Georgios on the E701, a signpost points off to the right – "Akamas Peninsula 18km". Following this, the surfaced road continues for about a kilometre, until you come to a large brown Forest Department sign announcing that "You are entering into the south coast of the Akamas Peninsula", with warning about litter, fires and camping, all of which are prohibited. Beyond it the road curves down into a valley where the **Aspros (White) River** disgorges into the sea. A beach sits at the foot of some white cliffs, and, upstream there's a taverna, the *White River Fish Tavern and Snack Bar*. Beyond this the road becomes a dirt track. After just over a kilometre of bouncing from rut to rut, you arrive at **Toxeftra Beach**, which is where the next river – the Avgas – runs out into the sea. Following a forestry department sign to the right, the river valley, full of citrus and banana plantations splits into two gorges. This is as far as you'll get on wheels. Park, and follow the path up the right-hand **Avakas Gorge**, which becomes increasingly spectacular the further you walk. After about fifteen to twenty minutes the going gets tough enough for casual walkers to turn back.

Back on the coast, the road continues north for 5km or so, hugging the shore, until it reaches Lara Bay.

Lara Bay

One of the most beautiful and most isolated beaches in Cyprus, **Lara Bay is** a haven for loggerhead and green turtles. During the turtle laying season (May–Aug) volunteers monitor the beach for female turtles and relocate their eggs to a fenced hatchery, protecting them from predators. These measures as well as the lack of light pollution mean thousands of baby turtles make it to the lapping waves of the Mediterranean. So far Lara Bay has escaped development – it is a protected area under a law passed in 1971, and also lies within the Akamas State Forest, but there's no room for complacency – a distressing amount of rubbish accumulates on the sand, despite the efforts of the volunteers. Contact with the Lara Bay Hatchery is in no way formalized, but those who run it welcome genuine interest and offers of help. Otherwise most people visit on a boat cruise or a 4WD safari (note that private vehicles are banned from approaching the beach during the laying season).

From Lara Bay you can either go back the way you came, take the **dirt road inland** to Ineia and Drouseia, or continue up the coast and strike **east** up to the Smigies picnic grounds, from where you can head east to Neo Chorio or south to Drouseia. Though these dirt roads are relatively well signposted, you're a long way from help if anything goes wrong.

Akamas from the north

Apart from Agios Georgios, the most popular way of getting onto the Akamas Peninsula, and by far the most convenient for the more remote northern part, is via **Loutra tis Afroditis** (the Baths of Aphrodite; see p.138) on the north coast. A good main road – the E713 – leads west from the outskirts of Polis to the baths, where it peters out at a car park and drinks kiosk. A poster with a map of the area provided by the

AKAMAS WALKING TRAILS

Walking trails through the Akamas are well marked, and in summer can be quite crowded. However, despite their user-friendliness, all the usual precautions should be taken – wear a hat, use plenty of sunscreen, carry bottles of water. Maps of the walks (and the excellent "Nature Trails of the Akamas" booklet which covers the routes below) are available from tourist offices, and copies are posted in several locations. If you get into difficulties phone the local police station number (☎ 26806285), tell them what trail you're on and the number on the last sign you passed. If you haven't got a phone, or there's no signal, you're on your own.

FROM LOUTRA TIS AFRODITIS (BATHS OF APHRODITE)

The Trail to Fontana Amoroza is the easiest walk from the Baths of Aphrodite, a 6km stroll which follows the coast to a small spring. The Fontana Amoroza ("Fountain of Love") was named by Italian poet-traveller Ludovico Ariosto, who probably mistook it for the Baths of Aphrodite (the contrast between the grandiloquent name and the actual tiny spring is a hoot). The route is hugely popular, and if you do this walk in summer try to set off very early or late in the day, not only to avoid the heat, but also the noise of speedboats, quad bikes and 4WDs. If you don't want to do the full 12km return walk, catch a boat from Lakki to Fontana Amorozo and walk back.

The Aphrodite Trail starts off along the same route as the one to Fontana Amoroza, but then swings west and climbs up to Muti tis Sotiras (370m), down to Pyrgos tis Rigainas (the indistinct ruins of either a Lusignan fortification or a Byzantine monastery), then back to the Baths of Aphrodite. Being a circular route (it's around 7.5km), it can be done in either direction. **The Adonis Trail** is also a circular route, again about 7.5km long, which loops south of the Baths of Aphrodite, then strikes north to Pyrgos tis Rigainas, where it joins the Aphrodite Trail for the return to the Baths.

Both the Aphrodite and Adonis trails involve a fair bit of ascent and are therefore quite strenuous.

FROM NEO CHORIO/SMIGIES

The Smigies Trail is a circular route to the north of the Smigies picnic site which has two variations – a short trail of 2.5km, and a longer one of 5km. The route offers terrific views both north across Chrysohou Bay and west towards Lara Bay, and includes some walking through dense forest. The route is classed as average difficulty, and does include a number of fairly steep climbs. The long trail links up with the Adonis Trail.

The Pissouromouttis Trail is a 3km circular route to the south of the Smigies picnic site, offering similar views and level of difficulty.

Forestry Department shows the main trails that start here (see box below). You can either go through the baths, or skirt them by following the "Fontana Amoroza 6km" sign. Beyond the baths, further signs welcome you ("You are entering into the North Side of the Akamas, Peninsula"), warn you that this is a wildlife conservation area, and give details (with map) of the cycling routes that crisscross the peninsula.

Akamas from the east

The Akamas Peninsula is also accessible along its eastern edge from several of the villages of the **Laona Pleateau** – from north to south **Neo Chorio**, **Drouseia**, **Ineia** and **Arodes** (Kato and Pano) and **Kathikas**. A number of these villages are worth visiting in their own right, and offer interesting **agrotourism accommodation** as a result of the work of the **Laona Foundation** (ⓦconservation.org.cy/laona.htm).

Neo Chorio

3

NEO CHORIO, a pretty stone village high on a hill south of the coast road, is a burgeoning agrotourism centre, with lots of traditional balconied houses being adapted for tourists to rent. There's also a solid stone church (Agiou Mina), and a memorial to three villagers who were members of EOKA and who died on the same day in 1956. There are superb views across Chrysohou Bay from here, too. Neo Chorio is the nearest easily accessible village to the **Smigies picnic site**, which is about 2.5km west of the village and the starting point of two marked trails (see box opposite). These are less popular, and therefore less crowded, than the ones that start at the Baths of Aphrodite.

Drouseia and Ineia

Hilltop **DROUSEIA** is set around an attractive eighteenth-century church. There's a small **Weaving Museum** (Mon–Fri 8am–2.30pm, also 2–5pm Mon & Thurs), a good selection of places to eat, and access to the southern part of the Akamas Peninsula on dirt roads – to Smigies and the Akamas Forest by driving northwest, and to the Pegeia Forest area to the south and west via Ineia.

Virtually part of Drouseia, **INEIA** has its own small **Basket Weaving Museum** (June–Oct Mon–Fri 11am–1pm & 4–7pm, Sat 11am–1pm; Nov–May Mon–Fri 11am–1pm & 3–6pm) with displays of one of Cyprus's oldest crafts. The museum is in the yard outside the village church.

Pano and Kato Arodes

PANO ARODES, and its neighbour **KATO ARODES**, have suffered, both from the exodus of Turkish Cypriots as a result of intercommunal violence and the 1974 invasion, and from an earthquake in 1995. They stand at the heart of a network of dirt roads which strike west into the southern part of the Akamas.

Kathikas

KATHIKAS is a large village packed with traditional houses (stone walls, shuttered windows, balconies) and narrow paved streets. It has become popular with visitors, particularly those who want to stay in the houses, and teeters on the edge of commercialism. It has a useful visitor centre, a donkey sanctuary, and some excellent places to eat. The village is surrounded by vineyards and has two wineries (Sterna and Vasilikon) just outside, and is another gateway to the Akamas – a dirt road heads west towards Agios Georgios, roughly parallel to the main E709/E701 which covers the same ground, but a lot more quickly and a short marked trail – the **Agiasmatos Trail**, which starts about a kilometre from the village on the road to Pegeia, ends in Kathikos, and is an easy 2km (45min) walk.

Polis and around

The north coast of Pafos district is dominated by the small town of **POLIS** (or *Polis Chrysochous*, to give it its full title) which sits on the banks of the Chrysochou River where it empties into wide **Chrysochou Bay.** A small, appealing and unpretentious market town, Polis became a favourite with backpackers in the 1980s. Since then reservations about its rate of development have been expressed but appear a little premature – while the town centre is full of restaurants and bars, it's still a delightful place at which to fetch up, has an interesting and varied hinterland, and represents an important counterweight to brash and breezy Pafos.

There's not a huge amount to see in town – a venerable old church, a neat little archeological museum and a rather old olive tree (aged 700, according to the sign) – yet just to the north is a good sandy **beach** with a campsite and views across to the Akamas Peninsula. Along the western coast road is the busy little port of **Lakk**i, and where the road ends, the **Baths of Aphrodite** from where you can access the Akamas Peninsula. East of Polis is a sweeping bay with the villages of **Pommos** and **Pachyammos** and, beyond the Turkish Cypriot **Kokkina Enclave**. Further east is the small town of **Kato Pyrgos**, long isolated from the rest of Cyprus but, since 2010, a border town with the opening of the most recent crossing point on the Green Line. South of Polis is an upland area dotted with **villages and vineyards**, easily accessible from the main B7 Polis to Pafos road.

Brief history

According to tradition, the Mycenean Akamas, son of Theseus, first established a city here, having landed nearby on his way back from the Trojan War. Whatever the truth of this, it is likely that the Chrysochou Bay was indeed first settled by the Myceneans more than a thousand years before Christ. By around 750 BC it was one of Cyprus's great city-kingdoms, called **Marion**. It flourished because of its copper and gold mines and traded closely with the Aegean islands, Corinth and Athens. The city fell to the Persians but was freed by Kimon in 449 BC. Following the death of Alexander the Great, it backed the wrong horse during the struggle between his successors, and in 312 BC the victor, Ptolemy I, destroyed the city and resettled its inhabitants in Pafos. A new city was built near or over the ruins of Marion by Ptolemy II and named in honour of his wife (who also happened to be his sister) **Arsinoe**. As far as we know the city continued to be inhabited, though it suffered from Muslim coastal raids during the seventh century. Now called Polis (simply the Greek word for "town"), it continued as a small rural settlement, a remote part of a remote district, and didn't hit the headlines again until the explosive "Kokkina Incident" in 1964 (see box below).

THE KOKKINA INCIDENT

The events of 1964 surrounding the village of Kokkina on the north Cypriot coast was in many ways a rehearsal for the Turkish invasion ten years later. This part of Cyprus had a high proportion of Turkish Cypriots, and after independence in 1960, the village of Kokkina, 27km west of Polis, became in effect an armed Turkish Cypriot enclave where TMT paramilitaries landed arms and goods from Turkey. EOKA, unsurprisingly, took exception to this and – despite being warned not to by President Makarios – attacked the town on August 6, 1964. On August 10, with the Turkish Cypriots facing defeat, Turkey intervened by sending jets over to strafe and napalm villages and towns, including Polis, causing heavy casualties. All-out war was avoided only by UN intervention. From then on, Kokkina became a Turkish military area – all Turkish Cypriot civilians were relocated elsewhere. After the full Turkish invasion of 1974 effectively divided the island, the Green Line between the two armies was established just east of Kato Pyrgos. This left the Kokkina Enclave separate from the rest of north Cyprus, a situation which continues to this day.

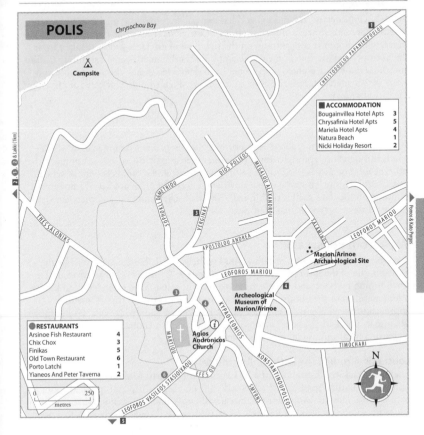

The Church of Agios Andronicos

Mon–Fri 10am–1pm, Sun 8.30am–4pm • Free

West of the town centre, and in a small park (with kids' play area) that's ideal for a picnic, stands the tiny, sixteenth-century **Church of Agios Andronicos** (not to be confused with the more modern church in the town centre). The church was used as a mosque during the Ottoman period, and continued to be attended by local Turkish Cypriots during the British occupation. It has a rather odd look from the outside, its simple traditional architecture compromised by a lean-to addition as big as the original church, used as an anteroom by Muslim worshippers. Abandoned in 1963 as Turkish Cypriots moved away, it has since 1974 been renovated, revealing important **Venetian frescoes** that had been hidden by whitewash. Officially open only to organized groups, arrangements seem to be very flexible, and you might find the church not only open but unattended. If in doubt, phone the archeological museum (see below).

Archeological Museum of Marion-Arsinoe

Archiepiskopou Markariou III Avenue •Tues & Thurs–Fri 8am–3pm, Wed 8am–5pm, Sat 9am–3pm • €1.70 • ☎ 26322955

On the road that heads east from the town centre (opposite a brand-new Lukoil filling station) is the **Archeological Museum of Marion-Arsinoe**, founded in 1998 and the place to see artefacts from the ancient city-states that once flourished here. The Museum is housed in a Neoclassical building, and has two galleries that lead off a central atrium: Room I covers the history of the area from its early Neolithic roots right up to medieval times, while Room II concentrates on the rich haul of artefacts that were taken from the necropolis at Marion. Some of the amphorae and statuettes are of stunning quality, and the ceramics are painted with scenes from daily life. There's also lots of gold and some stylish ancient Greek and Roman jewellery which wouldn't look out of place on the catwalk today.

The beach

Polis's expansive **beach** is about 1km north of the town, down a tarmac road which winds through eucalyptus groves and becomes increasingly rutted as you approach the sea. The sand quality is good, there's a lifeguard tower and a **campsite** with attached restaurant. The site has that backpacker-friendly feel that's rare in Cyprus (though camping on the sand itself is prohibited). The sea is clear and safe, and there are views westward towards the Akamas Peninsula.

West from Polis: Lakki

A couple of kilometres west of Polis, **LAKKI** (widely called "Latchi" or "Latsi" by the locals) is one of the most picturesque little villages in Cyprus. It's clustered around a small fishing harbour, and the quayside is a mass of restaurants, cafés, bars and kiosks offering cruises in glass-bottomed boats, watersports and diving trips. On either approach to the village there are wide sandy beaches surrounded by villa developments. Despite its popularity it hasn't lost its charm, and is still a laidback place to stop for a coffee or a meal and watch the boats coming and going.

Loutra tis Afroditi (The Baths of Aphrodite)

The main road west from Polis (the E713) ends at **Loutra tis Afroditi** or "**The Baths of Aphrodite**", natural pools where supposedly the goddess bathed and splashed about with Adonis. Despite its romantic name, it's all rather underwhelming. That said, if you want some easy walking along cleanly paved paths, through shady trees to a pool ringing to the sound of running water, then you might just enjoy its understated charm. This is also the start of several walks onto the Akamas Peninsula, and beyond the baths you might be greeted by the welcome sight of an ice-cream van. Back at the car park, on the opposite side of the road, the *Baths of Aphrodite* restaurant (see opposite), run by the CTO, offers stunning views of the cove below.

ARRIVAL AND INFORMATION   POLIS

By bus The main bus route between Polis and Pafos is the #645 (Mon–Fri hourly, Sat & Sun less frequent; 1hr). Buses start from Kyproleontos, southeast of the main square.
By car For motorists, there is ample parking in the town – either in pay-and-display car parks or on the streets.

Tourist office The tourist office is on Vasileos Stasioikou, opposite the bus terminal (Mon–Fri 8.30am–4pm; first week of each month Mon–Fri 9am–3.30pm, Sat 9am–2pm; ☏ 26322468).

ACCOMMODATION

Bougainvillea Hotel Apartments Veryinas ☏ 26812250, ⓦ bougainvillea.com.cy. A 5min walk north of the centre of Polis on the road to the beach, the *Bougainvillea* has six studios and 26 apartments which sleep up to four. Staff are friendly and helpful, accommodation is adequate if a little Spartan, and there's a bar, pool, and a reception desk open from 9am to 2am. Look out for extra charges, especially for breakfast and air conditioning. **€65**

★ **Chrysafinia Hotel Apartments** Prodromi ☏ 26321180, ⓦ chrysafinia.com. Set in well-tended gardens, in quiet Prodromi on the outskirts of Polis about a 15min walk from the centre. Apartments are clean and serviceable, all have balconies, and communal facilities include a bar, pool, and free wi-fi throughout. Portable air-conditioners on request. **€48**
Mariela Hotel Apartments 3 Arsinoe Street

26322310, marielahotel.com. A substantial block, recently renovated, on the southeast edge of Polis, the *Mariela* has a pool, and all apartments have a balcony. Family-owned and very friendly. Breakfast and air-conditioners extra. **€70**

Natura Beach Christodoulou Papanikopoulou Street 26323111, natura.com.cy. Just behind the beach east of Polis amid olive and citrus groves (and goats), the *Natura Beach* was renovated in 2011 and offers a choice of rooms or villas, all with balconies or verandas. The hotel has a bar and restaurant, a gift shop and swimming pool, mini-gym and sauna, and free wi-fi (though only in the lounge). Villas have their own swimming pools. **€99**

Nicki Holiday Resort PO Box 26322226, nickiresort.com. Lying conveniently halfway between Polis and Lakki, and 2km from each, *Nicki Holiday Resort* has two restaurants and bars, a floodlit tennis court, fitness centre and gym and two pools. Accommodation ranges from studios through a variety of different sized apartments, all with the usual TV, balcony and kitchenette. **€70**

Paradisos Hills Hotel Lysos 26322287, paradisoshills.com. Peaceful, smallish (fifteen-room) hotel in a picturesque village on top of a hill with extensive views over land and sea. The *Paradisos Hills* boasts attentive staff, spotless rooms, good food – and cookery classes if you fancy learning Greek cuisine. **€102**

EATING AND DRINKING

None of Polis's restaurants can claim to be outstanding, and your experience can vary according to how busy they are, but all are agreeably set, either in the cheerfully crowded central square or looking across the sea or the harbour in Lakki, a couple of kilometres west.

Arsinoe Fish Tavern Grigoriou Digeni 26321590. Just south of the central square, and inconspicuously located next to a large estate agents, *Arsinoe Fish Tavern* is popular with locals as well as tourists. The fish is fresh (the menu depends on what has been caught that day) and the service friendly. Main courses around €12 to €16, Dinner only.

★ **Baths of Aphrodite Restaurant** 26322070, bathsofaphrodite.com. With killer views across the bay below the Baths of Aphrodite and well-priced food, this CTO-run restaurant is frankly more interesting than the baths themselves. Mains from €10–17, fish meze €17.50. Daily April–Sept 11am–11pm; Oct–March 11am–8pm.

Chix Chox Central Square 26322366. Right at the heart of things, the *Chix Chox* (try saying that after a few glasses of wine) offers Cypriot specialities, grilled meat and fish, meze and, not always present in Cypriot restaurants, a few vegetarian dishes. Seating is under canopies in the village square, facing a lion fountain – a great spot to watch the world go by. Mains €10–22, with meze, fish or meat at €18. Breakfast, lunch and dinner.

★ **Finikas** Central Square 26323403, finikasrestaurant.com. Housed in a fine old building right on the central square, *Finikas* has the air of being a cut above the usual tourist joint. It does a complete range of meals – fish, meat, charcoal grills, steak, Cypriot dishes, pasta, salads – and has kids' and vegetarian menus. House

specials (from €9.50) include a delicious chicken dish topped with mushrooms and cheese, and kebabs using beef rather than the more usual pork or lamb. Dinner only.

The Old Town 9 Georgiades Kyproleontas 26322758. Not the cheapest option in Polis (mains around €16 to €24), but good locally sourced food in a classy setting. Its courtyard is shaded and cool, even on hot days, and tables are well spaced out. Nicely understated service too. 6–11pm (closed Wed).

Polis Camping Site Polis 26815080. Cheap and cheerful beach taverna knocking out burgers, omelettes, pizzas, pastas and grills (€4–8). Breakfast, lunch and dinner.

Porto Latchi Lakki 26322530. Housed in a centuries-old carob warehouse (renovated after a 2004 fire), the *Porto Latchi* specializes in fish, though it does offer meat dishes as well. Main courses range from €8 to €20. The fish meze is particularly good, as is the house wine, though service can be slow. Daily 10am–10pm.

★ **Yiangos and Peter Taverna** Akamantos Avenue, Lakki 26321411. Another great seafood option in Lakki well-patronized by locals, the *Yiangos and Peter Taverna* does excellent battered fish dishes, and good salads. Main courses range widely in price – €10 to €35, depending on type of fish (and you need to order fries etc separately). Daily 8.30am–11pm.

East of Polis

East of Polis, the road – the E704 – follows the coast around a large bay, and with the exception of a diversion inland to avoid the Kokkina Enclave, runs right up to the official crossing point from the republic into north Cyprus just beyond Kato Pyrgos.

Pomos

The first village of any size, 20km east from Polis, is **POMOS**. It straggles along the main road, and although there's a tiny boat haven, several restaurants, and a small **natural history museum** (in the Municipal Hall), you're only likely to stop here if staying in one of the local villas. The high point of the Pomos calendar is the **Paradise Beach Jazz Festival** held every July/August at the *Paradise Place* bar-restaurant (ⓦparadiseplace productions.com), an event now in its thirteenth year.

Pachyammos

About 5km beyond Pomos is the village of **PACHYAMMOS**, hard up against the fortifications of the Kokkina Enclave. Its main claim to fame, which attracts coachloads of Cypriots, is the large modern church of **Saints Rafael, Nikolaos and Eirini**, and within it the shrine of St Raphael, who is reputed to be able to heal the sick and disabled. The church stands on a wide terrace which overlooks the dunes and the beach, and contains several war memorials, including one to members of the National Guard and civilians killed during the Kokkina incident in 1964 (see box, p.258). If several coaches arrive simultaneously, the whole terrace and church can become very busy.

Kato Pyrgos

The final Republic of Cyprus village on this stretch of the north coast is **KATO PYRGOS**, in some ways a place that time forgot, and certainly one with a unique atmosphere. To reach it you need to drive inland from Pachyammos (effectively the end of the coast road), around the Kokkina Enclave's fences, guard towers and Turkish and UN troops; what should be a short hop is now a 23km drive along serpentine mountain roads. When you return to the coast, it's another 6km into the unexpectedly large village, which occupies a wide hill-girt bay. Squeezed between the Kokkina Enclave to the west, north Cyrprus to the east, and to the south Tilliria, the largest wilderness area in Cyprus, Kato Pyrgos has been pretty well isolated since the mid twentieth century. However, the opening of the new crossing point just east of the village in October 2010 has gone some way to ending this, since there is now a direct route to Lefkosia through the TRNC. Kato Pyrgos has three hotels, the westernmost of which the *Tylos Beach*, overlooks the modern harbour, home to a small fishing fleet. Either side of the harbour is a rocky shore often waist-deep in dried seaweed. Incidentally, it was in Kato Pyrgos that Makarios was based when he made desperate and ultimately futile attempts to stop Grivas and the National Guard attacking the Kokkina Enclave.

CROSSING INTO THE NORTH FROM KATO PYRGOS

The Kato Prygos crossing point, scenically sited among low hills 4km east, is the most recent to open, and is perfect for those staying around Pafos district. The roads are good, and this venture into the north can make for an interesting cross-cultural experience. Unlike some of the other crossings, it is easy to find on both sides of the border – the road has nowhere else to go. Once over the Green Line (the actual crossing takes 5–10min), the road, although marked on the maps as a very minor one, is in fact of good quality and makes for an exhilarating drive. The first Turkish Cypriot village you get to is Yesilirnak/Limnitis, and beyond this are the two ancient sites at Vouni and Soli, on the left and right of the road respectively, followed by Xeros where you join the main road to Güzelyurt. From there you can bear left for Kamlibel and Girne, or continue straight towards Lefkosa. For the return to the south, you can either retrace your steps to Kato Pyrgos, or cross back through the Astomeritis/Zodhia or the Agios Dometios/Metehan crossing just outside Lefkosa. For this part of north Cyprus, see pp.226–230.

Tilliria

The forest wilderness of **TILLIRIA** lies south of the coast between Polis and Kato Pyrgos and northwest of the Troodos Massif. The region makes for an exhilarating drive – passengers will be able to enjoy the endless forest vistas, but the driver won't be able to lift his eyes from the asphalt for a second, not only because of the bends but also because of rocks fallen from cliff faces above. Despite what it says on older maps, which show it crisscrossed only by 4WD tracks, there is now a well-surfaced road (the **F740**) that cuts right through the forest from the road around the Kokkina Enclave. Apart from Stavros tis Psokas there are no settlements (or petrol stations), and only the very occasional picnic site (though there's a beautiful one deep in the forest at Livadi). During the summer you're likely to come across a fair amount of traffic – especially coaches, jeeps on safari and forest warden's vehicles – but outside the main holiday season you might not see another vehicle for hours.

Stavros tis Psokas Forest Station

3

Though a working forest station, **Stavros tis Psokas** is also a popular destination for walkers and tour groups. It lies in a beautiful setting 3km off the road to Kykkos, along a side road which drops down through a wooded valley. A collection of buildings lie scattered under the trees – wooden cabins, the Chapel of the Holy Cross ("Stavros" means "cross"), a large "rest house" or **hostel** (☏26722338) and a picnic site with children's playground and a café/restaurant. There is also a large, hilly and wooded **mouflon enclosure**, where, if you're lucky, you may see these iconic wild mountain sheep, the emblem of Cyprus. You can't go into the pen (a man who climbed the fence and goaded the animals was gored in 2011), but a path up some steps from the road runs around the perimeter fence. Elsewhere in the forest station a fairly rudimentary campsite nestles under the trees. From Stavros dis Psokas there are several **forest walks** from 3–5km (the station is a stopping point on the E4 European Long Distance Path). Beyond the forest station a road (marked "earthen road", so you've been warned) eventually leads to Polis.

Cedar Valley

Cedar Valley is one of Cyprus's best known beauty spots, it attracts hordes of visitors during the summer and contains the largest collection of Lebanon cedars outside, the Lebanon itself. It's 21km east of Stavros tis Psokas and 18km west of the Kykkos Monastery. If you don't know your cedar from your silver birch, then after a long drive through impenetrable forest the unique nature of Cedar Valley might be lost on you, but it's certainly pretty to look at. Facilities are, though, a little threadbare – a drinking fountain, a few paths and a row of wooden benches plonked next to the road. Like Stavros tis Psokas, Cedar Valley is on the E4 Long Distance Path.

South of Polis

South of Polis, and accessible from the main roads that fan out from the town (especially the F723 and the B7), lie numerous villages that might not be worth a specific visit, but certainly merit looking out for, or making a short detour to.

Steni

The first thing you notice in **STENI**, 7km south of Polis on the F723, is its large war memorial. Rather than statues representing the fallen, it consists of a simple wall with parts dedicated in turn to the two World Wars, the campaign against the British and the Turkish invasion of 1974. Directly across the road is the **Museum of Local Life** (April–Oct 10am–6pm, Nov–March 10am–4pm: free, though donations welcome), which covers the usual ground – rural life, local crafts, and domestic equipment from 1800 to the end of World War II. Outside a wide piazza is a row of picnic tables and a small children's playground. Elsewhere in the village is a good restaurant, the *Steni* (☎26322506) and the *Neromylos* coffee shop (☎26352059, ⓦneromyloscafe.com). Many of the villagers emigrated to South Africa after the Turkish invasion, and some are now returning to do up their ancestral homes. Surrounding the village are several walking paths.

Peristerona

Also on the F723, 10km from Polis, is **PERISTERONA** whose traditional and in many cases renovated houses lie on a hill which is dominated by the buildings of the Bishopric of Arinsoe, a diocese which was subsumed into that of Pafos in the thirteenth century, but re-established in 1996 after centuries of ecumenical wrangling. The church buildings, set in a courtyard that has an old olive mill and press (and with modern mosaics of goats set into the crazy paving), contain a **Byzantine Museum** (April–Oct Mon–Fri 10am–1pm & 3–6pm; Nov–March 10am–4pm; €2) which has more than sixty icons and a good range of woodcarvings, vestments and manuscripts dating back to the sixteenth century. Just down the hill and on the same side of the road, a lane branches off to the right. This leads to the comely **Aetofolies Gorge**, haunt of eagles according to the name and pigeons according to the evidence of one's own eyes (in fact the village name derives from "*peristeri*" or pigeon). A sign also alerts the visitor to the presence down this road of "Fighters Dens", EOKA hideouts, dating from the 1950s.

Lysos

Some 12km from Polis, on the F733, lies **LYSOS**, one of the largest villages in the area. The fifteenth-century church of **Panagia Chryselousa**, dominated by its freestanding campanile, is interesting in that its architecture is largely Lusignan, with coats of arms of the local Lusignan overlords above both the north and south doors. Elsewhere in the village, a concerted effort is being made to develop the local tourist trade, especially through the *Paradisos Hills Hotel* (see p.139) which offers guided hikes, cooking classes and wedding packages. Horseriding (including overnight treks) is available from Ride in Cyprus (☎99777624, ⓦrideincyprus.com). A track near the hotel leads to the abandoned Turkish Cypriot village of Melandra, largely destroyed by shelling in 1974.

Evretou Dam

In a valley between the F723 and the B7, and accessible from both, lies the **Evretou Dam**, whose opening in the late 1980s transformed the lives of people in the surrounding villages by providing a reliable source of water. It offers total peace and quiet, and atmospheric views of the surrounding hills. There's little else bar a lonely bench looking out across the water. A good-quality road leads across the top of the dam but it's blocked to traffic – the dam overflowed in March 2012 and repairs are ongoing.

Kritou Terra

Up a narrow road to the right shortly after Skoulli, if you're travelling south on the B7 (and also accessible from the parallel E709), you'll come to the village of **KRITOU TERRA** which has a few unique attractions. Most startling is an early **casino,** opened in the 1870s and closed in the early 1900s. Featuring belly dancers from Syria and Lebanon, the casino catered largely for Turkish Cypriots and visitors from the Middle East. The whitewashed building, now maintained by the Department of, Antiquities, contains murals dedicated to a hero of the Greek War of Independence, Athanasios ("Diakos") Massavetas, who was executed by impalement in 1821. Also of interest is the variety of ways in which the four streams which flow through the village have been harnessed – look out for the **washing holes** down a turning just before the Co-op bank (local women didn't use soap, but a mixture of ash and water called *alusiva*). There's also a **restored watermill**, one of seventeen that once operated in the area.

Loukrounou

Four kilometres south of Skoulli on the B7 is the remains of the village of **LOUKROUNOU**, which briefly held out as a Turkish Cypriot enclave after the 1974 invasion. The last remaining forty or so villagers were finally escorted into the occupied north by UN troops in 1975. Today buildings damaged in the fighting, roofless and windowless, are slowly crumbling and returning to nature.

Skarfos Bridge

Worth a detour off the B7 and then the E712, and well signposted, is the elegant little single-spanned medieval **Skarfos Bridge.** Carrying the main Lusignan Pafos to Polis road across the Stavros tis Psokas stream, the bridge is in an isolated valley full of almond trees and loud with the sound of running water (in spring, at least), and is easily accessed via a path and steps. The remains of the road up to the bridge can be clearly seen, and on the north bank, some distance away, is a ruined watermill.

Kouyiouka Watermill

Museum and coffee shop daily 7.30am–5pm; restaurant Sun only from noon, or by appointment • ☏ 26632847, ⓦ kouyiouka .com/19409964

Some 15km from Pafos, along the B7, a couple of kilometres from the village of **GIOLOU**, is the **Kouyiouka Watermill** which is a lot more interesting than it sounds. The complicated multilevelled mill is a listed building which has been thoroughly renovated – check out the website to see how completely dilapidated it was before this process began. The mill contains a fascinating museum displaying all the bits and pieces used in the production of bread, oil and wine (labelling is only in Greek). There's also a delightful restaurant, coffee shop, and a shop selling bread freshly baked on the premises.

The Troodos Mountains

PEDOULAS, MARATHASA REGION

The Troodos Mountains

If you look at a satellite image of Cyprus, you'll see a large block of green stretching across the southern half of the island, speckled with white. This is the Troodos Massif, a massive plug of igneous rock, now carpeted with forest which, millions of years ago, rose like Aphrodite from the sea. Here, even at the height of summer, you will find cool, pine-scented air, quiet mountain villages and lonely monasteries, with the odd bird of prey circling above. This is Cyprus, but not entirely as we know it.

Rich in minerals, especially copper, the mountains have been extensively **mined**, though otherwise they were for centuries synonymous with isolation and poverty. Conversely, it was this very rugged seclusion that saved the area from the worst excesses of marauding invaders experienced elsewhere on the island. The Troodos became a haven for dissidents and rebels and a stronghold for the Orthodox chuch, as evidenced by its wealth of **monasteries** and **painted medieval churches**. Of all the various rulers of Cyprus, the British made the biggest inroads here, mainly in search of summer retreats in which to escape the relentless heat of the coast.

Today, with villages losing their young people to the coastal towns or even abroad, the Troodos region is relying more and more heavily on **tourism**. Many traditional homes have been adapted into small hotels, restaurants and agrotourism endeavours. And there's plenty to reward a few days' stay here – the south-facing foothills are draped in vineyards, with the higher mountains dotted with hiking and skiing trails, and picnic areas in spectacular settings. Declared a **national park** in 1992, and containing four specified nature reserves, the Troodos Mountains also contain over eight hundred species of plant, twelve of which are endemic; among its birds and animals are the rare Bonelli's Eagle and the iconic Cypriot mouflon (a species of wild sheep).

Within the park are five distinct **areas**: the village/resort of **Troodos** itself which surrounds **Mount Olympos** (2000m), the island's highest peak; **Marathasa** to the northwest, home to the village of **Pedoulas** and Cyprus's greatest monastery **Kykkos; Solea** to the northeast, with **Kakopetria** and other villages lining the main road to Lefkosia; largely treeless **Pitsilia** whose main villages are **Agros** and **Palaichori** to the east, and **Machairas** further east still, notable for the **Machairas Monastery** and the charming village of **Fikardou**. For the greatest concentration of frescoed churches, walks and picnic areas, hotels and restaurants, go for the first three, for a more laidback taste of the mountains, the last two.

ARRIVAL AND GETTING AROUND

If you just want to get a flavour of the mountains, a day-trip from your base in Agia Napa, Larnaka, Lemesos, Pafos or Lefkosia will probably be enough. Tours are available from all these places. If, however, you'd like to explore the region in more depth, hiring a car is the best option.

KYKKOS MONASTERY

Highlights

① Walking A good range of hiking trails traverse the mountains, often visiting waterfalls or circling the peaks themselves – for a start try the Artemis trail. **See p.151**

② Pedoulas A particularly scenic mountain village, also hosting a fine museum and a famous church. **See p.154**

③ Painted churches Ten churches in the region have been declared UNESCO World Heritage Sites owing to the stunning medieval frescoes they contain. **See p.156**

④ Kykkos Monastery A fine example of a modern Greek Cypriot monastery, with the added interest of its links with Archbishop Makarios III – also a great place to pick up souvenirs. **See p.157**

⑤ Picnics There are lovely picnic areas all over the Troodos Mountains, particularly on the way to major monasteries - one of the best is at Xystarouda near Kykkos. **See p.159**

⑥ Fikardou A mountain village meticulously preserved by the Department of Antiquities – a snapshot of the past. **See p.166**

HIGHLIGHTS ARE MARKED ON THE MAP ON P.148

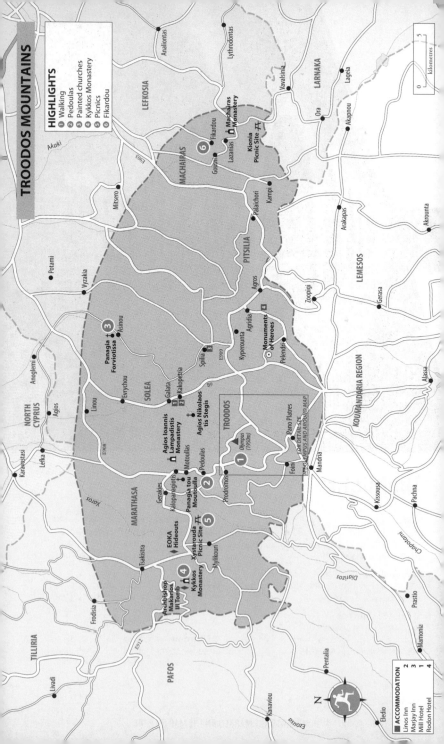

TROODOS MOUNTAINS

HIGHLIGHTS

1. Walking
2. Pedoulas
3. Painted churches
4. Kykkos Monastery
5. Picnics
6. Fikardou

LEFKOSIA

Analiontas

Lythrodontas

Vavatsinia

LARNAKA

Lageia

Ora

Akapnou

Machairas Monastery

Fikardou ⑥

Gouri

Lazanias

Kionia Picnic Site

MACHAIRAS

Akaki

Potami

Vyzakia

Mitsero

Palaichori

Kampi

PITSILIA

Agros

Zoopigi

LEMESOS

Geraxa

Arakapas

Akrounta

Panagia Forviotissa ③

Asinou

SOLEA

Evrychou

Galata

Kalopetria

Spilia ③

Agridia

Kyperounta

Monuments of Heroes ④

Pelendri

KOUMANDARIA REGION

Alassa

Linou

Agios Ioannis Lampadistis Monastery

Agios Nikolaos tis Stegis

Moutoullas

Pedoulas

TROODOS

Olympus (1952m) ▲

Pano Platres

Fotini

NORTH CYPRUS

Anoglemi

Agios

Lefka

Karavostasi

Gerakies

Kalopanagiotis

Panagia tou Moutoulla

Prodromos

MARATHASA

EOKA Hideouts

Xystarouda Picnic Site ⑤

Myllikouri

Isakistra

Archbishop Makarios III Tomb

Kykkos Monastery ④

Frodisia

Mandria

Kissousa

Pachna

Chapotami

Diarizos

TILLIRIA

Livadi

Pentalia

Prastio

Mamonia

Kanaviou

Eledio

Ezousa

N

ACCOMMODATION

Linos Inn	2
Marjay Inn	3
Mill Hotel	1
Rodon Hotel	4

0 — 5 kilometres

FOR DETAILS SEE MP OLYMPUS AND AROUND MAP

By car or motorcycle Given the lack of public transport (a few local taxis serve the villages), your best bet is to rent a car or motorbike. Bear in mind that the roads are convoluted and in some cases of poor quality, so journeys could take longer than you might expect from the distances marked on the map.

By bike Road cycling is a popular way to get around the Troodos Mountains, though given the terrain, you need to be fit. Mountain biking too is gaining in popularity, and the CTO has developed the "Troodos Cycling Route", a comprehensively marked and signed 57km trail that circles the National Park. You can pick up a copy of "Cyprus Cycling Routes" from tourist offices; it covers routes all over the Republic, including two starting at Troodos Square. Or just wander as the spirit takes you – the mountains contain hundreds of kilometres of side roads and dirt tracks.

On foot The Troodos range is an ideal place to enjoy walking on the many signed routes, the best of which are in the area around Troodos village.

Troodos village and around

At 1750m **TROODOS** village is only 250m below the island's highest point – Mount Olympos. It has the longest history of catering for visitors (during the winter it doubles as a ski resort), and therefore has the best infrastructure, with numerous hotels and restaurants, extensive hiking and cycling trails, and a tourist office serving the whole region. It's not particularly attractive – basically a clutch of tourist services housed around a central square – but if you want to get a taste of the mountains without roughing it too much, this is the place for you.

Troodos Square

The focal point of the village is **Troodos Square**, best described as functional rather than aesthetic. There's ample parking for cars and buses (but even this becomes strained at the height of the season) next to the large *Troodos* hotel (see p.152), a good choice of restaurants, plus a shopping area – a series of unlovely hexagonal brick buildings selling everything from ice cream and preserved fruit to wind chimes and postcards. Across the road, horse rides are on offer.

The Forestry Department Visitor Centre

200m west of Troodos Square • Nov–March Mon–Fri 10am–3pm; April–May Mon–Fri & Sun 10am–3pm; June Mon–Fri 10am–3pm, Sat & Sun 10am–4pm; July & Aug Daily 10am–6pm; Sept & Oct Mon–Fri & Sun 10am–3pm • €1 • ☎ 25420144, ⓦ moa.gov.cy/forest

In an appropriately rustic stone-and-timber building, the **Forestry Department Visitor Centre** provides an indispensable introduction to the Troodos National Forest Park. A scale model of the mountains is useful for orientation, while other displays fill you in on geology, (down to mushrooms and bats) and the impact of humans. Presentations on various aspects of the park are given in the film and lecture theatre, and you can follow a short (250m) circular botanical and geological trail.

Platres

Seven kilometres south of Troodos village is **PLATRES** an archetypal hill station left behind by the British. It's split into two sections – Kato (Lower) and Pano (Upper) Platres, with hotels dotted around both. If you're used to high-end acommodation, you might find it wanting, but you should still enjoy its faded air of imperial grandeur. At the height of the season Platres can become very crowded, with its facilities creaking under the strain, but off season it has the feel of any Cypriot village, where everybody seems to know everybody else.

On the main square is a post office, a police station, the main CTO tourist office for the region, a bike-hire office and, just below, a small amusement arcade (grandly called "Lunar Park"). Look out, too, for the **Chocolate Workshop** (☎ 99766446, ⓦ cypruschocolate.com; book in advance; €50). Here you can spend an afternoon crafting your own luxury confections (at a suitably luxury price). Platres is a good base for exploring the mountains, and offers a couple of popular and easily manageable walks (see box opposite).

Foini

A worthwhile short (4km) excursion to the west of Platres is the meandering village of **FOINI**, famous for its **pottery** and its *loukoumi* (see box, p.125) or "Foini Delight" as it's known here. There's a lovely viewpoint on the way into the village which provides a good map of the surroundings. Foini is a busy little community with a school, playground, banks, barbers' shops and two diminutive village squares. Traces of the past are everywhere – you'll see *pithoi* wine jars decorously positioned throughout and there are pretty **medieval bridges** to the west of the village.

To try the local *loukoumi*, ask for the **Pilavakis** family who welcome visits to their small home factory in the northern outskirts. They also run the **Pilavakion Museum** (daily 9am–5pm, closed Sun in winter; €1), which is housed in a venerable 400-year-old house

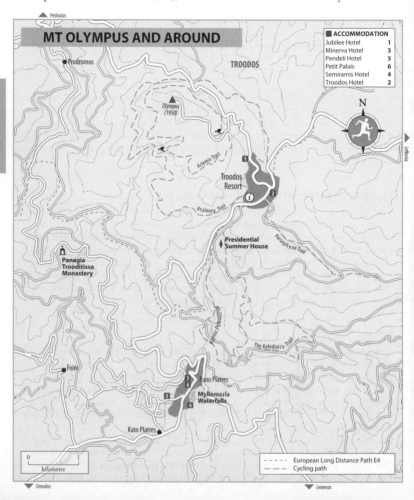

▲ Pedoulas

MT OLYMPUS AND AROUND

■ ACCOMMODATION

Jubilee Hotel	1
Minerva Hotel	3
Pendeli Hotel	5
Petit Palais	6
Semiramis Hotel	4
Troodos Hotel	2

● Prodromos

TROODOS

▲ Olympus (1950)

Artemis Trail

Troodos Resort

Atalante Trail

◆ **Presidential Summer House**

Persephone Trail

🏛 **Panagia Trooditissa Monastery**

Kryos Potamos

The Kaledonia Trail

● Foini

Pano Platres

Myllomeria Waterfalls

Kato Platres

0 ———— 1
kilometre

- - - - - European Long Distance Path E4
— — — Cycling path

▼ Omodos   ▼ Lemesos

N

WALKS AROUND TROODOS VILLAGE AND PLATRES

THE MYLLOMERIS TRAIL

The easiest walk in the area, the 1.5km Myllomeris Trail is a one-hour return stroll which starts opposite and just north of the church at the bottom end of Pano Platres to the base of the Myllomeris Falls, an attractive cascade when the river contains enough water.

THE KALEDONIA TRAIL

Accessible either at the top end from Troodos village or from the bottom near the *Psilo Dendro* trout farm/restaurant, halfway between Platres and Troodos, the 3km Kaledonia Trail follows the Kryos Potamos river (one of the few in Cyprus that flows year-round) and takes in the eponymous waterfall which, at 15m is the highest on the island. The trail is well signposted, and drops down from the Presidential Summer House (built by the British as a summer residence for the High Commissioner), crossing the river along log bridges or sets of stepping stones, and passing through a variety of woodland. Pick up the pamphlet detailing the walk from the Forestery Dept visitor centre. Allow one to two hours each way. To avoid retracing your steps, start at the bottom end, then return instead of climbing on to Troodos.

THE ARTEMIS TRAIL

A 7km route whose start from a car park off the road to the summit is signposted from Troodos village, the Artemis Trail is particularly satisfying as it circumnavigates Mount Olympos at around 1850m and offers tantalizing views (including interesting rock formations and the remains of several Venetian fortifications), yet doesn't involve much climbing. Again, a pamphlet produced by the Forestry Department explains everything in detail, including exactly what you can see from the various viewpoints. There's no water along this trail, so bring your own. Allow two to four hours, depending on fitness and how long you stop to admire the views.

THE ATALANTE TRAIL

Similar to the Artemis Trail but at 1750m it's slightly lower (and therefore longer by a couple of kilometres). It has the advantage of starting right in the centre of Troodos village, and passes a spring with drinkable water. It's not, however, a fully circular route.

THE PERSEPHONE TRAIL

A there-and-back 90min to two-hour 3km hike to the top of Makria KontarkaHill, with extensive views.

4

(signposted as the "pottery museum", or "Finoi Local Folk Art Museum"), and crammed with artefacts from the village's past. The curator will be happy to talk about the contents at considerable length. If you have got time, it's also worth taking the narrow road north from the top of the village to the **Chantara Waterfalls** and eventually, after tortuously winding route, to Trooditissa Monastery (see below).

Trooditissa Monastery

Just west of Troodos village, off the Platres to Prodromos road, is the **Trooditissa Monastery**, at 1200m the highest working monastery in Cyprus. Scenically set amid orchards and pine groves, its buildings, though not spectacularly ancient (they're mainly eighteenth century) are pretty and harmonious, with tiled roofs, triangular dormers and gables, and much use of timber and stone.

The story of how the monastery was founded is even more outlandish than most, and tells of an **icon of the Virgin Mary** floating over from Asia Minor in the tenth century to escape destruction by the iconoclasts, finding its way into a cave and then being discovered thanks to its heavenly glow. The monastery grew up around the icon (hence its full name "Panagia Trooditissa"), which developed a reputation for helping childless women conceive; in the past there was a tradition that any male born from the Virgin's intervention would become a monk. You can visit the **cave** in which the icon was found – it's signposted up a short climb off the main road about 200m east of the turning down to the monastery.

Incidentally, don't be put off by the sign at the entrance to the monastery saying "Entry is not allowed to tourists". During the 1990s there were concerns about the influx of coach parties disturbing the monks (part of the same austere sect as at Stavrovouni; see p.78). Individual visitors are welcomed with great charm (indeed even the odd coach tour is granted permission to drop by).

ARRIVAL AND INFORMATION

TROODOS VILLAGE AND AROUND

By bus The Troodos region is served by buses from Lefkosia (Mon–Fri 6.45am and 2pm, return 9am and 4pm; Sat 8.15am and 2.05pm, returning 10am and 4pm; Sun 7.30am and 2pm, return 9.30am and 4pm) and Lemesos (daily 9.15am, return 3.30pm); both services are to Troodos Square.

Tourist offices There is a tourist office on the main square in Pano Platres (4B Olympus Street; ☎ 25421020, ⊛ mytroodos.com) and the Troodos Environmental Information Centre (Troodos Square; ☎ 25420144, ⊛ moa .gov.cy/forest) is also a good source of information and maps.

ACCOMMODATION

TROODOS VILLAGE

Jubilee Hotel Troodos Square ☎ 25420107, ⊛ jubileehotel.com. Named after King George V's jubilee in 1935, when the hotel was built, the *Jubilee* is all about location: it's the highest hotel in Cyprus, about 500m from Troodos Square (and therefore clear of the coach-tour crowds), and close to the ski slopes. Rooms are pretty basic, though all have central heating and en-suite facilities. There's a bar/café, a pool table, and that's about it – most guests are out all day hiking, mountain biking or skiing. **€110**

★ **Troodos Hotel** Troodos Square ☎ 25420000, ⊛ troodoshotel.com. A low modern building with stone walls and green-tiled roof facing the main square, the *Troodos Hotel* has open log fires and rooms with clean minimalist lines. Its terrace overlooks the shops and restaurants of the square and there are great views to the rear. Facilities include, lounge, cafeteria bar and restaurant. Again, it's mostly aimed at outdoor enthusiasts. **€70**

PLATRES

Petit Palais Pano Platres ☎ 25421723, ⊛ petitpalaishotel.com. A balconied chalet-type building slap bang in the centre of the village. Warm and welcoming, and used to catering for families. A lift leads to all floors, and all rooms have balconies, most with views of wooded valley below the village. There's also a shaded terrace restaurant (burgers €6, mixed grills €14) where you can watch the world go by. **€65**

Pendeli Hotel 12 Archbishop Makarios III ☎ 25421736. A medium-sized hotel beginning to show its age (especially in the rooms), but with a fair range of facilities (café, bar, restaurant, outdoor pool, kids' play area). Good location in the centre of Platres, and friendly and helpful staff. Internet available, but slow, some off-street parking available. **€65**

Semiramis Hotel 55 Spyrou Kyprianou ☎ 25422777, ⊛ semiramishotelcyprus.com. Small, quiet hotel in a quirky, architecturally interesting Edwardian building, renovated in 2006 to provide modern facilities and decor. Agreeable multilevel terrace, atmospherically lit after dark. **€70**

EATING AND DRINKING

TROODOS VILLAGE

Troodos Hotel Troodos Square ☎ 25420000, ⊛ troodoshotel.com. Plain, wood-clad restaurant with outdoor terrace right on Troodos Square. Good range of sandwiches, pasta dishes, pizzas and grilled fish and meat. Most main courses €10; trout and steak more expensive. Daily 7am–10pm, and continues as a bar after the kitchens close.

PLATRES

Kalidonia Restaurant ☎ 25421404. On the main road up through the village, the *Kalidonia* offers the usual Greek dishes of souvlakia and *mezedes*; the presence of numerous Greek Cypriots appears to vouch

for its authenticity. Main courses from €10. Daily, lunch and dinner.

★ **Psilo Dendro** 13 Aedonion ☎ 25813131, ⊛ psilodendro.com. Restaurant attached to a trout farm between Platres and Troodos – follow the signs from the bottom end of the Kalidonia Trail. As you'd expect, the charcoal-grilled trout is excellent (€10 or thereabouts) though the rest of the menu is pretty standard. There's a large indoor room as well as outdoor eating area under the trees, loud with the sound of the water running through the fish tanks. Daily 9am–5pm; closed Dec–Feb.

Skylight 524 Arch. Makariou III ☎ 25422244, ⊛ skylight.com. On the left as you climb up towards the main square, the *Skylight* offers the usual range of Cypriot

KALEDONIA FALLS NEAR TROODOS (P.151) >

and international meat and fish dishes (main courses from €10) in cool but warmly lit indoor surroundings and a roofed terrace. Its USP, though, is the swimming pool just outside, which customers can use for free. Daily 9am–6pm all year.

★ **Village Tavern** 26 Arch. Makariou III ☎ 25422777. Just west of Pano Platres village centre, this is a traditional taverna owned and run in tandem with the *Semiramis Hotel*. Meze recommended, and it sells its own wine. Mains from €10, meze around €35 per couple. Daily 9am–8pm.

Marathasa

The **MARATHASA** region, lying north and west of Mount Olympos and the Troodos region, is dotted with villages and is relatively unspoilt. Apart from its three painted Byzantine churches in successive villages along the Marathasa river, it hosts the richest and most famous monastery on the island at Kykkos. It is also famed for its cool-weather fruit, particularly cherries and apples, and is particularly attractive in spring when the trees are in full blossom.

Prodromos

On travelling north into the Marathasa, the first village of any size you reach is **PRODROMOS**, a former hill resort, the jewel in whose crown was the massive *Berengaria Hotel*. The hotel catered for the glitterati from the 1920s onwards, but has been derelict since the 1980s. Prodromos (the top end of the village at least) is now essentially a cluster of restaurants, a bank and a petrol station gathered around a roundabout, there to service pilgrims on their way to the monastery at Kykkos. The village was named after John the Baptist (or the "forerunner") and, at 1400m above sea level, is officially the highest village in Cyprus.

Pedoulas

The next stop north down the Marathasa Valley, **PEDOULAS**, is an attractive place tumbling down a hillside in a series of terraces, only slightly marred by the rusted corrugated iron roofs on some of the houses. The village, notable mainly for its painted church, was established during the Byzantine period by refugees fleeing Arab coastal raids, though the origin of its name is somewhat in doubt – perhaps it refers to the shoe and sandal makers who once plied their trade here ("pedila" being the word for sandal). Pedoulas packs in all the services you might need including restaurants and shops, a petrol station and banks with ATMs, though, like many settlements in these mountains, its serpentine lanes are something of a maze – probably the easiest way to get orientated is from the huge white **Church of the Holy Cross** in the centre (not the painted church for which the village is famous). As you explore, look out for the statue of **Archbishop Makarios III** on the main (upper) street, the large monument to **Aristides Charalambous**, a local man who died during the independence struggle, and in particular (you can't miss it – it dominates the skyline above the village) the white 25m-high **Cross of Fithkia**, which stands next to a modern chapel.

Archangelos Michaelis Church
Daily, sunrise to sunset • Free

Pedoulas's **Archangelos Michaelis Church** (accessed down a steep lane from the Church of the Holy Cross) is one of the ten "painted churches of the Troodos Region" that have been declared by UNESCO as being a collective World Heritage Site (see box, p.156). Distinctive because of its tiled roof, which on one side sweeps down almost to ground level, the church is easy to date – a dedication over the north door says that it was built by "the most honourable priest Lord Basil, son of Chamades" and painted in 1474. The dedication also seeks forgiveness of sins for Basil, his wife and two daughters – a

TROODOS FESTIVALS

Villages in the Troodos Mountains celebrate all the usual religious festivals, plus a few devoted to local produce. Because of the weather up in the mountains, those worth seeing tend to be concentrated into the spring/summer/autumn.

MAY

Agros Rose Festival Displays, activities, demonstrations coinciding with the blossoming of the village's rose bushes. On sale are perfumes, rose water, rose brandy and even rose-based sweets.

Korakou Herb Festival Celebration of herbs, whether used in food, medicine, perfume or aromatherapy. Free buses run to Korakou from Germasogeia in Lemesos.

JUNE

Sports and Fun Festival (last weekend of June). Cycling, rock climbing, downhill racing, archery and much more, in Platres.

AUGUST

Pano Platres Festival (mid-Aug). Music, dance, drama, craft and farming exhibitions in and around the village.

Dormition of the Virgin Mary (Aug 14–15). A big religious celebration across the republic, but particularly worth seeing at the big three Troodos monasteries – Kykkos, Machairas and Trooditissa.

SEPTEMBER

Raising of the Cross (Sept 13–14). A particular feature in Omodos and Platanistasa.

Local Products Festival Held in Galata to celebrate bread, sweets and other local produce. Not exactly a snappy title, though.

OCTOBER

Cyprus Herb Event Similar to Korakou Festival above, but held in Pano Platres.

Apple Festival Displays, exhibitions, and tastings, all apple related, held in the villages of Amiantos, Dymes and Kyperounta, accompanied by much music and dancing.

NOVEMBER

Kakopetria Festival Choral festival, but with plenty of other music, singing and dancing.

Zivania Festival Displays on the way in which this fierce firewater is distilled, together with the opportunity of drinking some of it. Held in the villages of Alona and Pelendri. Inexperienced drinkers beware.

4

portrait of them donating the church to the Archangel provides an illustration of the fashions of the time. A further dedication (on the beam across the west wall) reveals that the artist was "Menas from Myrianthousa" (ie the Marathasa Valley). As is usually the case in these churches, the walls are divided into a lower zone populated by a host of individual saints and an upper one illustrating scenes from the Bible, including the Birth of the Virgin, Her Presentation to the Temple, the Annunciation, the Birth of Christ, His Baptism, Betrayal, Crucifixion and so on. The more you know your Bible, the more you'll appreciate the murals, but even the non-religious can't help but be impressed by the vividness of the colours, despite some fading over the centuries.

The Byzantine Museum

Daily: April–Oct 9.30am–1pm & 2–6pm; Nov–March 10am–1pm & 2–5pm • €1.70 • ☎ 22953636

Directly across from the Archangelos Church and housed in the old village school building, the **Byzantine Museum** contains icons and other religious objects from the thirteenth to the twentieth centuries. These include not only holy pictures, but also coins, painted altar doors, printed books, objects such as censers, and informative information boards. Interesting without being riveting: if short of time give it a miss.

The Folkloric Museum

10am–4pm; closed Mon • €1.70 • ☎ 22673375

Just along the street and back towards the centre of the village from Archangelos Church and the Byzantine Museum, is the **Folkloric Museum**, better than many of its ilk. Its low stone and timber house contains exhibits which illustrate the history of Pedoulas, and include the interior furnishings of a typical dwelling, local costume and

THE PAINTED CHURCHES OF THE TROODOS

In its stock of simple but exquisitely painted rural churches the Troodos Mountains is truly blessed. You can come across these little gems across the region, but especially on the north slopes of the range, sometimes in villages, sometimes in remote wooded areas. They are modest in construction, with steeply sloping wooden roofs (to shed snow during the winter) above stout rough stone walls. Inside, they are decorated with wonderful frescoes (and in some cases mosaics) which offer a glimpse of life and beliefs during the almost thousand years of the Byzantine Empire. Ten of these churches (listed below) are collectively included on UNESCO's World Heritage List.

Photography is not allowed inside the churches, but most sell guidebooks and/or postcards of the most notable paintings. For in-depth background get hold of "The Painted Churches of Cyprus" by Andreas and Judith A. Stylianou (see p.264) which gives detailed descriptions and illustrations of the wall and ceiling paintings of all the Troodos churches (and many others across the island).

Agios Nikolaos tis Stegis, Kakopetria
  (see p.159)
Agios Ionannis Lampadistis Monastery,
  Kalopanayiotis (see p.157)
Panagia Forviotissa (Asinou), Nikitart
  (see p.161)
Panagia tou Arakou, Lagoudera

Panagia, Moutoullas (see below)
Archangelos Michaelis, Pedoulas
  (see p.154)
Timios Stavros, Pelendri (see p.144)
Panagia tis Podythou, Galata
Stavros Agiasmati, Platanistasa
Agia Sotira tou Soteros, Palaichori

displays on the work of the villagers: the farmer, the winemaker, the blacksmith, the tanner, the boot-maker and more. Where the Folkloric Museum scores over many elsewhere is in its detailed information boards, in English as well as Greek.

EATING AND DRINKING
PEDOULAS

To Vrysi Corner of Pelopida & Hadjiloannou ☎ 22952240. A small family restaurant on a backstreet near the main road. Home cooking, local wine. Try the wild trout if available. Mains from €6. Daily 7am–9.30pm.

★ **Platanos** Vasou Hadjiloannou ☎ 22952518. Next to the Folkloric Museum, the *Platanos* is a traditional *estiadorio*, with a terrace canopied by large plane trees (hence the name). Much frequented by locals, who drink coffee, play tavli and eat Cypriot food. A shady place to see local life and watch the world go by. Main courses from €7. Daily 10am–6pm.

Moutoullas

Some 4km north of Pedoulas stands **MOUTOULLAS**, another village draped across a hillside, with tiled or corrugated iron roofs and outward facing balconies and terraces. This one is known for its mineral water (sold all over Cyprus), and in the past for producing carved wooden objects, particularly feed troughs, bread boards and threshing sledges. Moutoullas's crowning glory is, however, the church of Panagia tou Moutella.

Panagia tou Moutoulla Church
Daily sunrise to sunset • Free

Panagia tou Moutoulla is the oldest of the painted Troodos churches, with a steeply pitched, tiled roof which covers not only the nave, but also a covered walkway around the building. Not easy to find, the church stands next to the cemetery at the highest (northern) point of the village, up a paved ramp that climbs from the signposted dirt road. As is common in many of the Troodos churches an inscription and portrait (in this case on the north wall) tells us who stumped up the cash: "erected by the donation and the great desire of John (son of Moutallas) and of his wife Irene on the fourth of July in the year 1280 AD". The wall paintings follow the usual pattern – saints on the bottom half, stories from the Bible above, though the small size of the church means that the latter have been cut to a minimum. It's interesting to note that some things haven't changed for over seven centuries – Joseph, watching the approach of the Magi, is sitting on a donkey saddle of a type which you can still see in use today. Some of the paintings have suffered the ravages of time, others were damaged by British soldiers during a 1950s raid against EOKA fighters.

Agios Ioannis Lampadistis Monastery

Tues–Sun 9am–1pm & 4–6pm • Donations suggested

Below Moutoullas, in the village of **KALOPANGIOTIS**, known for its fine old buildings and bridges and its sulphur springs, lies the third and best of the Marathasa's ecclesiastical treasures, the **Monastery of Ioannis Lampadistis**. The monastery is accessible across a bridge in the valley's floor. Altered and added to over the centuries, the main building consists of the eleventh-century Church of St Herakleidius to the south (which you enter first), the Church of Agios Ioannis Lampadistis in the middle, the common narthex (entrance lobby) to the west, and what is thought to be a Latin chapel to the north, all of it under a massive second timber-and-tile pitched roof. The interior walls of these buildings are a riot of Byzantine art and cover many stories from the New Testament. Among the most vivid of the paintings are the *Triumphal Entry of Christ into Jerusalem* (in the western vault of St Herakleidius), *Christ Carrying the Cross along the Via Crucis* and *The Entombment* (in the northern vault), the series in the east wall of the narthex depicting *Christ Healing the Sick* (the paralytic, the man with the dropsy, the blind man) and the Italian-influenced paintings in the Latin Chapel. There is also a small Byzantine Museum in the monastery.

4

Kykkos Monastery and around

June–Oct 10am–6pm; Nov–May 10am–4pm • Free • ☎ 22942435

The monastery of **Panagia tou Kykkou**, widely known simply as "**Kykkos**", is the most famous in Cyprus. Located on the far edge of the Troodos area, 15km west of Pedoulas and the Marathasa valley, it's often dismissed rather scathingly by guidebooks but will tell you more about Greek Cypriots and their religion today than all the more venerable churches of Troodos put together. Add in President Makarios's tomb and the nearby EOKA hideouts and you have a a must-visit for anybody trying to get a handle on modern Cyprus.

The original monastery was established at the end of the eleventh century by the Byzantine Emperor, though none of the original buildings have survived the numerous fires that have swept through the region. Nothing in the current monastery predates the last fire in 1831, and much of it is later than that, though the famous icon of the Virgin Mary seems to have miraculously survived.

The Kykkos Monastery is the richest on the island and it shows. Its buildings are pristine and immaculately maintained, its murals vivid and bright, its monks numerous. This wealth grew partly because of the pulling power of the icon, and partly because, during Ottoman times, many people donated their money to the church rather than see it whittled away by heavy Ottoman taxes. On entry, through a highly decorated porch (even the cover-up clothes provided for visitors are a cut above the ones you'll find elsewhere), you walk into a handsome courtyard with a museum at the far left and, above the monastery roof, a wooded hillside with a recently built bell tower.

The Monastery Museum

June–Sept 10am–6pm; Oct–May 10am–4pm • €5 • ⓦ www.kykkos-museum.cy.net

The Monastery Museum is organized into antiquities (that is pre-Christian artefacts) and documents (on the left as you enter), vessels, vestments and ornaments from the early Christian and Byzantine periods and after in the main room, then icons, frescoes and woodcarving (on the left) and manuscripts, documents and books (on the right).

THE ICON OF THE VIRGIN AT KYKKOS

According to tradition, the Kykkos Monastery was established in the twelfth century AD by a hermit called Esaias, who lived a life of simple piety in the region's woods. One day the Byzantine governor of Cyprus, Manuel Voutoumites, was hunting in the area and got lost. Coming across Esaias, he asked the way, only to be ignored by the holy man, whose mind was on higher things. As you might expect, the politician took offence at the perceived slight, berating the hermit, or even, according to some versions, giving him a good hiding. Having returned to Lefkosia, Voutoumites contracted a terrible disease and, surmising that this was his punishment for his maltreatment of the holy man, appealed to God to cure him so that he could seek forgiveness. This wish met with divine agreement, but when Voutoumites finally tracked down the hermit and apologized, Esiais set him a task. A famous icon of the Virgin Mary, painted by the Apostle Luke while the Virgin was still alive, and lodged in the Imperial Palace at Constantinople, must be brought to Cyprus. The governor and the sage set off for Constantinople on what Voutoumites considered to be a wild goose chase – he could see no way in which the emperor would accede to the request. But the almighty intervened again. The emperor's daughter contracted the same disease that had laid Voutoumites low, and he was forced to agree to the icon's export to Cyprus in order to save her. The icon has been lodged in the monastery ever since.

Though of limited lay interest, nobody could fail to be impressed by the comprehensiveness of the collections and the lush complexity of the exhibits. A detailed account of the contents of the museum is available on the website, whose epilogue – "An exhibition that does not talk loudly but speaks suggestively" – probably doesn't quite mean what it says.

The church

Beyond the main courtyard the visitor is free to explore a series of passageways and flights of steps and paved courtyards that can't seem to muster a right angle between then. Domed roofs and white walls of corridors bear colourful murals, stone and tile floors are buffed to a high polish. The **monastery church** is opulent even by Greek Orthodox standards, and is lined with icons (including the famous one of the Virgin, in its own silver, tortoiseshell and mother-of-pearl protective case), usually busy being kissed by a line of supplicants. Nearby is a brass or bronze arm, the result of a punishment, it is said, meted out by the Virgin to a Turk who had the temerity to light a cigarette from one of the sanctuary lamps, and, a more cheerful story, the blade of a swordfish, presented by a sailor who was saved from drowning by the Queen of Heaven. The church and the courtyard outside it often becomes packed with people at weekends – some attending weddings or christenings, some making pious pilgrimage, others simply having a day out.

Tomb of Archbishop Makarios III

Above Kykkos Monastery is the tomb of Cyprus's most famous son, **Archbishop Makarios III**, first president of the republic. As you follow the road that climbs up beyond the monastery, past the bell tower and a giant communications "golf ball", the Troodos Mountains open up around you. After a couple of kilometres you reach a car park and a huge statue of Makarios welcomes you to the summit of Throni (the "throne" of the Virgin). In his youth Makarios served time as a novice at Kykkos, and this is where he chose to be buried. A paved path loops upwards from the car park, lined with mosaics of numerous saints, then doubles back to the tomb, guarded by a small military post. Twists of paper and pieces of cloth are attached to several bushes ("wish trees") as supplications for help and intervention from the saints. The tomb, just below the summit of the hill, is a simple slab of black marble on a stone plinth, with a picture of the archbishop before it, flanked by cut flowers, the whole protected by a low, arched stone roof. (For more on Makarios, see box, p.160).

EOKA Hideouts

As you leave Kykkos Monastery, you'll see a sing about 3km back along the main road, that points leftwards to "**EOKA Hideouts** 2km", accessed along a rough track best handled by a 4WD. The hideouts themselves are little more than holes in the ground with, up a steep and rather unstable path, a "headquarters", simply a larger hole, above them. But their proximity to Makarios's tomb and to Kykkos Monastery, where units of the Gordon Highlanders were stationed during anti-EOKA activity in 1956, emphasizes the strong links between the political and military fight for independence and the Orthodox church. At the last visit, though the sign still indicated the hideouts, a stout fence blocked off the road.

Xistarouda Picnic Site

Some 6km east of Kykkos, on the right of the E912, lies one of the picnic sites at which the Troodos Mountains excel. **Xistarouda** has a roofed barbecue area, numerous picnic tables on a series of stone-faced terraces under tall and shady trees, and toilets. Because it's on the main route to the Kykkos Monastery, it gets very busy, especially at weekends, with families erecting gazebos and portable barbecues and setting themselves up for the afternoon.

Solea

East of Marathasa, the **SOLEA** region straddles the main road to Lefkosia, ensuring its popularity as a day-trip and weekend destination for the capital's residents. Progressively less hilly the further north and east you travel, the region is mainly popular for its village life, and for its wealth of painted churches. The main village, **Kakopetria**, has enough hotels, restaurants and services to make it a good base from which to explore.

4

Kakopetria

KAKOPETRIA sits astride the Karyotis river on the main B9 road to Lefkosia, 50km from the capital, and allies the convenience of hotel, restaurant, bank and petrol station with a pretty (and now protected) old town of alleys and tottering houses. Busy with tourists at the height of the season, but pretty and relaxing around the main square, it has a soundtrack of whispering or roaring waters, depending on where in the village you are.

The name "Kakopetria" means "bad stones", deriving, it is said, from the numerous large rocks swept down from Olympos in primordial times, which you can still see in the foundations of some of the houses. One such stone ("the Stone of the Couple") had a reputation for bringing good luck to newlyweds: they would walk around its base, climb onto it, and make a wish. That reputation was somewhat dented when the stone shifted, killing a young couple in the process (it has since been underpinned by concrete and stone).

Agios Nikolaos tis Stegis

Tues–Sat 9am–4pm, Sun 11am–4pm • Donations

Just a couple of well-signposted kilometres southwest of Kakopetria along the F936 stands another of the region's ten UNECO World Heritage Site churches, **Agios Nikolaos tis Stegis** (St Nicholas of the Roof). Make sure you visit during opening hours – it's completely fenced off, and you won't get even a glimpse of it from the road. The church building has a rough-and-ready, lopsided look, prompting speculation that the eleventh-century masons who built it weren't quite up to the job. The steep-pitched roof, added to protect the early cross-in-square building from

FATHER OF THE NATION: MAKARIOS

Born on August 13, 1913, in the village of Panagia in eastern Pafos district, Makarios (then known as Michaelis Mouskos) became a novice at Kykkos Monastery at the age of 13, before continuing his education at the Pancyprian Gymnasium in Lefkosia. After graduation, he went on to study in Greece and Turkey (hence his rather unexpected facility with the Turkish language), and finally Boston in the US.

In 1948 he became Bishop of Kition (Larnaka), and two years later **Archbishop of Cyprus**. It was at this time that he took the clerical name of Makarios III. He was now not only the religious leader of the Greek Cypriot community in Cyprus, but their de facto political leader. One of his first actions was to carry out a plebiscite on union with Greece ("**enosis**") – 96 percent of Greek Cypriots voted in favour. It goes without saying that the Turkish Cypriot community were against enosis from the start, fearing for their position if the island became a province of Greece.

As the 1950s progressed, the so-called "**Cyprus Problem**" became increasingly high profile, with EOKA (the right-wing organization led by George Grivas) carrying out a guerrilla war from April 1, 1955 within Cyprus, and the Greek government pushing hard in the UN for an end to British rule and unification with Greece. Makarios, strongly identified with this opposition to British rule, was eventually exiled to the Seychelles in March 1956. After a year, he was released with the proviso that he did not return to Cyprus. He settled instead in Athens, from which base he travelled the world, drumming up support for his cause, particularly among non-aligned countries and the Soviet Union.

In 1959, amidst continued violence across the island, Makarios accepted an offer from the British of **independence**, but without enosis. This provoked predictable disgust and fury among EOKA, and accusations that he had sold out, even that he'd been blackmailed into acceptance by the British Secret Service. No such scenario is needed, though, to explain his actions. Faced with a choice of leading a distant province of Greece or a proudly independent country, it really was a no-brainer. Makarios was duly elected **president** of the new Republic of Cyprus on 14 December.

As the new decade dawned, Makarios realized he was presiding over an unenviable situation. Turkish Cypriots, supported by Turkey, would accept no move towards enosis, while the Greek Cypriot right, supported by Greece, would accept nothing less. The imposition of a virtually unworkable constitution didn't help either. He also had little control over the hawkish General Grivas who was intent on military action against Turkish Cypriot armed enclaves, which were becoming almost a state within a state. Finally, when a right-wing junta seized power in Greece in 1967, the left-leaning Makarios came out openly against enosis, explaining that it would be beneficial to have two Greek voices at the UN rather than one. He began to try to build bridges with the Turkish Cypriots.

Between 1970 and 1974 there were numerous attempts by the junta and the CIA to assassinate Makarios (Nixon allegedly called him "Castro in a cassock"). Finally, on July 15, 1974 the National Guard and EOKA B rose up in rebellion, deposed Makarios (who fled abroad), and set up a right-wing administration. This provoked the catastrophic response of a full-scale **Turkish invasion** of the north, and partition. When the dust had settled, Makarios returned from abroad to resume as president of a now divided island. He died suddenly of a heart attack in August 1977.

Makarios undoubtedly made many mistakes during his period of office, though it seems unlikely anyone could have managed the ticking time bomb that he inherited. Certainly, blame for the 1974 Turkish invasion could not be laid at his door. His pragmatism, his undoubted political skills and above all his commitment to the people of Cyprus have ensured that he is held in widespread and lasting affection in the modern republic, something which cannot be said of his militaristic rival George Grivas. On the other hand, unsurprisingly, he was not popular among Turkish Cypriots. While his body was lying in state in Agios Ioannis Cathedral in Lefkosia, the capital suffered an unprecedented August downpour. Greek Cypriots quoted an old Greek saying – "God cries when a good man dies". Turkish Cypriots came back with one of their own – "When an evil man dies, the heavens try to wash away his crimes".

the harsh winter weather, led to the name. The church was once part of a monastery, but the rest of the buildings disappeared in the late nineteenth century. The paintings range from the eleventh to the seventeenth centuries and therefore represent a remarkable history of the development of Byzantine art. The oldest paintings (for example, the *Transfiguration* and the *Raising of Lazaros*, both early eleventh century) may not look as impressive and colourful as later ones, but are extremely important. Note the number of life-sized saints in the nave and the narthex, and the larger-than-life-sized St Nicholas in the entrance to the diaconicon (the chamber to the south of the apse in which the books, vestments and no or used in the services are kept). Look out, too, for the painting of St Peter on one of the east piers supporting the dome, and in particular for the graffito (in ink) written by Russian monk and early travel writer **Basil Moscovorrossos** in 1735 in which he outlines his recent travels in the region – vandalism, it's true, but interesting vandalism nonetheless.

ACCOMMODATION
KAKOPETRIA

★ **Linos Inn** 34 Palea Kakopetria ☏ 22923161, ⓦ linos-inn.com.cy. A labyrinthine complex of old houses in the heart of Kakopetria's old town, the *Linos Inn* was restored with the help of the CTO, and falls under the umbrella of agrotourist accommodation, though it is actually big enough to be considered a hotel. It offers a range of rooms, studios and suites, all with a traditional feel yet modern facilities, some with four-poster beds, some with jacuzzis. Take a look at what's available before committing. Its atmospheric restaurant offers international and Cypriot food. **€95**

★ **The Mill Hotel** 8 Mylou ☏ 22922536, ⓦ cymillhotel.com. Across the river and overlooking the centre of Kakopetria, *The Mill Hotel* incorporates bits of an ancient water mill within a large modern building. Its size disguises the fact that the accommodation is quite limited – at thirteen rooms, it's half the size of the much smaller Linos Inn. Access to the hotel and restaurant is by lift, with reception, sauna and accommodation on the middle two floors. Wood and stone rooms are clean and chunkily furnished, en-suites adequate, though the balconies have lovely river views. **€90**

EATING AND DRINKING

Argentina Tziellari Cyprus Restaurant 72 Palaias Kakopetrias ☏ 22922522. Owned and run by an Argentinian/Cypriot couple, this popular restaurant offers a fusion of each country's cuisine, with meze, steaks and *asado* (barbecued meats and sausages) specialities. Traditional interior, small terrace. Main courses from €8. Closed Mon.

Linos Inn 34 Palea Kakopetria ☏ 22923161, ⓦ linos-inn.com.cy. Rustic restaurant attached to the hotel of the same name. Deceptively large (it seats 100 indoors and another 70 on the terrace), it has a widespread reputation for both Cypriot (at the associated *Mesostrato Tavern*) and international cuisine. Hugely popular so you must reserve a table. Not cheap – mains from around €14. Restaurant daily 10am–midnight; tavern Fri & Sat 10am–10pm, Sun 10am–1pm.

★ **Mylos Restaurant** 8 Mylou ☏ 22922536, ⓦ cymillhotel.com. WIth open fires in winter, great views across the village from the balcony and a tradional feel, this hotel restaurant is a firm favourite. The menu is extensive and wide-ranging, with Cypriot specialities and international food, though it's best known for its trout. Mains from €15. Mon–Fri 12.30–10.45pm, Sat & Sun noon–3.30pm & 7.30–10.45pm. Advance booking of at least 4 days is required. Closed for the month running up to Christmas.

Zoumos Restaurant ☏ 22922154, ⓦ zoumos restaurant.com. The *Zoumos* in the centre of the village, might not look like much, with its cane furniture and picture menus, but the food is fresh and well cooked, the wine is local and plentiful, and the service is good. Sit out on the rear balcony if you can – it overlooks the Karkotis river that flows through the village. Main courses from around €8. Daily, lunch & dinner.

Panagia Forviotissa (Asinou) Church

9.30am–1pm, 2–4pm • Free • ☏ 99830329; contact Father Kyriakos Christofi in Nikitari if closed

Compared with the other painted Troodos churches, **Panagia Forviotissa** is rather isolated, but worth the extra effort because of the beauty of its setting, close to a lovely picnic site and hiking trail. At the top of a slope in the northeastern Troodos foothills, surrounded by wooded hills, it lies about 4km southwest of the village of Nikitari, off the main B9 Lefkosia to Troodos road.

THE LONELIEST RAILWAY STATION

As you travel north on the B9 from the heart of the Troodos Mountains towards Lefkosia, a string of villages present themselves, sitting on the slopes of sharp-crested hills, their houses deep in trees or perched on ridges – particularly **GALATA** with its numerous old balconied houses and several old churches, all worthy of note but of interest mainly to enthusiasts. A further 6km brings you to **EVRYCHOU**, a sizeable village just off the main road, unique on the island for having a railway station. Evrychou Station is in fact one of the few remains of the **Cyprus Government Railway (CGR)**, built by the British authorities to link the port of Famagusta to Lefkosia and the copper mines of the northwest. The 2ft 6in gauge line was not an economic success, and was progressively wound down between 1932 and 1951. Odd buildings and bits of equipment survive, mostly in Northern Cyprus. However, in 2004 it was decided to restore Evrychou Station, pave the road to it and open a museum of the CGR. Progress so far appears to have been substantial on the restoration, but not on the paving or the museum. It is very clearly signposted, but the road to it is little more than a track, would require a 4WD, and was, at the time of writing, closed.

A great clutch of the church's wall paintings (about two-thirds of the original decoration) date from when it was built in 1105. Note in particular the picture over the nave's south entrance of the church's founder Ischyrius handing over a model of the church to Christ via the Virgin Mary. It is noticeable that the model lacks a narthex (western entrance hall), which indicates that this was a later addition. The paintings – saints on the bottom half of the walls, scenes from the scriptures on the top half and ceilings – are amazing in their rich use of colour. There's also a touch of macabre humour – look out for the murals depicting the fate of the renegade monk and nun, the thief, the slanderer, the dishonest miller, the woman who refuses breast milk to infants, the one who diverts water from another's land, all of whom are pictured, in almost cartoon form, in chains being tormented by serpents. The whole church is a reminder of one of the purposes of religious art – to provide a biblical education to a largely illiterate population, and to warn them of the wages of sin.

Panagia Forviotissa is one of the best of a brilliant bunch of Troodos decorated churches. But it's not just the church that draws visitors. Just before you get to it the **Asinou Picnic Site** offers the opportunity of al fresco dining, with shaded seating and a small playground. Directly across the road from the church is a well set-up **restaurant** *Estiatorio Stavros tis Asinou*, and the start of a hiking trail to Agios Theodoros is just beyond. Lunch, a walk, a visit to the church – it makes for a splendid day out.

EATING AND DRINKING   **ASINOU**

Estiatorio Stavros tis Asinou Asinou ☎ 22852000. A great spot for some al fresco Greek Cypriot food served in a lovely wooded area. There's also a more fomal restaurant indoors. €8–15. Daily 9.30am–6pm.

Pitsilia

Mountainous **PITSILIA** is one of the remotest parts of the Troodos Massif. Spreading eastwards from the main B9/B8 Lefkosia to Lemesos road that loops through the mountains, the region is sparsely forested, with large areas of hazel and almond trees and grapevines. Little visited or known, it has a character and charm all its own, and is beginning to make attempts to attract tourists, with a small but growing number of places to stay and eat. Like other parts of the Troodos Mountains, Pitsilia is associated with the struggle for independence and enosis, memorials to EOKA fighters are encountered in many villages, and the Greek (as opposed to the Cypriot flag) is still much in evidence.

Agros

AGROS, the main village of Pitsilia, is an attractive spot, its red-roofed houses (many of which are on stilts) cupped by the mountains at the head of the **Agros valley**. It's known across the island for its **rose petal products**, sold at several shops along the serpentine main street (for example Venus Rose at 12 Triantafillou ☎25521893, ⊕www.venus-rose.com). You'll also find several tavernas raucously popular with locals and shops selling the village's **traditional sweets** (try Nikis at 5 Triantafillou ☎25521400. During the first half of May the area's dedication to roses is celebrated in the **Rose Festival**. Just across from the main square are two churches – one, **Panagia Eleousa**, built at the beginning of the twentieth century, the other, **Timon Sprodromos**, slightly older and encased in modern stone walls and a wooden roof.

Agros feels remote, yet is eminently accessible, being thirty minutes from Lemesos along the E110 and twenty minutes from Troodos east of the B9. And the surprising presence of a very large hotel, sited high on the hill with extensive views both south across the village and north across the mountains, makes it the perfect base for exploring the region.

The Frangoulides Museum

Daily Aug 10am–noon & 5–7pm or by appointment • Free • ☎25521201

Situated in the undercroft of Panagia Eleousa is the **Frangoulides Museum**, dedicated to the work of a well-known artist, Solonas Fragoulidi, who lived in Agros for two years in the 1930s. Lots of his pictures adorn the church above, and the museum, once the local cinema, has rough drafts and sketches and additional finished work by the artist.

Agridia

About halfway between Agros and the B9, the village of **AGRIDIA** makes little impression on the tourist literature of the area, yet is really well worth a stop. It's a typical mountain settlement, untidy yet appealing, with a large modern church, a small ecclesiastical museum and a preserved olive mill. However, the thing which really makes it worth a visit are its recently completed **picnic site** and **viewpoint**, both well signposted in the area. The picnic site, on the right as you enter the village from the south, climbs up a steep-sided little gorge, and has wooden tables, little picket fences, a stream with a wooden bridge, a children's playground, water fountains, a toilet, even a small modern amphitheatre, all stretching upwards under the trees. Above the site, a steep but driveable concrete road leads to the little **Chapel of Profitis Ilias**. This pretty church, built in 1998, is usually open, and the modern icons within and mosaics around the door positively glow. Sharing the hilltop (1090m) with the church is a **viewing point** with a (free) telescope through which you can see the tops of Mounts Olympus, Madari and Papoutsa, the villages of Agridia, Dymes, Chandria and Kyperounda, and on a good day Akrotiri Bay.

Spilia

Just off the B9, on the F929 is **SPILIA**, a small village dominated by a large war memorial consisting of four full-sized statues of **EOKA fighters**. Oddly, the statues – showing men brandishing automatic weapons – seem to be dedicated to some hapless bombmakers who blew themselves up, rather than commemorating one of EOKA's greatest victories over the British which happened in the hills nearby. In December 1955 the cream of EOKA fighters, including its leader General Grivas (see box, p.165) and its second-in-command Grigoris Afxentiou (see box, p.167) were caught in a pincer movement by British troops advancing from the north and the south on their mountain HQ. As the Cypriots retreated towards the summit, a fog descended, under cover of which they avoided the closing trap by marching quickly to the west. When the British troops reached the mountain top each group believed the other to be EOKA paramilitaries, and in the fog and confusion opened fire, suffering a number of casualties (Grivas claimed around fifty, the British admitted to three). Spilia today is a sleepy and peaceful village, with a small hotel and a single restaurant (see opposite) – a relaxing base, perhaps, for walking in the surrounding hills.

Pelendri

About 7km along the E806 southwest of Agros lies the village of **PELENDRI**, which in **Timios Stavros** has not only one of the best of the region's painted churches, but also one of the most accessible. As you enter the village, the church is clearly visible a few metres left off the main road – it stands between a reservoir and gardens and vineyards. Although usually locked, the key-holder lives in the cottage next to the church, and he's likely to rush out to open up as soon as he sees that there are visitors.

When built in the twelfth century it was a single-aisled domed church, but all that remains of the original building is the apse, the west wall and some of the colonnades. An unknown catastrophe destroyed the bulk of the rest of it in the early fourteenth century. It is, though, the wealth of wall paintings that are the glory of the church, especially some rare **twelfth-century paintings** that were discovered in the early 1970s, having previously been over-painted. These are in the apse, and consist of a "deisis" (Christ with the Virgin Mary on one side and St John the Baptist on the other) and portraits of six prelates with an altar and chalice between them. Inscribed above the apse window is a note from one of the artists "the sinful and humble servant Monmachos" and a date "6686" (1178 AD according to the modern calendar). Thought to be the work of four artists, the paintings are pretty crude and have sustained some damage, but their survival at all is a miracle. The excellent guidebook to the church by Dr Nektarios Zarras (€10) gives a detailed account of all the paintings (140 are listed).

The only other thing likely to grab the attention as you enter Pelendri is the inevitable **monument** to local heroes, consisting of full-sized sculptures of local men – Sotiris Tsaggaris who died in 1957 during the EOKA struggles, and Nikos Karasamani who died in 1974, presumably during the Turkish invasion. Neither is well served by their representations: the former looks distinctly nerdy, the latter has a flamboyance that the sculptor surely didn't intend.

The Monuments of Heroes

On a hilltop between Pelendri and Kato Amiantos to the northwest, the activities of EOKA in this part of Pitsilia are comprehensively commemorated in the **Monuments of Heroes**, a heavily symbolic clutch of linked memorials in a natural woodland setting. Entrance is through the "Porticos", which places the fight against the British against the backdrop of Greek history, and includes portraits of Makarios and Grivas, together with marble rolls of honour. This is followed with the **Room of the Fighters** which has artwork and a big-screen film presentation, and the **108 Steps of Freedom**, each representing a fallen EOKA fighter. The steps lead up to a large paved hilltop capped with the **Monument of Freedom** and the little **Chapel of Panagia Eleftherotria**, representing the large part played by the Greek Orthodox Church in the struggle. It's all a bit florid, yet the natural setting lends it a certain gravitas.

ACCOMMODATION   **PITSILIA**

AGROS

★ **Rodon Hotel** ☎ 25521201, ⓦ rodonhotel.com. An unexpectedly vast hotel at the top of Agros, about 1km from the centre, the *Rodon* comprises 123 doubles, six studios, fifteen family suites, ten executive suites, one presidential and one honeymoon suite, all in a village of

CYPRUS'S OLD WARHORSE: GENERAL GRIVAS

Together with Archbishop Makarios III, **General George Grivas** (whose nom de guerre was "Digenis") is the person most associated with the "Cyprus Problem" between the 1950s and 1970s. Born in Trikomo (now Iskele) in northeast Cyprus on May 23, 1898, he, like Makarios, studied at the Pancyprian Gymnasium in Lefkosia. When he graduated he fled to Athens, apparently to avoid an arranged marriage and it was here that his military education began. Having joined the **Greek army** as an officer, he served in the catastrophic campaign in Asia Minor which ended with the expulsion of the Greeks from Turkey in 1922. Despite this setback Grivas gradually moved up the ranks, making captain by 1925 and major by 1935.

During the German occupation, Grivas was involved in what can only be described as the murky deeds of the far-right organization "Khe" – the Greek letter usually represented as an "X" – which he founded and led. It was said to be far more concerned with attacking Greek communist guerrillas than the occupying forces. Indeed, there have been accusations of collaboration with the Nazis – at many times during his career, Grivas's political hatred of the left seems to have outranked his patriotic Hellenistic pride.

After the war Grivas played a significant part in the Greek Civil War (1946–49), fighting for the government against the communizts. He stood unsuccessfully in the Greek elections of 1951, one of several times when his attempts to turn to politics failed, perhaps owing to a distinct lack of the common touch. Following his dream of enosis (unification of Cyprus with Greece), he returned to his homeland. He met Makarios, and the two of them, together with other supporters, formed **EOKA**, the Ethniki Organosis Kyprion Agoniston or "National Organization of Cypriot Fighters", pledged to the overthrow of British rule in Cyprus and union with Greece. If there was any disagreement between the two men at this stage, it was that Grivas favoured full-scale armed rebellion, while Makarios wanted to limit action to the destruction of property.

In November 1954 Grivas landed in a caique loaded with arms and explosives on the west coast of Cyprus, near Pafos, and on April 1 the start of the **armed struggle** was announced by explosions all over the island. Grivas led the rebellion from a series of hideouts, in Lemesos, and later, the Troodos Mountains, attracting a price of £10,000 on his head. After Makarios was exiled in March 1956, Grivas led both the military and the political struggle from a hideout back in Lemesos. Finally, when the archbishop accepted a British offer of independence without enosis in 1959, Grivas decamped in disgust to Greece – his exile was part of the final agreement. In Greece he was deliriously greeted as a hero, and promoted to general.

The deteriorating situation in the new Republic of Cyprus attracted him back to the island in **1964**, where he led Greek hardliners in the National Guard and a division sent by Greece. Attacks on leftists and on Turkish Cypriots became increasingly outrageous, until the massacre of 27 Turkish Cypriots, many unarmed civilians, in Kofinou and Agios Theodoros caused worldwide revulsion. The Greek division, and Grivas, were withdrawn. The general returned once more to Cyprus in 1969, and re-established EOKA, now called EOKA B, whose aim this time, in addition to achieving enosis and suppressing Turkish Cypriot opposition to it, was also to combat the Greek Cypriot left. Virtual civil war broke out between **EOKA B** and the left, while Turkish Cypriots formed heavily armed enclaves. Finally, in January 1974 and still in hiding in Lemesos, Grivas died of a heart attack, thus avoiding the disastrous Turkish invasion that his actions had done so much to precipitate.

less than a thousand people. All rooms have full facilities, central heating and a/c, and access to veranda or balcony, while public areas include a gym, saunas, swimming pools (one for adults, one for children) and tennis courts. Plenty to do then, and also ideal for exploring Pitsilia. Look out for deals. €88

SPILIA
Marjay Inn ☎ 22922208, ⓦ marjay.com. Small,

comfortable hotel owned and run by a married couple in the centre of Spilia, near the EOKA memorial. There are six rooms, each different, with one on two levels, all en suite and (important in winter and on cool spring or autumn nights) centrally heated. The food's good – the *Marjay* started as a restaurant which expanded into accommodation. If you really like the hotel, why not buy it – at the time of writing, it was up for sale. €56

Machairas

East of Pitsilia, **MACHAIRAS** feels even more remote, a fact that is reflected in its total lack of hotels – even villages are few and far between. It is, however, a favourite day-trip destination for Lefkosians, and does have a number of attractions, including a monastery very much associated with EOKA, and a museum village, while its mountains and forests have more of an alpine feel than anywhere else in the Troodos range.

Machairas is signposted along the E902 from Strovolos on the outskirts of Lefkosia, from where an invigorating forest drive via Politiko and Pera brings you to its monastery via the extensive picnic grounds at Mandra Kambiou.

Machairas Monastery

9am–noon Mon, Tues & Thurs (groups only) • Free

Commanding wonderful views of the surrounding mountains, **Machairas Monastery,** like Kykkos, is very well maintained and exudes a sense of prosperous decorum. The story of its foundation follows the usual formula – a miraculous icon, one of seventy painted by the Apostle Luke, was brought here from Asia Minor by an unknown ascetic during the iconoclastic period. Hidden in a cave, it was discovered (probably by revealing itself with a divine glow) by two hermits – Neophytos and Ignatios – who'd arrived in the area from Palestine. To reach it, they needed to hack away the undergrowth, and a divine hand kindly provided the sword or "machairi". Ignatios founded the church in 1172 AD, which later expanded into a monastery. Fire destroyed the buildings in 1530 and 1892, but the icon, encased in silver, survived.

The monastery also played a role in the fight for Cypriot independence. EOKA's second-in-command, **Gregoris Afxentiou**, hid here, disguised as a monk, and eventually met a martyr's death at the hands of the British (see box opposite) – the cave in which he was trapped lies about 1km below the monastery, and is marked with a flag and commemorative tablet. There's a small **museum** dedicated to his short life (it's to the right of the ramp that leads down to the monastery terrace from the road), and on the terrace itself stands a gigantic statue of the man and the bird (an eagle) from which he derived his nom de guerre. Dashing and heroic though Afxentiou undoubtedly was, his statue may remind British visitors of Rik Mayel's Lord Flashheart.

Fikardou

The carefully conserved mountain village of **FIKARDOU** lies northwest of Machairas Monastery, and can be approached from there via Lazanias or from the west via Gourri. Either way, you enter the village on the E916. Though somewhat "preserved-in-aspic", it provides an excellent idea of what a Cypriot mountain village of the eighteenth or nineteenth century would have looked like.

The first building you encounter when you finally climb up into the village is the **Church of the Apostles St Peter and St Paul** on the left. A pretty little stone and clay-tiled-roofed building, it is set into the hillside below the road. In front of it lie graves which must have some of the best views in Cyprus. Across the road, on the hillside and with equally fine views, stands a memorial to four local men who died during the 1974 invasion. Immediately ahead is the village's coffee house and restaurant *Yiannakos*, tucked into a steep hairpin bend. Two-storey traditional houses are stacked up the hillside, each with straw-flecked mud walls and capped by mellow red/brown tile roofs. (The ground floor was used for making and storing wine and other farm produce, the first floor housed the people.) The organic nature of the village speaks for itself – the buildings seem to grow out of the hillside.

GRIGORIS AFXENTIOU: THE GENTLEMAN SOLDIER

While the names of Archbishop Makarios III and George Grivas loom large in the fight for Cypriot independence, within the Greek Cypriot community **Grigoris Afxentiou** is probably the man held in the greatest honour and affection. Even his notional enemies in the British Army held him in high regard – one British officer is reported as saying to Afxentiou's father, "I want to congratulate you on having such a splendid son". Grigoris Afxentiou is a clear-cut, old-fashioned, uncomplicated popular idol whose early death at the age of 29 in a heroic last stand against the occupying forces is the stuff of legend.

Afxentiou was born on February 22, 1928 in the village of Lysi (now in the north and called Akdogan) and became committed to Cypriot independence and eventual enosis from an early age. He joined the Greek army as a volunteer in 1949, and reached the rank of second lieutenant. When he heard that **EOKA** were recruiting, he joined up. His intelligence and potential were immediately recognized by Grivas, who took him under his wing and saw to his training in guerrilla warfare personally. Afxentiou was entrusted with blowing up the Cyprus Broadcasting station in Lefkosia during the night of simultaneous explosions that kicked off the fight against British rule on April 1, 1955. Having been recognized, he went on the run with a group of fighters in the Kyrenia mountains where he became Grivas's second-in-command.

For the next two years Afxentiou moved around the Troodos Mountains, training guerrillas and attacking British positions and convoys. He became one of the British Army's "most wanted", with a price of £5000 on his head. He narrowly evaded capture at the Battle of Spilia (see p.163), and again at Zoopigi a year later. His time ran out in March, 1957 when he was tracked down to the **Machairas Monastery**, where, with the help of the abbot, Irineos, he had been living disguised as a priest. Hiding below the monastery in an underground hideout, he ordered the four men who were with him to surrender, but decided to fight to the death himself. Unable to capture him without serious losses, the British soldiers finally poured petrol into the hideout, ignited it, and followed up with explosives. Afxetntiou had finally been killed.

His widespread popularity since his death can be explained by a number of factors. Compared to Grivas, he was a careful strategist, planning actions to minimize loss of life. He was even understanding towards informers, refusing to execute one man on the grounds that his wife had recently had a baby. His commitment to the cause of freedom and union with Greece was simple and straightforward, without the ferocious hatred of the left that consumed Grivas. And finally, by dying when he did, his reputation was never compromised by the sorts of fudges that post-independence politics invariably required.

Two of Fikardou's old houses have been opened to the public – the **House of Katsiniourou**, named after its last owner and owing its plan and features to the sixteenth century, has been turned into a rural **museum** (Daily April–Oct 9am–5pm; Nov–March 8am–4pm; €1.70; ☏22634731). Furnishing, tools and utensils from the past are on show, together with photographs, plans, drawings and texts illustrating the process of preservation. The **House of Achilleas Dimitri** has been furnished as a weaver's workshop and also acts as a guesthouse.

EATING AND DRINKING

FIKARDOU

★ **Yiannakos** Fikardou ☏22633311. Traditional two-storey building with roof terrace overlooking the village. The decor is also traditional (as you'd expect, it specializes in Greek Cypriot cuisine, with meze at €15 per person, and main courses like *stifado* and *koupepia* at €8, *kleftiko* €12. Wise to book – if it's full, as it often is, there is no alternative in the village. Daily 9am–5pm.

Lefkosia (South Nicosia)

LEFKOSIA ROOFTOPS

5

Lefkosia (South Nicosia)

The city of Lefkosia (still widely called Nicosia by locals, on signposts and on maps) is by far the largest settlement on Cyprus, though by international standards it is still pretty small, with a total population of little more than 250,000. Until 1974 Nicosia was the capital of the unified island; now the southern half, Lefkosia, forms the capital of the republic while the northern half, known as Lefkoşa (see p.198) is the capital of the Turkish occupied, self-styled TRNC – when the Berlin Wall fell, Nicosia became the last divided capital in the world.

A political and financial centre, not just for the republic and the Eastern Mediterranean, but for the whole of the Middle East, Lefkosia is less dependent on tourism than anywhere else on the island. Yet there is still a great deal to see and do in the southern, republic-controlled half of the city. Within the forbidding **Venetian Walls** of the old city are the excellent **Cyprus Museum**, the **Leventis City Museum**, as well as the **Shacolas Tower** which offers unparalleled views to the north. You'll also find some of Cyprus's best restaurants and its most sophisticated shopping. Much of interest also exists in the newer parts of the city and beyond – especially the **Police and Coinage museums** and the **Cyprus Handicrafts Centre** in the suburbs, and the ancient city of **Tamassos**, a short drive to the south.

While the capital remains divided, the opening of **checkpoints** between the republic and the occupied north (the most accessible being **Ledra Street**) enables you to sample two cultures in a singe day. The division is still "in your face", particularly in the derelict areas of the Buffer Zone, and a journey between south and north offers you a real perspective on the Cyprus Problem. For coverage of the Turkish-controlled northern half of the city, as well as other areas of north Cyprus within striking distance of Lefkosia see p.196.

Brief history

Thought to have originated in a small town (Ledra) established by Lefkonas, son of Ptolemy I in 300 BC, Nicosia grew significantly under the Byzantines. Its inland position, protected by the island's two main mountain ranges, kept it safe from attack from the sea, and well placed for the political and religious administration of the country. The Lusignans fortified the city and it was under them that Nicosia experienced a "**golden age**" during which numerous palaces, churches and monasteries were built. This has left an impressive, if patchy, legacy of Gothic Crusader remains. Lusignan prosperity, however, ended with a series of **attacks** – by the **Genoese** in 1372 and the **Mamelukes** in 1426, and finally, after the **Venetians** had hastily thrown up the massive walls you see today, by the Ottomans who sacked the city in 1570. There then followed a period of three centuries when, although the population were better off financially than they had been under the Venetians, the city settled into a kind of quiet decrepitude, interspersed with bouts of extreme violence – in 1764 Turkish riots against rule from Constantinople led to the death of a particularly hated governor; in

THE CYPRUS MUSEUM

Highlights

❶ The Venetian walls These beautifully preserved walls may have failed to stop the Ottoman advance but are well worth exploring today, not least for their impressive views. **See p.173**

❷ Laiki Geitonia The old city's quaintest area, all narrow alleys and overhanging old buildings, is perfect for window-shopping and aimless wandering. **See p.173**

❸ The Postal Museum Hidden down a side-street, the diminuitive Postal Museum is a little gem, whether or not you're into stamps. **See p.173**

❹ Shacolas Tower Though it no longer offers the frisson of peering over the Green Line into

forbidden territory, the Shacolas Tower still offers fabulous views of both sides of the city. **See p.176**

❺ The Cyprus Museum By far the best museum on the island, this is a world-class attraction whose rather fusty presentation in no way detracts from its spectacular contents. **See p.179**

❻ Archbishop Makarios Centre Part of the sprawling Archbishop's Palace, the Byzantine Galleries of the Archbishop Makarios Centre are rich in colour and atmosphere. **See p.181**

❼ The Royal Tombs, Tamassos Wonderfully atmospheric burial chambers dating from the time of Homer. **See p.192**

HIGHLIGHTS ARE MARKED ON THE MAP ON P.172 & P.178

5

1821 the authorities indulged in mass executions of leading Greek citizens to discourage support for the Greek War of Independence.

In 1870 the **British** took over the island and continued with Lefkosia as capital. It was during their watch that the city finally burst out of the Venetian battlements, especially after World War II when colonial administrative offices moved outside the walls. During the fight for independence the city's **Pancyprian Gymnasium** was a hotbed of EOKA involvement and sympathy among teachers and students. While the fight against the British intensified, intercommunal violence built up to such an extent that even before the Turkish invasion of 1974, de facto **partition** was well under way, with the north of the city becoming mainly Turkish, the south mainly Greek. In 1963 the British bowed to the inevitable and made the division official – a line (in green pencil, hence the name) was drawn on the map of the city, dividing it into Greek and Turkish areas. The 1974 invasion simply confirmed the division and caused an influx of refugees from the north. As a result, there was extensive further development of the area outside the walls to house displaced Greek Cypriots.

Over the years various practical initiatives have tried to cope with the fact that the city is split in half. In 1979 a joint sewerage plan was drawn up, followed in the 1980s by the **Lefkosia Master Plan**, promoted by both the UN and the EU, under which planners from both sides have started to cooperate on such things as renovating buildings along the Green Line and pedestrianizing streets in the city centre. Much of this is based on the assumption of the eventual **reunification** of the city; and the opening of the Ledra Street crossing in 2008 has gone at least some way towards achieving this.

Ledra Street and around

Within the walls, South Lefkosia's main tourist area lies between **Ledra Street** (also known as Lidras), which runs north from the D'Avila Bastion to the checkpoint into north Cyprus (see box, p.176), and **Aischylou** which parallels it to the east. Much of this area is pedestrianized, and contains the **Laiki Geitonia** traditional quarter (where you'll find lots of bars, restaurants and small shops, together with the tourist office) with its maze of narrow streets and alleys, the **Leventis Museum**, the **Shacolas Tower**,

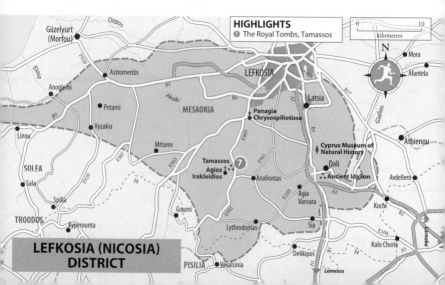

HIGHLIGHTS
7 The Royal Tombs, Tamassos

LEFKOSIA (NICOSIA) DISTRICT

5

ORIENTATION: THE CITY WALLS

The principal aid to orientation in Lefkosia is the **Venetian walls** – an aerial view of the city shows their absolutely regular star or snowflake shape punctuated by eleven bastions. What it doesn't show is the eyesore of the Buffer Zone – dilapidated buildings with boarded-up windows, barricaded streets, weeds growing everywhere – that separates South Lefkosia from the Turkish-occupied north. Taking the whole of the walled city, the Green Line cuts it into two roughly equal parts. As a general rule of thumb, most of the old city lies within the walls, which remain relatively complete, and most of the modern sprawl created by the city's expansion during British rule and then after independence lies outside. The scale of the city is such that you don't need to worry about getting around – it's easily walkable, apart from a couple of suburban sights.

---

within which is the Ledra Museum and Observatory, the **Bank of Cyprus Cultural Foundation and Museum**, and the **Faneromeni Church**. Just to the east of Aischylou is the **Cyprus Postal and Philatelic Museum**.

Laiki Geitonia

Laiki Geitonia is the focus of tourist Lefkosia. Pedestrianized during the 1980s as part of the Lefkosia Master Plan, this area to the east of Lidras Street and north of the D'Avila Bastion is a mishmash of alleys and lanes, where the tables, chairs and parasols of bars and restaurants have colonized the spaces between the buildings and racks of tourist souvenirs spill out of shops onto the pavements. This creates a veritable rabbit warren where, thankfully, given how hot Lefkosia can become, the sun barely penetrates. The area's shops, cafés and restaurants get an A for vitality, an E for value-for-money.

The Leventis Museum

15–17 Ippokratous • Tues–Sun 10am–4.30pm • Free • ☎ 22661475, ⓦ leventismuseum.org.cy

The **Leventis Museum** (one of the many projects of a foundation named after Cypriot philanthropist Anastasios Leventis) provides a brilliantly organized introduction to the history of the republic's capital. Housed in a stunning Neoclassical mansion in the heart of Laiki Geitonia, it starts with three rooms which give a broad sweep of the city's development from the earliest times. This is followed by a chronological series of galleries covering the Byzantine years, the Frankish period and so on up to the British period, and is interspersed with exhibits dealing with particular subjects (Gothic architecture for example, or maps, jewellery, pottery). Presentation is smart, up to date and effectively lit, and you're not overwhelmed with case after case of similar objects. If you're pushed for time, check out the museum's "mini guide" which promises to introduce you to all the important stuff in less than an hour. There's also a classy shop that's good for souvenirs. Photography is allowed (ask for a permit), but you mustn't use a flash.

Cyprus Postal and Philatelic Museum

Agiou Savva • Mon–Fri 9am–3pm, Sat 9am–1pm • Free • ☎ 22304711

Housed in an unassuming little building tucked away down a side street to the east of Aischylou, the **Cyprus Postal and Philatelic Museum** is surprisingly interesting, even for those who find the attractions of philately inexplicable (a school pupil wrote in the visitors' book "it is the only museum where I did not feel bored"). Although it covers postal services on the island since Venetian times, the bulk of the exhibits refer to the period of British rule, when a modern mail system was established, and the period since post independence. Brits will find some of the exhibits (the Victorian post boxes,

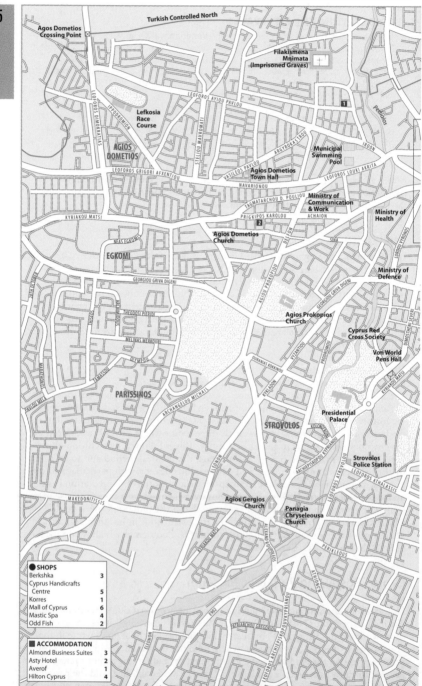

Turkish Controlled North

Agios Dometios
Crossing Point

Filakismena
Mnimata
(Imprisoned Graves)

LEOFOROS AYIOU PAVLOU

Lefkosia
Race
Course

AGIOS
DOMETIOS

Municipal
Swimming
Pool

LEOFOROS GRIGORI AFXENTIOU

Agios Dometios
Town Hall

LEOFOROS LOUKI AKRITA

NAVARIONOU

Ministry of
Communication
& Work

KYRIAKOU MATSI

PRIGKIPOS KAROLOU

ACHAION

Ministry of
Health

NEAS EGKOMIS

Agios Dometios
Church

EGKOMI

Ministry of
Defence

GEORGIOU GRIVA DIGENI

Agios Prokopios
Church

Cyprus Red
Cross Society

Von World
Pens Hall

MELINAS MERKOURI

OLYMPOU

PARISSINOS

ARCHANGELOU MICHAIL

STROVOLOS

Presidential
Palace

Strovolos
Police Station

MAKEDONITISSIS

LEOFOROS ATHALASSIS

Agios Gergios
Church

Panagia
Chryseleousa
Church

PERIKLEOUS

PATRIARCHOU GREGORIOU

● SHOPS	
Berkshka	3
Cyprus Handicrafts Centre	5
Korres	1
Mall of Cyprus	6
Mastic Spa	4
Odd Fish	2

■ ACCOMMODATION	
Almond Business Suites	3
Asty Hotel	2
Averof	1
Hilton Cyprus	4

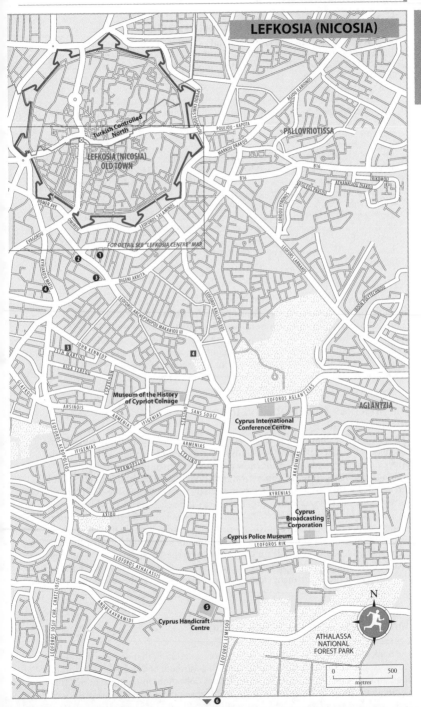

LEFKOSIA (NICOSIA)

Turkish Controlled North

PALLOVRIOTISSA

LEFKOSIA (NICOSIA) OLD TOWN

FOR DETAIL SEE "LEFKOSIA CENTRE" MAP

Museum of the History of Cypriot Coinage

AGLANTZIA

Cyprus International Conference Centre

Cyprus Broadcasting Corporation

Cyprus Police Museum

Cyprus Handicraft Centre

ATHALASSA NATIONAL FOREST PARK

N

0   500
        metres

5

VISITING THE NORTH FROM SOUTH LEFKOSIA

Three of the seven **Green Line crossing points** are in Lefkosia: two pedestrian-only ones at the Ledra Palace and Ledra Street, and one for vehicles and pedestrians at Agios Dometios. This means that Lefkosia is the best place from which visitors can get a taste of northern Cyprus while being based in the south. Red tape is minimal – if you're on foot, all you need is your passport. If you're concerned that having a TRNC stamp in your passport might cause you grief on any future visit to Greece or Cyprus, ask that a separate slip of paper be stamped rather than the passport itself. You can then use this slip for any subsequent forays into the north. The most convenient place to cross on foot into north Lefkosia is the **Ledra Street crossing** (see opposite) from where the whole of the northern part of Lefkosia can be explored on foot.

Though getting into the north by car is a little more complicated, formalities are still minimal – you'll need your passport, plus proof that you have motor insurance which is valid in the north. Some car hire companies will arrange this for you when you pick up your rental car; otherwise, you can get insurance at the border. But it still only takes a matter of minutes. The Agios Dometios crossing point is west of the city centre. It's not well signposted (this is common on both sides of the Green Line) – when driving west along Leoforos Agiou Pavlou, when the road bears sharply to the left (immediately after Lefkosia Racecourse), look out for the crossing on the right. From the Agios Dometios crossing it's no more than half an hour's drive to Kyrenia (Girne), Cyprus's most picturesque town, and to its spectacular mountain backdrop.

---

for example) very familiar. But then there are the stamps themselves, which, as well as showing what Cyprus considered worth commemorating (the great Pafos mosaics, for example, or the indigenous mouflon), are also miniature works of art in their own right. Stamps bearing portraits of President Makarios inevitably loom large and are used as a case study to illustrate "How a stamp is born". The curator (Ploutis Loizou) is happy to talk on all things stamp-related for as long as you've got, and you can of course buy packets of stamps and commemorative issues.

The Shacolas Tower Observatory

171–179 Lidras • daily 10am–6pm • €1

The eleven-storey **Shacolas Tower,** owned by multi-millionaire philanthropist Nicos Shacolas, is the tallest building in Lefkosia. Once used by Cypriots to peer over the Buffer Zone into northen Cyprus (now rendered redundant by the pedestrian crossing), the views from the tower's eleventh-floor **observatory** are still remarkable, and detailed information boards tell you precisely what you're gazing down on (you can borrow binoculars if you want a closer look). It's the best place from which to view the gigantic and inflammatory TRNC flag painted on the hillside to the north of the city. A fine aerial photo of the city provides orientation, and the whole floor is air-conditioned – that alone is worth the low price of admission. The first five floors are occupied by Debenhams, while on the sixth floor is the *Venue Cafeteria*, a good place to have a coffee while continuing to enjoy the views. Note that you can't reach the observatory via the department store – a separate entrance can be found down the side street to the right.

Bank of Cyprus Cultural Foundation

86–90 Fanoremenis Street • Daily 10am–7pm • Free • ☎ 22128157, ⓦ boccf.org

The **Bank of Cyprus Cultural Foundation** is more interesting than it sounds. Just off Lidras, to the east, it contains two museums – a **Museum of Coinage**, on the ground floor, and the **George and Nefeli Giabra Pierides Collection** on the mezzanine. The former is an elegantly mounted collection of Cypriot coins; the latter, equally well displayed, covers pottery, ceramics and sculpture from 2500 BC to the sixteenth century AD. Don't miss the hi-tech "digital archeological explorer" in the Pierdes collection where you can place an artefact on a rubber membrane and an explanation pops up on a screen. Note that while the building may be a cultural foundation, it's also a bank with a useful ATM.

Faneromeni Square

Faneromeni Square, which is worth a little wander around, lies between Lidras and Aischylou, and was the centre of pre-1974 Lefkosia. It has several buildings of passing interest. **Faneromeni Church** (7am–1pm, 3–6pm), the largest in Lefkosia, has no great pretensions to architectural or historic importance, but is notable for the marble mausoleum on its eastern side which contains the remains of the four clerics executed by the Ottoman authorities in 1821. The **Faneromeni School**, whose Neoclassical facade faces the square, was established by Archbishop Makarios I in 1852, and was the first all-girls school in Cyprus. Today it's a mixed secondary school, clearly subject to all the strains of adolescent angst (sample graffito: " x is a shallow little bitch trying to make a scene").

The Ledra Street crossing

Open since April 2008, the **Ledra Street crossing** provides pedestrian access to the north Cypriot part of the city (and indeed of the island) with the minimum of fuss. There are no formalities on the part of the republic's officials, except that you might be searched for contraband on your return. On the northern side (all of 20m beyond the southern office) you need to queue at the row of kiosks, fill in a visa form (which you keep, and have stamped as you come back across), and off you go. In the past there was considerable propagandist posturing at the crossing, but now it's all much friendlier. For example, on the southern side of the crossing a comprehensive display of photographs focuses on joint north–south ventures, such as the clearing of land mines, and police cooperation. It's all a far cry from the UN-manned barrier, boarded-up buildings, barbed wire and no-photography signs that used to be here.

Pafos Gate and around

A short walk west of Lidras, the area around the **Pafos Gate**, where the Green Line and the Venetian walls intersect, has a clutch of minor attractions, both inside and just outside the walls. The **Holy Cross Catholic Church**, the **Maronite Church** and the **Kasteliotissa Hall**, together with the **Cyprus Classic Motor Cycle Museum**, are concentrated in an area which epitomizes the depressing effects of partition – barbed wire, armed guards, no-photography signs. Just outside the walls in this uninspiring corner of the city lies one of its greatest glories – the **Cyprus Museum**, at the edge of a **Municipal Park** which also contains the **House of Representatives** and the **Municipal Theatre**. On the Pafos Gare roundabout look out for the statue of **Markos Drakos**, a hero of the War of Independence.

Holy Cross Roman Catholic Church

Not of any great interest in itself, but something of a curiosity in its location, the **Holy Cross Roman Catholic Church**, a few metres inside the Pafos Gate, has a facade in South Lefkosia, a body lying in the Buffer Zone, and a rear end that sticks out into the Turkish-controlled north. By agreement, as long as the back door in the north is kept sealed, the church is allowed to function.

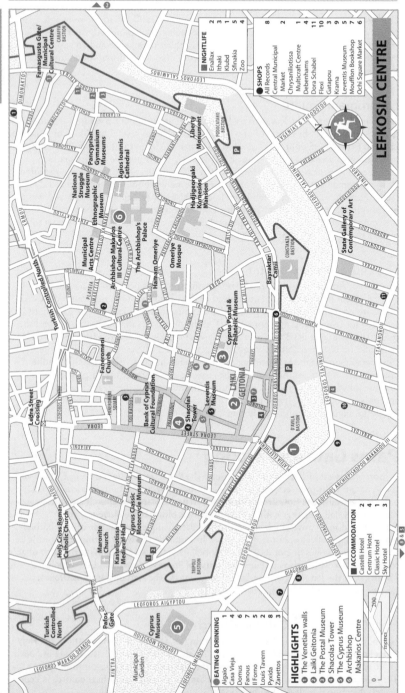

LEFKOSIA CENTRE

■ NIGHTLIFE
Enallax	2
Ithaki	3
Klubd	1
Sfinakia	5
Zoo	4

● SHOPS
All Records	8
Central Municipal Market	2
Chrysaniliotissa Multicraft Centre	1
Debenhams	4
Dora Schabel	11
Flexi	10
Gatapou	3
Krama	9
Leventis Museum	5
Moufflon Bookshop	7
Ochi Square Market	6

■ ACCOMMODATION
Castelli Hotel	2
Centrum Hotel	4
Classic Hotel	1
Sky Hotel	3

● EATING & DRINKING
Aigaio	1
Casa Vieja	4
Domus	6
Fanous	7
Il Forno	5
Louis Tavern	2
Pyxida	8
Zanettos	3

HIGHLIGHTS
❶ The Venetian walls	
❷ Laiki Geitonia	
❸ The Postal Museum	
❹ Shacolas Tower	
❺ The Cyprus Museum	
❻ Archbishop Makarios Centre	

Maronite Church

5

A hundred metres south of the Holy Cross Church stands another reminder of Cyprus's religious diversity, the **Maronite Church**. The Maronites are descendants of a Christian sect that originated in Syria and was probably brought to Cyprus between the seventh and thirteenth centuries (see ⊕maronitesofcyprus.com). Having kept their separate identity for more than a millennia and a half, they have tried to stay neutral in the struggle between the Orthodox and Muslim communities on the island. The vast majority of Maronites live in the republic.

Kasteliotissa Medieval Hall

Agiou Marona • ☎ 22800970

Across the road from the Maronite Church, the Gothic **Kasteliotissa Medieval Hall** was originally part of a Lusignan Palace dating from the thirteenth/fourteenth centuries. You can only admire it from the outside unless a concert or some other cultural event is going on inside.

Cyprus Classic Motorcycle Museum

44 Granikou • Mon–Fri 9am–1pm & 3–6pm; Sat 9am–1pm • Donation • ☎ 22680222, ⊕ argino.org/motormuseum

Established and run by a motorcycle-nut, Andreas Nicolaou, the **Classic Motorcycle Museum** is a true labour of love. Housing over 150 bikes from World War I onwards, its old-school marques are full of romance – Norton, BSA, Harley Davidson, Triumph, Motor Guzzi, Royal Enfield. Cypriot exhibits include a police bike used in President Makarios's motorcade, an EOKA bike used to transport guns and ammunition, and a World War II military bike. If you were a mod in the 1960s, the scooters will bring tears of nostalgia to your eyes. This is a real hands-on museum, with not just a gift shop but also an area selling spare parts and leathers. If you're in any doubt about its petrol-head credentials, have a look at the website which provides audio samples of, for example, "two Harley Davidson bikes going slow" or "Police motorcycle pulls away".

The Cyprus Museum

1 Mouseiou • Tues, Thurs & Fri 8am–4pm, Wed 8am–5pm, Sat 9am–4pm, Sun 10am–1pm • €3.40 • ☎ 22303112, ⊕ tinyurl.com/cyprusmuseum

Outside the walls and the Pafos Gate, at the top of Mouseiou and to the left of the Municipal Gardens, is the **Cyprus Museum**, the single most important attraction in Lefkosia. Here you'll find a trove of archeological treasures representing the many cultures which have inhabited the island. It's all slightly old-fashioned – you won't find a touch screen in sight and the collection is beginning to outgrow the current building. But the information boards tell you just enough to make sense of what you're seeing, and the labelling of cases and objects is clear and is in English as well as Greek.

The first few rooms take you through objects from earliest (Neolithic) times to the arrival of the Romans. As well as local **pottery** you can see Mycenaean, Phoenician, and Greek designs, a reflection of Cyprus's trading position between Europe and the Middle East. Highlights from rooms IV to VI include the hundreds of clay figurines and statues from the Sanctuary at Agia Irini, Egyptian and Assyrian finds, and some stunning **Greek and Roman marbles** and bronzes. Room XI, not to be missed, has the rich pickings from the **Royal Tombs of Salamis**, including an impressive, ivory-decorated bed, two thrones, a large bronze cauldron on a tripod and much else. Also from Salamis, in Room XIII, are the sculptures which came from the gymnasium, together with photographs of the excavations (pre-1974 – Salamis is now, of course, in north Cyprus, see p.238). A brief summary can't do justice to the

5

richness and variety of the exhibits on show so it's best to take your time and focus on a couple of areas. There's plenty of background material, postcards, etc, on sale in the museum shop.

East Lefkosia

The eastern side of Lefkosia has a number of sights, from the Ottoman-era **Omeriye Mosque** and baths to the magnificent **Hadjigeorgaki Kornesios House**. Further east are several attractions key to Greek Cypriot identity, concentrated on the **Archbishop's Palace**. Continuing east you come to the imposing Venetian walls and bastions that incorporate some fairly workaday buildings including the post office, public library and the Town Hall, before you reach the florid **Liberty Monument** at the Caraffa Bastion. The areas fringing the walls contain a mixture of public gardens, playing fields, and the best car park (between the D'Avila and Constanza bastions) for access to the city centre. Just outside the Constanza Bastion is the estimable **State Collection of Contemporary Art**.

Hamam Omeriye

8 Platia Tillirias • Tues–Sun 9am–9pm, Mon noon–9pm • €20 • ☎ 22750550, ⓦ hamambaths.com

Originally part of the same fourteenth-century Augustinian church as the mosque across the square (see below), the **Hamam Omeriye** (Turkish Baths) was fully renovated in 2002–04 as part of the communal Lefkosia Master Plan. It is an interesting building (with characteristic dome) but the wonderful baths themselves are currently closed. It remains to be seen if their planned opening under new management goes ahead: call ahead for information.

Omeriye Mosque

Platia Tillirias • Mon–Sat 10am–12.30pm, 1.30–3.30pm • Donations

The **Omeriye Mosque** started life as the fourteenth-century church of St Mary, an origin which is clear from the Gothic lines of its barn-like main building. It was largely destroyed during the Ottoman invasion of 1570, and rebuilt the following year as a mosque (based on the belief that the Muslim prophet Omer, who came to Cyprus in the seventh century, was buried here). It is used today by Muslim immigrants and visitors from the Middle East (disagreements between some of them, possibly Shia and Sunni, led to a violent and widely reported clash here in 2009), and can be accessed subject to the usual dress code for mosques. You can even, with permission, and if you've got a head for heights, climb the minaret for views across the city, though they're not quite as good as from the air-conditioned Shacolas Tower (see p.176). St Mary's was a favourite burial place for the Lusignan ruling class, and a number of their gravestones can be seen in Lemesos Castle.

The Municipal Arts Centre

19 Palias Ilektikis • Tues–Sat 10am–3pm & 5–11pm, Sun 10am–4pm • Free • ☎ 22797400, ⓦ nimac.org.cy

While its periodic exhibitions of contemporary art are of interest, the **Municipal Arts Centre** is also worth visiting for its extremely beguiling ambience. It has a library (10am–2.30pm & 5–8pm), a superb restaurant (the *Old Power House*) with airy room and courtyard alfresco dining, and the Guerrilla Shop (same hours as the centre). The centre, located since 1994 in the old power house of the Electricity Authority and partly financed by the Pierides Foundation, stands beyond an extensive archeological dig north of Platia Tillirias along Peiraios.

Hadjigeorgakis Kornesios Mansion

5

20 Patriarchou Grigoriou • Tues, Thurs, Fri 8.30am–3.30pm, Wed 8.30am–5pm, Sat 9.30am–3.30pm • €1.70 • ☎ 22305316

The **Hadjigeorgakis Kornesios Mansion**, a short walk east along Patrarchou Grigoriou from Platias Tillirias, is a wonderful old house, once the property of a famous eighteenth-century "dragoman" or representative of the Greek Cypriot community in its dealings with the Ottomans (see box below). Although billed as the "Ethnographic Museum" its actual contents are really not of much interest, and it shouldn't be confused with the "Ethnographical Museum" marked on the CTO map next to the Archbishop's Palace (on the ground, the latter is actually called the "Folk Art Museum"). But the airy architecture, the shady arches and courtyard, the covered stairway, the huge rooms with flagstone floors, and in particular the large sitting room with large rug, low-cushioned seating on three sides and central hubble-bubble pipe give a feeling of how the Ottoman elite and their Greek administrators lived.

The Archbishop's Palace

Five minutes' walk north of the Hadjigeorgaki Kornesios Mansion stands a rather grand complex of buildings centred on the **Archbishop's Palace** (closed to visitors). Built in the early 1960s to celebrate independence and rebuilt in the 1980s following virtual destruction during the 1974 Nikos Samson coup, it seems to be modelled for no good reason on a Venetian palace. It does, however, give a sense of spaciousness that is missing in much of the rest of the city. Until 2008 a gargantuan **statue** of Archbishop Makarios III stood before the palace, but it was moved (perhaps as a result of negative comments about its artistic merit, or as an attempt to signal a willingness to consider reconciliation) and now overlooks the car park at Makarios's tomb (see p.158). The two busts which remain in front of the palace are those of archbishops Kyprianos and Sopronios – the former was executed, together with over four hundred prominent Greek Cypriots, by the Turks in 1821, the latter was in office when the British took over the island, and was the first to articulate the demand for enosis or union with Greece.

The Archbishop Makarios III Cultural Centre

Plateia Archiepiskopou Kyprianou • Mon–Fri 9am–4.30pm, Sat 9am–1pm • €1.70 • ☎ 22430008

In the northwest wing of the palace is the **Archbishop Makarios III Cultural Centre**, which, apart from a library and a church music school, houses the impressive **Byzantine Museum and Art Gallery**. This contains the largest collection of icons in Cyprus (the second largest in the world), and includes, in a separate annexe, the famous **Kanakaria Mosaics**, infamously stolen from the church of Panagia Kanakaria in north Cyprus in the late 1970s (see box, p.246). Vividly coloured, if a little rough in the execution, the occasional sense of distorted perspective is is explained by the fact that originally they were mounted on the curved apse of the church, whereas here they are mounted flat. Elsewhere in the museum are 150 icons and numerous frescoes from all over Cyprus and beyond.

THE GREAT DRAGOMAN

Hadjigeorgakis Kornesios was the Great Dragoman of Cyprus from 1779 until 1804. Although the word "dragoman" simply means "interpreter or guide" the Great Dragoman wielded considerable political clout, being the main link between Greek Orthodox subjects and Ottoman authorities. One of the principal responsibilities was the collection of taxes. By creaming off his own cut, being personally tax-exempt and amassing large estates, Kornesios became the richest man on the island. But his comeuppance arrived in 1804 when a revolt against the authorities drove him and his family to seek asylum in Constantinople. From there, he organized troops to put the rebellion down. When he returned to the island, further political skulduggery led to his downfall. He was called back to Constantinople, found guilty of embezzlement and maladministration, and beheaded.

5

Agios Ioannis Cathedral

Plateia Archiepiskopou Kyprianou • Mon–Fri 8am–noon, 2pm–4pm; Sat 8am–noon • Free

Within the Archbishop's Palace precinct is the church of **Agios Ioannis**, which doubles as the city's cathedral. In its scale and simplicity it seems to put to shame the extravagant architecture of the palace itself. Built in 1662 on the site of a previous Lusignan Benedictine abbey, it wasn't actually promoted to cathedral status until 1720. The interior is as splendid as its exterior is modest, boasting an original set of frescoes (including one of the finding of St Barnanas's tomb in Salamis), a carved and gold-leaf adorned iconostasis and four large icons, all dating from the eighteenth century. The cathedral contains the throne on which the archbishop is crowned, together with seating for the president and the Greek ambassador to be used on state occasions.

The Ethnographic Museum

Plateia Archiepiskopou Kyprianou • Mon–Fri 9am–5pm, Sat 11am–1pm • €1.70 • ☎ 22432578

Once called the Cyprus Folk Art Museum (and still named as such on the sign outside) the **Ethnographic Museum** is housed in a mellow galleried and colonnaded two-storey building which originates from as far back as the fifteenth century (though with many additions); it's right next to the cathedral. Displays include a wide range of Cypriot folk art and decoration from the nineteenth and early twentieth centuries – carved wood and leatherwork, metalwork, lace, tapestry and embroidery, basketry, woven fabrics, pottery and regional costume, and rustic art. Outside the museum are some giant *pithoi* (earthenware jars), a millstone, and a two-wheeled wagon.

The National Struggle Museum

Agiou Ioannou • Mon–Fri 8am–2pm, 3–5pm • Free • ☎ 22304550

In a newish building next to the Ethnographic Museum is the **National Struggle Museum**, dedicated to those who fought for independence from the British during the period 1955 to 1959, and to highlighting the brutality of the oppressors. As such it can make for an uncomfortable half-hour for the UK visitor. Items on display include photographs of British soldiers searching old women and schoolchildren, the personal belongings of EOKA fighters (including leader Grivas), weaponry, details of torture methods used by the British authorities, full-sized mock-ups of a guerrilla hideout and a prison cell (containing a fighter awaiting execution), plus the gallows used to execute nine men in Lefkosia's central prison in 1956 (see p.185). English labelling is patchy, but this really doesn't matter – the museum's displays rely on visual impact to get their message across.

The Pancyprian Gymnasium

Agiou Ioannou • Mon, Tues & Thurs, Fri 8am–2pm, Wed 8am–2pm & 3–5.30pm • Free • ☎ 22466014

Across the road from the National Struggle Museum stands the imposing edifice of the **Pancyprian Gymnasium**, a secondary school which has had a huge influence on Cypriot history. Established in 1812 by Archbishop Kyprianos, it has educated generations of prominent Cypriots – both Grivas and Makarios attended (at different times), and other illustrious alumni include former presidents Tassos Papadopoulos and Grafkos Clerides. English author Lawrence Durrell taught here in the 1950s, when the school was beginning to earn a reputation as a hotbed of EOKA membership. It is still a functioning secondary school, with no entry for casual visitors. However, there is a **museum** (or museums) signposted to the left of the main school building, which consists of some twelve rooms displaying a hotch-potch of archeological finds, coins, natural history and a huge Gothic sculpture. One gallery displays paintings by staff and pupils of the school.

5

The Famasgusta Gate

Athina Avenue • Mon–Fri 9am–1pm & 4–7pm • Free • ☎ 22430877

Northeast of the group of buildings around the Archbishop's Palace, next to the Caraffa Bastion, stands the squat, solid and well-preserved **Famagusta Gate**, the best-preserved of Lefkosia's Venetian gates. Constructed by Guilio Savorgnano in 1567 and an approximate copy of one in Iraklion in Crete, it has now, after a long period of neglect, been tidied up, and is used as a venue for concerts and as an exhibition space. The building consists of an inner and outer gate, joined by a long passageway or tunnel with, about halfway along, a cupola to admit natural light. During the long Ottoman occupation which immediately followed its construction only Muslims were allowed through the gate on horseback – everybody else had to walk – and the gates were locked on Fridays. Following renovation in the 1980s, the gate building has been used as a venue for exhibitions.

The Liberty Monument

Dominating the Podocataro Bastion is the **Liberty Monument**, erected in 1973 to commemorate the release of EOKA prisoners in 1959 in preparation for independence. A female statue representing Liberty stands above two EOKA fighters hauling on chains to open the prison gates below, out of which stream figures representing Cypriot fighters, civilians and clergy. The triumphalism of the statue was rather overtaken by the events of the year following its construction, and it's now considered a bit of an embarrassment by many Greek Cypriots.

Bayraktar Camii

On the Constanza Bastion stands the **Bayraktar Camii** – "the Mosque of the Standard Bearer", which throws light on two separate eras in the capital's history. The mosque was built where a soldier bearing the Ottoman colours was killed by defenders (and subsequently buried), having clambered up onto the bastion during the 1570 siege. The mosque and tomb figured in the intercommunal violence that followed independence in 1960 – bombs in 1962 and 1963 damaged the building. The assumption was that these were EOKA atrocities, but it has since been established that they were carried out by Turkish Cypriot agents provocateurs. The mosque precincts are now kept locked, to prevent any further trouble.

The State Gallery of Contemporary Art

Leoforos Stasinou and Kritis • Mon–Fri 10am–4.45pm, Sat 10am–12.45pm • Free • ☎ 22458228

Next to the Constanza Bastion, but outside the walls, stands the **State Gallery of Contemporary Art**. Its interestingly convoluted Neoclassical building houses a collection of paintings and sculptures by twentieth-century Cypriot artists. There are also one or two modern art pieces in the grounds. It's worth a visit for both building and content.

The suburbs

Most of the things that are worth seeing in the capital are inside or just outside its Venetian walls, and within walking distance of each other. However, the city suburbs also merit a visit – the area of Strovolos, for example, wasn't established until 1986, yet is now almost as big as Lemesos. Dotted around these recently developed outskirts are a number of attractions worth visiting, but realistically you'll need a car or taxi to get around.

THE LEFKOSIA MASTER PLAN

Ever since the Turkish invasion of 1974 and the partition of the island peace plans have foundered on the opposition of one or other of the communities. However, behind the scenes, a number of initiatives have gone ahead, involving north–south cooperation. The best example of this is the Lefkosia Master Plan. Beginning with a distinctly pragamatic agreement for the construction of a common sewerage system in 1978 it quickly flowered into a more general agreement on a development plan for Lefkosia. In 1981 a "bi-communal multidisciplinary team" was set up to further the plan. Efforts were concentrated on the old city contained within the walls. Neighbourhoods on both sides of the Green Line were designated for restoration, shopping and artisan zones identified and traffic improved. A start was even made on rescuing the many imposing buildings stuck in the Buffer Zone, which have been decaying for nearly forty years. Though the Lefkosia Master Plan has concentrated on a clutch of practical initiatives, it implies that reunification is, in the long term, the only sensible solution for both the city and the island.

Filakismena Mnimata (The Imprisoned Graves)

8am–1pm Mon–Fri • ask at the gate • Free

West of central Lefkosia stands the city's grim Central Prison, somewhere most visitors to Cyprus (and indeed Cypriots) would wish to avoid. However, within its confines are the **Filakismena Mnimata** or "Imprisoned Graves". In a small patch of land, next to what had been cells and gallows, are buried thirteen Greek Cypriot fighters – nine (all aged between 19 and 24) hanged by the British between May 1956 and March 1957, four who died during or shortly after fire fights with the British Army. The latter includes Gregoris Afxentiou, Grivas's second-in-command (see box, p.167). In order to prevent the funerals of these men, widely considered by Greek Cypriots to be martyrs, to become the focus of demonstrations and riots, their bodies were hurriedly buried in secret in the depths of the prison. Since independence, the "Imprisoned Graves" have become a place of pilgrimage for Greek Cypriots, particularly the young.

Von World Pens Hall

37 Demostheni Severi Avenue • ☎ 22463204

Von World Pens Hall, on the road out to the Presidential Palace, is housed in a delightful if dishevelled Art Deco building which is not easy to find – if you reach the new EKO filling station, you've gone too far. The museum covers pens from all the world's great manufacturers, and includes dip pens, special edition pens, and Victorian pencils, with examples from all the world's greatest manufacturers, from Mont Blanc to Waterman, Sheaffer to Conklin. It also has a small shop and, on the roof, a club for enthusiasts. However, at the time of writing the museum was closed, and looked distinctly down-at-heel.

The Museum of the History of Cypriot Coinage

80 Kennedy Avenue • Mon–Fri 7.30am–2.30pm • Free • ☎ 22714100, ⓦ eshop.centralbank.gov.cy

The **Museum of the History of Cypriot Coinage**, though widely advertised in Lefkosia's tourist literature, is in fact rarely visited. A display put together to celebrate Cyprus's adoption of the euro, it is lodged in the basement of the Central Bank of Cyprus. There's ample parking, and if you announce yourself at the main entrance, you'll be given a temporary badge by security staff and asked to wait until they're able to track down somebody to show you around. The emphasis is on modern coinage so it'll help if you're something of a numismatist – those more interested in ancient coins would be better off visiting the Coin Museum in the Bank of Cyprus Cultural Foundation (see p.176). Collector's issues can be bought via the bank's online shop.

5

The Cyprus Police Museum

Evangelou Floraki • Mon–Fri 8am–2pm • Free • ☎ 22808793, ⊕ police.gov.cy

Just east of, and visible from, the main road (Leoforos Lemesou) into Lefkosia from the motorway, is one of those small specialist museums that can be an absolute delight. The **Cyprus Police Museum** is housed in a clean white building with appropriate blue trim which sits inside the main police HQ. You approach from Evangelou Floraki, a small street which runs parallel to the main road – if you can't find the way in, ask at the main gate and they'll give you directions. When you get to the entrance, just ring the bell. The museum was founded by the British in 1933 as the "Criminal Museum", and was seen as the Cypriot equivalent of the Metropolitan Police's famous "Black Museum". After independence, it moved around, eventually settling in its current building in 2004. It includes all the sort of stuff you'd expect, from badges, truncheons, helmets, guns, riot shields and uniforms up to motorcycles, Black Marias and armoured cars, and some that you wouldn't – for example, a room full of musical instruments. If you're lucky the curator – a serving officer and very knowledgeable – will show you around.

Cyprus Handicraft Centre

186 Athalassa Avenue • Mon, Tues & Thurs, Fri 7.30am–5.30pm, Wed 7.30am–1pm, Sat 9am–1pm • Free • ☎ 22305024 • Bus #16; free parking

About 500m south of the Police Museum, but off the opposite side of Leoforos Lemesou (it's well signposted off the main road), is the **Cyprus Handicraft Service** complex, consisting of a range of workshops turning out craft items using traditional methods. Established by the Ministry of Commerce, Industry and Tourism with the support of the UN Refugee Agency, it represents a determined attempt to revive traditional folk art. In a low-key modern building laid out around a shady central garden, craftspeople can be seen hard at work producing clothes, leatherwork, woodwork, basketry, metalwork, pottery, tapestry and embroidery. You can chat to the workers, buy quality-assured items without fear of being ripped off, and feel that you are supporting a worthwhile enterprise. This is the flagship of other such schemes across the island (for example in Larnaka, Lemesos and Pafos), and you'll find plenty of information on Cypriot crafts, such as the traditional pottery of Fini, or Lefkara lace.

Athalassa National Forest Park

Daily 8am–sunset • Free • ☎ 22805533

Some 2.5km due east of the Cyprus Handicraft Centre and the Police Museum, and again well signposted from Leoforos Lemesou, **Athalassa National Forest Park** represents an invaluable open space only 2km from the city centre. There are two picnic areas, footpaths, bicycle tracks, a children's playground, a kiosk and ample free parking. There's also an Environmental Information Centre, a bird observation point overlooking the Athalassa Dam and a botanical garden. A smaller park-within-the-park, **Agios Georgios**, with its pretty lake and footpath which is lit at night, is particularly charming – you'll find it and all the facilities on the detailed map in the car park.

ARRIVAL AND DEPARTURE   LEFKOSIA

By plane The nearest international airport to Lefkosia is Larnaka (Nicosia Airport, closed in 1974, now languishes in the UN Buffer Zone). A regular shuttle bus runs from Larnaka Airport to the *Philoxenia Hotel* in Lefkosia roughly every hour (€8; journey time 50min). The *Philoxenia* is in

the suburbs so you'll most likely need a taxi from there into town (there's a rank nearby).

By bus Intercity buses run from to and from Lefkosia from all the republic's main towns. From the bus station in Solomos Square there are services to Finikoudes in Larnaka

5

(hourly; 1hr), the New Port in Lemesos (hourly; 1hr 45min) and Karavella in Pafos (5 daily; 2hr).

By car You're likely to approach the city from the south on the A1 motorway or from the west on the A9. Either way, you will find yourself in a fast one-way system for which your main orientation aid will be the Venetian walls. The most useful car park is the one between the D'Avila and Constanza Bastions, from where there's direct access from up a flight of steps to the main tourist area of the city. Parking is cheap, starting at €1.50 for 2 hours then increasing by €0.50 for each additional hour.

By shared taxi A shared taxi service (☎ 77777474) links Lefkosia and Larnaka (€8.20-one way) and Lefkosia and Lemesos (€10.90). Fares are slightly higher on Sundays.

GETTING AROUND

On foot Lefkosia is small enough for you to explore the main city, within the walls, on foot. Walking is also the best way to access North Lefkosia (see p.176).

By bus Bus services throughout Lefkosia and the surrounding district are provided by OSEL (🖥 osel.com.cy) from their terminus on Solomos Square.

INFORMATION AND TOURS

Tourist office 11 Aristokyprou ☎ 22674264. Located deep within labyrinthine Laiki Geitonia, the tourist office is nevertheless well-signposted and easy to find (Mon–Fri 10am–1pm & 4–7pm, Sat 10am–1pm). They offer a range of free walking tours of the city departing Mon & Thurs at 10am.

Tours For trips further afield try Aeolos Sightseeing Tours (☎ 22881222, 🖥 www.aioloscyprusexcursions .com) at 6 Zenas Kanther, Elpis Travel and Tours (☎ 22353401, 🖥 elpistravel.com) at 39 Elia Papakyriakou, or Tamasos Tours (☎ 22762683, 🖥 tamasostours.com.cy) at 30a Chytron.

ACTIVITIES

Basketball and squash Eleftheria Indoor Hall Makariou Athletic Centre Avenue, Engomi. Home to the Cyprus National Basketball team, with facilities also for badminton, gymnastics, volleyball, squash and much else. Also used as a venue for concerts.

Bowling Kykko Bowling, Theodosi Pieridi Egkomi ☎ 22350085. Ten-pin bowling, with the usual fast-food accompaniment.

Horse racing Lefkosia Race Club Agios Dometios ☎ 22782727, 🖥 www.nicosiaraceclub.com.cy. Horse racing and betting Wed & Fri in summer, Wed & Sun in winter.

Swimming Lefkosia Public Swimming Pool 4 Loukis Akritas Avenue, Agios Andreas ☎ 22771544. Olympic-sized outdoor pool open during the summer months (May–Sept).

LEFKOSIA FESTIVALS

MARCH

Lefkosia International Documentary Film Festival 🖥 cyprusdocfest.org. Documentary films from around the world, shown at the Melina Merkouri Hall.

APRIL

Ledra Music Soloists International Festival Two-week festival of chamber music held at the PASYDY Auditorium.

JULY

International Festival of Ancient Greek Drama (🖥 cyprus-theatre-iti.org) Held in Lefkosia, Lemesos and Pafos.

AUGUST

Pharos International Contemporary Music Festival (August/September; 🖥 pharosartsfoundation.org) Twentieth-and twenty-first century avant-garde music at the Shoe Factory and the Olive Grove.

SEPTEMBER

Ice Cream Festival Free ice creams and entertainment at the Famagusta Gate Moat.

Septemberfest Beer festival held at the Constanza Bastion. As well as a good range of ales there's music and dance, plus children's events.

OCTOBER

Cyprus International Film Festival (🖥 cyprusfilmfestival.com) Established film festival with screenings followed by Q&A sessions with directors.

NOVEMBER

Rainbow Festival International music and dance. Festival run by Action for Equality, Support and Antiracism. Also held in Lasnaka and Pafos.

5

ACCOMMODATION

Hotels in Lefkosia are mainly aimed at business customers – despite the city's many attractions, visitors tend to come in for the day rather than to stay over. If you're travelling by car, it's better to avoid the hotels within the walls – parking can be a problem.

OLD CITY

Castelli Hotel 38 Ouzounian ☎ 22712812, ✉ reservations@kennedy-hotels.com. The *Castelli Hotel* has a useful location tucked into the southwest corner of South Lefkosia, within a 5min walk of Ledra Street. Part of the *Holiday Inn* chain, customers can use some of the much more expensive mother ship's facilities just along the street. The hotel is beginning to look a little worn, and it can be noisy on lower floors (however, the higher up you go, the weaker the free wi-fi). **€150**

Centrum Hotel 15 Pasikratous ☎ 22456444, ⓦ centrumhotelcyprus.com. The clue to this hotel's USP is in the name – it's bang in the centre of the Laiki Geitonia district within easy walking distance of shops, restaurants and sights. This, of course, has its drawbacks – it can be noisy into the small hours. Partly occupying a nineteenth-century mansion, its recently renovated rooms are modern and comfortable, though standard rooms can seem a little cramped. There are coffee and tea-making facilities (not always the case in Cyprus), and the mini-fridge can come in handy on hot days. **€115**

Classic Hotel 94 Rigenis ☎ 22664006, ⓦ classic.com.cy. In the same corner of the city as the *Castelli*, the *Classic* offers a good range of in-room and hotel facilities aimed at business customers. It is less suited to families with children. Facilities include a rooftop gym and spa, a café/bar and restaurant, and, (oddly) an art gallery. **€105**

★ **Sky Hotel** 7c Solonos Street ☎ 22666880, ⓦ skyhotel.ws. A good-value choice in the heart of Laiki Geitonia. You won't find luxurious fixtures and fittings, and it can get noisy, but its perfectly comfortable and its restaurant (*Fanous*) is Lebanese/Arabian, which adds interest. **€72**

OUTSIDE THE WALLS

Almond Business Suites 25 March St, Agios Omologites ☎ 22879131, ⓦ almond-businesshotel.com. Although intended largely for business people – it's located in an area which contains the bulk of government offices, embassies and consulates – it is also an attractive alternative for other types of traveller. Suites are top-end regarding comfort, all include a well-equipped kitchenette, and decor is cool and modern. Despite being away from the city centre, there are plenty of shops and restaurants within walking distance. **€130**

★ **Asty Hotel** 12 Prince Charles St, Agios Dometios ☎ 27773030, ⓦ astyhotel.com. Located in a quiet residential area to the west of the city centre, the recently renovated *Asty* is, for a city hotel, family-friendly, with a children's play area, mini-golf, a pool table, games room and babysitting services. Rooms are clean and comfortable, wi-fi is free, and the hotel is just a 5min drive from the Agios Dometios crossing point into North Cyprus. **€130**

Averof 19 Averof St, Agios Andreas ☎ 22773447, ⓦ www.averof.com.cy. Plus points for the *Averof* are that it's in a quiet residential area yet only a 10min walk from the Venetian walls, its staff are friendly and helpful, and its rates are rock bottom for a hotel in the capital. Currently, its downsides are the lack of a restaurant (though it has a supply of takeaway menus and an area in which you can eat your own food), a fairly minimal bar, and dated decor. After a recent change of hands, renovation is planned, so check the website before visiting. Like the *Asty*, a 5min drive from the Agios Dometios crossing place into the north. **€65**

Hilton Cyprus Archiepiskopou Makariou III ☎ 22377777, ⓦ hilton.com. The only five-star hotel in Lefkosia, the *Hilton* is hard to miss on the main approach from the motorway. Though it claims to be within walking distance of the city centre, it's a fair slog, though buses are frequent. There are some facilities which you might not expect in a city hotel – outdoor pool, tennis court – and if you're overlooking the pool, you could almost believe you're in a resort rather than the capital. A word of warning – bar prices are eye-watering. **€220**

EATING AND DRINKING

Aerikon 86–90 Faneromenis ☎ 99641244. Above the Bank of Cyprus Cultural Foundation (there's a sign leading to it just outside), the *Aerikon* is a café/bar as well as a restaurant offering good Greek Cypriot food (the lamb, pork and chicken meze is excellent) and great city views from a cool (in both senses of the word) terrace. Daily 10am–midnight.

Aigaio 40 Ektoros ☎ 22433297. Classy Greek Cypriot restaurant in the old city with an open-air courtyard that often hosts live traditional music. It's good for a treat (allow around €17 for meze) and has an excellent wine list. Popular, so you'll need to book a table. Mon–Sat 7pm–1pm.

Casa Vieja 3 Archangelou Michael ☎ 22673371, ⓦ casaviega.com. Smart tapas bar with three dining areas plus patio. Choose from, at the last count, nearly forty tapas dishes and four types of paella. Most dishes between €4 and €9 (paellas €10–14), with wines from around €15. Warm in winter, cool in summer, and with excellent service. Daily 7.30–11.30pm.

★ **Domus** 5 Korae ☎ 22433722, ⊛ domusloungebar .com. Fine dining restaurant with attached lounge (or vice versa) in a rather sedate old building in the area of the city around the Archbishop's Palace. Slightly self-conscious decor in the lounge with lots of wood and arty photographs, cooler and classier in the restaurant and its attached bar. Reservations necessary for restaurant meals, though there is a bar menu in the lounge. Main courses €18–30. Daily 8pm–2am.

★ **Fanous** 7c Solonos ☎ 22666663, ⊛ fanous.eu. Lebanese-style restaurant attached to the *Sky Hotel*. You can't miss it – cane tables, chairs and sofas spill out onto and across the alley next to the hotel entrance, where customers smoke hookahs (or *narghiles*), giving the whole place a really Middle Eastern atmosphere. With its long opening hours, it's as good for a quick coffee and a cake as for as full meal (meze €15). You can buy *narghiles*, tobacco and much else in the *Fanous* shop, and on Saturdays enjoy belly dancing (watching, not doing). Daily 11am–midnight.

Il Forno 216–218 Ledra St ☎ 22456454. Does what the best Italian restaurants do so well – provide comfort food in a warm, busy atmosphere. There's quality pasta and pizza as well as all the staple main courses, and delicious sweets. Not for calorie-counters. Overflows onto Ledra Street in the summer, and is always busy – better book a table. Main courses €9–11. Daily 11.30am–11pm.

Le Café Archiepiskopou Makariou III ☎ 22466566. One of the most fashionable cafés in the capital, with a busy outdoor terrace and a stylishly designed interior. Great coffee. Daily 9.30am–2am

★ **Louis Tavern** 84 Agiou Andreou, Pallouriotissa ☎ 22345881. Highly rated family-run restaurant east of the city centre. Good grilled meat and fish in convivial surroundings, and a cosy atmosphere (some online reviews go over the top for what is a solid but not outstanding restaurant). Main courses from €10. Daily 7–11pm.

Old Power House Restaurant Palia Elektriki ☎ 22432559. Attached to the cultural centre next door, this sophisticated restaurant serves a mixture of Cypriot (especially grills) and more eclectic meals (main courses around €10–20) in what was once the Nicosia Electricity Authority building. If you can get a table, try to eat in the leafy courtyard. Tues–Sat 11am–2.30pm & 7pm–midnight; Sun 11am–3pm.

★ **Pyxida** 5 Menandrou Street ☎ 22445636, ⊛ pyxidafishtavern.com. Popular fish restaurant offering a 19-dish seafood meze and mains featuring everything from swordfish to sardines (mains from €12). A big patio offers formal alfresco dining, and the interior decoration is suitably nautical. Southwest of the old town, out beyond the Cyprus Museum. Popular, so you'll need to reserve a table. Daily 12.30–3pm & 7.30–11pm.

Zanettos 65 Trikoupis ☎ 22765501, ⊛ zanettos.com. *Zanettos* has been going since 1938, so it's obviously doing something right, particularly its traditional meze, washed down with lashings of wine. Not easy to find (it's just west of the Omeriye Mosque and Hamam), but everybody knows where it is, and it is heavily patronized by locals. Main from around €9. Daily 6pm–midnight.

NIGHTLIFE

More than in any other large Cypriot town, Lefkosia's nightlife is largely for local youth rather than for visiting holiday-makers. There are lots of bars, pubs and clubs, many contained inside the old town, others along the inner and outer ring roads that follow the walls.

Enallax 16–17 Athinas Avenue ☎ 22430121. At the eastern edge of the walled city, near the Famagusta Gate *Enallax* concentrates on live and recorded Greek music (Thurs & Sat) with rock on Fri. Thurs–Sat, usually from 11pm.

Ithaki 33 Nikiforou Foka ☎ 22434193, ⊛ ithakivenue .com. South of the Famagusta Gate. Indoor venue with outdoor area open during the summer. Latin, rock, theme nights. Wed–Sat. Student night Wed.

★ **Klubd** 33 Ammochostou ⊛ klubd.net. Near the Famagusta Gate (close to *Enallax* above), this is perhaps the most sophisticated club on the island – the main room glories in a "sky" made up of tiny LEDs. Techno with minimalist industrial decor. International DJs sometimes feature. Fri & Sat midnight–4am.

New Division 2 Vasilissis Frederikis ☎ 22679957. Laid-back and down-to-earth rock bar with the atmosphere of a students' union. Mon–Sat 5pm–2am, Sun 9.30pm–2am.

Sfinakia 1 Kyriakou Matsi Avenue ☎ 2276666110. Popular Greek dance/house club with rooftop access during summer. When crowded, a (bookable) table or couch is a plus. You'll find it in the Gabrielides Building, where Spyrou Kyprianou and Themistocle Dervi cross. Wed–Sun 11pm–4am.

Versus 2 Archiepiskopou Makariou III, Capital Centre 3rd floor ☎ 99393009. Just south of the D'Avila Bastion. Top-end light and sound systems, progressive, house, dance, some live music. Wed–Sat 11.30pm–late.

★ **Zoo** 15 Stasinou Avenue ☎ 22458811. East of *Versus*, and popular with the younger clubbing crowd, the *Zoo* has a bar on the ground floor (and serves food), with the dancefloor upstairs. International and Greek music, super views of the city. Lounge Bar Wed & Thurs 9pm–2am, Fri & Sat 9pm–3am; Club 11pm–3am Fri & Sat (though start time varies according to what's on).

5

SHOPPING

Lefkosia offers the closest you'll get to big-city shopping in Cyprus. Apart from the usual souvenirs (leather goods, textiles, jewellery, wines and spirits, lace), you'll find plenty of designer shops and a number of modern shopping malls. Two areas are particularly worth concentrating on: the streets either side of Ledra Street, and the area outside the walls to the southwest, on either side of Archiepiskopou Makariou III and Diagorou/Themistocle Dervi. Look out also for Stasikratous, the smartest and most stylish street in the city, which runs between the two. This is the area which contains the Louis Vuitton, Versace and Gucci stores. For fruit and vegetables, head for the Central Market.

BOOKS

Moufflon Bookshop 3 Sofouli ☎ 22665155. Good general bookshop with extensive English-language section. All aspects of Cypriot life and history well covered. Mon, Tues, Thurs & Fri 9.30am–7pm; Wed 9.30am–2pm, Sat 9.30am–3pm.

CLOTHES, SHOES AND ACCESSORIES

Bershka 48B Archiepiskopou Makariou III ☎ 22763434, ⓦ bershka.com. Stylish clothes for teens and young adults at affordable prices in eye-catching surroundings. Another brand from the Spanish Zara/Massimo Dutti group. Mon, Tues, Thurs & Fri 9am–8pm, Wed 9am–2.30pm, Sat 9.30am–7.30pm.

Dora Schabel 14B Electras ☎ 22757740. Quality leather shop selling a variety of bags and accessories in way-out modern styles and unconventional leathers – python, ostrich, even fish-skins – some featuring national flag designs. Mon–Fri 9am–6pm, Sat 10am–2pm.

★ **Flexi** 23 Aphrodites ☎ 22767003. Specialist boutique which carries ranges by a number of Cypriot designers who have an international reputation, among them Joanna Louca and Elena Pavlou. Mon, Tues, Thurs & Fri 10am–7pm, Wed 10am–1.30pm, Sat 10am–2.30pm.

Krama 3E Arnaldas ☎ 22761655. Original designs of necklaces, bracelets, rings and earrings in silver and gold by local designer Skevi Afantiti (ⓦ skeviafantiti.com). June–Aug Mon, Tues, Thurs & Fri 9.30am–1pm & 5–8pm, Wed 9.30am–1.30pm, Sat 10am–1.30pm; Feb–May Mon, Tues, Thurs & Fri 9.30am–1pm & 3–6pm, Wed & Sat 10am–1pm.

Odd Fish 11K Mnasiadou ☎ 22660181. Clothes, shoes, bags and accessories – a one-stop shop with lines from Europe and South America. Mon, Tues, Thurs & Fri 9.30am–1.30pm & 3–6.30pm, Wed 9.30am–1.30pm, Sat 9.30am–2.30pm.

CRAFTS, GIFTS AND SOUVENIRS

★ **Chrysaniliotissa Multicraft Centre** 2 Dimonaktos ☎ 22347465. Human-scale little arts and crafts centre, with eight workshops and a coffee shop facing a central courtyard. Mon–Fri 10am–1pm & 3–6pm, Sat 10am–1pm.

★ **Cyprus Handicrafts Service** 186 Athalassa Avenue ☎ 22305024. Tat-free source of genuine Cypriot craft items (see p.186). Mon, Tues, Thurs & Fri 7.30am–5.30pm, Wed 7.30am–1pm, Sat 9am–1pm.

Gatapou Stoa Georgiou Papadopoulou ☎ 22667741. This shop overflows with ornaments, bookmarks, greetings cards, coasters, key-rings, dress jewellery, photograph frames and more. If efforts to find suitable gifts have come to naught, this is the place to go. Mon–Tues, Thurs–Fri 11am–2pm & 4–7.30pm, Wed 4–7.30pm, Sat 11am–4pm.

★ **Leventis Museum** 15–17 Hippocrates Stree, Laiki Yitonia ☎ 22661475, ⓦ leventismuseum.org.cy. The attached shop to one of Cyprus's best museums, selling quality replicas of pottery, jewellery and other items from the collection – ideal for gifts. Tues–Sun 10am–4.30pm.

HEALTH AND BEAUTY

Korres Galaxias Centre, 33 Archiepiskopou Makariou III ☎ 22375730. Natural beauty products from Greek skincare brand Korres (usually only available at Liberty and House of Fraser in the UK).

Mastic Spa 9D Themistocle Dervi ☎ 22667771. Beauty products based on (the clue's in the name) mastic (the gum from the mastic tree). Clearly all the rage – another shop (Mastiha) across the road offers a similar range. Mon, Tues, Thurs & Fri 9.30am–7pm, Wed & Sat 9.30am–2pm.

MALLS AND DEPARTMENT STORES

Debenhams 171–179 Ledra St ☎ 22679369. One of ten department stores in Cyprus identical to the UK Debenhams chain though run by Cypriot company Ermes/Shacolas. Offers the usual mix of fashion, lingerie, accessories, cosmetics and homeware. This is the main branch which also incorporates the Shacolas Tower (see p.176); there are two more stores on Archiepiskopou Makariou III. Mon, Tues, Thurs & Fri 9am–8pm, Wed 9am–3pm, Sat 9am–7.30pm.

Mall of Cyprus Shacolas Emporium Park, 3 Verginas St ☎ 77776255, ⓦ themallofcyprus.com. Large shopping mall just east of (and well signposted from) the A1 motorway south of the city. You'll find everything from Accessorize to Zara here (as well as yet another Debenhams) plus a Carrefour supermarket, a five-screen cinema and a food hall and ample parking. April–Oct Mon, Tues, Thurs

& Fri 9am–8pm, Wed 9am–3pm, Sat 9am–7.30pm; Nov–March Mon, Tues, Thurs & Fri 9am–7.30pm, Wed 9am–3pm, Sat 9am–7pm.

MARKETS

Central Municipal Market Diogenous. Rather bleak concrete covered market selling fruit and veg, nuts, honey, fish. Mon, Tues, Thurs & Fri 6am–3pm.

Ochi Square Constanza Bastion. Open-air fruit and vegetable market. Wed 6am–5pm.

MUSIC

All Records Chanteclair Building, 30–32 Sefouli ☏ 22663251, ⓦ allrecords.com. Good range of music – new releases on the ground floor, together with ethnic, R&B, electronic, easy listening, film soundtracks and Greek music, classical, jazz and blues on the first floor. There's also a wide range of DVDs. This was the first of a chain of music stores (known as "Play" outside Lefkosia) now found across the Republic. Mon, Tues & Thurs 9am–6.30pm, Wed & Sat 9am–2pm, Fri 9am–7pm.

DIRECTORY

Banks and exchange As the financial hub of the republic, Lefkosia is very well supplied with banks – not only of the main Greek Cypriot and Greek banking chains, but also of UK and global banks such as HSBC and Citibank. You're rarely more than a minutes' walk from an ATM.

Consulates and embassies Australia, Block A, Level 7, Alpha Business Park ☏ 22753001 ⓦ cyprus.embassy.gov .au; Canada, 1 Lambousa St ☏ 22775508; Ireland, 7, Aiantas St ☏ 22818183, ⓦ embassyofireland.com.cy; New Zealand, 6 Kondilaki, ☏ 22818884; South Africa, 101m Archiepiskopou Makariou III ☏ 22374411; UK, Alexander Pallis Street ☏ 22861100, ⓦ ukincyprus.fco.gov.uk; US,

Metochiou & Ploutarchou Street ☏ 22393939, ⓦ cyprus .usembassy.gov.

Internet Lefkosia has the island's best free wi-fi coverage, with dozens of hotels, restaurants, bars and cafés, and some buses, offering hot spots.

Medical Lefkosia General Hospital (A&E) ☏ 22603000. Night pharmacies ☏ 11892, ☏ 90901412 (automatic recording).

Police Next to the Ledra Street crossing ☏ 22477434.

Post Office The Central Post Office is at Constantinos Palaeologos St, just off Eleftheria Square (on the D'Avila Bastion).

Around Lefkosia

There is much to see around **Lefkosia**, and it would be a mistake to concentrate solely on the capital. Most of the district's wilder areas of mountain and forest are considered part of the Troodos Mountains, but there are also a few worthwhile sights beyond the (seemingly endless) industrial estates and suburbs to the south and west. The areas to the east and north of Lefkosia, of course, lie in the Turkish-controlled zone, though these are now also easily accessible.

Panagia Chrysospiliotissa

Kato Deftera • All year • Free

Situated on the E903 which strikes southwest of the capital (from the B9), the village of **Kato** Deftera has an oddity which is worth a stop. **Panagia Chrysospiliotissa** (Our Lady of the Golden Cave) is an early Christian cave-church of a type common in the rest of the Middle East but rare in Cyprus. Its entrance is halfway up a crumbling ochre cliff face above the (usually dry) Pediaios River. Fortunately, it now benefits from a modern flight of steps and a couple of benches either side of the entrance on which to rest after the climb. The cave consists of two main chambers connected by tunnels, the whole being at once in good order but also slightly eerie. There are modern icons and church furnishings, but the original frescoes have been largely washed away by flooding – appropriately, this is the place to pray for rain. The Virgin here also helps to find husbands for unmarried women, ending a different sort of drought. The church is not easy to find, however, despite a brown and yellow sign opposite Kato Deftera's village church. The road it points down is rough enough for you to think you're lost. Keep going, and look out for a large cross at the top of a cliff – the entrance is directly below. There's ample parking, a fountain and plateia, and even a small seasonal food and drink kiosk, all at the base of the cliff.

5

Politiko and Ancient Tamassos

On the same road (the E903) as Kato Deftera but 7km further south is the large modern village of **POLITIKO** which stands on the site of the ancient city-state of **Tamassos**. A mention of "Temessis" in Homer's *Odyssey* is thought to refer to it, and other sources indicate a large and prosperous city whose wealth was based almost entirely on the production of copper. The study of Tamassos is very much a work in progress, with German excavations during the 1970s having unearthed a sanctuary dedicated to Aphrodite (who else) next to the remains of early copper production. Finds from the area include the "Chatsworth Head" – a bronze head of Apollo, purchased by the Duke of Devonshire (and named for his residence) and now in the British Museum – and a group of six large limestone statues of sphinxes and lions now on show in the Cyprus Museum (see p.179).

The Royal Tombs

April–Oct 9.30am–5pm, Nov–March 8.30am–6pm • €1.70 • ☎ 22622619

The star attraction of the Tamassos remains are its pair of **Royal Tombs** dating from the sixth century BC that stand on the northeastern edge of Politiko, their entrance steps protected by wood-and-tile louvred structures. Once down the steps – direct in the first, dog-legged in the second – and through modern Perspex doors, the simplicity of the design of the tomb chambers and the quality of the stonework give them the feel of the interior of Egyptian pyramids. This minimalism is slightly misleading – the tombs undoubtedly had great piles of statuary, gold and other goods, long pinched by grave-robbers (in one of the tombs there's a still-visible hole in the roof). Look out, too, for the skilful carving of the stone to simulate wood. The site itself is on raised ground which gives views of fields, poplars, cypresses and vineyards of the surrounding areas.

Agios Irakleidios

8.30am–6pm (5.30pm in winter) • Free

On the other side of the village from the Royal Tombs is the convent of **Agios Irakleidios**, a popular destination for Greek Cypriots. Irakleidios was the son of a pagan priest ordained by Cypriot Christianity's two founders Saints Paul and Barnabas. Martyred at the age of 60, he was buried in the cave in which he'd lived. In 400 AD a monastery was erected over his grave, subsequently much destroyed and rebuilt – the present one dates from 1773. The monastery has been occupied by nuns since 1962. Entry is through a gatehouse trustingly decked with modern icons, beyond which a drive curves up across vineyards and olive groves to the convent itself. Between the usual bright mosaics of saints, the entrance leads through a pointed arch to the cloisters and cells arranged around a verdant garden, in the centre of which is a medieval chapel built over the tomb of Irakleidios himself. The main church contains some early frescoes and the skull of the saint in a jewelled reliquary. The whole atmosphere of the convent is one of self-contained peace and quiet.

Cyprus Museum of Natural History

Carlsberg Breweries • Mon–Thurs 9am–noon, 2–4pm, Fri 9am–1pm • Free • ☎ 22585834, Ⓦ natmuseum.org.cy

The privately run **Cyprus Museum of Natural History** requires a determined effort to visit – it's in a brewery complex deep in a business park east of the A1 motorway. The location is thanks to its benefactor, Cyprus Carlsberg, who helped set up the cultural foundation to which it owes its existence. Though usually visited by tour groups rather than individuals, it is possible to gain access by arrangement. The first hall contains a comprehensive treatment of the geology of Cyprus, the second a similarly thorough account of the island's marine life. Further halls deal with fossils, insects and rural life with a specific exhibit on Pafos Forest and Larnaka's salt lake. There are also collections

5

of semi-precious stones, corals and shells, and, in the surrounding gardens, a group of replica dinosaurs.

Ancient Idalion

Dali • Mon, Tues, Thurs & Fri 8am–3pm, Wed 8am–5pm • €1.70

In the angle between the A1 and A2 motorways halfway between Lefkosia and Larnaca lies the city of **Ancient Idalion** which was, it is said, established by Chalcanor, one of the Greek heroes who besieged and in due course destroyed Troy. Although there is evidence of occupation of the area going back to 1800 BC, the city itself dates from around 700 BC, and flourished from then until around 500 BC when it was captured by the Phoenicians under Kition. There's no longer a huge amount to see on the ground – the remains of walls, the ground plans of buildings – the most important parts of which are now protected by wooden canopies. This is partly because it was so thoroughly looted in the past, particularly by **Luigi Palma di Cesnola** (see box, p.118) who boasted that he had excavated (plundered) that is, 10,000 graves here. The archeological investigation of Idalion continues, especially of several sanctuaries discovered recently. The site **museum**, opened in 2007, provides a fine introduction to the city's development, featuring the results of excavations old and new. It does, alas, rely on photographs for the more illustrious finds, the originals having long found their way abroad. A second gallery deals with the Phoenician conquest and administration of the city.

Early Industrial Workshop of Agia Varvara

Agia Varvara • Wed 8am–1pm, Sat 3–6pm • Donation • ☎ 99365774

A good example of efforts made by idealistic young people to conserve local history can be found in the village of Agia Varvara, just west of the A1/A2 motorway junction. **The Early Industrial Workshop of Agia Varvara** (clearly signposted from the main village street) is a collection of tools, contraptions and workshops that once belonged to a certain Gregoris Theocharous (1887–1991). The well-travelled Theocharous became a sort of pioneer industrialist, having learned to build and repair machines in Egypt and Greece. On his death at the age of 104, his house, its contents and a variety of inventions (including a water recycling pump), were bequeathed to the community and are preserved by a local history group. You can learn more at ⓦtinyurl.com /industrialworkshop.

North Cyprus

GIRNE (KYRENIA) CASTLE

North Cyprus

For many visitors crossing into Turkish-controlled north Cyprus is akin to time travel. Gone are the busy resorts, malls and familiar international chains of the south, replaced by remote villages and a slower place of life – "the Mediterranean as it used to be" in the words of the local tourist board. This sense of suspended animation can be dated precisely to the Turkish invasion of 1974, when the north, stripped of its Greek Cypriot population, became cut off from the rest of the world, a self-styled republic recognized by no one but Turkey itself (see box, p.201).

While tourism in north Cyprus remains a sore point in the south (see p.37 for the republic's stance on "legal" entry points and property ownership), it is now commonplace – Greek Cypriots themselves come in their thousands, both on day-trips and for overnight stays. This is largely due to the gradual opening up of the **Green Line**, the de facto "border" between the two communities. Consequently, it is perfectly feasible for travellers staying in the south to see as much of the north as they wish, with many attractions little more than half an hour's drive away from the south's major resorts. Others choose to spend their whole trip in the north, though this necessitates travelling via Turkey.

There is certainly plenty to draw you here. North Cyprus boasts two of the island's best-looking **towns** (Girne and Gazimağusa), half the **capital city** (Lefkosia/Lefkoşa), three of its mightiest **crusader castles** (St Hilarion, Buffavento and Kantara), and arguably the island's most significant archeological site at **Salamis**. Its wilderness areas, particularly the **Kyrenia Mountains**, are a hiker's paradise and many of its **beaches** remain mercifully free of high-rise resorts. Furthermore, any visit to Cyprus which includes both sides of the island offers the unique experience of two very different cultures: Orthodox, Greek Cypriot and Muslim, Turkish Cypriot. There's also the small matter of **cost** – being outside the Eurozone the north can feel a cheaper place to means that visit than the south, while its tourist infrastructure is gradually improving.

As for sightseeing in the north, you might find that many **museums** and other places of interest seem rather neglected and old-fashioned (dusty old mannequins seem to be a particular favourite), while its **hotels** and **restaurants** lack the sophistication of the south. You might also come across a cavalier attitude to published **opening times** – if something's really important to you, if possible phone ahead or check with the tourist office. Finally, if you haven't had a chance to obtain **Turkish Lire**, don't worry: euros and dollars are widely accepted.

ST HILARION CASTLE

Highlights

❶ Mevlevî Tekke Museum, Lefkoşa Learn about the origins and beliefs of the "whirling" Dervish sect in the setting of a seventeenth-century monastery. **See p.200**

❷ Büyük Han (Great Inn), Lefkoşa Take refreshment and shop for souvenirs at this beautifully renovated traveller's inn. **See p.205**

❸ Girne Harbour People-watch while strolling around the prettiest harbour in Cyprus, or while sitting in one of its many cafés and restaurants. See p.212

❹ St Hilarion Castle Clamber around this fairy-tale Byzantine/Lusignan castle, while imagining the medieval courtly life it played host to. **See p.220**

❺ Bellapais This bustling village, the location for Lawrence Durrell's travel classic *Bitter Lemons*, is a lovely spot to while away an afternoon. See p.224

❻ Soli A well-excavated Roman town with a Byzantine basilica famous as the site of St Mark's christening. **See p.228**

❼ Gazimağusa old town Relish the unique ambience of this delicately ruined old town surrounded by crumbling Venetian walls. See p.233

❽ Salamis Marvel at the remains of one of Cyprus's greatest ancient cities, followed by a visit to the equally significant Royal Tombs (or perhaps a swim). See p.238

HIGHLIGHTS ARE MARKED ON THE MAP ON PP.198–199 & P.202

Lefkoşa (North Nicosia)

LEFKOŞA (the northern half of what was, before 1974, Nicosia), is the capital city of north Cyprus. As with its southern counterpart, most of Lefkoşa's modern buildings and administrative machinery lie outside the Venetian walls, and most of what visitors will want to see are in the old town within the walls. Compared to the southern part of the city, Lefkoşa is noticeably less vital, with the air more of a sleepy provincial town than a national capital. While the city feels safe, wandering in areas away from the centre is best avoided at night.

Foreign tourists usually enter from the south through the **Ledra Street crossing** (see box, p.176). Once across, you're faced with an attractively **pedestrianized area** packed with shops, cafés and restaurants. Clear signposts indicate where the nearest attractions

lie. Beyond here the main street – **Girne Caddesi** – leads north to the **Girne Gate**, the best place to start a walking tour of North Lefkoşa. If you're short of time, though, it's probably worth heading straight to the **Büyük Han**, a beautifully renovated sixteenth-century merchants' inn. **Museums** to look out for include the Mevlevî Tekke and Lapidary Museums and the Dervis Paşa Mansion, each worth an hour or so of your time. Other places of interest include the **Samanbahçe Quarter**, an early experiment in social housing, and the the dishevelled but improving **Arabhmet Quarter**. Religious sites include the huge **Selimiye Mosque**, visible north and south of the Green Line. Beside it is the ornately Gothic **Bedestan**, once a Christian church, now a performance venue. Other sights, among them the **National Struggle Museum**, the **Museum of Barbarism** and of course the **giant flags** looming on the hillside behind the city, provide uncomfortable reminders of the island's division.

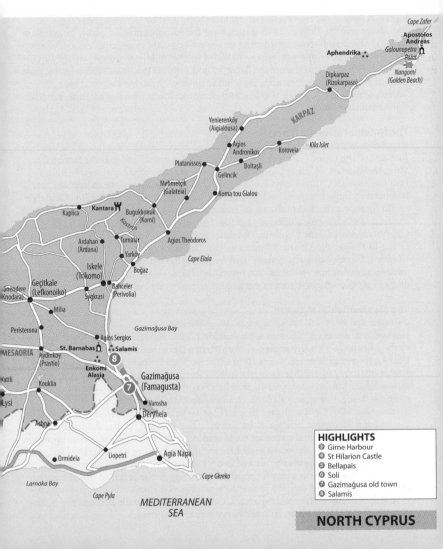

HIGHLIGHTS
❸ Girne Harbour
❹ St Hilarion Castle
❺ Bellapais
❻ Soli
❼ Gazimağusa old town
❽ Salamis

NORTH CYPRUS

6

> ## ENTRY POINTS, VISAS AND TRANSPORT
>
> For information on travel between south and north Cyprus see the box on crossing points on p.28. If using the north's Ercan Airport see p.23 & p.208. Using public transport in the north is not recommended. For information on car rental see p.27. Note also the need for a map using Turkish place names. We have used these names throughout this chapter, giving original Greek names also where relevant.
>
> Remember too that if you think having a TRNC stamp in your passport might cause you problems, you can ask for it to be recorded on a separate piece of paper, which you can continue to use until it's full. For more information see entry requirements, p.36.

The Girne Gate and around

Of the various entrances into the walled city on the northern side, the **Girne (Kyrenia) Gate** is the best preserved, and has been used by the Venetians, the Ottomans and the British, all of whom have left inscriptions that adorn its exterior. In 1931 the British demolished parts of the wall on either side to allow traffic into the city. As a result, the gate is now stranded in the middle of a dual carriageway, with worthy statues to the north (Ataturk) and south (Dr Küçük, with adoring little girl), and an open space on all sides – **Inonu Square** – which now sometimes becomes the focus of political rallies and demonstrations. For more on the Venetian walls themselves see p.173.

The National Struggle Museum

Musalla Bastion • Daily 8am–3.30pm • Free

Just east of the Girne Gate, on the Barbaro (or Musalla) Bastion, is the **National Struggle Museum** which, while inevitably partisan, does offer considerable insight into the Turkish Cypriot (and Turkish) perspective on events since the 1950s. You will need to show photo ID to the soldiers that guard the site. Opened in 1989, it might be seen to be a response to its namesake museum in the south (see p.182), though, of course with a different agenda: focusing on the struggle of Turkish Cypriots against Greek Cypriots, especially between the Turkish TMT and the Greek EOKA in the 1960s. Artefacts on display include guns and improvised weapons, broadcasting equipment used by Radio Bayrak, gung-ho art work, and, outside, some military vehicles and ordnance. The invasion (or "Peace Operation") of 1974 is, of course, covered in detail.

The Mevlevî Tekke Museum

Girne Caddesi • Mon–Wed & Fri 8am–3.30pm, Thurs 8am–1pm & 2–6pm (winter 5pm) • 5TL

Just south of the Girne Gate on Girne Caddesi is the **Mevlevî Tekke Museum**, devoted to the Muslim sect widely known as the **Whirling Dervishes** and housed in what is left of a seventeenth-century dervish monastery. The Mevlevî Order was founded in Konya in Turkey by the Mevlana Jelal al-Din Rumi (1207–1273) and quickly spread through Asia Minor. Central to their beliefs was the *sema* – the characteristic whirling dance, thought to achieve a transcendental forgetting of the self and communion with God, a process that UNESCO has declared to be a "masterpiece of the oral and intangible heritage of humanity". The museum depicts the *sema* in its central hall where a set of mannequins in traditional dress are frozen in time spinning to a mannequin band above. Beyond here are the tombs of past Mevlevî Sheiks, archive photographs, prayer beads and other ephemera as well as a few gnomic quotations that give you pause for thought: "A stingy Vizier is forced to pay a high price to a poor potter" or "The candle Mevlana lights is smaller, but keeps burning long after the others have melted away". One sums up the whole point of the dervishes – "Mevlana whirls in humble reverence".

THE STATE WITHIN A STATE

The Turkish Republic of North Cyprus (TRNC), as it has called itself since 1983, is still in many ways a pariah state, and this lack of international recognition continues to starve it of investment. Global chains such as McDonald's and Starbucks are conspicuous by their absence and its tourist industy is still dwarfed by that of the south. In part this is self-inflicted: the shabbiness of many of its museums and attractions contrast markedly with the magnificence of its totalitarian-style military monuments and the regular sight of Turkish troops and bases, often incongruously close to tourist attractions, can be a jolt to the senses. The empty shells of Orthodox churches and monasteries that dot some parts of the landscape are also an uncomfortable reminder of the wonton destruction that followed the invasion or "intervention" as the Turks put it. While the north remains in political limbo, its future seems to hang on demographics – with Turkish settlers now outnumbering Turkish Cypriots, north Cyprus increasingly feels like an offshore province of Turkey rather than the independent state that it claims to be.

6

The Dr Küçük Museum

Girne Caddesi • Summer 9am–1pm & 2–4.45pm; winter 9am–2pm • Free

Housed in a 1920s-era building on Girne Caddesi, the **Dr Fazil Küçük Museum** gives an insight into one of the key figures in Cypriot politics (see box, p.203). Dr Kücük is held in the same respect by Turkish Cypriots as Archbishop Makarios is by Greek Cypriots and his home and surgery has been converted into a diverting museum containing plenty of photographs and personal possessions which help humanize the man. A brief pamphlet of notes is available on request from the custodian.

The Tekke Bahçesi Şehitlği

East of Girne Caddesi and a few metres south of the Dr Küçük Museum is the **Tekke Bahçesi Şehitlği**, a graveyard which contains the remains of Turkish Cypriots who died during the troubles in 1963 and the invasion of 1974 – it's signposted "Tekke Bahçesi Şehitlği Martyrdom". It's an affecting spot which draws attention to the cost of political upheaval and war, but its overt agenda can be a turn-off: the photographs of the corpses of men, women and children, and the inflammatory language of the dedication risks provoking the response that it's simply time to move on.

The Samanbahçe Quarter

On the other side of Girne Caddesi from the Tekke Bahçesi Şehitlği is an interesting example of early town planning – the **Samanbahçe Quarter**. Built in a grid pattern from the 1890s onwards on land which was once a market garden called "Straw Field", and financed by a Muslim religious trust or *vakif*, the quarter was social housing designed for the poor, and consisted of 72 dwellings made of mud brick with tile roofs. With uniform white walls and green shutters and doors, the houses are arranged along five parallel stone-paved streets with a domed stone fountain at the centre. Unlike, say, London mews flats which once housed lowly grooms and are now the preserve of the well-heeled, the Samanbahçe Quarter is still reserved for low-income families whose pride in their houses is reflected in the profusion of potted plants that line its lanes.

Ataturk Square

Ataturk Square (Meydani) is the nearest thing to a hub that North Lefkoşa has, with its large paved and pedestrianized central island, fitted out with benches, around a circular wall surrounding the fenced-off **Venetian Column**. Incidentally, if you ask for directions to "Ataturk Meydani" you're likely to be met with blank stares – all the locals call it **Sarayönü** after the palace ("saray") that once stood on the square, the same derivation appearing in the nearby Moorish-style **Sarayönü Camii** and the ugly, 1960s-built *Saray Hotel*, which does at least offer fine views from its roof terrace.

6

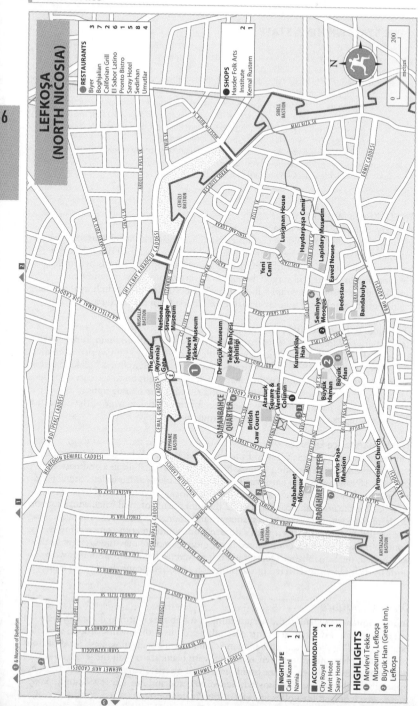

LEFKOŞA (NORTH NICOSIA)

RESTAURANTS
Biyer	3
Boghjalian	7
Califorian Grill	2
El Sabor Latino	6
Pronto Bistro	1
Saray Hotel	5
Sedirhan	8
Umutlar	4

SHOPS
Hasder Folk Arts Institute	2
Kemal Rustem	1

NIGHTLIFE
Cadi Kazani	1
Narnia	2

ACCOMMODATION
City Royal	2
Merit Hotel	1
Saray Hotel	3

HIGHLIGHTS
1. Mevlevi Tekke Museum, Lefkoşa
2. Büyük Han (Great Inn), Lefkoşa

DR FAZIL KÜÇÜK

In contrast to many of the leaders of both north and south Cyprus, Dr Fazil Küçük was an engaging, larger than life figure, a journalist and bon viveur much given to bad language, carousing with friends, and playing practical jokes. Born in Nicosia in 1906, he trained as a doctor in Turkey, Switzerland and France, returning to practise in Cyprus in 1938. As friction between Greek and Turkish Cypriots developed, he emerged as a leader of the Turkish Cypriot community, setting up his own political party, establishing the first Turkish trade union and launching a newspaper – *Halkin Sesi* – which is still published today. He led the Turkish Cypriot faction during talks leading up to independence, and became the first vice president of the republic. He was increasingly eclipsed by Rauf Denktaş (see box, p.206) as the intercommunal strife of the 1960s progressed, and was replaced by him as the leader of the Turkish Cypriots in 1973. He died in London in 1984. True to character, his last request was that a glass of his favourite tipple be regularly poured onto his grave.

The Venetian Column

The **Venetian Column** was pilfered from Ancient Salamis by the Venetians in 1489, and erected with a lion of St Mark on the top and at the base the coats of arms of prominent Venetian families. It was toppled by the victorious Turks during the Ottoman invasion in 1570, and re-erected by the British in 1915, with a bronze globe replacing the lion on the top.

The British Law Courts

A dominant feature of the square are the **British Law Courts**, built right at the end of the Victorian period and an elegant example of colonial architecture. Now used as government offices, they have a colonnaded ground floor with an open, veranda-style first floor and a red tiled roof – look out for the royal coat of arms that adorns the wall facing the square, put there to mark the coronation of Queen Elizabeth II in 1953.

The Arabahmet Quarter

Some 600m west of Ataturk Square is the **Arabahmet Quarter**, named after Arab Ahmet Paşa who governed the city from 1584 to 1587. A warren of narrow streets and alleys, old houses with balconies and arched doorways, the area is now being renovated bit by bit and gradually being settled by mainland Turks. Some houses are therefore in immaculate condition while others, mostly still inhabited, look about to fall downs. Indeed, if you get off the beaten track, and see families sitting out in the backyards of tumbledown houses, you might well feel as if you've been transported to an Anatolian village. It's good for a quick wander (though don't expect too many cafés or restaurants) and there are several attractions worth seeking out.

The Arabahmet Mosque
Open outside prayer times • Free

The **Arabahmet Mosque** which serves the quarter was probably built in the late sixteenth century on the remains of a Lusignan church – the floor of the mosque is partly made up of Lusignan tombstones. It was heavily restored in the mid-nineteenth century, and is of interest more for its lush and peaceful graveyard than for the building itself.

The Derviş Paşa Mansion
8am–3.30pm • 5TL

Two minutes' walk south of the Arabhmet Mosque, is the **Derviş Paşa Mansion**. The two-storey house with overhanging upper floor was built at the start of the nineteenth century for one Derviş Paşa, the editor of *Zamam* or "Time", Cyprus's first Turkish-language newspaper. Since 1988 it has been a museum which, like the

6

A POLITICAL LANDSCAPE

From the Shacolas Tower in South Lefkosia or the *Saray Hotel* in North Lefkoşa (and indeed, from any other vantage point which has a clear view north) you can't help but see two enormous **flags** on the nearest south-facing hillside. One represents the TRNC (red crescent and star on a white background with red bar above and below) the other Turkey (white crescent and star on red background). The story behind them is rather dispiriting for those who would like to see the island reunited. Officially created to honour the great Turkish leader Ataturk (the slogan below the Turkish flag – "How happy is he who can say he is a Turk" – is attributed to him), the position of the flags seems to indicate that this explanation is disingenuous. A more believable version says that the Turks created the flags by painting boulders at night, turning them face down during the day then, on the eve of August 15, a national holiday in the Greek Cypriot calendar but also the anniversary of the 1974 Tochni massacre of Turkish Cypriots, turned them face up so that they could be seen in the south. In other words, a taunt or a memorial, depending on your point of view.

Hadjigeorgakis Kornesios Mansion in the south, offers an insight into Ottoman-era living. Set in palm-fringed gardens, the house is cool and colonnaded, with steps leading up to a first floor furnished in contemporary style. There's plenty of decorative glassware, rugs, pottery, swords and the odd mannequin. As well as a dining room and bedroom there's what's billed as the "main room", a large area for entertaining, with bench seating around the outside, rugs on the floor and hookahs and coffee cups dotted around.

The Armenian Church

A couple of minutes south of the Derviş Paşa Mansion is the **Armenian Church**, a ruin that is gradually being restored. Until the troubles in the mid-twentieth century, the Arabahmet quarter was largely populated by Armenians. In return for their support of the Ottomans during the sixteenth-century invasion, they were given an old Benedictine monastery to use as their place of worship. In 1963, having been perceived as favouring the Greeks during that troubled year, the Armenians were expelled by the TMT and their church fell into disrepair. Based on the initial renovation work financed by the UN, it should be a splendid addition to the quarter when complete.

South of Ataturk Square

South of Ataturk Square, and north of the pedestrianized shopping streets that greet you on passing through the Lokmaci Gate (that is the Ledra Street crossing from the south), is an area of busy traffic and impressive buildings.

Büyük Hamam

You can't miss the **Büyük Hamam** (Great Baths) – it's a fine stone building that looks as if it has sunk into the ground (whereas, of course, it's the ground that has risen up from its original medieval level as successive layers of building have taken place). The baths were converted by the Ottomans from a Lusignan church, St George of the Latins, whose front portal is still the main entrance, and is approached down one of two flights of stone steps. Though it would be a particularly atmospheric place in which to bathe, it rarely seems to be open.

Kumarkilar Han

A minutes' walk east of the Büyük Hamam is the **Kumarkilar Han**, or "Gamblers' Inn". Also called "The inn for merchants using donkeys" and "the inn for travelling musicians" the Kumarkilar Han is now in a sad state of neglect. Built around 1700, with 44 of its original 56 rooms surviving, it is crying out for renovation; only the front Gothic archway and door – probably dating from an earlier building – are in a good state of repair. Take a look from the street (you can't get into the building), imagine what it would look like after renovation, then pass swiftly on to the Büyük Han down the street.

Büyük Han

The **Büyük Han** (Great Inn) is a graceful and harmonious building which is somehow more affecting because it was built, not to glorify God or the power of princes, but as practical lodgings for traders and merchants. Appropriately, this is not a frozen-in-time relic, but a vibrant collection of shops, restaurants and small businesses that do its origins proud. It was built on the orders of the first Ottoman governor general of Cyprus, Mustafa Paşa, in 1572, just after the conquest. Used by the British as a prison, and later to house destitute families, it was sensitively restored between 1992 and 2002. The two-storey building consists of 68 rooms on two vaulted galleries looking onto a courtyard, and ten shops which open outwards to the street. In the centre of the courtyard a *mesjid* or miniature mosque stands on columns under which is a *sadirvan* or fountain, used for ritual ablutions. There are two entrance gates to the east (the main one) and west, and inside the courtyard stone stairways lead to the upper floor (once used for accommodation). The courtyard of the Büyük Han is an ideal place to sit in the shade, have a drink or a meal and, on Tuesday or Friday evenings, listen to live music (see p.210).

Selimiye Cami

West of the Büyük Han, the **Selimiye Cami** is not only Lefkoşa's biggest mosque, but also one of its most historically significant. Built by the Lusignans between 1208 and 1326 as the Roman Catholic St Sophia's Cathedral, it was adapted into a mosque shortly after the Ottoman invasion by the addition of the two impressive minarets (between which, these days, Turkish and TRNC flags are suspended). This combination of Lusignan and Ottoman architecture is best appreciated in detail from the café in the garden or as a whole from some distance away – there's a particularly good view of it from the Shacolas Tower in South Lefkosia.

The Selimiye Mosque (it was renamed in 1954 after **Selimiye II**, sultan at the time of the Ottoman conquest) is still a working place of worship into which visitors are welcome as long as they are dressed appropriately. The whitewashed interior is simple and spacious (all the Roman Catholic furnishings were removed immediately after the Ottoman conquest) except for an elaborate and flamboyantly painted *mihrab* (prayer niche) in the southern wall, and a green-painted *minbar*, or pulpit in the north transept. The south transept has a women's gallery. The cathedral was used for coronations during the Lusignan period, and several royal tombstones are incorporated into the floor, now obscured by the Mecca-orientated carpets. Around the back of the mosque is a splendid, roofed *sadirvan* (ablution fountain) in its own courtyard.

The Bedestan

Mon, Tues, Thurs & Sat 10am–1pm, Wed 2.30–5pm • 5TL

Right next door to the Selimiye Mosque is the **Bedestan**, a building which even by Cypriot standards has had a chequered past. Starting as a twelfth-century Byzantine church, it was reincarnated as St Nicholas Roman Catholic Church during Lusignan times, became an Orthodox church during the Venetian occupation, and under the Ottomans was converted into a covered food and textiles market by subdividing the internal space. Towards the end of the Ottoman period the Bedestan fell into disrepair, but was revived as a market under the British. Only part of the north face of the building, including a magnificent Gothic entrance, was preserved complete, though the whole edifice is currently being renovated using EU funding. Inside, information

6

"MR NO" – RAUF DENKTAŞ

Turkish Cypriot leader Rauf Denktaş was born in 1924 in Pafos. He studied law in England and returned to practise as a solicitor in 1947. He quickly became involved in politics, helping to found the Turkish resistance movement the TMT during the 1950s. He rose further to prominence during the troubles that followed independence in 1960, became known for strong-arm tactics, even against fellow Turkish Cypriots with whom he disagreed, and finally replaced his mentor Dr Fazil Küçük as the leader of the Turkish Cypriots in 1973. In 1974 he welcomed the Turkish invasion, became head of the "Turkish Federated State of Cyprus" and oversaw the foundation of the Turkish Republic of North Cyprus in 1983. His uncompromising support for a **"two-state solution"** (he once claimed that there were no such things as Greek and Turkish Cypriots, saying that the only true Cypriots were the island's donkeys) made him the darling of the Turkish military and the Turkish Cypriot community and the bane of a succession of Greek Cypriot, UN and US negotiators (he became known as "Mr No" for his intransigence). However, during the early years of the twenty-first century his unchanging views began to look outdated, with Turkish Cypriots in the north becoming increasingly frustrated by their isolation from the rest of the world, a situation only exacerbated by the republic's accession to the European Union. Even Turkey began to find his inflexible views difficult as the north started to experience serious economic problems, and as Turkey began to nurture their own hopes of joining the EU. Though Denktaş reluctantly presided over the easing of restrictions on crossing the Green Line, he looked more and more out of touch, and finally left politics in 2005. Known as a dog lover and keen amateur photographer, he died in January 2012.

panels fill you in on the history and renovation. The Bedestan is now used as a venue for performances and for exhibitions.

Bandabuliya/Belediye Pazari

Mon–Sat 7.30am–6pm

Around 100m east of the Büyük Han is the **Bandabuliya** or covered market, a handsome building of great character; its Art Deco entrance gate has "Belediye Pazari" engraved on its lintel and the date 1932 worked into the decorative ironwork below. Closed for renovation at the time of writing, the actual buying and selling at the moment goes on in nearby Kutuphane Street and the surrounding alleys, now covered by canvas. The goods are the same as you'd find in the Bandabuliya – fruit and veg, preserves, meat and fish, clothes, hats, bags, belts, scarves, rugs, baskets.

The Eaved House

Mon–Wed & Fri 8am–3.30pm, Thurs 8am–1pm & 2–6pm (winter 5pm) • Free • ☎ 227 75 47

Stretched out along Kutuphane Street/Yeni Cami, the road that heads north after threading its way between the Bedestan and the Bandabuliya, are several establishments that are worth visiting, the first of which is the **Eaved House**. Now an arts and cultural centre which mounts periodic exhibitions, its eaves are indeed noticeable, jutting out far enough beyond the walls to require wooden struts to support them. The ground floor was built by the Lusignans, the first floor added during Ottoman times. Though its restoration in the 1990s was so thorough that there's not much of architectural consequence to see (the only inscribed date is 1932), the graceful arches, galleries, verandas and white painted walls make it a cool refuge from the heat of the day.

The Lapidary Museum

Kirlizade Sokak • Mon–Wed & Fri 8am–3.30pm, Thurs 8am–1pm & 2–6pm (winter 5pm)

A minute's walk north of the Eaved House is the tiny **Lapidary Museum**, contained in a perfect little fifteenth-century Venetian house and courtyard. Featuring a hotchpotch of stone carvings and architectural details from all over Cyprus assembled by the British, it offers an irresistible hint of times past and a sense of crumbling grandeur. A valiant attempt has been made to categorize and contextualize the exhibits, so that, for example, a jumble of pieces of window tracery and archways in the courtyard have design outlines above them, and exhibits inside the house, on two floors, are accompanied by notes and sketches.

Haydarpaşa Camii

Open during exhibitions Mon–Fri 9am–1pm & 2.30–5pm, Sat 9am–1pm • Free

A short stroll north of the Lapidary Museum is the **Haydarpaşa Camii**, notable for its mixed architectural ancestry – a tall, Gothic, clearly Lusignan nave (formerly St Catherine's Church) with a minaret at its prow. The whole building is out of proportion – too narrow, too high for its length – presumably because of bits that have been demolished, and as with many converted churches, the minaret just doesn't look comfortable. The mosque is now a private art gallery open only during exhibitions.

The Lusignan House

Mon–Wed & Fri 8am–3.30pm, Thurs 8am–1pm & 2–6pm (winter 5pm) • 5TL

An impressive fifteenth-century **Lusignan House**, not a mansion but obviously the abode of somebody of singular wealth, can be found a short walk beyond the Haydarpasa Camii. An arched gateway boasting several Lusignan coats of arms leads into a secluded courtyard, from which stone steps lead up to an immaculate first floor with, again, an arched entrance into the building. Though over 500 years old, few of us in the twenty-first century would object to living in it. Though the house closed for renovation at the time of writing, staff have no objections to visitors looking around the outside.

Yeni Cami

North of the Lusignan House, on the street named after it, the **Yeni Cami** ("new mosque") is more notable for its history than for what you can see of it today. An eighteenth-century governor, so the story goes, had a dream that the original mosque (which was itself a Lusignan church) had treasure buried beneath it, so he had it demolished in order to secure the riches for himself. Not only was there no treasure, but local indignation at the desecration of the mosque provoked the sultan into having the delinquent paşa executed. His tomb stands next to the minaret which survives from the mosque he destroyed, together with a Gothic arch from the original church. The "new mosque" stands a few metres away in the gardens. Incidentally, the domed old Turkish tombs nearby are those of the family of the first Ottoman chief judge.

The Museum of Barbarism

Irhan Sokak 2 • 8am–3.30pm • Free

Outside the walled city, in the northwestern suburbs of Lefkoşa, stands an unassuming suburban bungalow, once the home of a Dr Ilhan, a major in the Turkish Army. It has been converted into the **Museum of Barbarism** to commemorate the fate of his unfortunate family. In December 1963, while the doctor was on duty, armed Greek Cypriot irregulars burst into the house and gunned down his wife, three children and a next door neighbour. With graphic descriptions and photographs, bullet holes and bloodstains, this is not a museum for children or the faint of heart. Its purpose is, of course, to draw attention to the sort of terrorism that was perpetrated by EOKA during the period after independence in 1960. You can't help feeling the simple memorial in the garden outside is a more fitting reminder.

6

NORTH CYPRUS FESTIVALS

Whatever the festivals are called, in North Cyprus they usually include a wide variety of activities and events, not all directly relating to the subject contained in the title. So the tulip festival includes a pinball competition, an olive festival a darts competition. And many also throw in a beauty contest for good measure.

MARCH

Tepebasi Tulip Festival Walks and displays to celebrate the Cyprus tulip (Tulipa Cypria) and a wide range of activities – including bicycle tours, dancing and a pinball competition, in villages near Lapta.

MAY–JUNE

International Bellapais Music Festival (ⓦ bellapaisfestival.com) A festival of chamber and choral music and dance in one of North Cyprus's most beautiful settings – Bellapais Abbey.
International Famagusta Art and Culture Festival (ⓦ magusa.org) Huge music, theatre, ballet, visual arts festival held at various venues in Gazimağusa.

JUNE–JULY

Girne Living Culture and Art Festival Turkish and Cypriot drama and music festival held in Girne's amphitheatre.
Iskele International Folk Dance Festival Folk dancing groups from all over the world take part in this festival, with evening performances over a week.

Lapta Tourist Festival (June) Huge range of competitions aimed at and put on by the expat community – pool, table tennis, remote-controlled boats – there's even an "alcohol-drinking competition" (details at ⓦ cyprusscene.com).
Lefke Walnut Festival (June) Festival of walnut-based sweets in the village in the western part of North Cyprus.

AUGUST

Gecitkale Hellim (Halloumi) Festival A variety of events and demonstrations revolving around the Cypriot cheese halloumi – cooking, photography (not just photographs of cheese), beauty and fashion competitions.

OCTOBER

International Girne Olive Festival (Oct) Dance and drama, music, food (with an olive theme) and drink, shooting and darts competitions. Starts in Kyrenia Castle, then moves to the village of Zeytinlik. ⓦ girnebelediyesi.com.

ARRIVAL AND DEPARTURE

By plane Ercan Airport (ⓣ 228 32 00, ⓦ aircanairport .co.uk; see p.23) is 12km east of the city, to which it is linked by a good dual carriageway road. Scheduled airport buses (provided by Kibhas, with five buses a day) while cheap, rarely coincide with flights, and you're better off renting a car or taking a taxi (around €30 to Lefkoşa or Girne).

By bus The long-distance bus station in Lefkoşa is on the intersection of Ataturk Caddesi and Gazeteci Kemal Asik Caddesi, due north of the old city. There are no

through buses to the south.
Destinations Gazimağusa (every 20min; 1hr); Girne (several per hour, but departs when full; 30min); Güzelyurt (every 30min; 45min).

By car Wherever you are arriving from by car, you will end up at the Girne Gate. Once in the city, on-street parking is relatively easy, and there are several car parks.

By service taxi and minibus Service taxis and minibuses travel to Gazimağusa and Girne, from the main bus station and from stops within the old city.

GETTING AROUND

On foot Lefkoşa is small enough to explore on foot – there really is no need to use taxis or buses.

By car For car rental, try Bicen Rent a Car (ⓣ 227 16 80) or Kosezade Rent a Car (ⓣ 228 52 22).

INFORMATION

Tourist office The main office is in the Girne Gate, at the northern end of the main north–south street Girne Cad (Girne Gate, Mon–Fri 9am–5pm, Sat & Sun 9am–2pm; ⓣ 227 29 94). There's also a kiosk at the

Ledra Street crossing and where you can pick up the "Nicosia Walled City: Walking Route Map" published by the Lefkosia Master Plan (see box, p.185).

ACCOMMODATION

There are no hotels that can be unreservedly recommended in Lefkoşa – they tend to be rather dated and in need of renovation, and the fact that they offer casino facilities can attract the odd unsavoury character. Consequently, most who wish to visit stay south of the Green Line and cross over to shop or sightsee. Of the three large hotels that can be used, two lie north of the old town, while the other is very central.

City Royal 19 Kemal Asik Cad ☎ 228 76 21, ⓦ city-royal.com. North of the old town, about a 20min walk from the centre, near the bus station. A slightly monolithic business and gamblers' hotel, with full range of services, casino gym and pool (closed in winter). Ask for a room away from the main street. **€65**

Merit Hotel Bendrettin Demirel Street ☎ 650 32 00, ⓦ merithotels.com. Northwest of the city centre, about twenty minutes' walk. A substantial tower block with a Byzantine/Ottoman feel and the inevitable casino. Rooms are well-appointed, bathrooms spacious, food good, and there's a pleasant fountain and terrace. Sweeping views from the fourteenth floor. **€150**

Saray Hotel Ataturk Meydani ☎ 228 31 15. The only choice if you want a central hotel in the old town. It has good views, and, being on the city's main square, is at the heart of things. However, it's expensive and very down-at-heel (though renovation was apparently imminent). Caesar's Casino, which is part of the hotel, is also pretty shabby. **€210**

EATING AND DRINKING

Many of the most popular restaurants in North Lefkoşa are in the old city, within the walls. Otherwise try the Dereboyu district to the northwest.

OLD CITY

Boghjalian Salahi Sevket Sokak ☎ 228 07 00. Beautiful restored building, once owned by a rich Armenian, in the Arabahmet area on the western edge of the city. High banqueting hall and courtyard in the Turkish style. Kebab-style dishes, especially mixed kebab and meze. Good-quality food, highly popular. Meze around 10TL a dish. Daily Noon–3.30pm & 7–11pm. Closed Sun.

★ **El Sabor Latino** Selimiye Meydani (next to the mosque) ☎ 228 83 22. As the name suggests, *El Sabor Latino* offers Italian food, but with an additional strangely eclectic mix of tapas and Chinese. The setting is fashionable – open kitchen, wood, leather, hanging lamps, photographs on the walls, there's live jazz Wed & Fri, and the coffee is famous. Though much frequented by tourists, it is also popular with locals from both sides of the Green Line. Mains around 12–15TL. If there's any criticism, it's that service can be a little slow. Mon–Sat 11am–midnight.

Saray Hotel Ataturk Meydani ☎ 228 31 15. The main selling point here is the view from the roof restaurant of North Lefkoşa's tallest building. Drink in the view and the cocktails, eat only if you must – food has a reputation for poor quality and high prices. Cocktails 10–15TL. Lunch and dinner.

★ **Sedirhan** Büyük Han ☎ 228 14 39. Good selection of traditional Turkish snacks and meals served in the beautifully restored Büyük Han. Don't be put off by the picture menu – it's very useful if you don't know the cuisine. Most meals 15–17TL. Even if you're not hungry, stop for a drink – it's such a marvellous setting. Mon, Wed & Fri 9am–5pm, Tues, Thurs & Sat 9am–1pm, but hours can vary – restaurant stays open if there's live music on.

Umutlar 51 Girne Cad ☎ 227 32 36. Traditional Cypriot food, kebabs and soups (4TL upwards) on edge of the Samanbahçe estate, with indoor and outdoor seating in the lane. 9am–11pm (though in summer appears to be open 24/7).

DEREBOYU DISTRICT

Biyer 61 Mehmet Akif Cad (opposite Califorian Grill) ☎ 228 01 43. A good-value restaurant for the younger crowd, modelled perhaps on the sort of street cafés you might get in Istanbul. Turkish food with the emphasis on kebabs and cold and hot meze, accompanied on some days (usually Wed & Sat) by live music. Café and snacks downstairs, more formal dining on the first floor. Breakfast, lunch and dinner and takeaway on offer. Mains from 15TL. Daily 10am–1am. Closed Sun.

Califorian Grill 74 Mehmet Akif Cad ☎ 227 07 00. American-style fast food together with Chinese, Italian and Turkish dishes (12–18TL). Trendy when opened, now a part of the scene. The missing letter "n" is no mistake – it was dropped to avoid trademark issues. Daily 8am–midnight (no Sunday lunch).

Pronto Bistro Dereboyu ☎ 228 65 42. Five minutes' walk north of the British High Commission, *Pronto Bistro* offers a good mix of pizzas, Chinese, Italian and Tex-Mex. Pizzas around 10TL. Music Wed, Fri & Sat. Daily 10am–1am.

NIGHTLIFE AND ENTERTAINMENT

Lefkoşa is not known for its nightlife. Apart from eating and drinking, the main entertainment is gambling – all three of the hotels listed above have casinos attached. Casinos also put on entertainment, though this can often resemble a kind of "north Cyprus's got talent". Otherwise, it's a matter of looking out for live music in bars and other venues – the Büyük Han, for example, has live music on most Tuesdays and Thursdays.

★ **Cadi Kazani** 77 Tanzimat Sokak ☎ 229 23 71, ⓦ cadicazanicafe.com. A bar tucked away in the up-and-coming Arabahmet area on the western edge of the old city, Cadi Kazani is owned and run by an artist whose paintings decorate the walls. Gentle background music, mellow atmosphere. Tues–Sat 5pm–1am, Sun 6pm–1pm.

Narnia 23 Nuri Efindi Sokak ☎ 859 71 15. A bar in an old building in the Arabahmet area, *Narnia* has live music up to three nights a week – rock, blues, jazz and electronic music. Daily 6pm–late.

SHOPPING

Serious shoppers tend to stick to South Lefkosia. However, quite a few head north in search of bargains – especially cheap copies of designer goods on sale on the other side of the Ledra Street crossing. The temporary open market, filling in until the renovation of the Bandabuliya is complete, is in Kutuphane Street. Büyük Han, too, is a good place for all sorts of souvenirs and arts and crafts objects. Bear in mind that there are restrictions on what you can bring back into the south: 200 cigarettes, 1 litre of alcohol and no more than €100 worth of other goods.

Erdal Jewellery and Silver Kadinlar Pazari 20 ☎ 227 44 34. Jewellery at affordable prices.

★ **Hasder Folk Arts Institute Craft Centre** Selimiye Square. Excellent range of craft output – basketry, bags, glassware, lace, furniture, textiles etc. Mon–Wed 8am–12.30pm & 1.30–5pm, Thurs–Fri 8am–7.30pm, Sat 8am–1pm.

Kemal Rustem Girne Cad 22–26 ☎ 228 35 06. Decent range of English-language books, new and secondhand, together with magazines. It's opposite the Saray Hotel, and has a coffee shop.

Mentes Ozsakin Devlet Hastanesi Karsisi ☎ 223 29 40. Fashion shoes and accessories, including boots and shoes with the highest heels you've ever seen.

DIRECTORY

Banks and exchange There are numerous currency exchange offices (including one at the Ledra Street crossing) and banks with ATMs in the city, especially on Sarayönü and Girne Cad. But don't forget that, if you're crossing from South Lefkosia, euros are widely accepted in the north. Bank opening hours are 8am–noon in summer, with additional afternoon (2–4pm) opening in winter.

Consulates and embassies Turkey is the only country that recognizes the TRNC, and therefore has a full embassy. Other countries have liaison offices. Australia, Guner Turkmen Sokaki 20 ☎ 227 73 32; Germany, Kasim Sokak 15 ☎ 227 51 61; Turkey, Bedreddin Demirel Cad ☎ 227 23 14; UK, Mehmet

Akif Cad 23 ☎ 288 38 61; USA, Saran Sokak 6 ☎ 227 82 95

Emergencies Ambulance (☎ 112), Fire Brigade (☎ 199) or Police (☎ 155). Nicosia Hospital (☎ 228 30 36).

Internet Though wi-fi is getting more and more available, it is still not as common as in the south. If you can't find wi-fi in a hotel or restaurant try the *Fistik Net Café* on Sht Salih Cibir Sokak 15 ☎ 227 37 27. Failing that, ask at the tourist office.

Medical Burhan Nalbatanoglu Devlet Hastahanesi ☎ 228 33 11; Cyprus Life Hospital, Ataturk Cad 13 ☎ 680 80 80 ⓦ cyplh.com.

Post Office Sarayönü Sok just off Ataturk Meydani (Mon–Fri 8am–1pm & 2–5pm, Sat 8.30am–12.30pm).

Girne (Kyrenia)

GIRNE (still widely known by its Greek name **Kyrenia** or *Keryneia*) is the most beautiful town in Cyprus, owing to its ravishing harbour, mighty Venetian castle, and a backdrop of sharp and craggy mountains. It even has a pleasant climate, courtesy of those mountains, which bring cooler air and a greener landscape than in the rest of Cyprus. Away from the harbour area, the town is less appealing – some parts are run down, others beginning to succumb to characterless tourist development. But for all that, it's a place that all visitors to the island should try to take in, for the day if not longer.

Apart from the harbour and the castle, there's much else hidden away amongst Girne's steep serpentine alleys. The Anglican Church, the **Cafer Paşa Camii**, the **Ottoman Cemetery** and the **Chrysopolitissa Church** attest to the spiritual life of the town, the tiny **Folk Art Museum** and **Icon Museum** to its cultural life, and the **Bandabuliya** together with a host of shops to its commercial side. Finally, Girne's

VISITING GIRNE FROM THE SOUTH

The best place to cross over from the south if travelling to Girne is at the Agios Dometios checkpoint west of Lefkosia city centre. It's not well signposted – drive west along Leoforos Agiou Pavlou, and when the road bears sharply to the left immediately after Nicosia Racecourse, look out for a sharp right turn. The crossing is a few metres up this side street. Once across, you're in Metehan, and it's no more than half-an-hour's drive to Girne. But do memorize the route after the crossing so that you can find your way back – the signposts are for Metehan, and there's no mention of it being a crossing point.

numerous **cafés** and **restaurants** offer the opportunity to eat, drink and socialize with friendly locals, or just enjoy the views and the chance to people-watch in comfort.

Brief history

Girne was established in the tenth century BC by the first Greek invaders of Cyprus, the **Myceneans**, and can therefore claim to be the settlement with the longest history of continuous occupation anywhere on the island. During the time of Classical Greece it was one of the ten kingdoms of Cyprus. In the seventh century AD, **Arab raids** led to the building of a castle by the **Byzantines**, possibly on the site of an earlier Roman fort, later added to and strengthened by the **Lusignans** and then the **Venetians**. Although the castle was never taken by force of arms, it was starved into surrender by the **Ottomans** in 1570. During the occupation that followed, Girne declined and stagnated, but saw something of a renaissance during the **British period** as the new rulers built roads and developed the harbour. It became a busy port, exporting carob pods, importing goods from Greece and Turkey, and building ships. Prosperous and with a delightful climate, it was no wonder that British civil servants, streaming back from the collapsing empire, saw it as a paradise to which they could happily retire. However, this Levantine Shangri La changed as Cyprus gained its independence in 1960, and was then riven by intercommunal friction. Girne was one of the first places to fall during the 1974 Turkish invasion. With properties being looted, and then confiscated during the early post-invasion years, British expats left in droves, their number falling from 2500 to a couple of hundred. The spaces left by them, and even more by departing Greek Cypriots, were filled by Turkish Cypriots relocating, mainly from the Lemesos, and by Turks coming in from the mainland. Since then, the **Brit expat community** has burgeoned once more, though issues over property ownership in the north has stifled the second-homes market.

The harbour and around

Busy with excursion boats, laced with wooden pontoons and bristling with masts, Girne's medieval **harbour** is one of the most picturesque in the Mediterranean. Almost perfectly circular, its western side is dominated by the massive Venetian castle (see below), while the harbour entrance is now protected by a long breakwater built after independence. The horseshoe-shaped quay is taken up with restaurants and small hotels, some in converted carob warehouses, others in modern buildings, with balconied upper stories and canopied ground floors. Nearby is the **Customs House**, converted by the British from a medieval tower to which, during troubled times, a chain was slung from the castle to prevent access to the harbour. It is now occupied by the tourist office. There's an even older, ancient harbour immediately to the east (you can see it from the Venetian tower of the castle) and a much newer, modern one even further east beyond that.

Girne Castle

March–Nov 8am–8pm, Dec–Feb 9am–2pm • 12.5TL

Girne Castle has a confusing architectural history, having been adapted, destroyed, rebuilt and improved so many times. The Byzantines first built a castle here, perhaps on

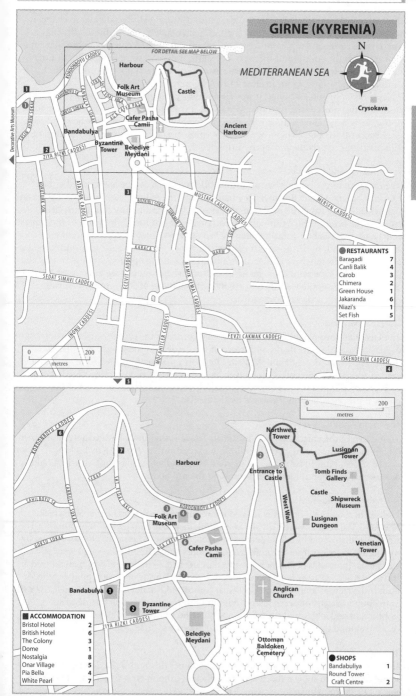

GIRNE (KYRENIA)

N

MEDITERRANEAN SEA

FOR DETAIL SEE MAP BELOW

Harbour

Castle

Crysokava

KORDONBOYU CADDESI

SAHILBOYU SK.

CAFER PASA

Folk Art Museum

Cafer Pasha Camii

Ancient Harbour

GÖKSU SOKAK

Bandabulya

Byzantine Tower

Belediye Meydani

Decorative Arts Museum

YASIN AYDIN SOKAK

ZIYA RIZKI CADDESI

KÖRDÜNK SK.

AZALJUK CADDESI

ECEVIT CADDESI

BOZKIRLI SOKAK

TURKMEN SOKAK

KARACA S.

MUSTAFA CAGATAY CADDESI

ZISS SOKAK

MERSEN CADDESI

MARM.

NAMIK KEMAL CADDESI

SEDAT SIMAVI CADDESI

INÖNÜ CADDESI

MUCAHITLER CADDESI

FEVZI CAKMAK CADDESI

ISKENDERUN CADDESI

● **RESTAURANTS**	
Baragadi	7
Canli Balik	4
Carob	3
Chimera	2
Green House	1
Jakaranda	6
Niazi's	1
Set Fish	5

0 200
metres

5

---

0 200
metres

KORDONBOYU CADDESI

Northwest Tower

Lusignan Tower

Harbour

Entrance to Castle

Tomb Finds Gallery

Castle

Shipwreck Museum

West Wall

Lusignan Dungeon

Venetian Tower

Folk Art Museum

KORDONBOYU CADDESI

CARBILLA SOKAK

SERAP

SAHILBOYU SK.

GÖKSU SOKAK

NACA CAFER PASA

Cafer Pasha Camii

Anglican Church

Bandabulya

Byzantine Tower

ZIYA RIZKI CADDESI

Belediye Meydani

Ottoman Baldoken Cemetery

■ **ACCOMMODATION**	
Bristol Hotel	2
British Hotel	6
The Colony	3
Dome	1
Nostalgia	8
Onar Village	5
Pia Bella	4
White Pearl	7

● **SHOPS**	
Bandabuliya	1
Round Tower Craft Centre	2

the remains of an earlier structure, in the tenth century AD. Rectangular in shape, it was reinforced and extended during the Lusignan era, with the addition of living quarters and a moat. Its present form took shape under the Venetians in the sixteenth century, with the addition of the west and south walls and the construction of three new bastions. The British used the castle as a prison and as a police academy, and, during the late 1950s, to incarcerate EOKA fighters.

Never taken by force (though it was almost destroyed by the Genoese in 1373), the castle did succumb to the Ottomans in 1570. It is said that the Venetian commander of the castle negotiated a truce with the Ottomans until it became clear how the siege of Nicosia turned out. When the Ottomans presented him with the severed head of his Nicosian counterpart, he promptly surrendered.

The entrance and courtyard

The entrance to the castle is across a stone **bridge**, which can be approached either from the central square **Belediye Meydani** through the police station yard, or up (clearly signposted) steps from the quayside. Either way, you need to buy tickets just before crossing the bridge. Once through the entrance gate, a tunnel brings you to the **central courtyard**, with its bits of broken masonry, palm trees, piles of stone catapult ammunition and, in the northeast corner, the rather pleasant *Kybele Cafe* and a souvenir shop from where all the castle's attractions are signposted. Be sure to take the steps up to the **viewpoint** over the harbour from where you can see as far as St Hilarion castle. Notice, too, the twelfth-century **Byzantine Chapel of St George** which was swamped by the castle as it expanded.

The Lusignan Tower

The **Lusignan Tower** standing at the northeast corner of the castle contains two floors of displays illustrating the medieval history of the castle. On the lower floor there are drawings by English academic William Dreghorn, mannequins dressed in armour and various weapons (crossbow, canon, even an early sort of machine gun), clearly labelled by period – Lusignan, Venetian, Ottoman. There are also details of some of the political prisoners held in the castle by the British.

The Tomb Finds Gallery

To the east of the entrance to the Lusignan Tower is the **Tomb Finds Gallery**, showcasing Neolithic and Bronze Age objects found in excavations at **Vrysi** (Agios Epiktitos), 10km east of Girne, **Kirni** (near modern Pinarbasi) and **Akdeniz** (Agia Irini). The highlight is a reconstruction of an underground tomb on the top floor.

The Shipwreck Museum

Housed in rooms that originally housed the royal guard, is the fascinating **Shipwreck Museum**. The chief exhibit is a 15m-long Greek merchant ship dating from 300 BC. The wreck was discovered by a local sponge diver off the coast of Girne in 1965 and raised by marine archeologists from the University of Pennsylvania. Among the cargo were 400 wine amphorae, thousands of almonds preserved in jars and 29 millstones which also served as ballast. Archeologists were able to deduce that the ship, made of Aleppo pine sheathed in lead, had a crew of four, and had docked at Samos and Rhodes on its final voyage. As well as the ship itself, the museum has exhibitions of the goods found on board, artists' impressions and a life-sized cross section to show how it was built, and is worth the price of admission to the castle on its own (see also the "sister" attraction in Agia Napa, p.60).

The Venetian Tower

In the southeast corner of the castle, a gallery slopes down into the depths of the **Venetian Tower** to show a mock-up of a Venetian cannon crew in action. There are also more Dreghorn paintings.

The Lusignan Dungeon

Halfway along the western wall, the between the southwest bastion and the exit, lies the entrance to the **Lusignan Dungeon**, which delivers all the ghoulish thrills that any bloodthirsty schoolchild could ask for. Waxwork displays show some of the types of torture used in the dungeons in the early 1300s when a purge of royalty and nobility was carried out. These include a particularly graphic model of a naked man being stretched on a wheel. The detail on the victims is grisly in itself – for example Joanna L'Aleman, who was tortured while pregnant and one John Visconti, who wound up starving to death in Buffavento Castle.

Ağa Cafer Paşa Camii

Just uphill from the waterfront west of the castle is Girne's main mosque, the **Aga Cafer Paşa**. Dating from 1589 it has been renovated and adapted many times, most recently after an EOKA-B bomb damaged it in the 1950s. Although the minaret is fairly short and stumpy, it's remarkable how visible it is from wherever you are in the harbour area. Open to visitors, the mosque contains three main rooms, each with an air of simplicity and space. Outside is the unused yet lavishly named "Hasan Kavizade Huseyin Effendi Fountain" built in 1841.

Chrysopolitissa church

West of the mosque (take a right then a left), early fourteenth-century **Chrysopolitissa**, Girne's oldest church, stands forlorn, flotsam left behind by the sea of history. Its main entrances and windows are bricked or boarded up, weeds sprout below its eaves, the occasional tourist is photographed in front of it. Restoration is, apparently, planned, but there's no sign of it at present.

The Folk Art Museum

Mon–Fri 8am–3.30pm (Thurs closes 5pm) • 5TL

On the waterfront, facing the harbour, is the **Folk Art Museum** (Harup Ambari Ve Kibris Evi) which stands in a fine Venetian-era house, once used as a carob store and donated to the city by a British expat in 1966. The building has been beautifully preserved and is distinctly more impressive than the contents – a motley collection of kitchen utensils, textiles and a few items of contemporary furniture.

The Icon Museum

Canbulat • Mon–Fri 8am–3.30pm • 5TL

Located on the western arm of the harbour up steep steps from Canbulat Sok, the **Icon Museum** is worth a quick visit (if it can be found open – its hours seem to be particularly irregular). The icons are largely seventeenth to nineteenth century, gathered from unnamed churches and stored in the castle until 1991 when the museum was opened. They are now displayed on three floors in the Archangelos Michaelis Church, built in 1860 with the blessing of the Turkish authorities, and with a bell donated by a local Muslim. The bell tower has long been a landmark for sailors, but the whole building, with its peeling white paint and rotting stucco, now looks in urgent need of attention. Opposite the steps up to the entrance are some Greco-Roman **rock-cut tombs**, a rare sight in Girne as many others have been built over.

Belediye Meydani and around

If the harbour is the tourist face of Girne, **Belediye Meydani** (Town Hall Square) reflects its ordinary Turkish Cypriot life. It's only a couple of hundred metres up the hill from the waterfront, yet it has a totally different feel – buzzing with pedestrians and traffic, and with a mall joining it to the main shopping street, **Ziya Rizki Caddesi**. If you raise your eyes above the bustle, you can see the snaggle-toothed outline of

6

St Hilarion Castle in the distance. The only thing to spoil the atmosphere is the very building that gives the square its name – an ugly modern municipal town hall, plonked right in the centre.

The Ottoman Baldoken Cemetery

With busy Belediye Meydani on one side and a large car park on the other, the little **Ottoman Baldoken Cemetery**, all that's left of a once huge graveyard, looks a little overwhelmed. It started as a place outside the castle to bury soldiers killed during the Ottoman siege, and later, during the seventeenth century, began to take civilians. It has also, at different times, been known as the Islamic Graveyard or the "Graveyard of the Forlorn". At its heart is a **domed tomb** called the Osmanli Baldoken Mezarligi. It is, given its surroundings, a surprisingly serene place in which to relax.

St Andrew's Anglican Church

Services Sun 8am & 10am, Thurs 9.30am • ☎ 2815 43 29, ⓦ standrewskyrenia.org

Part of the vast Anglican diocese of Cyprus and the Gulf, **St Andrew's Church** stands just beyond the Ottoman Cemetery's northern edge, and just southwest of the castle. A pretty white single-storey building with shuttered windows, it could be mistaken for a colonial bungalow if it wasn't for its understated little bell tower. Celebrating its centenary in 2013, the church is is still a functioning place of worship, welcoming Christians of any denomination.

The Byzantine Tower

Walking west from Belediye Meydani along Ziya Rizki Caddesi, you'll see the **Byzantine Tower**, squat and ancient-looking, with a busy café at its base and the "Round Tower Art Gallery and Craft Centre" upstairs. It's worth a visit to see the inside of one of the remaining city wall towers – if you spot souvenirs to buy, that's a bonus.

Bandabuliya

Next to the Byzantine Tower, with the main entrance on Canbulat Sok, the **Bandabuliya** is another old building that's been dragged into the twenty-first century. Once the town's bazaar, it's now an upmarket shopping mall with cafés, restaurants and gift shops.

Crysokava

To the east of the castle, and not easy to find (head for the New Harbour, signposted "Turizm Limani", and turn left at the harbour gates), is an eerie area of Roman tombs called **Crysokava** (or, more correctly, the "Crysokava Open Air Museum"). Now overlaid in parts with allotments, and with domestic animals occupying at least one of the tombs, the necropolis became a quarry under the Lusignans and Venetians. The main reason to visit is the **Church of Agia Mavra**, rock-cut, crumbling, and with some frescoes still intact, probably dating from the tenth century.

The Decorative Arts Museum

Mon–Sat 8am–3.30pm • 5TL • ☎ 815 21 42

To the west of the harbour/castle area, on Paşabahce Street, is Guzel Sanatler Muzesi, or the **Decorative Arts Museum**, which is housed in an interwar building. A rather diverse jumble of paintings, embroidery, porcelain and bric-a-brac, it might while away a few minutes if you're short of something to do.

ARRIVAL AND DEPARTURE   **GIRNE**

With excellent roads connecting it to the south, west and east, Girne is an easy place to get to, wherever you're staying on the island.

By bus The long-distance bus station can be found just off Halim Hocadglu Cad, southwest of the medieval harbour. Shared minibuses (dolmuş) set off from the central square, Belediye Meydani.

Destinations Gazimağusa (every 30min; 75min); Lefkoşa (every 30min; 20min).

By car Girne is connected to Lefkoşa by a dual carriageway, and to Gazimağusa and Güzelyurt by good main roads. On arrival, head for the car park next to the central square, Belediye Meydani, or look out for (often more expensive) private car parks on waste ground. Away from the old town, on-street parking is also a possibility.

By ferry Ferries connect Girne with the Turkish mainland, and run to and from the new harbour, east of the medieval harbour. They are run by two companies: Fergun (☎815 32 44, ⊛fergun.net, in Turkish only) and Akgunler (☎815 35 10, ⊛akgunler.com.tr), both on Belediye Meydani.

GETTING AROUND

On foot Girne is best explored on foot. Other places worth visiting in the region (St Hilarion, Buffavento and so on) will need a car, or can be visited using service taxis (from the bus station) or on tour buses.

By car For car rental try Cyprus Pines Rent a Car ☎815 02 90; Pia Bella Rent a Car ☎815 53 21; Ship Inn Rent a Car ☎815 67 01.

INFORMATION

Tourist office At the back of the Old Customs House at the western end of the medieval harbour (daily 8am–6pm ☎815 21 45).

ACTIVITIES

GOLF

Korineum Golf Club Esentepe, Girne ☎600 15 00, ⊛korineumgolf.com. New par-72 golf course – the first full golf course in north Cyprus. Has a golf academy, driving range, spa and gym, pro shop. Low/high season green fees €55–85, plus a range of equipment hire.

PARAGLIDING

Tandem paragliding (no experience needed) is offered by Highline Tandem Paragliding Old Harbour, Girne; ☎855 56 72, ⊛highlineparagliding.com. Experienced paragliders are also catered for.

WALKING

There's good walking in the Kyrenia mountain range just south of Girne – ask for a trail map at the tourist office, or consult ⊛kyreniamountaintrail.org, where you can buy downloadable GPS files for your mobile phone and a range of paper maps. As ever in Cyprus, the best walking weather is in spring and autumn, though the altitude in the mountains extends the walking season somewhat.

WATER SPORTS

Numerous watersports/boat trips/fishing trips are advertised around the harbour. There's usually no need to book. For example: African Queen ☎876 36 66 (six-hour boat trips, with stops at beach clubs for watersports) Aphrodite Boat Trips and Water Sports ☎868 09 43 (boat trips, fishing trips); Karabetca ☎862 62 70 (fishing trips); Marina Makina ☎873 21 00 (parascending); Ladyboss ☎855 56 72 (offshore fishing); The Princess ☎877 08 30 (daily boat tours).

SCUBA DIVING

Blue Dolphin ☎851 51 13, ⊛bluedolphin.4mg.com. Full range of scuba diving and tuition, based at the *Jasmine Court Hotel*.

Turtle Bay Dive Centre ☎0533849 6266, ⊛turtlebaydivecentre.com. Dives and training (dive sites include the Zenobia, near Larnaka).

ACCOMMODATION

Girne has a growing stock of hotels, villas and apartments split between the town and big package resorts along the coast. Another option is to stay in Bellapais village in the hills above town.

GIRNE TOWN

Bristol Hotel 114 Ziya Rizki Cad ☎815 65 70. Good budget option right in the centre. Small and friendly. Rooms have choice of bath or shower. There's a restaurant, bar and patio garden. Good views from top floor. Parking available. **€50**

British Hotel Kyrenia Yacht Harbour ☎815 22 40, ⊛britishhotelcyprus.com. Boutique-style hotel in centre of town with fine views from roof terrace. Following renovation, all rooms have plush interiors (deep purple throws and chairs add a bit of colour) with bath or shower, and there's a bar, restaurant and 24hr room service. **€60**

★ **The Colony** Ecevit Cad ☎815 15 18, ⊛thecolonycyprus.com. Back from the harbour area, this is a smart newish hotel which aims at a classy ambience, with a choice of restaurants and bars, rooms and suites.

6

Facilities include the inevitable casino, a fitness suite and spa (personal trainers are available) and a rooftop pool and terrace. Mostly aimed at Turkish business clientele rather than holiday-makers, but a good choice if you fancy a splurge. **€180**

Dome Kordon Boyou ☏815 24 53, ⓦdome-cyprus.com. Just out of the central harbour area, on the western promontory, within easy walking distance of the castle, this is the most famous colonial hotel in Girne. It dates back to the 1930s, and was where Lawrence Durrell stayed when he first arrived here. Stately public areas are complemented by comfortable modern rooms (renovated 2006). Smart bar with sea view, well-trained and friendly staff. Freshwater and sea-water pools. **€150**

Nostalgia 7, Cafer Paşa Sok ☏815 30 79, ⓦnostalgiaboutiquehotel.com. Old-fashioned (hence the name) hotel in the centre of Kyrenia – behind the Bandabuliya and the Byzantine Tower. Facilities include a/c and en-suite bathrooms in all rooms (though en suites can be a bit basic), and there's a small pool, and a restaurant and bar. The hotel occupies two townhouses, one slightly more modern than the other, so check the room on offer if this matters to you. This is a hotel with a slightly eccentric feel – you'll either love it or hate it. And there's a fair amount of street noise. **€55**

Onar Village Girne-Lefkoşa road ☏815 58 50, ⓦonarvillage.com. Nicely set hotel on the hill above Girne, with rooms in two wings plus villas around the pool, in lush gardens. There's a sauna/Turkish bath, solarium, indoor pool, restaurant, bar, library, even a small museum (and wi-fi throughout). Villas have full kitchens, so can be self-catering. There's a free daily shuttle into town (essential as it's several kilometres from the town centre up a steep hill). Lovely coastal and mountain views. **€70**

★ **Pia Bella** Iskeriderun Cad ☏815 53 21, ⓦpiabella.com. Clean, attractive modern family-run hotel with caring friendly staff. Quiet gardens with palm trees and mountain backdrop, pool, restaurant, café and several bars (though pool bar sometimes not open). Rooms are comfortable and have central heating and a/c, mini-bar and coffee-making wherewithall. **€85**

White Pearl 23, Eftal Akca Sok ☏815 04 29, ⓦwhitepearlhotel.com. Well-placed small hotel (ten rooms with heating, a/c and en-suite facilities, free wi-fi) on Girne harbour, with great views from room balconies and a roof terrace bar/restaurant which is open April–Oct. Rooms vary in size, so ask to see first if this is an issue. Refurbished 2007. **€68**

BEACH HOTELS

Acapulco Holiday Resort Çatalköy, Girne ☏650 45 00, ⓦacapulco-cyprus.com. Large resort hotel (200 rooms, 230 bungalows) with casino, 8km east of Girne. The *Acapulco* has a good range of facilities, including a beach restaurant, children's funfair and mini water park, kids' club, fitness and health centre. It claims to have the biggest pool in north Cyprus. Main restaurant uses locally sourced food, and there are several bars (including an "English Pub"). Good sandy beach, though the army camp on the western promontory is a bit intimidating. Free daily shuttle bus to Girne. **€245**

Mercure Kervansarsy Karaoğlanoğlu ☏650 25 00. This new business and tourist hotel just west of Girne is the only large global chain hotel in the north, and offers comprehensive hotel facilities, both personal and business. It offers a wide choice of rooms and suites, all with sea or mountain views, three restaurants, a range of bars, a beach club on its own beach and a casino. **€185**

EATING AND DRINKING

★ **Baragadi** Dogan Turk ☏815 94 81. Just up from the harbour, the *Baragadi* has an elegant colonial interior and a cool shady garden. It offers all the usual Turkish kebabs and the like, plus fish caught in the bay daily. Mains 20–28TL. Daily 9pm–2am. Closed Sun.

Canli Balik Eski Liman ☏815 21 82. This is a good fish restaurant down by the harbour (roughly halfway around, below the Folk Art Museum) and cheaper than many. The menu includes a wide selection of main courses, including lamb shank, bass and sea bream, kebabs and kleftiko, and snacks like omelettes, egg and chips and burgers, together with set menus. Around 20TL. Daily 10am–12.30am.

Carob Eski Liman ☏815 62 77. As the name implies, this restaurant is accommodated in a converted carob warehouse on the dock. Italian and Turkish cuisine is on offer – eat or drink downstairs, or enjoy the commanding views of the harbour from the balcony (full meals only). There's live music Fri & Sat. Around 25TL. Daily 9am–midnight.

★ **Chimera** Eski Liman ☏815 43 94. On the harbour side, at the castle end. French and Turkish cuisine served by attentive, friendly staff. Expect to pay 40TL per person for three courses and wine. English breakfasts. Occasional live music. Daily 9am–late.

Green House Kordon Boyu Cad ☏815 29 90. Busy restaurant serving massive portions of Turkish, Italian and Mexican food, indoors or alfresco (mains 10–15TL on average). It's on the small bay to the west of the main harbour, near the Dome Hotel. Daily 11am–midnight.

Jakaranda 2 Cafer Paşa Sok ☏815 60 08. Right next door to the Cafer Paşa Mosque, the *Jakaranda* is set in beautiful little terraced courtyard, with access either end. Has changed its name from the rather less evocative "Set Italian" – which still hangs on a sign over the upper gateway. Classic Italian set menu of pasta, seafood and steaks (35–55TL). Food noon–3pm & 6–11pm, drinks 11am–3pm "photos anytime".

Niazi's Kordon Boyn Cad ☎ 815 21 60 (take away ☎ 815 8460), ⓦ niazis.com. Hugely popular with locals and visitors *Niazi's* is famed for its "full kebab" (25TL) which packs in *kofte*, *şeftali* (North Cypriot sausage), plus a lamb chop, and comes served with accompanying meze and sweets from the open buffet. They also do takeaway. Daily 11am–midnight.

Set Fish Eski Liman ☎ 815 23 36. In an attractive stone building with balconies, on a terrace above the harbour road. 25TL upwards. Good-value fish restaurant which used to be the sister restaurant to "Set Italian", now *Jakaranda* (see above). Two sets to one, you could say. Daily 10am–11pm.

NIGHTLIFE AND ENTERTAINMENT

Girne is no Agia Napa though there are numerous bars around the harbour area and even a beach club (a rarity in north Cyprus). Otherwise nightlife and entertainment revolves around hotel casinos – with over twenty in the area, Girne is the casino capital of the north.

Café 34 Girne Limani. This place, in an old harbourside building, is a laidback café during the day, with more of a music scene at night. Young clientele.

★ **Escape Beach Club** Yavuz Cikarma Plaji, Alsancak ☎ 821 83 30. Set right on the beach 5km west of Girne, the *Escape* is a bar/club/restaurant complex. Music veers between R&B, hip-hop and Turkish.

Ice Lounge Yavuz Cikartma Plaji. Just outside Alsancak, above Cikarma Beach, west of Girne. International DJs during the summer, drinking, dancing and a decent sound system. 9pm–2am.

SHOPPING

There's not much in the way of exciting shopping available in Girne, though a couple of places offer a good range of souvenirs and gifts in interesting historical surroundings.

Bandabuliya The old indoor market (see p.216), now a source of souvenirs and gifts – handbags, candles, cards, textiles, pottery and jewellery. There's also a restaurant, juice bar, and coffee shop. Free wi-fi, too, and sometimes live music. Closed Sun.

Round Tower Ziya Rizki Cad. Good place to get art and craft goods like pottery, jewellery and pictures, in the setting of a Lusignan tower. You can also buy books. 10am–5.30pm.

DIRECTORY

Banks and Exchange Turk Bankasi, Ziya Rizki Cad; Is Bankasi, corner of Ziya Rizki Cad and Ataturk Cad.
Emergencies Ambulance (☎ 112), Fire Brigade (☎ 199) or Police (☎ 155). Girne Hospital (☎ 815 22 66).

Internet *Café Net*, Efeler Sokak ☎ 815 92 95; *Bright Star Internet Café*, Vakifler Paşaji 7, ☎ 844 93 93.
Post Office Off Belediye Meydani Mon–Fri 8am–1pm & 2–5pm, Sat 8.30am–12.30pm.

Around Girne

Although there's plenty to see in Girne, its possibilities are likely to start running out after a few days. Fortunately, its sandy coastline offers some excellent beaches while inland are some heavyweight sights including St Hilarion Castle and Bellapais village. Indeed, it shouldn't be forgotten that Lefkoşa and Güzelyurt are also within easy reach.

Karaoğlanoğlu (Agios Georgios)

Landings monument and cemetery open access • **Museum** June–Sept Mon–Sat 9am–1.30pm & 4.30–6.30pm; Oct–May 8am–1pm & 2.30–5pm • Free

About 8km west along the coast from Girne is the village of **Karaoğlanoğlu** (previously the Greek village of Agios Georgios), now a run-of-the-mill resort also home to the campus of the American University (and thus busy with students during termtime). It's mainly notable as the place where the **Turkish forces landed** on 20 July, 1974.

The landings are commemorated by a **monument** and museum west of town – stay on the main road, straight through three roundabouts (the first and third of which have signs for Karaoğlanoğlu pointing off to the right), and the monuments and museum are on the right. A large paved area leads to a small **Muslim cemetery** in which the 71 Turkish soldiers who died during the landing are buried, backed by a modern sculpture and the flags of Turkey and the TRNC. Karaoğlanoğlu was named in honour of an infantry colonel who was killed on the beach – his photograph and biography are mounted on a plinth.

Next to the plinth and cemetery is the **Peace and Freedom Museum**, a small collection of uniforms and photographs with some military vehicles on show outside. The actual **landing point** is marked by a huge concrete monument, nicknamed "the Turkish erection" by locals. The beach where it all happened was called "Five Mile Beach" by the British, presumably because it's five miles from Girne. It's one of the more attractive in the area, with the *Ada Beach Hotel* on one side, and on the other a pretty cove with golden sand, a little offshore island, and the *Escape Beach Club*.

Hazret Omer Tekke

9am–4pm, closed Fri • Free

On a rocky shore, 10km east of Girne, sits the **Hazret Omer Tekke**, built to house seven Muslim martyrs. The story goes that the seven (the commander Omer and six of his men), now regarded as saints, were killed in the seventh century, and their bodies put in a cave. Centuries later, after the Ottoman conquest, their bodies were discovered, still in a miraculous state of preservation, and moved to a mosque and mausoleum specially built to receive them. The beautifully designed mosque is in a spectacularly pretty setting, with views across a bay towards the mountains, but the effect is somewhat spoilt by the towering modern lamppost above it and intrusive modern toilet in the car park. The mosque itself badly needs a fresh coat of paint, having been battered and buffeted by wind and rain each winter.

Acapulco Beach

Around 10km east of Girne are a series of bathing possibilities, the best of which is **Acapulco Beach**, heavily colonized by a large hotel and casino complex (see p.218). It's a nice little cove with rocks just off the strand, and has all the facilities you'd need for an all-inclusive beach holiday. The resort is open to non-guests, free out of season but with a charge (20TL at the time of writing) during July and August. The holiday mood might be blighted somewhat, however, by the military camp, bristling with flags and barbed wire, which occupies the western headland of the bay.

Alagadi Protected Area

8am–8pm • Free • ⓦ seaturtle.org/mtrg/projects/cyprus

East of Acapulco Bay is a beach of a totally different type. **Alagadi** is a "Protected Area" because of the green and loggerhead turtles which nest here. A large noticeboard indicates some of the wildlife to be seen – plants, lizards, butterflies, and, of course, the sea turtles. During July and August a visitor centre operates, and it's possible to watch baby turtles hatching in the evening (see the website above). Although there are signs to deter litter and driving on the beach, a barrier which is shut overnight, and attempts to limit bathers to certain parts of the shore, there is often rubbish strewn across the sands. Overall it's a pretty bleak and unattractive spot except, presumably, to turtles.

St Hilarion Castle

June–Sept 9am–6.30pm, Sept–May 9am–12.30pm & 1.30–4.45pm • 7TL

Of the three magnificent castles in the Kyrenia mountains, by far the most accessible, popular and most complete is **St Hilarion**. Dramatically sited on a rocky crag with

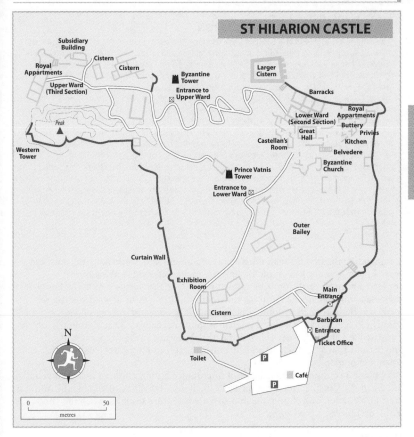

ST HILARION CASTLE

Subsidiary Building

Royal Appartments

Cistern

Cistern

Upper Ward (Third Section)

Byzantine Tower

Entrance to Upper Ward

Larger Cistern

Barracks

Royal Appartments

Lower Ward (Second Section)

Buttery

Privies

Peak

Great Hall

Kitchen

Castellan's Room

Belvedere

Western Tower

Byzantine Church

Prince Vatnis Tower

Entrance to Lower Ward

Outer Bailey

Curtain Wall

Exhibition Room

Main Entrance

Cistern

Barbican Entrance

Ticket Office

Toilet

P

P

Café

N

0   50
metres

6

elegantly ruined turrets, towers and windows, it certainly fires the imagination – in Rose Macaulay's words it's a "picture-book castle for elf kings" – and formed the template for both the fairy-tale castles of King Ludwig in Bavaria and Walt Disney's Magic Kingdom. If possible, visit in spring when the surrounding landscape is a riot of wild flowers.

To reach the castle from Girne you need to drive south along the Lefkoşa motorway as it climbs up into the mountains, and just before it gets to the top of the pass and begins its descent to the Mesaoria plain, follow the yellow signpost off to the right. A 3km side road snakes up through a **military camp**, past a large statue of a soldier in battledress at its entrance. (The firing range on the left was once the site for medieval tournaments.) Up a sharp hill, you arrive at a small car park outside the castle gate. The whole trip from Girne takes about 20min. On this road bear in mind that you're in a restricted military area, and not allowed to stop, let alone take photographs. This is a pity because it's as you approach the castle that you get by far the best view.

Brief history

St Hilarion was originally a **monastery** dedicated to an obscure fourth-century Syrian hermit who lived in a cave on Mount Didymus ("Twin peaks"). An ascetic of the most extreme kind, **Hilarion** reputedly never washed and built up a following thanks to banishing demons and performing miracles. The monastery's strategic position,

6

DASTARDLY DEEDS AT ST HILARION

On January 17, 1369, **Peter I, King of Cyprus** was stabbed to death as he slept in his palace in Nicosia, supposedly by three of his own knights. He was succeeded by his son, Peter II. **Queen Eleanor** – now the Queen Mother – became convinced that her husband had been killed on the orders of Peter's brother **Prince John**. Despite rumours of her infidelity in the king's absence she vowed to avenge his murder. John had taken up residence in St Hilarion Castle, which he held with a force of Bulgarian mercenaries, while Peter's other brother James held Kyrenia. A Genoese invasion, possibly at Eleanor's instigation, led, in 1374, to the surrender of Kyrenia, and James ended up as a prisoner in Genoa. Eleanor now turned her attention to John. Having persuaded him that all was forgiven, she warned the prince that his Bulgarian force were planning to overthrow him. John responded by throwing several of them to their deaths from Prince John's Tower. Eleanor's accusations were almost certainly untrue – a Machiavellian plan aiming to both bring him closer and weaken him. The drama concluded when Eleanor invited John to dine with her and the young king in Nicosia. They ate in the very room where Peter I was murdered and, when the final dish arrived, she dramatically flung back the cloth to reveal her dead husband's blood-stained shirt. This was the signal for retainers to appear and stab Prince John to death in his turn. Eleanor was not someone you'd want as an enemy.

commanding the pass through the Kyrenia mountains and overlooking the northern coastal plain, was not lost on the Byzantines. Facing repeated Arab raids, they converted it into a castle, probably sometime in the eighth century AD. The Lusignans improved and strengthened it in the thirteenth century – most of what you can see today was built in 1228 by John d'Ibelin – and it became not only a military stronghold but also a **palace** for Lusignan royalty, nicknamed "Dieu d'Amour", loosely translated as Cupid's Castle. This was the castle's heyday, an era of tournaments, knights and courtly intrigue, especially under the rule of **King Peter I** and **Queen Eleanor of Aragon** (see box above).

St Hilarion continued to be a castle of importance during the latter Lusignan period, but when the Venetians took over in 1489 it fell into disrepair and became the ruin it is now, to see action only during the mid-twentieth-century troubles, when the Turkish TMT occupied it.

The site

Once through the castle entrance – which includes a barbican – you will find yourself in the large **outer bailey** originally built by the Byzantines. Follow the sign to the right for the first of many wonderful views then continue upwards along the "Main Road". It's a well-made path with occasional steps, and you'll see as you climb a watchtower and, to your left, the impressive curtain wall that rises steeply to the upper parts of the castle. This outer bailey was the area into which peasants and livestock could be withdrawn when the castle was under attack.

The castle stables are now used as a small **visitor centre** which offers lots of sketches, and information about the Lusignans. Beyond the stables, the path winds steeply upwards to the tunnel-like gate of what is described as the "second section", perhaps the **Lower Ward**. It's a warren of alleys, buildings and rooms opening off a central tunnel, some of which were part of the original tenth-century monastery. The first structure, up to the right, is the monastery **church**, now open to the elements, but with a well-preserved apse. North of here is the **Great Hall**, now home to the *Café Lusignan*. Along one side of the hall is a wooden balcony hanging over a staggering view of the coast below – on a clear day you can see Turkey, some 100km away.

Beyond the hall are a group of rooms which serviced it – **kitchen**, **buttery** and **privies** – and a **belvedere**, a shaded vaulted terrace with picnic tables and arches, again with those superb views. To the left (west) of the hall are more workaday rooms and the **castellan's quarters**, which contain displays with mannequins illustrating medieval life.

Continuing along the path which tunnels through this clutch of lower ward rooms, you emerge into the sunlight to signs pointing one way (off to the right) to the **barracks**, and **Royal Apartments**, and the other way, onward and upward, to the third section.

You pass a very large cistern which appears to have been built rather than hewn out of the rock (it has stone buttresses), and then the path, partly steps, partly rock-strewn tracks, soars upwards. Just before you reach the top, a fork leads left to the isolated **Prince John's Tower**, where several of John's Bulgarian mercenaries were murdered (see box opposite). Turning right instead of following the path to Prince John's Tower brings you to the main gate of the **Upper Ward**. Once through the gate, there are, in succession, a Byzantine tower, a kitchen, a cistern and a group of subsidiary buildings. Beyond them are a further set of Royal Apartments and the famous **Queen's Window** at which Queen Eleanor is said to have sat. From here glorious views to the west open out, with, in the foreground, the village of Karmi. All that remains to be seen is the **Western Tower** and the **Zirve** (summit) of the mountain, marked with a sign: "732m – Congratulations! You are at the peak".

6

Buffavento Castle

Open access • Free

Buffavento Castle is the second of the three great fortresses that are strung out along the Kyrenia mountains (the other is Kantara, far off to the east; see p.245). Whereas St Hilarion is easily accessible, Buffavento is more remote, with the result that you may well be the only visitor – a major plus in terms of atmosphere. However, don't expect refreshments, information leaflets or the like – there's not even a ticket kiosk. Part of the excitement is the drive up to the castle along mountain roads revealing views across the whole island (see box below).

Brief history

Though never a monastery, Buffavento like St Hilarion was a Byzantine fortification built during the Arab raids, much developed and improved by the Lusignans. Indeed, it was the surrender of Buffavento to Richard the Lionheart by the daughter of Isaac Comnenos, the then ruler of Cyprus, that signalled the end of resistance to the English King and, a year later, the beginning of the Lusignan age. The castle had some high-profile residents – **John Visconti**, for example, who was the knight who informed King Peter I that his wife Eleanor was having an affair and was incarcerated for his

---

THE ROAD TO BUFFAVENTO

The castle is accessed from the main coast road east of Girne. Look out for the sign ("Buffavento 6km") on the right, past Acapulco Beach. From Lefkoşa, take the main Gazimağusa road east, then take a left (signposted "Girne") at a roundabout after 14km. Ignore earlier signs for Buffavento via Taskent – you're better off sticking to the main roads. After the turn-off, a good road climbs for 13km up towards an impressive blade of a mountain (called Pentadaktylos because its five peaks look something like a hand) past a large quarry – you may have to overtake heavily laden lorries grinding along at barely walking speed – to the Buffavento turning.

The mountain road to the castle looks narrow and uninviting, and is easy to miss, but it's well surfaced (not gravel as is sometimes reported) and meanders fetchingly off into the mountains. It certainly doesn't, as some guidebooks say, require four-wheel drive. There are stretches where there are steep drops to the left and no guardrail, and in places you might have to dodge rocks that have fallen off the cliffs to the right, but it's easy enough driving if you ignore the amazing views and keep your eyes on the road. After 6km a clear sign points up a steep hill to the castle car park.

6

pains, first in Girne Castle then at Buffavento, where he starved to death. Another story tells of a woman (variously identified as a Byzantine Queen or the Lusignan **Eschive of Montbeliard**) who locked herself away in the castle to prevent others being infected with her leprosy. Her only companion was her dog (which also had the disease). The mutt started to go missing for a time every day, and miraculously began to get better. One day she followed him to a natural spring, where he splashed in the water. She too bathed in the spring and was cured. In thanks, she built a church over the spring – **Agios Ioannis Chrysostomos** – and around it grew a monastery. It's still there (though deconsecrated) below the castle, but can't be visited, since it's well within one of the area's military camps.

The site
Though at 940m above sea level the highest of the three castles, Buffavento is also the smallest and worst preserved, more a romantic Gothic ruin than a sturdy fortress. The castle was much damaged by the Venetians to prevent its future use, and badly eroded over the centuries by elements (though its name means "not yielding to winds").

From the car park a path and steps rise steeply towards the ruins that you can see lining the clifftop high above. Bear in mind that it requires a fair bit of hard climbing (though there are plenty of hand rails) and there's little shade (if you get into trouble dial 155). As you climb, the views south are particularly impressive. As at St Hilarion, the hillside is carpeted with flowers in spring.

Incidentally, in the car park is a sad little **monument**, almost completely demolished by vandals. It commemorates the victims of an **air crash** in February 1988 when a Boeing 727 chartered by a Turkish airline heading for Ercan Airport hit the mountain here. All fifteen people on board were killed. The vandalism has been the subject of numerous complaints from visitors, but nothing has yet been done, either to remove or repair the ruined monument.

Bellapais
Almost exactly halfway between St Hilarion and Buffavento is the flower-bedecked village of **Bellapais**, a tangle of narrow lanes and steep hills, with fine views down to Girne's modern harbour. The village is synonymous with its **medieval abbey**, one of the most beautiful in the eastern Mediterranean. Yet, it's not just the abbey that makes Bellapais so popular – one of its principal cheerleaders was English author **Lawrence Durrell**, who lived here in the 1950s and included detailed descriptions of the village and its inhabitants in his book *Bitter Lemons*. Bellapais is one of the principal tour-stops on the island, so it is often packed. Try to avoid high season and late morning/early afternoon.

Brief history
Bellapais abbey was founded by the second Lusignan ruler **Aimery** to house Augustinian monks expelled from the **Church of the Holy Sepulchre** when Jerusalem fell to Saladin in 1187. Known as the "Abbaye de la Paix" or the Abbey of Peace, most of what remains dates from the period 1267–84, with the cloisters and refectory being added in 1324–59. In its early years the monastery adopted strict Premonstratensian beliefs, but as time went on it started to earn a name for a variety of **corrupt practices**, where monks ate and drank to excess, took wives (sometimes two or three), had children, and would then only accept their own sons into the monastery as novices. Though it built up considerable wealth, its treasure was plundered by the **Genoese** in 1373. After the **Ottoman Conquest** in 1571 the abbey became derelict, and was raided for its dressed building stone – only the church escaped, as it continued to be used for worship by the local Greek Orthodox community. Vandalization of the monastery continued under the British, who even used the refectory as a rifle range.

Bellapais Abbey

March–Nov 8am–6.15pm, Dec–Feb 8am–2.15pm • 9TL

Bellapais Abbey stands on a small square with trees, lawns, flowerbeds and park benches. Having bought tickets, you can walk through the **entrance gateway** whose ruins indicate that it was once heavily fortified. Nearby is the enviably sited *Kybele Restaurant*, which occupies the abbey's kitchen court, and a set of steps to the abbey's lofty **medieval tower**, topped by the vivid red and white of the Turkish and TRNC flags; despite signs warning that it's not safe to climb, the tower is far too seductive a photo opportunity for most visitors. Beyond here a tree-shaded **courtyard** leads to the **church**, the most complete part of the monastery. Unlike Western monasteries it is flat roofed, with a rather dark, gloomy interior. To the north of the church are the **cloisters**, the most atmospheric part of the abbey, three sides of which are in reasonable condition, but the fourth (western) side is ruined. The four rather large poplar trees in the quadrangle, planted in 1940, are home to a loud colony of sparrows. To the north of the cloisters, with access through a superb doorway with dog-tooth edges and three Lusignan coats of arms, is the **refectory**. Some 30m long, 10m wide and 12m high, it is covered by a single-span stone vaulted roof, an architectural triumph considering that it stands right at the edge of a cliff. At the far end (the end with the small rose window) stood the Abbot's high table, with, along the length of the north and south walls, the long tables of the ordinary monks. On the north wall is a small **pulpit** from where scriptures would be read to the diners silently munching below. Outside the refectory is a fountain where the monks would wash their hands before eating. If you look carefully you can make out the Roman sarcophagus into which it has been incorporated.

Lawrence Durrell's House

Lawrence Durrel lived in Bellapais from 1953–56, detailing his experience in *Bitter Lemons* (see p.263). To find his home, walk up from the abbey square along Aci Limon Sokak which climbs past the Tatlisulu market – there is a small hand-painted sign "Bitter Lemons 400m up on left" attached to a telegraph pole and pointing skywards. Another sign further up indicates that you're nearly there but should really visit the *Gardens of Irini* guesthouse. Durrell's house (dated 1893) is large and yellow, with brown doors and window shutters and a wooden-fenced roof terrace. In case you were in any doubt, there's a ceramic plaque above the door. Across the road is the public water fountain (marked "ER 1953") which played a prominent part in the tortuous and hilarious process of buying the house – the sale takes up a whole chapter in the book.

Another chapter of the book is devoted to the "**Tree of Idleness**" that stands opposite the abbey. Durrell was warned never to sit under it because "its shadow incapacitates one for serious work", a belief that arose from the idle hours spent by many villagers under the tree. It is now the centrepiece of a rather good restaurant.

ACCOMMODATION AND EATING · BELLAPAIS

★ **Bellapais Monastery Village** Bellapais Yolu ☎815 90 53, ⓦbellapaismonasteryvillage.com. Located 3km east of Girne, within walking distance of the village of Bellapai, this is a Byzantine/Ottoman-style modern buildings, with rooms, suites and "mini villas" all with a/c and en-suite facilities, and with a sun terrace, indoor and outdoor pool, rooftop restaurant and bar. Great views throughout. A hotel that prides itself on peace and quiet (therefore no children under 12). **€90**

★ **Gardens of Irini** Bellapais ☎815 28 20, ⓦgardensofirini.com. Run by long-term expats (one of them an artist whose paintings decorate the place), the *Gardens of Irini* is located at the top of Bellapais village – head for Lawrence Durrell's house (see above), and you'll see the sign. Tiny and delightful, the guesthouse consists of a small converted cottage and a studio backing onto a lovely garden. **€360** per week

★ **Tree of Idleness** Bellapais ☎815 33 80. Good-quality Turkish food in a restaurant through which grows the "Tree of Idleness" immortalized by Lawrence Durrell (though there is another pretender to the title elsewhere in the village). The stairs to the first floor climb up through its branches. Main courses 20–30TL. Live Turkish music Fri & Sat. Daily 10am–midnight.

Güzelyurt and the west

The western part of north Cyprus is not much frequented by visitors, yet it's easy to access following the opening of more **crossing points from the south** (see box below). The region's main town, **Güzelyurt**, is worth a brief wander for its archeological museum and the Agios Mamas Church. But it's the twin ancient sites of **Soli** and **Vouni** that are the real draw.

6

Güzelyurt (Morfou)

GÜZELYURT (called Morfou before 1974, a name that is still widely used), 40km west of Lefkoşa, is the principal town for the western part of north Cyprus. Once hugely prosperous, it has suffered badly first from the demise of the copper-mining industry and, subsequently, the impact of the 1974 invasion which devastated the surrounding citrus groves and strawberry fields, once tended by Greek Cypriot farmers – still a cause of immense bitterness in the south. The fruit farms are, at last, recovering and the main impression that you get now as you approach is a sea of orange and lemon trees stretching as far as the eye can see.

On the way into town on the Girne road, look out for **Engine No 3** of the Cyprus Government Railway. A saddle engine, it was built in the USA in 1924, and looks a little sorry for itself compared to Engine No 1 in Gazimağusa. Rearing up on the town's main roundabout (along with a memorial to Turkish Cypriots killed by EOKA) is the imposingly large, white **Fatih Camii** mosque, built with Saudi Arabian money. Nearby is the **archeological museum** and the town's main highlight, the church and monastery of **Agias Mamas**. The rest of Güzelyurt, with its prosaic buildings, and heavy traffic, is simply somewhere to pass through on your way to the attractions further north or west.

The Museum of Archeology and Nature

Summer 8am–7pm, winter 8am–3.30pm • 7TL

Güzelyurt 's **Museum of Archeology and Nature** is housed in an impressive white colonial building that stands just behind the main roundabout. Broadly, the ground floor contains the "nature", the first floor the "archeology". The former consists of a miscellany of stuffed animals (including a frankly disturbing lamb with two heads), plus a small collection of mounted butterflies and geological samples. Upstairs things start to look up. **Neolithic** and **Bronze age artefacts** occupy the first room; the next two are devoted to finds from Tumba tou Skuru, and the last two display objects from the Archaic to the Byzantine eras. Particularly fine is a nicely mounted gold diadem (though with no indication of its provenance), finds from Salamis and some votive figures from the seventh century BC. Around the back of the museum are some lovely **gardens** (a perfect spot for a picnic) behind which the church of Agios Mamas and the minarets of the mosque rise in becoming fashion.

VISTING GÜZELYURT FROM THE SOUTH

There are two crossing points in the Güzelyurt region. The **Astromeritis/Zodia crossing** opened in August 2005, is one of the better-signposted ones, and is also one of the quietest. Astromeritis is a fast 30km west on the A9/B9 motorway/dual carriageway from the outskirts of Lefkosia. Once across into Zodia, it's only 3km to Güzelyurt. The **Yeşilirmak/Limnitis/Kato Pyrgos crossing** (see box, p.140) is the most recent, built jointly by the north and south and opened with great fanfare in October 2010. Again, it is easy to find – a ten-minute drive east from Kato Pyrgos brings you to the crossing point, after which it's a scenic 32km drive to Güzelyurt. This makes possible a number of enjoyable routes through the north. Lefkosia–Girne–Güzelyurt–Kato Pyrgos, for example, is certainly feasible in a day, either direction, or try Astromeritis–Güzelyurt–Kato Pyrgos.

Agios Mamas Church and Monastery
Key available from Museum of Archeology and Nature • Free

To the left of the museum is a gate offering direct access to the cloisters of **Agios Mamas**. The story of St Mamas is a colourful one. A hermit who lived in a cave, he refused to pay taxes to the Ottomans. Soldiers were sent to bring him before the authorities. As they took him to Nicosia, they came upon a lion attacking a lamb. Mamas commanded the lion to spare the lamb, then hopped on the lion's back and (lamb safely in his arms), rode the beast all the way to the governor's palace. The governor, much impressed by the manner of his arrival, granted Mamas immunity from local taxation for the rest of his life. Some accounts say that the grateful saint then gave the lamb to the governor.

6

Today the monastery and church are, of course, unused (except for intermittent permission for the saint's name day to be celebrated) but are in very good condition compared with many such Orthodox sites in the north. Cool colonnades surround a paved courtyard in the centre of which is the church which contains, partly inside and partly outside, the sarcophagus of St Mamas. Inside the church a rather good iconostasis survives, as does an ornate 1711 pulpit. The star of the show, though, accessible from both within and without, is the saint's marble sarcophagus on the left of the north entrance. A scented nectar is said to ooze out of it on occasion, and is apparently excellent for curing earache – hence the ear-shaped votive offerings – and for calming stormy seas.

The Koruçam Peninsula
Due north of Güzelyurt, separating the north Cypriot coast from Morfou Bay, is the **Koruçam Peninsula**, similar in size to the Akamas to the west. Though it offers superb sunsets, a dramatic, rock-strewn and wave-lashed coastline (often, alas, heavily littered) and beautiful views back to the Kyrenia mountains, there's not much here to tempt the passing tourist, though a point of interest is the age-old **Maronite community** that still keeps a precarious toe-hold in the area (see box below).

You can access the peninsula via the loop of road, mostly good, that leaves and rejoins the Girne to Güzelyurt route just before the garrison town of **Çamlibel** (Myrtou). The only landmarks on the coast road are **Horseshoe Beach**, which has a few basic facilities on a bluff above a stony shore, **Kayalar (Orga)**, with its regimented villas, **Sadrazamkoy (Livera)**, a clutch of white houses and a café and the last village on the peninsula, and beyond that a dirt track to the tip, with little **Kormakitis Island** beyond. On the inland

---

THE MARONITES OF THE KORUÇAM PENINSULA
A **Maronite** community has existed on the Koruçam Peninsula for at least nine hundred years, though it has now shrunk to a few hundred people. Maronite Christian beliefs originated in Syria and the Lebanon, and arose from an arcane seventh-century dispute about the nature of Christ. The Maronites lost the argument, were declared heretical, and had to take to the hills. They came to Cyprus, it is said, on the coat-tails of the Crusaders: they'd helped their fellow Christians against the Muslims in the Holy Lands (though one theory postulates that they were simply joining a Maronite community which was already on the island). The Maronites congregated on the Karpaz and Koruçam peninsulas – the former disappeared through emigration and intermarriage, the latter are, just about, still there. During the troubles of the 1960s the Maronites sided with the Greeks, and following the Turkish invasion in 1974, were harassed, issued with identity cards, and refused citizenship. Most left for the south, or went abroad. Since the progressive opening of the Green Line since 2003, however, Maronites who had made their lives in the south can now visit freely. The future of their distinctive language, a fusion of Aramaic and Arabic, is less rosy, and its demise as a living language is predicted within a few decades.

road the only settlement is **Koruçam/Kormakitis** itself, dominated by its large Maronite church and the gaunt frame of a modern, and abandoned, school.

Çamlibel (Myrtou) and around

Çamlibel (Myrtou), inland from the Koruçam Peninsula and about 20km from Güzelyurt, is best used as a navigation aid rather than as a place to visit in itself. It's at the heart of an extensive series of **Turkish army camps**, and any attempt to navigate through it will founder on barbed wire and sandbagged entrance gates. However, a couple of places around it are worth a look.

Pigades Shrine

Open access • Free

Just off the main Çamlibel to Lefkoşa road, about 2km past the turn off for Güzelyurt, is **Pigades**, a Bronze Age shrine which it might just be worth slogging along a 250m path to see. There is a sign on the main road, though it's easy to miss, and you can identify where the shrine is by the clump of trees in the middle of a field. It's an open site, the remains of a temple that dates from 1600–1050 BC, the centrepiece of which is a pyramidal stone altar topped by Minoan-style stone bull-horns. The rest of the temple consists of two blocks of rooms, one around a garden, the other around a hole in the ground.

The Blue Villa

Tues–Sun 9am–5pm • 0.5TL

A little way west of Çamlibel is the clearly signposted **Mavi Kosk** or **Blue Villa**, a bizarre 1970s pleasure palace now within a Turkish military area. You need to hand over your passport to the guards at the gate in order to drive up to the house (no getting out and walking) – note that if you're in a rented car from the south, you will be politely but firmly turned away.

The villa was built a year before the Turkish invasion by Greek Cypriot **Byron Pavlides**, a successful car dealer with friends in high places (particularly high in the case of Archbishop Makarious III). Something of a playboy (he had a sunken pool built in the lounge and a secret tunnel to his bedroom), rumour has it that he also dabbled as an EOKA gun-runner and chose this location, with its unimpeded views out to sea, in order to keep an eye on his contraband boats. Having relocated from the equally fabulous "White House" near St Hilarion when that area became predominantly Turkish Cypriot, Pavlides was forced to flee once again as the Turks invaded and commandeered the Blue House in 1974 (he died in mysterious circumstances in Italy in 1986). Aside from its sense of intrigue, the house has a gorgeous blue-themed interior and offers some unbeatable ocean views.

West of Güzelyurt

The main road west from Güzelyurt to Yeşilirmak and the Kato Pyrgos crossing is of good quality all the way along its length, whatever your map says. It gets to the coast just before Gemikonaği – a quick detour up to **LEFKE (Lefka)** is worthwhile, for its lush vegetation, old Turkish houses and colonial British storehouse. Back on the coast you reach **GEMIKONAĞI (Karavostasi)**, which, with its derelict ore-handling jetties has an appealing air of shabby dereliction – one, in particular, looks like a beached Chinese dragon. Beyond Gemikonaği are the unmissable archeological sites of **Soli** and **Vouni**.

Ancient Soli

Summer–7pm, winter 8am–3.30pm • 7TL

The site of the ancient city of **SOLI** has few equals in north Cyprus, possibly on the whole island, thanks to its instant comprehensibility and the quality of information

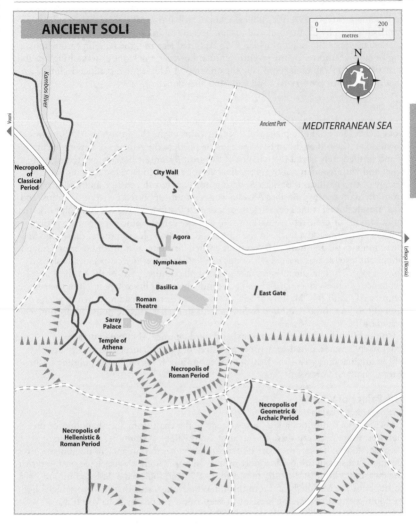

ANCIENT SOLI

0   200
metres

N

6

Kambos River

Vouni

MEDITERRANEAN SEA

Ancient Port

Necropolis
of
Classical
Period

City Wall

Agora

Nymphaem

Basilica

Roman
Theatre

East Gate

Saray
Palace

Temple of
Athena

Necropolis of
Roman Period

Necropolis of
Geometric &
Archaic Period

Necropolis of
Hellenistic &
Roman Period

Lefkoşa (Nicosia)

provided. It offers a detailed picture of life in late Roman and early Byzantine times, in a city set on a hillside overlooking the Mediterranean.

You'll find the site just after leaving Gemikonaği, travelling west on the coast road. Look out for a small sign pointing to the left just after the announcement that you're in Yedidalga (Potamos). The sign is easy to miss, but the huge roof covering part of the site isn't.

Brief history

Soli was originally settled in the eleventh century BC – its first mention in written records is as "Si-il-lu" in an Assyrian tribute list. According to legend it was named after the Athenian philosopher **Solon**, who, while visiting his friend King Philocypros, suggested he built a new capital here, pointing out the excellent natural harbour and fertile soil. Soli soon flourished, though siding with the Ionians against the Persians led to it being sacked in 498 BC. Biblical scholars will also recall Soli as the site of St Mark's baptism by St Auxibius and it soon became an important **Christian centre**, particularly once the Edict of Milan (313 AD) had legalized the religion throughout the Byzantine empire. By the seventh century, however, the harbour was silting up, and a succession of Arab raids, especially the one in 653 AD, led to a gradual decline, such that by the ninth century AD Soli had been abandoned.

6

The site

Soli is vast, and only part of it has been excavated. Once you've parked and bought your ticket (get hold of a plan) you'll see the ruins of the third-century AD Roman town down the hill to the right – the agora, a portico, the remains of a nymphaeum – and immediately ahead the remains of the great **Byzantine basilica**, protected by a roof, and with wooden walkways to allow visitor access. In fact, the remains you can see are of two basilicas – Basilica A, dating from the fourth century, and Basilica B from the sixth century. **Basilica A** had a wooden roof supported on stone columns, and had **mosaic floors**, some geometrical, others with the figures of birds and dolphins. The most famous of these representations is of a swan against a blue background, with flowers, dolphins and a duck. In the apse is a dedication "Jesus, protect those who had these mosaics made". **Basilica B** was built entirely of stone, and instead of mosaics made of cuboid tesserae was floored with opus sectile tiles (larger pieces specifically shaped for the job). Though the mosaics take pride of place, other parts of the basilicas are also explained – a presbytery, an atrium, a column which still lies where it fell in the eighth century AD, and the "**Mystery of Soli**" – a staircase or ramp leading down to what's thought to be a tomb dedicated to St Auxibius or even a treasure house (unfortunately sealed off).

Up the hill behind the basilica is an early third-century AD **Roman theatre**, extensively renovated and sometimes still used for performance. There's very little left of the original masonry – the British pilfered most of it for use in the building of the Suez Canal and Port Said.

The Palace of Vouni

Summer 8am–5pm, winter 8am–3.30pm • 5TL

Crowning the summit of a hill 5km west along the coast from Soli (look out for the sign pointing up a steep drive) is the mysterious **Palace of Vouni**. It's mysterious because, despite its size, there are no known references to it in ancient documents. Even the name tells us nothing – it simply means "hilltop". Archeologists have surmised that the palace was built in the early fifth century BC, and followed a design common throughout the Middle East. From this it has been suggested that it was originally built by a king sympathetic to the Persians to keep an eye on nearby Soli. Vouni was eventually destroyed by fire in around 380 BC.

You'll have to use your imagination to visualize the "palace". However, you're given an excellent pamphlet with annotated ground plan, photographs and notes when you buy your ticket. Each part of the site is labelled – entrance hall, main room, cistern, courtyard, bathrooms, storerooms, private rooms and so on. In the centre of the courtyard is a very distinctive piece of masonry, which looks like a time-worn statue. It is located above the entrance to the cistern, and was in fact intended to hold a windlass for raising water – the slots for the handles are there, but the intended decoration of a goddess is unfinished, leading to the conclusion that the palace was destroyed before it could be completed. At the top of the site are the remains of a Temple of Athena, indicating that the palace had been adapted to Greek taste at some point in its history.

Despite being a little underwhelming in terms of its remains, the views towards the little island of Petra tou Limniti, the surrounding countryside and back towards Gemikonağı, are spectacular.

Gazimağusa (Famagusta)

The charming city of **GAZIMAĞUSA** (Famagusta), is second only to Girne in the north's tourism league table. Like Girne it boasts an atmospheric old town surrounded by crumbling Venetian walls, a legacy of its strategic position facing the Middle East. Its shops, restaurants and cafés are threaded through and between the photogenic remains of **churches** destroyed or damaged during the Ottoman siege of 1570–71. Immediately to the south lies the ghost town of **Varosha**, once the heart of Famagusta's tourist trade, now isolated by the Turkish invasion of 1974. To the north lie a clutch of historically important sites – ancient **Enkomi/Alasia**, the monastery of **Apostolos Varnavas**, the **Royal Tombs**, and above all ancient **Salamis** – and the miles of beaches that line Gazimağusa Bay.

Confusingly, Gazimağusa is known by a host of different names. The city was renamed Gazimağusa (sometimes shortened to **Mağusa**) by the Turks in 1974, having been known as **Famagusta**, from French (Famagouste) and Italian (Famagosta), since Lusignan/Venetian times. In Greek it is known as **Ammochostos**. If that wasn't puzzling enough the name Famagusta/Ammochostos is also used by the republic for the district across the Green Line to the east, of which the city is the notional capital.

Brief history

The current site of Gazimağusa was established during the Byzantine era by refugees from Salamis, after that city was destroyed by Arab raids. The new city reached its zenith under the Lusignans, especially after the Fall of Acre to the Saracens in 1291 AD brought an influx of Christian merchants and craftsmen. When the pope banned direct economic ties with the infidel, Gazimağusa became a major entrepôt for the whole of the Middle East, famous for its wealth and as a melting pot of different cultures and beliefs – hence the huge variety and number of churches (one, it was said, for every day of the year). It went into something of a decline from the late fourteenth century onwards, but was fortified under the Venetians as they tried to meet the growing threat from Ottoman expansion. As at Girne and Lefkosia, this did them little good – the city fell in 1571 after a nine-month siege, thus completing the Ottoman conquest of the island. It is said that 100,000 cannonballs crashed into the city during the siege and, since no attempt was made by the Ottomans to repair the damage, the remains still stand today. Three years after the siege, Greek residents were expelled from within the walls. Many of them resettled just to the south, creating what later became Varosha.

VISITING GAZIMAĞUSA FROM THE SOUTH

To get to Gazimağusa from the south, there are two convenient crossings, both in the Dekhelia Sovereign Base area. The first is the most useful if you're staying in Larnaka, and is known variously as the **Pyla/Beyarmudu/Pergamos crossing** (see box, p.70). From Larnaka, take the coast road or the A3 motorway towards Agia Napa, and follow the signs off to the left, signposted Pyla. Drive through Pyla, and up the hill on the other side. The crossing is a couple of kilometres along this main road. Once across, you're in the village of Beyarmudu – remember the name, since you'll need to head towards it on your return. Drive for 9km to an intersection, cross it, and continue for another 9km till you hit the main Lefkoşa–Gazimağusa highway. Turn right, and you hit the dual carriageway all the way to Gazimağusa. On your return, make sure you don't miss the turn off the highway towards Beyarmudu.

The second option, especially handy if you're staying in the Agia Napa/Protaras area, is the **Agios Nikolaos/Akyar/Strovilia crossing**. This is closer than the Pyla crossing, but a lot harder to find. Drive through Paralimni and head for Dyrenia. Turn left at the traffic lights, heading for Frenaros along the main E305 road, then follow the signpost right to Vrysoulles. Turn right at the T-junction, and the crossing point is about 3km beyond. If lost, stop and ask directions. Once across, Gazimağusa is just 5km beyond.

GAZIMAĞUSA (FAMAĞUSTA)

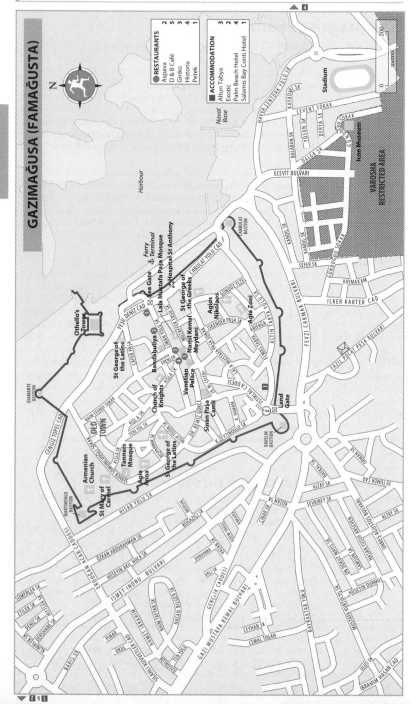

N

RESTAURANTS
Aspava 2
D & B Café 5
Ginko 3
Historia 4
Petek 1

ACCOMMODATION
Altun Tabya 3
Exotic 2
Palm Beach Hotel 4
Salamis Bay Conti Hotel 1

Naval Base

Stadium

VAROSHA RESTRICTED AREA

Icon Museum

Harbour

Othello's Tower

Sea Gate
Ferry & Terminal
Lala Mustafa Paşa Mosque
Hospital
St Anthony

St George of the Latins

Bandabuliya

St George of the Greeks

Agios Nikolaos

Agía Zóni

Namik Kemal Meydani

Venetian Palace

Church of Knights

OLD TOWN

Armenian Church

Tanners Mosque

St George of the Latins

Agía Anna

St Mary of Carmel

Sinan Paşa Camii

Land Gate

During the 1960s and early 1970s, Varosha and its beaches were at the heart of massive tourist development, only to be frozen in time by the Turkish invasion.

The city walls

Originally built by the Lusignans, Gazimağusa's **city walls** owe their present impressive dimensions and design to the Venetians, who spent half a century up to 1540 remodelling them for medieval battle, for example, building ramps up which to haul cannons, and making square towers round, so that they were proof against artillery fire. A dry moat was cut around three of the four sides – the fourth faces the sea. Unfortunately you cannot make a complete circuit of the walls – the northern bastions (Diamante and Martinego) are restricted areas. This was not the case under the British who played golf along the ramparts in the 1930s.

The Land Gate and Ravelin Bastion

In the southwest corner of the walls is the **Land Gate**, one of the two original main gates (the other being the Sea Gate) to the old town. As you approach across the bridge, look to the right for a good view of the stretch of wall to the first "Santa Napa" bastion. Once inside you'll find the tourist office to the left. The **Ravelin Bastion** (or Rivettina Bastion) in front of the gate was heavily involved in the Siege of Famagusta, and when it finally seemed bound to be taken by the attackers, the Venetians blew it up, killing, it's said, a thousand Ottoman soldiers and a hundred of their own. This was also where the white flag of surrender was flown, prompting the victors to rename it Akkule, or "White Bastion". The innards of the bastion, a warren of passages, rooms and flights of steps, are open to the public.

The Canbulat Bastion

Museum: June–Sept 9am–7pm, Sept–May 9am–12.30pm & 1.30–4.45pm • 5TL

As you circle the walls in an anticlockwise direction, the next major bastion – the **Canbulat Bastion** – is in the southeast corner. It is named after one of the Turkish heroes of the siege of Famagusta, Canbulat, the Bey of Kilis. Faced with a fearsome

THE SIEGE OF FAMAGUSTA

Fresh from its victory over Nicosia and the surrender of Kyrenia, the Ottoman army approached Famagusta in confident mood in September 1570. Before them lay a small garrison of Venetians, no match it would seem for thousands of battle-hardened Turkish troops. Having blockaded the port (thus preventing relief from the Venetian navy), the Ottoman commander **Mustafa Paşa** ordered his artillery to pound the city while his engineers built trenches and a huge earth ramp to scale the walls. The Venetian defenders, hopelessly outnumbered, put up a gutsy resistance under the command of **Marcantonio Bragadin** and his lieutenant **Lorenzo Tiepolo**, cunningly moving soldiers about so that the invaders were tricked into thinking them a far more formidable force. The Venetians managed to hold out for ten months before the citadel was breached in July 1571. Bragadin agreed to a negotiated surrender where all civilians could leave the city and his soldiers could sail for Crete.

Things went largely to plan until during the hand-over ceremony when Mustafa Paşa, up until then courteous towards his opponent, suddenly exploded with rage, killing several Venetian officers and cutting off Bragadin's ears and nose. A **massacre** of the remaining Christians in the city followed. Bragadin, after several weeks' imprisonment, was publicly **executed**, his body quartered, and his skin, stuffed with straw, sent riding on an ox through the town before being sent to the sultan in Constantinople. The treatment of Bragadin so incensed the Venetians that it was said to inspire their forces at the Battle of Lepanto a couple of months later, halting Ottoman expansion in the Mediterranean. Bragadin's flailed skin was rescued from Constantinople in 1596 and returned to Venice, where it still rests in the Basilica di San Zanipolo.

defensive device consisting of knives attached to a rapidly rotating wheel, Canbulat rode his horse full tilt into it, killing both himself and his steed, but jamming the wheel and making it ineffective. His tomb, which is in the bastion, once had a fig tree growing out of it, whose fruit, if eaten by young women, would not only ensure conception, but also that the resulting children would be as brave as Canbulat. There's a small **museum** containing oddments of costume, artillery and Venetian and Ottoman ceramics.

The Sea Gate

After the Canbulat Bastion, the walls swing north, parallel to the sea. Note to the left of the wall, the remains of the **Hospital of St Antony**, which was built using stone taken from the ruins of Salamis. Beyond them is the **Sea Gate**, which once provided access from the port. A squat and solid-looking fortification with a signature statue of a Venetian lion at its base, it has massive iron-clad wooden gates, Ottoman in origin, and a heavy Venetian iron portcullis (both shrouded in tarpaulin at the time of writing). The top of the Sea Gate is accessible via a steep flight of steps from inside the town at the end of Liman Yolu; the views across the town one way, and the port the other, are worth the climb. Looking north from the Sea Gate you can see a variety of ships in the harbour, many of them Turkish naval vessels (which is why the northern parts of the walls are off limits). Incidentally, the Venetian lion is said to open its mouth once a year – if you're nearby when it does so, plunge your hand down its throat and you will retrieve treasure.

Othello's Tower

June–Sept 9am–8pm, Oct–May 9am–12.30pm & 1.30–4.45pm • 7TL

Beyond the Sea Gate stands the massive **Othello's Tower**. The name is a little fanciful, bestowed by the British on the strength of the locations mentioned in Shakespeare's play: "A seaport in Cyprus" and "a hall in the castle". Indeed its alternative name, "**The Citadel**", is a better description. Above the entrance in the southwest corner is a large relief of the Lion of St Mark, the Venetian emblem. Despite its Venetian exterior you can still make out the original Lusignan fortress beneath: the large central courtyard on the north side is the Great Hall, still used for concerts and performances. The views from the battlements are as good as those from the Sea Gate. Look out, too, for the ventilation shafts designed to clear smoke from the cannons inside the tower; a few of these were filled in with rubble prompting rumours that the Venetians had buried their gold here rather than see it fall into the hands of the Ottomans.

The old town

Within the walls, the **old town** of Gazimağusa is an appealing jumble of ruined churches, odd bits of medieval masonry, cafés, restaurants and shops, tree-shaded and flower-bedecked and much of it pedestrianized. The best approach, once you've entered through the Land Gate and perhaps visited the tourist office, is to head up the main street **Istiklal Caddesi** towards the central square, **Namik Kemal Meydani**, perusing shops and cafés as you go. East and south of the main square is a maze of narrow streets and alleys, good for souvenir hunting, and overlooked by picturesque ruins. You can imagine a similar scene in medieval times, though with the great Gothic churches intact, rising above people's homes.

Sinan Paşa Camii (Church of St Peter and St Paul)

Open access • Free

As Istiklal Caddesi bends to the right, just before the central square, the first of Gazimağusa's ruined churches sails into view like a galleon under full sail. A great lump of Lusignan architecture, **Sinan Paşa Camii**, originally the **Church of St Peter and St Paul**, is impressively massive, with wide flying buttresses shoring up its bulk. It was built in the mid fourteenth century and financed, it is said, by a merchant from the proceeds of a single transaction. As one of the few larger buildings to survive the 1570 Turkish bombardment relatively intact, it has gone through a number of reincarnations – under the Ottomans as a mosque, under the British as a potato and grain store, and more recently as a public library and performance venue. In its precincts are several tombs – one is of Yirmisekiz Mehmet Cheleb, who was the first Ottoman ambassador to France.

6

The Venetian Palace
Open access • Free

Just as you enter the square, you'll see on the left what remains of the **Venetian Palace** which housed the governor. There's not a lot to see – the east facade consisting of a couple of two-storey high walls, and three arches supported by four columns taken from Salamis. This was the palace in which the ill-fated Bragadin lived, and in front of which he so horribly died (see p.233).

Namik Kemal Meydani
Namik Kemal Museum: June–Sept 9am–2pm, Sept–May 9am–12.30pm & 1.30–4.45pm • 5TL

At the heart of old Gazimağusa is the central square **Namik Kemal Meydani**. Surrounded by mellow, ruined buildings, it is dotted with cannons and piles of cannonballs (the iron ones were fired, the stone ones flung from catapults), and lined with the tables, chairs and parasols of several cafés – a delightful spot to stop for refreshment. The square is named after dissident Turkish poet and playwright **Namik Kemal** (1840–1888) who was exiled to Cyprus when one of his plays, performed in Constantinople, was considered seditious. He was imprisoned from 1873 to 1876 in the small building that faces into the square. His "dungeon" is now a small museum – there's also an impressive bust of the man in front of the cathedral.

Lala Mustafa Paşa Mosque (St Nicholas Cathedral)
Open to public when no services are on • Donation requested

On the eastern side of Namik Kemal Meydani, and dominating all around it, is the impressive bulk of **Lala Mustafa Paşa Mosque (the Cathedral of St Nicholas)**. Though

---

ECCLESIASTICAL GEMS – A WALKING TOUR

Dotted around the old town are numerous minor churches, often in a poor state of repair but full of interest. A good place to start is just off Namik Keymal Beydani, on Kisla Sokagi opposite the distinctive glass-dotted dome of a hamam, where, next to each other, two little fourteenth-century churches stand. They are invariably identified as the churches of the **Knights Templar and Knights Hospitaller**, the latter based on the Hospitaller coat of arms above the western door. One is now a cultural centre and art gallery, the other, surprisingly, is a bar. A short walk northwest, by the Othello Tower, is the ruined **St George of the Latins**, one of Gazimağusa's oldest churches. Based on the height off the ground of its surviving windows, and the presence of a parapet, it has been speculated that it was a fortified church predating the Lusignans. There's little left now but a single wall with large lancet windows, precarious but undoubtedly romantic. Beyond St George of the Latins, a walk along Gengiz Topel Cad then left onto Server Somuncuoglu Sok brings you to the northwest corner of the town. Here the churches of **Agia Anna** and **St Mary of Carmel**, the **Armenian Church** and the converted **Tanners Mosque** are clustered together in the angle between the walls that meet at the Martinengo Bastion. Since this is near a military zone, access can be tricky, and photography is definitely a no-go. Back at Namik Keymal Beydani, a stroll due south brings you to **St George of the Greeks** which is (or was) a large Byzantine Orthodox Church (all that remains are three apses and a flying buttress at one end and the entranceway on the other) – while a little further southeast takes you to **Agios Nikolaos** and **Agia Zoni** which are small and pretty, the first a ruin, the second pretty much intact.

badly damaged during the siege, its western facade is still largely intact, looking like a cathedral lifted out of northern France and dropped here in the Levant. Built during the first half of the fourteenth century, and designed by architects brought from France (it's said to be modelled on the "royal" cathedral at Reims), it was an ostentatious celebration of the huge wealth of the town after the influx of merchants fleeing the fall of Acre. Once the site of Lusignan coronations, its twin towers were destroyed by the Turkish shelling and by later earthquakes. While converting it into a mosque the victorious Ottomans ripped out its interior Christian decorations and memorials, and added a rather inconsequential minaret to the northwest corner. Inside, it is cool and spacious and impressively simple. Outside are two typical **Ottoman shrines**, those of Mehmet Omer Efendi and Mustapha Zuhtu Efendi, both past imams, the bust of Namik Kemal and, beside the mosque, the Famagusta **medrese** dating from around 1700. Also worth noting is the huge **fig tree** (allegedly in situ when the cathedral was built, making it over 750 years old), and the **Venetian loggia** which now houses the ablutions fountain.

The Bandabuliya

Just north of the cathedral/mosque, across Liman Yolu is the old covered market or **Bandabuliya**, restored and painted a delicate shade of yellow; it contains cafés, restaurants, stalls and a stage – look out for the elegant arches down one side.

Maras (Varosha)

If the old town of Gazimağuza is full of ruins dating from the Ottoman siege, the "new town" of **Varosha**, now officially **Maras**, is a sad reminder of a more recent conflict. Having been expelled from the old town in the 1570s, the Greeks established a prosperous settlement here, surrounded by orange groves. Over the years the population of the new town eclipsed that of the old and in the twentieth century its beach area, **Glossa**, became an upmarket **resort**, "The Monte Carlo of the Middle East", visited by the likes of Elizabeth Taylor and Paul Newman. During the 1974 invasion, the Turkish army seized Varosha in its entirety, forcing its Greek population to flee to the south. Today, sealed off by fences, barbed wire and checkpoints, it festers in the sun, its high-rise hotels crumbling, its cracked tarmac claimed by weeds and scrub.

The only part of Varosha open to visitors is the **icon museum** in the 1960s-built church of **Agios Ioannis**, but this really isn't worth negotiating the checkpoint to see. Instead you can simply walk or drive down Fazil Polat Paşa Bulvari (once Independence Avenue) to see the ruins. On the way you'll notice a little green tank engine (dating from 1904) standing outside what was the Famagusta terminus of the **Cyprus Government Railway** (see box, p.162). The converging street of Ilker Karter Caddesi and the streets east of here offer views of Varosha, as do the streets around the Dr Fazil Küçük Stadium, though it's is probably best seen as a whole from the Cultural Centre of Occupied Famagusta (see p.69) across the Green Line.

ARRIVAL AND DEPARTURE   GAZIMAĞUSA

By bus The bus station (☏ 366 63 47) is on Gazi Mustafa Kemal Bulvarı, the main road that heads northwest from the Victory Monument roundabout – it's a 5min walk from the Land Gate.

Destinations Girne (every 30min; 1hr 10min); Lefkoşa (every 30min; 1hr). You can also pick up minibuses to Lefkoşa and Girne from the large roundabout outside the Land Gate.

By car All roads into Gazimağusa lead to the old town. This area is mostly pedestrianized, so park outside the walls and walk. From the south, two crossing points are convenient (see box, p.231).

By ferry Ferries sail between Gazimağusa and Mersin on the Turkish mainland. (Mersin–Gazimağusa Mon, Wed & Fri; Gazimağusa–Mersin Tues, Thurs & Sun; 10hr). The ferry port is right next to the Old Town's Sea Gate. Tickets available from Cyprus Turkish Shipping ☏ 366 45 57 or at the passenger terminal.

VAROSHA – A BRIDGE TO PEACE?

For almost forty years the fate of Varosha has been a painful source of resentment among Greek Cypriots and a strong bargaining tool for the Turks who have deliberately avoided any development of the resort. Various proposals have been put forward to end the impasse – the latest to turn the town into a UN-administered buffer zone which would allow Greek Cypriots to return as an act of goodwill, rather than a prelude to reunification. This would, it is thought, help grease the wheels of Turkey's accession to the EU. In August 2012 President Demetris Christofias said Varosha "can, as in the past, be a bridge of peace, hope, cooperation and cohabitation". Though with Turkey boycotting negotiations during Cyprus's presidency of the EU in 2012 its future seemed stuck in sun-bleached stalemate.

GETTING AROUND

On foot Most of what you'll want to see in Gazimağusa is within the walls and mostly within a pedestrianized area, so all you'll need to get around is your feet.

By taxi If you want to go further afield, look to the taxi rank next to the Sea Gate (Ulas Taksi ☎ 988 12 76).

INFORMATION

Tourist office Just inside the Land Gate, on the left (Istiklal Cadis, Mon–Sat 8am–5pm; ☎ 366 28 64).

ACCOMMODATION

With a few notable exceptions, most of Gazimağusa's hotels languish in a kind of 1970s time warp and are aimed principally at Turkish visitors. In general you are better off staying in Girne (see p.217).

Altun Tabya Altun Tabya Sokak ☎ 366 53 63. One of the very few hotels within the walls of the old town – follow the signs from the Land Gate. Rooms are distinctly down-at-heel, though do at least have en-suite facilities, and you can elect to have a/c for an extra charge. It's on a busy street, though, so don't expect peace and quiet. **€37**

Palm Beach Hotel Nadir Yolu, Deve Limani ☎ 366 20 00, ⓦwww.arkinpalmbeach.com. Recently renovated large hotel, just southeast of the walled city. Helpful staff, good facilities – pool, beach club, fitness suite, restaurants, bars, health club and so on. Rooms are modern and comfortable, decor classy and understated. The elephant in

the room, though, is its position right next to ruined Varosha (some guests, perhaps those who don't realize its location, want to leave as soon as they've arrived). And don't take photos of the devastation – it's forbidden. Half board. **€250**

Salamis Bay Conti Hotel ☎ 378 82 00, ⓦsalamisbay-conti.com. Beachside luxury hotel 10km north of Gazimağusa. Good range of rooms and suites with full facilities, three bars and a main restaurant, kids' club, sports facilities, evening entertainment, casino (though what's offered may be restricted out of season – check with the hotel). It's a bit isolated, though – it's a 45min walk to the site of Ancient Salamis. **€136**

EATING AND DRINKING

The best area to eat in Gazimağusa is in and around the central square – Namik Kemal Meydani. There is very little in the way of nightlife and entertainment except that put on by hotels and casinos.

Aspava 19 Liman Yolu Sokuk ☎ 366 60 37. The *Aspava* looks out onto the main town square and mosque and offers not only grills and meze, with food served in a shady garden, but is a prime people-watching site. Kebabs 10–15TL. Noon–midnight. Closed Sun.

D&B Café Namik Kemal Meydani ☎ 366 66 10, ⓦdbcafe.net. One of the many restaurants on the main square, D&B has ample seating outside, and an upstairs terrace. It advertises "world cuisine" – lots of pizzas (12–19TL), pastas (14–19TL), burgers (15–18TL) and grilled meats (22–29TL). Clientele is young, with many students from the local university, and there's free wi-fi for customers. Daily 9.30am–midnight.

Ginko 1 Liman Yolu Sokak ☎ 366 66 60. Next door to the mosque, housed in buildings that were partly the old Catholic building and partly a Muslim madrasa, the menu includes pasta, salads, fish and meat, and famously huge home-made burgers. Or they're happy for you to just have coffee and cake. Pasta and salads (10–13TL), kebabs (16–20TL), steaks (25–30TL). 10.30am–11.30pm. Closed Sun.

Historia Namik Kemal Meydani ☎ 367 01 53. A good range of meals is provided by the *Historia*, which faces the main square, and therefore is also a good place to watch

the world go by. Omelettes 10–15TL, burgers 14–15TL, kebabs 18–22TL, lamb dishes 25TL. Daily 9am–10.30pm.

★ **Petek** 1 Yesil Deniz Sokak (where it intersects with Liman Yolu Sokak, opposite the Sea Gate) ☎ 366 71 04, ⓦ petekpastahanesi.com. Part of a chain of patisseries (or *pastahanesi*), *Petek* offers a wide range of sweets, Turkish Delight, baklava, ice cream and various types of cake, most involving combinations of honey, chocolate and nuts. From 4TL. Housed in an odd-shaped building with terrace, balcony and potted plants, attractively cluttered interior (foreign newspapers often available to customers). Daily 11am–5pm.

SHOPPING

Gazimağusa is not known for its shopping. However, there are a number of attractive shops along Liman Yolu, mainly selling clothes, postcards, sunglasses, hats and souvenirs, etc. Otherwise head for the narrow tangle of lanes southeast of Namik Kemal Meydani and Istiklal Cad where you'll find music, jewellery and accessories.

DIRECTORY

Banks and exchange The most convenient ATM to use is right in the central square, Namik Kemal Meydani – it's an HSBC one at the back of *D&B Café's* outside seating area. Also in the square, right next to the HSBC ATM, is another, in a branch of Turkiye Bankasi.

Emergencies Ambulance (☎ 112), Fire Brigade (☎ 199) or Police (☎ 155). Gazimağusa Hospital (☎ 364 89 86).

Post Office Fazil Polat Paşa Bulvari (Mon–Fri 8am–1pm & 2–5pm, Sat 8.30am–12.30pm).

Around Gazimağusa

Some 8km north of Gazimağusa, and signposted from both the coast road to Boğaz and the main road to the capital, is a group of ruins which are among the most important and impressive in Cyprus, north or south. By far the most famous and most photographed are the remains, largely Roman, of **Ancient Salamis**. But within a couple of minutes' drive of this colossal seaside site are the **Royal Tombs**, the **monastery of St Barnabas**, now a museum, and the prehistoric remains of **Enkomi-Alasia**. Allow a day for a full inspection, or half a day for edited highlights.

Ancient Salamis

March–Dec 8am–7pm, Jan–Feb 9am–5pm • 9TL

One of the most significant archeological sites in the Mediterranean, **Salamis** is notable not only for the richness and extent of its remains but also for its agreeable beachside setting. The site itself is huge and, despite almost a century of archeological digging, has still not been completely uncovered. A plan of the site at the entrance (clearly signposted from Gazimağusa) offers **two walking routes**, one short, one long. Luckily the most important and most comprehensively investigated buildings are very close together just beyond the entrance. If you intend to view every single part of the city, it'll involve a lot of walking so come prepared.

Brief history

Founded around 1075 BC by Greek and Anatolian settlers and reinforced by refugees as Enkomi-Alasia was abandoned, Salamis was an important cultural centre throughout **Classical Greek and Roman** times, becoming the richest and most important city on the island for around 1700 years. Its kings claimed descent from its founder, the Trojan War hero Teucer, brother of Ajax and son of the King of Salamis, the island to the

6

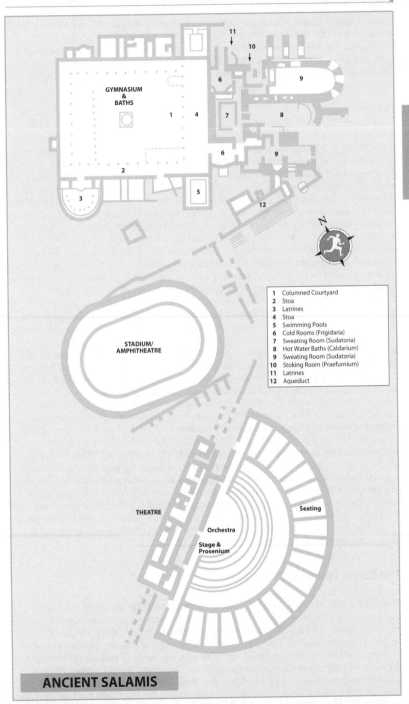

1 Columned Courtyard
2 Stoa
3 Latrines
4 Stoa
5 Swimming Pools
6 Cold Rooms (Frigidaria)
7 Sweating Room (Sudatoria)
8 Hot Water Baths (Caldarium)
9 Sweating Room (Sudatoria)
10 Stoking Room (Praefurnium)
11 Latrines
12 Aqueduct

GYMNASIUM
&
BATHS

STADIUM/
AMPHITHEATRE

THEATRE

Seating

Orchestra

Stage &
Prosenium

ANCIENT SALAMIS

south of Athens (hence the name). Destroyed by earthquakes in 332 and 343 AD, the city was rebuilt by Byzantine **Emperor Constantine II**, who modestly renamed it Constantia. But the harbour silted up, there were further earthquakes, and the coup de grace was delivered by the **Arab raids** which plagued Cyprus from the seventh century AD onwards. The inhabitants of Salamis moved south to where modern Gazimağusa now stands.

The site

The first impressive group of remains are the **Gymnasium and Baths**, built originally by the Greeks and substantially modified by the Romans and Byzantines. At the heart of the building is the huge open courtyard surrounded by columns, and with the remains of a plinth in the centre. This is the **palaestra**, where people exercised or stood gossiping in the shade of the surrounding colonnaded *stoa*. Much of the tessellated marble flooring remains, with clearly legible inscriptions in places. To the west of the palaestra are the remains of a number of shops. To the east are the **baths** with the usual series of rooms of escalating heat – from *frigidarium* to *caldarium*. In places the floor has collapsed, revealing the hypocaust (underfloor heating system) beneath. Plunge pools stand at either side of the baths, the northern one (through which you enter the site) rectangular and surrounded by headless statues. There are also latrines, several octagonal pools and an aqueduct for bringing in the water.

Leaving the baths via the south plunge pool, a column-lined path leads to the sketchy remains of an amphitheatre/stadium. Beyond here is the much more impressive **theatre**, one of the highlights of the site. Built during the reign of Augustus (27 BC–14 AD), it has the standard Greco-Roman semi-circular layout, though built upwards in the Roman manner rather than fitting into a hillside as the Greeks were wont to do. As you enter it from the north, the seating curves sharply to your left around the semi-circular orchestra, the stage and proscenium straight ahead. Much restored (the new seating is easily distinguished from the original – it's white instead of red/brown), it could originally accommodate 15,000 spectators in fifty rows of seats. In the orchestra was an altar to Dionysus, and the stage was backed by statues.

When you leave the theatre, the short route swings round through the second car/coach park back to the entrance. The long route continues south, past the remains of the largest **basilica** in Cyprus, founded by **St Epiphanius** in the fourth century AD – his empty marble-lined tomb can be seen at the end of the south aisle – to a large Byzantine **cistern** or vouta in which water, brought via an aqueduct 50km away, was stored before being distributed to the baths. Beyond this is the large Roman forum or **agora** (of which there's not much left apart from a single column) and the few remains of a **temple to Zeus**. Returning back past the St Epiphanius basilica, then turning off towards the sea, brings you past another Byzantine building called "**The Olive Press**" on the plans, but whose original purpose is unknown – it was used to house an olive press in the Middle Ages. Beyond this is the Byzantine **Basilica of Kampanopetra**, a slightly later, fifth-century AD building.

The Royal Tombs of the Kings

Mezarlik Alani 8am–3.30pm • 5TL

The eighth- and seventh-century BC **Royal Tombs of the Kings** should be considered an adjunct to any visit to Salamis, since they represent a part of the vast necropolis in which the dead – not necessarily kings but certainly the very wealthy – from the ancient city were interred. Despite centuries of looting and treasure hunting several finds from the site have caused great excitement in the world of archeology. However, the most stunning aspect about the graves is that they reveal **burial customs** virtually identical to those described by Homer in the *Iliad*. The dead were carried to the tomb

on a horse-drawn hearse accompanied by ceremonial chariots before being burnt on a funeral pyre or or *propylaeum*, the remains collected, put into jars, and stored inside the tomb. The horses were sacrificed as well as the occasional human according to the *Iliad*: "The mourners made a pyre and on it … laid the body. Four horses he (Achilles) laid on the funeral pyre. Twelve noble young Trojans he slew without mercy. Then he applied the relentless fire …. When the fire had been quenched with wine, they set up a circle of stone slabs … and shovelled earth within."

6

The site

When you return to the main road from the entrance to Salamis, turn left at the roundabout, then right at the next roundabout. The Royal Tombs of the Kings are to the left off this road a few hundred metres west: look out for the yellow sign – it's easy to miss. There's a small ticket office and a **museum** which includes some good reconstructions of some of the most startling finds, for example bronze chariots and horse armour still attached to equine skeletons. Outside, the tombs (each with a number), are dotted around a grassy plain, and are clearly signposted.

Within a minute's walk of the ticket office are tombs 47, 50 and 79. **Tombs 47 and 79** have a clearly defined *dromos* (the ramp down which the hearse was dragged) and *propylaeum* (the platform on which the dead were burnt). The incongruous-looking glass structures on the ramps are there to protect the skeletons of the sacrificed horses. **Tomb 50**, also known as St Catherine's Prison, is an oddity in that the original structure was adapted by the Romans to create a chapel in which, local legend maintains, St Catherine was imprisoned and martyred. Walking the other way from the ticket office brings you to **Tomb 1** (with steps instead of a ramp), **Tomb 2** (classic in structure but smaller than usual) and **Tomb 3** (very large and protected by a modern roof). A few hundred metres to the southeast of these tombs is the **cellarka,** a warren of small rock-cut chambers with truncated ramps, the burial ground of poorer Salamians, used between 700 and 300 BC. Finally, a long walk south brings you to **Nicocreon's Cenotaph** which isn't a tomb at all, but a memorial to King Nicocreon who, under segie by the army of Ptolemy I in 311 BC, opted for suicide rather than the dishonour of surrender. His wife Axiothea decided that first all their daughters should be killed (and persuaded the wives of Nicocreon's brothers to do likewise). If that wasn't tragic enough, the palace was then set ablaze. When the cenotaph was excavated in 1965, clay figures (presumably of the doomed royals) were found on a circular platform surrounded by steps.

The Monastery of St Barnabas

8am–3.30pm • 7TL

Continuing along the road west from Salamis, within another kilometre or so of the Royal Tombs (and built on the western edge of the necropolis) takes you to the **Monastery of St Barbabas**, once one of the most important Christian sites on the island, now an archeological and icon museum. This handsome monastery, said to have been built as the result of a divinely inspired dream (see box opposite) consists of the church of St Barnabas, behind which lie the monastery cloisters: a colonnade of pillars on three sides of a lush and well-tended garden. An extension – further colonnades and a campanile – though modern, fit in pretty well with the rest of the building. The **archeological museum**, housed in rooms that look out into the garden, is less than impressive – a miscellany of Neolithic axe-heads, Bronze Age pottery and Ottoman artefacts; the **Icon Museum**, housed in the church of St Barnabas, is a somewhat perfunctory collection of icons lit by domestic light bulbs. A few bits of the Orthodox furnishings remain in place – the pulpit, a chair, the iconostasis. Look out in particular for the four **frescoes** to the right of the entrance which tell the story of the finding of St Barnabas's body. Before leaving, visit the gift shop, which is particularly strong on rugs

> ## ST BARNABAS AND THE CHURCH OF CYPRUS
>
> One of the great figures of early Christianity, **St Barnabas**, was a Jew, born in Salamis, who became one of the earliest converts to the new religion and founded the Cypriot church. Together with his cousin **Mark the Evangelist** and the pivotal **St Paul**, he travelled extensively in both Cyprus and Asia Minor, spreading the gospel. In fact Barnabas was so successful that the Jewish elders in Salamis had him stoned to death around 75 AD. Mark retrieved his body and buried it secretly in a cave to the west of the city. Over time, the location of the cave was forgotten.
>
> Four hundred years later the Cypriot church under **Archbishop Anthemios** was faced with a takeover bid by **Antioch**, the patriarch of which claimed suzerainty over the island's Christians – a claim supported by Byzantine Emperor Zeno. In 478 AD, when all seemed lost, Anthemios was visited in a dream by the spirit of St Barnabas, who told him where his body was buried – beneath a distinctive carob tree on the western edge of Salamis. Here Anthemios discovered a skeleton along with a copy of **The Gospel of Matthew** written in Hebrew by St Barnabas himself. Anthemios shot off to Constantinople, donated the good book to the emperor and the Church of Cyprus was triumphantly granted autonomous or "autocephalous" status. Zeno also paid for a monastery to be built over the saint's final resting place. The independence of the Cypriot church was to become particularly important over a thousand years later when it was able to use its privileged position to shelter its flock from the worst excesses of Ottoman occupation.

and textiles, then take a look at what is said to be the **tomb of the Apostle Barnabas** himself, contained in a 1950s-built mausoleum. It's along a short track that heads east from the car park, past excavated rock-cut tombs, to the mausoleum's modern steps.

Ancient Enkomi-Alasia

June–Sept 8am–7pm, Oct–May 8am–3.30pm • 5TL

The archeological site of **Enkomi-Alasia** lies on the same road as the Monastery of St Barnabas, less than a kilometre further west. When you get to a T-junction, you'll see the rather inconspicuous entrance across the road, just to the right.

One of the earliest settlements on the island, Alasia (the "Enkomi" bit refers to the nearest Greek village) is thought to have been established around 2000 BC and is mentioned in clay tablets from ancient Egypt, Syria and Anatolia. When the city was excavated (by the British Museum from 1896 and by successive French, Swedish and Cypriot teams up to 1974), much evidence of copper smelting was discovered. Boosted by the arrival of Achaean migrants in the thirteenth century BC, Alasia was of impressive size, made up of straight streets on a grid pattern, with public buildings of dressed stone and with a stone-paved central square, all surrounded by massive walls. The town was levelled by invaders from the sea in 1200 BC, and most of what can be seen today arose from its rebuilding. Alasia never truly recovered, and when its river harbour silted up and it was rocked by an earthquake in 1075 BC, its people left, possibly to establish a new city at Salamis.

Despite its historic significance, **the site** is relatively underwhelming, especially after a visit to Salamis. A path slopes down to some jumbled masonry walls overgrown with grass and other vegetation. There are no explanatory information boards but the single-page information sheet, available from the custodian, helps with navigation. As you work north from the south, a series of "houses" are identified by what was found in them – the **House of the Bronzes**, the **House of the Pillar**, the **House of the Horned God** (all to the left as you approach along the path) and the **Sanctuary of the Ingot God**, another house in which many bronze objects were found. Further north is the main site of the extensive **copper works**. The best view of the site is from the air – if you can't afford to hire a helicopter, take a look on Google Earth.

> **THE WILD DONKEYS OF THE KARPAZ**
>
> At the easternmost end of the Karpaz Peninsula, beyond Dipkarpaz, hundreds of **wild donkeys** roam free. Though seemingly native to the region, their wild status goes no further back than the Turkish invasion of 1974 when, thousands of domestic donkeys, the mainstay of peasant agriculture on the island, were abandoned. The new administration of the north herded them together and let them loose on the Karpaz Peninsula, whose covering of marquis was felt to be ideal for their sustenance. The donkeys, however, preferred the more succulent crops being grown by local farmers, and made a thorough nuisance of themselves, even jumping fences to get at the crops. Understandably angry, the farmers put pressure on the authorities to do something about them, but a proposal to relocate the animals to mainland Turkey caused a storm of environmental and animal-rights protest. So the donkeys remain, and the farmers take what measures they can to keep them out. Perhaps 500 to 1000 feral donkeys survive here, and visitors are advised to treat them with respect – they have a notoriously bad temper.

The Karpaz Peninsula

Famous for its wild donkeys and relatively little else, the **Karpaz Peninsula (Kirpaşa)** stretches for 70km, a tapering finger of land pointing northeast towards Turkey and Syria. One of the most sparsely settled places on the island, road improvements have now made it more readily accessible and holiday villages are springing up along its otherwise pristine beaches. Greek Cypriots also make pilgrimages here to visit **Apostolos Andreas Monastery**, near the peninsula's tip. Where the Karpaz begins is anyone's guess but we've opted for **Iskele/Boğaz** on the south coast, and **Kaplica** on its north coast. On this basis the atmospheric castle of **Kantara** falls within its boundaries.

The only convenient way of exploring the peninsula is **by car**. Buses are infrequent and the route from Gazimağusa extends only to Yenierenköy.

Iskele

Just 3km inland off the main coast road from Gazimağusa, **ISKELE** is the administrative centre for the Karpaz Peninsula. For centuries called Trikomo, a name that reflected its creation by the amalgamation of three villages, it was renamed Iskele after the place in the south from which many Turkish Cypriots were resettled after 1974. There's not much to detain you – even its own tourist information map can muster only two places of interest, both churches. **George Grivas** was born in Trikomo, but you wouldn't expect much to be made of that in north Cyprus.

Boğaz

Continuing 4km up the coast road from the Iskele turn-off brings you to **BOĞAZ**, which is much more worth visiting. A pretty little harbour lined with fishing boats and pleasure craft, it has a well thought out pedestrianized area, lots of park benches and a fair-sized children's playground. It also boasts a couple of hotels and restaurants, making it a feasible base for exploring the peninsula.

ACCOMMODATION   **BOĞAZ**

Boğaz Hotel Boğaz ☎371 25 58, ⊛bogazhotel.com. The thoughfully named *Boğaz Hotel* is set around a private beach backed by a pleasant restaurant terrace. Despite some rather flattering photos on its website, it was in dire need of renovation at the time of writing. While it cannot therefore be recommended, it might do for a night if you get stuck. **€65**

Exotic Boğaz ☎371 28 85, ⊛cyprusexotic.com. For a smallish hotel away from the big towns, the *Exotic* offers a lot – adult and child pools with water slides, views of the sea from all rooms and decent facilities. The hotel's not on the beach, though – it's set back on the opposite side of the road. All the watersports, bars and restaurants of Boğaz are right on its doorstep. Half board. **€60**

Kantara Castle

June–Sept 8am–5pm, Oct–May 8am–3.30pm • 5TL

Kantara Castle is the third of the great mountain fortresses built originally by the Byzantines along the Kyrenia Mountains (see also St Hilarion p.220 and Buffavento, p.223). It is worth visiting not only for its Gothic architecture and atmosphere, but also for its views – from here, you can see both coasts of the Karpaz Peninsula stretching off to the east, and on a clear day the mountains of mainland Turkey. The first mention of Kantara Castle is in 1191 AD when, legend has it, Richard the Lionheart captured Isaac Komnenos here. Lusignan prince John, brother of King Peter I (see box, p.222) is said to have hidden out here from the invading Genoese in 1373. Later, his brother James I of Cyprus refortified the castle – the origin of much of the stonework that remains today. The nearby **village of Kantara** is a hill station which has seen better times.

The easiest route to the castle is along the north coast road **from Girne** to the Karpaz. At **Kaplica**, a fine, wide new road climbs up from the sea, and within minutes you've covered the 6km to the Karpaz village intersection. From here, there's a clearly signposted and good-quality tarmac road which takes you past a large picnic ground to the castle car park, some 4km from the village. You can also approach **from Gazimağusa**, turning off the east coast road just before Boğaz and following a vertiginous mountain road via Yarkoy and Turnalar. After around half an hour of white-knuckle driving (there are no safety barriers) you reach Kantara village.

The site

Access to the castle (750m) is up well-graded paths and steps, with a few safety barriers (though higher up the castle, barriers are not always present, so keep an eye on children). Once you're through the main gate, an inner entrance leads between the massive northeast and southeast towers to a path that leads westwards. A succession of **vaulted rooms** with arrow slits, probably the barracks, is followed by a latrine. Beyond here are several more chambers and ruined towers. At the southwest corner of the castle are more chambers and latrines, and a hidden gate. At the top of the castle is a **beacon tower** which could send warning of attack west to Buffavento, which in turn lit beacons to warn St Hilarion.

Kaplica

You can see **KAPLICA** clearly from the ramparts of Kantara Castle. The village, its white mosque prominent, stands back from two curved sandy beaches on the north coast of the peninsula. On the one to the west stands a large hotel and restaurant and a mobile home/caravan site, the one to the east a small boat harbour. Both beaches are pleasant enough spots to idle away an afternoon, and have fine sand and clear water.

Yenierenköy and around

Midway between Kantara and the tip of the peninsula is **YENIERENKÖY**, now populated by migrants from the Kokkina Enclave in the west. It has a bank, a petrol station and a tourist information office. Before reaching the village a turn-off some 11km west leads to the villages of **Gelincik** (Vasili) and **Boltasli** (Lythrangomi). Between them lies the church of **Panagia Kanakaria**, made famous by the theft of its mosaics after the 1974 invasion, and even more so by their return in 1991 (see box, p.246).

East of Yenierenköy are some fine beaches, though the view is now dominated by the luxury **Karpaz Gate Marina** (⊛karpazbay.com). Seemingly aimed at superyacht-owning oligarchs, the marina was opened in 2011 and boasts a 200-seat restaurant, dive centre and a 33m infinity pool among its attractions.

6

THE KANAKARIA MOSAICS

The widespread looting of religious art treasures from Orthodox churches in the north after 1974 is epitomized by the fate of the Kanakaria mosaics, whose story reads like a Hollywood thriller. At some point between 1974 and 1979, thieves raided the church of Panagia Kanakaria, about halfway along the Karpaz Peninsula, and made off with four sections of its sixth century mosaics. In 1988, Indianapolis art dealer Peg Goldberg ("Indiana Peg", perhaps) agreed to buy the mosaics from a Turkish art dealer for just over $1million. Goldberg soon began hawking the mosaics around museums and art galleries in the US, with a price tag of $20million. One museum, the Getty, became suspicious, and checked with the authorities in Cyprus. It confirmed that the mosaics were stolen and demanded their return. The Church of Cyprus followed up with a legal claim, and the Indiana Federal Court found in favour of their repatriation. In 1991 the mosaics were returned to the Archbishop Makarios III Cultural Centre in Lefkosia, where they can be seen today (see p.181).

The dealer who sold the mosaics, Aydin Dikmen, was tracked down to Munich in 1997 and his flat raided by police. They discovered a huge haul of Cypriot icons, frescoes, bibles and other artefacts worth some $40million. After a totrtous legal dispute with the German authorities the stolen artworks were eventually repatriated in 2010. For more on Cypriot icons see p.252.

On the edge of the village of **SIPAHI**, to the right off the main road about 5km after Yenierenköy (follow the yellow sign), are the remains of an impressive early Christian basilica, **Agia Trias** (summer 8am–5pm; winter 8am–3.30pm; 5TL) dating from the fifth-century AD. Particularly remarkable are its large geometric mosaics, with, at the northern and southern end, inscriptions acknowledging the men who financed the church. Further along the main road (8km from Yenierenköy) and occupying a terrace on the shore is the old stone church of **Agios Thyrsos**, in the crypt of which is a sacred spring said to have healing powers.

Dipkarpaz (Rizokarpaso) and around

Fifteen kilometres beyond Agios Thyrsos is **DIPKARPAZ**, the last village on the peninsula and your last chance to fill up with petrol. It's a prosaic kind of a place, reflected in the preponderance of vans and pick-up trucks on its streets, and is mainly notable for the fact that there are still Greeks living here among the largely Turkish incomers. In the centre is an Orthodox church overlooked by a very large mosque, and behind them arcaded shops. Around Dipkarpaz, to the north (follow the signs for the *Oasis Hotel*) lie the substantial ruins of the twelfth-century **Agios Philon** church, one of the few Orthodox churches in Cyprus built in the Romanesque rather than the Byzantine style (all of which are found on the Karpaz Peninsula). Standing in a cluster of palm trees, the church is characterized by a profusion of blind arches and windows. Beside and around Agios Philon are the remains of Greco-Roman **Karpasia** and a fifth-century AD cathedral built from stone plundered from it. From the beach you can see the remains of the ancient harbour, including a 100m-long breakwater stretching out to sea, while on the bluff above it is the *Oasis Hotel*.

The tip of the peninsula

Beyond Dipkarpaz there's a real feeling that you're approaching the edge of the world. This is a land of wild donkeys, open country, isolated beaches and wild geological formations. Along the north coast are the ruins of **Aphendrika,** one of the largest cities of Ptolemaic Cyprus, marked now only by the ruins of three later churches – Panagia Chrysiotissa, Agios Georgios and Panagia Asomatos. Along the south coast is one of the finest beaches on the island – **Nangomi**, or **Golden Sands Beach**. Backed by substantial dunes, the beach is some 6km long, with a hill at the end of the western promontory, and consists of fine sand and shallow pellucid water, with access down several paths at different points from the road. Besides being a fine bathing beach, Nangomi is also a **sea turtle nesting site** where the security of the eggs are ensured by particularly aggressive sand flies. It is also, as is the whole tip of the peninsula, a protected area.

Apostolos Andreas Monastery

Dawn to dusk • Donations requested

A couple of kilometres beyond **Galounopetra Point**, at the eastern end of Golden Sands Beach, is one of Cyprus's greatest pilgrimage destinations, the **monastery of St Andrew**. A kind of Cypriot Lourdes, its reputation for miracles comes from the tale of the **Apostle Andrew** who is said to have run aground here on his way to Palestine. St Andrew went ashore, the story goes, struck a rock with his rod, causing spring water to gush out. The ship's captain was blind (perhaps why the ship ran aground), but bathing his eyes in the spring water cured him. A chapel was built on the spot in the fifteenth century followed by a church in the eighteenth century and the monastery buildings in the nineteenth.

The monastery's miraculous reputation was boosted in 1895 by the story of Anatolian Greek **Maria Georgiou**, whose son had disappeared seventeen years earlier. She was told in a dream to visit the monastery to pray for her son's return. On the boat over she told her story to a young dervish, who asked how she would identify her son after all this time. She said that he had distinctive birthmarks on his shoulder and chest, at which point he threw his cloak back to reveal identical marks, prompting a tearful reunion (and, of course the reversion of the son to the Orthodox faith).

The monastery was the site of frenetic mass pilgrimages on the saint's name days, August 15 and November 30, until the events of 1974 caused its closure. Since the opening of the Green Line in 2003 it has been growing in popularity again, not only with the religious, but also as a general tourist attraction. There's a huge plaza surrounded by lodgings and stalls selling souvenirs and religious items. Towards the sea the dilapidated monastery buildings surround the church, which is topped by a bell tower. Inside, in addition to the usual icons, are numerous votive offerings. From the church, steps lead down to the chapel and the holy well. UN money has been granted for the refurbishment of the monastery, though there's not much to show for it so far. As with many monastery buildings in Cyprus, the whole place is overrun by cats.

Zafer Burnu (Cape Apostolos Andreas)

A further 4km from the monastery brings you to **Zafer Burnu (Cape Apostolos Andreas)**, which has a rocky shore and a small archipelago offshore – the Kleides ("Keys") Islands. A rock, hollowed out by caves and bearing Turkish and TRNC flags, marks Cyprus's northernmost and easternmost point.

ΚΥΠΡΟΣ

ΑΝΑΤΟΛΙΚΗ ΜΕΣΟΓΕΙΟΣ:
ΓΕΩΓΡΑΦΙΚΟΝ ΜΗΚΟΣ 33° ΚΑΙ ΠΛΑΤΟΣ 35°

ΤΟ ΚΥΠΡΙΑΚΟΝ ΖΗΤΗΜΑ ΕΜΦΑΝΙΖΕΤΑΙ ΠΕΡΙΠΛΟΚΟΝ. ΚΑΙ ΟΜΩΣ ΕΙΝΑΙ ΑΠΛΟΥΝ. Ο
ΛΑΟΣ ΜΙΑΣ ΜΕΓΑΛΗΣ ΕΛΛΗΝΙΚΗΣ ΝΗΣΟΥ ΖΗΤΕΙ ΑΠΟ ΤΑ ΗΝΩΜΕΝΑ ΕΘΝΗ ΑΔΕΣΜΕΥ-
ΤΟΝ ΑΝΕΞΑΡΤΗΣΙΑΝ ΜΕ ΔΙΚΑΙΩΜΑ ΑΥΤΟΔΙΑΘΕΣΕΩΣ. ΚΑΙ ΕΙΝΑΙ ΤΟ ΑΙΤΗΜΑ ΤΟΥ

MAP OF CYPRUS BY GREEK PAINTER SPYROS VASSILIOU (1965)

Contexts

History

The turbulent history of Cyprus arises directly from its geographical position in the Eastern Mediterranean (the "Levant") – a crossing point and melting pot between the three continents of Europe, Asia and Africa. This has resulted in successive waves of invaders each leaving behind traces of its culture in a complex patchwork of ancient burial sites, pagan temples, Byzantine churches and medieval castles, often built on or adapted from what has come before. What follows, therefore, comes with a health warning – it is a simplification. It should, however, offer a framework through which to interpret and appreciate the many historical sites described in the book. For a comprehensive history of Cyprus, try some of the books mentioned in the reading list (see p.263).

Prehistoric Cyprus

The earliest stone implements in Cyprus date from around 8000 BC and indicate the presence of a hunter-gatherer society who slowly developed the use of domestic animals and farming. Small amounts of copper started to be used for making ornaments, tools and weapons, probably by incomers, from around 4000 BC to 2400 BC, often called the **Chalcolithic Age** from the Ancient Greek "chalcos" – copper. They also used the serpentine mineral picrolite for making jewellery, in particular, small cross-shaped human figures. The people of this period lived in circular single-roomed dwellings and continued to use stone tools, drinking vessels and pots. They grew and ate cereals, raised domesticated animals (sheep and goats, but no cattle) for meat, milk and skins, and buried their dead within their settlements, usually under the floors of their huts. (see Tenta and Choirokoitia, p.75).

The Bronze Age (2400–1050 BC)

During the **Early Bronze** (2400–1900 BC) and **Middle Bronze** (1900–1650 BC) Ages, dwellings became oblong, and contained several rooms. Farming was revolutionized by the use of ploughs, copper jewellery became common, and the dead were buried in separate cemeteries. As the island moved into the **Late Bronze Age** (1650–1050 BC), domestic life was increasingly dominated by bronze implements, drinking vessels, pots and pans. Weapons could also be fashioned out of the new material. The **mining of copper** and other metals became more widespread, and the large reserves of copper found in the Troodos Mountains attracted envious looks from across the region as demand for the metal exploded. Coastal towns developed, and trading contact was made with all three nearby continents. Partly arising from these outside contacts and

c.7000–5000 BC	c.4000–2000 BC	c.2400–1900 BC	c.2400–1650 BC
First settlers arrive and establish Tenta and Choirokoitia	Copper starts to be mined and used to make tools	Beginnings of the use of bronze	Bronze jewellery becomes common (Early and Middle Bronze Age)

driven by the needs of commerce, a **written script** appeared – old inscriptions have been found on pottery shards and loom weights, for example, and a complete text on a sixteenth-century BC tablet from Enkomi-Alasia, just north of Famagusta. The script, possibly a version of the Minoan script from Crete (and therefore called Cypro-Minoan), and consisting of eighty characters, is yet to be deciphered.

From the latter part of the thirteenth century BC, waves of **Mycenaean Greeks** came to the island, probably driven out of their cities in the Peloponnese by invaders from the north. They established cities – for example, Maa-Palaiokastro and Kition in the west and Salamis in the east – and brought with them the Greek language, Mycenaean pottery and other influences.

The Iron Age (1050–480 BC)

During the Iron Age, bronze was progressively replaced by the much harder, stronger and more effective iron, at first only in jewellery, later in the making of tools and weapons. At the same time, the Bronze Age Mycenaean cities disappeared, probably destroyed by earthquakes, and were replaced by new **city kingdoms** built, according to legend, by Greeks returning from the Trojan Wars, or more probably by a late wave of Mycenaeans incomers. These cities included Salamis, Kition, Idalion, Amathus, Kourion, Paphos, Marion and Soli. Whatever the truth regarding their establishment, this was when Greek language and traditions became firmly entrenched on the island. Links, too, with other Greek islands grew, particularly Evvia and Crete.

The Iron Age is often divided into two eras, according to the type of pottery they produced – **Geometric** (1050–750 BC) and **Archaic** (750–480 BC). These two eras coincide with the incursion of two different groups of outsiders. From the Geometric era's first two centuries very little has survived, which is why the period is sometimes called a "Dark Age". But thereafter, from about 850 to 750 BC, Kition (Larnaka) was colonized by the **Phoenicians** from nearby Lebanon which sparked a renaissance in that part of the island. Setting up influential trading posts in other Cypriot towns, the Phoenicians introduced an alphabet for the first time.

The subsequent Archaic era saw conquest by the **Assyrians**, who had no interest in colonizing the island, but only in extracting tribute. The existing cities (Salamis, Kition, Amathous, Kourion, Idalion, Palaipafos, Marion, Soloi and Tamassos) retained effective independence, and continued in what was, economically and culturally, something of a golden age. Further incursions by the Egyptians (under the Emperor Amasis 568–525 BC) and the **Persians** (under Cyrus, from 525 BC) followed.

Classical Cyprus (480–323 BC)

The Classical period in Cyprus was contemporary with, though not as illustrious as, that of mainland Greece – Cyprus's main contribution being the establishment of the Stoic school of philosophy by **Zenon of Kition** (see box, p.51). Politically, because of its geographical position, Cyprus was very much pig-in-the-middle during the **Greco-Persian Wars**, with some Cypriot cities supporting Persia, some Greece. Dominated at first by the Persian empire, parts of Cyprus were freed briefly (450–449 BC) by the victory of the Athenian fleet under Kimon and the subsequent

c.1650–1050 BC	c.1200–1050 BC	c.1050–750 BC
Cypro-Minoan script developed	Mycenean settlers from the Greek mainland bring in Greek culture, art, language and religion, and establish cities	New city kingdoms established by, according to tradition, Greeks returning from the Trojan Wars

relief of Marion (Pafos) and of Kition (Lannaka). However, Kimon was killed during the siege of Kition, and Cyprus reverted to Persian rule, retaining, though, a fair degree of autonomy so long as tribute was paid. The Persians in no way diluted the island's Greek personality – it was during this period that the pantheon of **Greek gods** was adopted, and in particular that the Middle Eastern goddess of Astarte, long worshipped on the island, was Hellenized to become **Aphrodite**, the goddess with which Cyprus is most associated.

Hellenistic Cyprus (323–31 BC)

Persia's domination of Cyprus was emphatically ended by **Alexander the Great**'s defeat of the Persian Empire, but after his death in 323 BC Cyprus became a bone of contention between his generals. The War of the Diadochi ("successors") (323 BC–280 BC) was, as it affected Cyprus, between two of the successor states: the Egypt of Ptolemy and the Seleucid Empire in the Middle East, with **Ptolemaic Egypt** prevailing. There followed two hundred years of relatively peaceful rule from Alexandria, during which Hellenization progressed apace as the new rulers exploited the island's timber, olives, wheat and above all copper. They also used the island as a military base.

Roman Cyprus (31 BC–330 AD)

In 58 BC Cyprus was annexed by Rome, then reverted several times to Egyptian rule, finally becoming a full **province of the Roman Empire** in 31 BC. As with many other parts of the empire, the Romans' main interest was in exploiting natural resources – in this case copper (this is when Cyprus first got its modern name, being known by the Romans as "cuprum", the Latin for copper). However, unlike earlier rulers of the island, the Romans left a positive legacy. The answer to the question "What have the Romans ever done for us?" in Cyprus would include new roads and harbours, the expansion of trade, economic growth, greater prosperity and three hundred years of relative peace and stability. Exports flourished, especially copper, decorative pottery, jewellery and glassware. It was during the Roman hegemony that the island embraced what has come to be regarded as one of the cornerstones of Greek Cypriot identity – Christianity. The island was converted to the new religion by St Paul and St Barnabas (see box, p.243) from 45 AD onwards.

Byzantine Cyprus (330–1192)

In 330 AD the capital of the Roman Empire was moved by the Emperor Constantine to the new city of Constantinople (modern-day Istanbul) on the Black Sea. In 395 the declining empire was divided in two, the western half ruled from Rome, the eastern half from Constantinople. Cyprus fell firmly into the latter half, the so-called **Byzantine Empire**. This period, which was to last, with interruptions, for well over eight hundred years, left a a rich legacy of Christian art, architecture, ritual and legend on the island. Although the Cypriot church was ruled nominally from Constantinople, it was in reality independent, a status that was formalized by the granting of autocephalos status by the Emperor Zeno (see box, p.243).

c.750–480 BC	c.480–323 BC	c.323–31 BC
Archaic period: Assyrian conquest followed by Egyptian and Persian incursion	Classical Cyprus is in the front line in conflict between Greece and the Persian Empire	Hellenistic period: the (Greek) Ptolemies of Egypt succeed in struggle between the heirs of Alexander the Great and rule Cyprus

ICONOGRAPHY: RELIGIOUS ART IN CYPRUS

Most visitors to Cyprus will find themselves looking at icons in churches, monasteries, or in one of the island's many Byzantine **museums**. Though the word "icon" can cover a variety of types of religious image, its most common use is for figurative religious art consisting of representations of biblical figures and scenes, either painted on a simple wooden board, sometimes embellished with gold and silver, or made of small pieces of pottery or glass organized into mosaics.

Few icons date from before the eighth/ninth century AD. This was because, during the years between 725 and 842, the Byzantine Empire was split by a vicious struggle between **iconoclasts**, who considered icons to be idolatrous, and "iconodules", who viewed them as aids to worship rather than things to be worshipped. The iconodules eventually triumphed, but not before the iconoclasts destroyed icons in their thousands.

Icon painters in Cyprus adhered strictly to the formal style established in Constantinople – figures appear flat against a plain background, facing the viewer, with emphasis on eyes and hands. Although the influence of Italian Renaissance art can be detected in the later output of the **Cypriot School**, their loyalty to the traditional approach over many hundreds of years makes Cypriot icons hard to date. While many of the icons produced today are just cheap reproductions made for the tourist market, others are of high quality – those produced in Stavrovouni Monastery, for example.

After the **Turkish invasion** of 1974, many of the north's religious icons were **looted** and ended up either on the black market or auctioned off to collectors (see box, p.246). The Church of Cyprus has been successful in repatriating only a small proportion of the art (for images of stolen icons see ⊕ churchofcypruseu.com). In 2011 the singer Boy George returned an icon that he had bought in London in the mid-1980s. The authorities in the north have belatedly made some attempt to preserve the artworks in their care, for example setting up museums in Girne and Gazimağusa. However, their failure to prevent what amounts to the greatest large-scale theft of art since World War II remains a continued source of resentment in the south.

The early churches were simple wooden-roofed buildings based on the Roman basilica model, not dissimilar to those in much of Western Europe. But over time domes and arches were added, giving the more Levantine or Middle Eastern outline of modern Cypriot churches. Many were adorned with beautiful frescoes and mosaic **icons** (see box above) as well as plenty of gold and silver plate contributing to the opulent appearance of many Orthodox churches on the island today. Examples include the early frescoed, wooden-roofed **churches in the Troodos Mountains**, the gold and silver plates discovered in Lambousa and now in Nicosia's **Cyprus Museum**, the three surviving early **Christian mosaics** in Kiti, the Karpas Peninsula and Livadia.

In addition to this great flourishing of Byzantine art, **new cities** developed as others declined or were destroyed, often by earthquakes. The capital moved from Pafos to Salamis, and Ammochostos (Famagusta) grew up nearby. Lemesos (at first called Neapolis or Nemesos) was established, Lefkosia (Nicosia) replaced Ledra, and was eventually to become the capital in the eleventh/twelfth centuries.

Economically, the great innovation of the period was the introduction of the **silk industry**, based on secrets stolen from the Chinese and developed from the sixth century AD. Shipbuilding, gold and silversmithing all flourished.

31 BC	45 AD	330	468
Roman rule in Cyprus begins, bringing relative peace and prosperity. Theatres, gymnasia, roads and aqueducts built	St Paul and St Barnabas begin the conversion of the island to Christianity	Cyprus becomes part of the Byzantine Empire	Church of Cyprus granted autonomous status

There were, however, setbacks. The island was sacked in 649 by a Saracen army, with a garrison being left from 653. Periodic **raids by Arab pirates** drove the population away from the coast to seek safety in inland villages. A Byzantine/Arab agreement brought a sort of peace between 688–965 after which the intruders were cleared out by Emperor Nicephorus Phocas, re-establishing full Byzantine control. Add to all this a succession of earthquakes, plagues and famines, and it becomes clear that the great artistic successes of the period were achieved in the face of considerable misfortune.

The Byzantine Empire's hold on Cyprus ended in a welter of political intrigue. In 1184 **Isaac Komnenos**, King of Cyprus, declared the island independent of Constantinople, a move which might have been popular amongst his subjects had it not been for the king's substantial personal failings. His short reign was characterized by pointless cruelty and political ineptitude, which ended with the first incursion into the story of Cyprus by a country at the opposite end of Europe – England.

Lusignan (Frankish) Cyprus (1192–1489)

The successors to the long period of Byzantine rule arrived on the island almost by accident, courtesy of political chaos caused by the Third Crusade, started in 1187. A gaggle of European kings led by **Richard the Lionheart** of England, infuriated by Saladin's successes in the Middle East, set out to restore Christian access to the Holy Lands. Richard was on his way to the Middle East when his sister and his wife-to-be were shipwrecked on Cyprus. Isaac Komnenos took them hostage and tried to extract ransom from the English king. Angered by this impertinence, and mindful of how useful Cyprus would be for future Crusader activity, Richard invaded and conquered the island and imprisoned Komnenos. Not wishing to be sidetracked by the need to keep Cyprus in subjugation, Richard promptly sold the island to the **Knights Templar**. Their rule was short and not very sweet, so the island was in turn off-loaded to one **Guy de Lusignan**, a Frankish knight who had helped Richard conquer the island in the first place. It was this unlikely and rather disreputable chain of events that inaugurated the three hundred years of Frankish, or **Lusignan**, rule of the island.

The Lusignans, originally from Poitiers in France, introduced a feudal system of government which was in essence common to many countries in Western Europe – for example, that imposed by William the Conqueror on England in 1066. Numerous **knights** of French origin came in as the new ruling class, the island was divided between them, and the peasantry was expected to provide labour and military service in return for land on which to grow crops. The knights were allowed to build themselves fortified towers, for example the ones at Pyla, Alaminos and Kiti, while the great fortresses of Nicosia, Famagusta, Paphos, Limassol, Kyrenia, St Hilarion, Buffavento and Kantara were reserved for the royal family. These towers and **castles** are among the main survivals of the Lusignan era. Another change was the imposition of **Roman Catholicism**, although the Orthodox Church continued to worship in secret. As might be expected, the ruling class and the Catholic Church did very well during this period, the Cypriots and the Greek Orthodox Church less so. The ruling family themselves were an unprepossessing lot, long on luxurious living, short on political ability (see box, p.254).

647	649	649–965	965–1191
First of numerous Arab raids on coastal cities	Island invaded by Saracen army	Period of conflict between the Christian Byzantine Empire and the forces of Islam	Second period of relative peace within the Byzantine Empire

When, in 1291 Acre, the Crusaders' last major stronghold in the Kingdom of Jerusalem, fell to the Muslims, Cyprus became the only Christian land in the Eastern Mediterranean, and therefore even more important militarily and commercially. The two great trading city states of **Genoa** and **Venice** competed fiercely for favours, and both were granted trading rights by the Lusignan authorities. The cities of Nicosia and Famagusta flourished during this period, as did production and export of sugar, wine, textiles (especially lace) and ceramic ware.

Venetian Cyprus (1489–1571)

The continuing rivalry between Genoa and Venice finally ended in 1489 when the island was ceded by the Lusignans to the **Venetian Republic**. They immediately began to develop it as an entrepôt for their activities in the eastern Mediterranean. Conditions for ordinary Cypriots became, if anything, worse, with the island being viewed by its new rulers as little more than a military base and a source of tax revenue. Commercially, the island's main exports were sugar, wine, olive oil, wheat, barley and cotton, and it was this period that saw the beginning of **lace production** in Lefkara. The bulk of these exports were funnelled through **Famagusta**, which became by far the island's main port.

The **fall of Rhodes** to the Ottoman Empire in 1522 led to a feverish military building programme, with the Venetians rightly suspecting that Cyprus would be next. New walls were thrown up around Nicosia, and the existing walls of Famagusta were greatly strengthened. The onslaught didn't come immediately, but all these preparations in the end proved of little avail. **Nicosia fell** to the Ottomans after a seven-week siege in 1570 and Famagusta, after heroic resistance lasting almost a year, in July 1571. The cruelty meted out to the Famagusta's defenders – their leader, **Marcantonio Bragadin**, was flayed alive – boded ill for the island's future.

A perhaps apocryphal but amusing story says that the Ottoman invasion of Cyprus occurred partly because the splendidly and aptly named **Sultan Selim the Sot** was eager to get his hands on the source of the sweet Commandaria wine of which he was excessively fond. It was a case of be careful what you wish for: under the influence of the wine he fell in his bathroom, fractured his skull, and died.

1191	1192	1192–1489	1489–1571
Richard the Lionheart conquers Cyprus	Richard sells Cyprus first to the Knights Templar, then to his lieutenant Guy de Lusignan	Lusignan (Frankish) rule – Cyprus becomes a Crusader state	Cyprus is ruled by the Venetians, and becomes a trading base for their commercial activities

Ottoman Cyprus (1571–1871)

Ottoman rule was initially welcomed by the local population – they shed no tears for the Venetians. And indeed, things started well enough, with the new regime giving recognition and power to the Cypriot Orthodox Church. This was, however, more to do with greed than enlightened tolerance – the easiest way to collect taxes was through the church's established network. Administrators (among them dragomen, see box, p.181) had to pay the authorities hefty bribes to secure their posts, and were badly paid, the expectation being that they would make a profit by squeezing the population until the pips squeaked. When the tax burden became too great, there were periodic **rebellions** (for example in 1680, 1764, 1821 and 1833) which were put down with ferocious cruelty – the rebellion of 1821, for example, led to the execution by hanging or beheading of 500 prominent Greek religious leaders in Nicosia.

Some Cypriots, often those descended from the remnants of the previous Venetian occupation, were aware that Muslims enjoyed a variety of privileges, and converted, at least outwardly, while maintaining most of their Christian beliefs in private – many of today's "Turkish" Cypriots are in fact descended from these "**Linovamvaki**" (see box p.106). Others emigrated, many of them to the Anatolian region of Turkey or elsewhere in the Balkans. Yet more looked to Greece, particularly after it had shaken off Ottoman rule in 1823.

The **Greek War of Independence** had widespread, albeit implicit, support from **Great Britain**, the ascendent power of the time, whose ruling classes had often been schooled in the ancient Greek philosophy and language. Yet despite their Philhellenic tendencies, the British preferred to keep the status quo in Cyprus. The rise of nationalism across the Balkans and Eastern Mediterranean and the weakening of the Ottoman Empire, widely known as the "**sick man of Europe**", threatened to create a power vacuum. Mindful of Russian designs on Cyprus as a useful warm-water port, Britain continued to support the ailing empire, fighting alongside the Ottomans in the Crimea.

Despite the ill-governance of the Ottomans, Cyprus flourished as the nineteenth century progressed, with European traders establishing themselves in the main ports, and consular offices opening on the island, particularly in Larnaka. Cypriots were becoming increasingly educated and urban, and the seeds of "**enosis**" – union with Greece – began to flower. At the same time, Britain's continued support for the Ottomans on the international stage was recognized by London's increasing influence over the sultan, and, after British military support in the 1877–1878 Russo-Turkish War, was formalized in the **Cyprus Convention** of 1878. This allowed Britain to occupy Cyprus, with extensive administrative powers, though stopped short of outright sovereignty. British forces landed in Larnaka in July, 1878, and the period of British rule began.

British Cyprus (1878–1960)

The British takeover of Cyprus was popular with Greek Cypriots, who hoped that their new rulers would view eventual union with Greece more favourably than the Ottomans. The Cypriots had every reason to be optimistic – after all Britain had ceded the Ionian islands to Greece fourteen years earlier. For a variety of reasons, however, this didn't happen, despite the reduction in Cyprus's strategic importance after Britain's

1522	1571	1572
The fall of Rhodes to the Ottoman Empire leads to the fortification of the island against possible Muslim attack	Siege of Famagusta completes the Ottoman conquest of the island	Building of the Buyuk Han (Great Inn) in Nicosia by Mustafa Pasa

occupation of Egypt and the Suez Canal in 1882. When Britain finally offered to hand over Cyprus to Greece during World War I (in return for Greek entry into the war), the Greeks refused – the Greek king, Constantine I, being pro-German. The offer was one of cynical wartime political expediency, with a return to normal service (opposition to enosis) once the war was over.

Having ended up on the losing side in World War I, the Ottomans were forced to renounce all claims to Cyprus and the rest of their empire under the **Treaty of Lausanne** in 1923, in return for recognition of the new Turkish state. Two years later Cyprus became a full **British colony**. The British authorities continued to tax the population fiercely, and refused to countenance demands for enosis. In October 1931 there was a serious uprising which was harshly put down. Cypriots did their bit for Britain during **World War II** – 6000 Cypriot volunteers joined the newly formed Cyprus Regiment which fought in the Greek campaign. Greek Cypriots were hopeful that they would be rewarded by being allowed to join Greece, but again their hopes were dashed, though an offer of limited self-rule was made and turned down in 1947.

It is in some ways difficult for outsiders to understand the passion of Greek Cypriots for **union with Greece** – a country which was impoverished, chaotic and, at that time, right wing. It was, perhaps, an affair of the heart, not the head. The opposition of Turkish Cypriots, who made up around eighteen percent of the island's population, was easier to grasp. Whatever the practicalities, the demand for enosis reached new heights: on January 15, 1950 an unofficial referendum organized by the church was held among Greek Cypriots, who voted overwhelmingly (95.7percent) for enosis. The British authorities paid no attention. London's response was summed up by the Minister of State for the Colonies who said that "certain Commonwealth territories, owing to their particular circumstances, can never expect to be fully independent", a veiled reference to Cyprus's stategic signifcance. These concerns were confirmed when Britain moved its Middle East Command to Cyprus from newly independent Egypt in 1954. Armed **rebellion** against British rule began the following year.

EOKA and the fight for independence

The leader of the political movement for enosis was the head of the Greek Orthodox Church in Cyprus, **Archbishop Makarios III** (see box, p.160), while that of the military opposition to the colonial power was **George Grivas** ("Digenis"; see box, p.165), leader of right-wing paramilitary organization EOKA. Weapons and explosives were smuggled onto the island along the west coast north of Pafos, and British military installations and personnel were targeted, together with Turkish Cypriots and even left-wing or anti-enosis Greek Cypriots.

Violence, and British responses, escalated. In 1956 Makarios and two of his associates were **exiled** to the Seychelles, and in the same year nine EOKA fighters were executed, causing widespread demonstrations on the island and in Greece. In 1958 an explosion outside the Turkish press office in Nicosia sparked further intercommunal violence (though it was actually thought to have been caused by Turkish Cypriot agents provocateurs, not by Greek Cypriots). The British authorities recruited special constables exclusively from the Turkish Cypriot community, a move widely condemned as provocative. At the height of the disturbances, around 1200 EOKA guerrillas, located mainly in the Troodos Mountains, were tying down 25,000 British regulars and

1821	1878	1925	1942
Rebellion is violently suppressed, with over 500 prominent Greek Cypriots being publicly executed in Nicosia	Period of British rule begins	Cyprus becomes a Crown colony	British soldiers discover the Pafos mosaics

4500 special constables. Finally, hostilities ended in 1959 when independence (though not enosis) was granted.

Independent Cyprus (1960–present)

The independent **Republic of Cyprus** came into being on August 16, 1960, with Archbishop Makarios as its first president, and the Turkish Cypriot leader **Dr Fazil Küçük** vice president. Cyprus took its place at the United Nations, the Commonwealth and the Council of Europe, and became a member of the Non-Aligned Movement. The settlement was based on a hugely complicated formula which tried to secure the rights of both communities (a 1960 census revealed a population of 442,138 Greek Cypriots and 104,320 Turkish Cypriots), while Britain retained two sovereign military bases – Dhekelia and Akrotiri, totalling 158 square kilometres. Among several agreements made at the time of independence was the **Treaty of Guarantee**, by which Britain, Greece and Turkey were empowered to take action if the terms of independence were violated.

Suspicion between the Greek Cypriot and Turkish Cypriot communities was if anything exacerbated by independence, and divisions within the Greek Cypriot community also appeared, between the left and the right, and between those who were happy with independence and those who still wanted enosis. Grivas, rightly suspecting that Makarios's fervour for enosis had cooled, went into self-imposed exile in Greece.

Intercommunal violence and the beginnings of partition

The provisions of the new constitution never really worked, and in 1963, when Makarios suggested a number of changes, Turkish Cypriots and Turkey rejected them, and the Turkish Cypriot contingent withdrew from government and set up a "temporary Turkish Cypriot administration". Intercommunal violence (involving paramilitaries on both sides) escalated to the extent that the UN sent in a peacekeeping force in 1964.

Despite the presence of UN troops the violence continued, and a series of heavily defended **Turkish Cypriot enclaves** were set up, with their own administration, police forces and radio stations. Nicosia became a divided city, separated by the **Green Line**

THE CYPRIOT "COSTA DEL CRIME"

A combination of Cyprus's historic links with Britain, the camouflage offered by its large expat community, and the presence of the unrecognised Turkish Republic of Northern Cyprus, which has no extradition treaty with the UK, just minutes away, make Cyprus particularly attractive to members of the British criminal fraternity. In 2012 a UK Police campaign "**Operation Zygos**" targeted a list of the nine "most wanted" hiding out on the island. That said, the experiences of tycoon **Asil Nadir** will be both an encouragement and a warning to felons hoping to use Cyprus to evade justice. Having fled to north Cyprus from the UK in 1993 following accusations of false accounting and theft arising from the collapse of his Polly Peck International company, Nadir enjoyed a life of luxury in the north for seventeen years. Yet the restrictions on his freedom to travel anywhere apart from Turkey eventually led him to risk all by returning to the UK in 2010 to face trial. He was convicted in August 2012, and sentenced to ten years in prison.

1955–59	1957	1959	1960	1963–64
EOKA fights for union with Greece ("enosis")	*Bitter Lemons* by Lawrence Durrell published	Independence granted and elections held	Archbishop Makarios III elected president	Intercommunal violence leads to intervention of UN troops

(so-called because it was drawn by the British commander in green crayon on a map of the city) into northern Turkish Cypriot and a southern Greek Cypriot halves. An enclave centred on the village of **Kokkina** on the northwest coast became a landing point for men and supplies coming in from the Turkish mainland. In 1964 the Cypriot National Guard, led by the newly returned Grivas, attacked the enclave, despite pleas from Makarios not to do so. This almost provoked all-out war as Turkish air-force jets bombed and strafed the Greek positions and the nearby town of Polis. Far from preventing men and supplies coming in via the enclave, it subsequently became a Turkish military base. De facto partition was happening.

Coup d'etat and the Turkish invasion

By 1974 Makarios had lost the support of the military junta that had been ruling Greece since 1967, and of the Greek Cypriot right, including son-of-EOKA, EOKA-B, neither of which believed that he still wanted union with Greece. He was also opposed by the US, who considered him to be too left wing and too close to the USSR. All this came to a head in 1974 when on July 15 an extreme right-wing member of EOKA-B **Nicos Sampson**, led a coup d'etat with the backing of the Greek junta (and, it is claimed, the CIA). In response **Turkey invaded** the island on July 20, landing just west of Kerynia (near the village now called Karaoğlanoğlu), justifying the action by referring to the Treaty of Guarantee.

The Turkish military intervention ended both Sampson's brief rule in Cyprus and that of the longer-lived junta in Greece. A new government took office in Cyprus under President **Glafkos Clerides**, removing the ostensible reason for the invasion. But during the ensuing ceasefire, Turkey continued to pour reinforcements into the island and

---

CYPRUS HITS THE BUFFERS

With a population of less than a million, and a GDP of €18 billion (less than a tenth that of Greece), Cyprus has always been a minnow in economic terms. However, until recently the island was confident that it could ride out the economic storms of the recession. It was capitalizing on its geographical position, to become a financial hub for the region, and its tourist industry seemed to be going from strength to strength. There was even the hope that on-going **natural gas exploration** might turn the Eastern Mediterranean into a new North Sea.

In the last couple of years this confidence has evaporated. The explosion at the Vasilikos naval base in 2011 (see box, p.73) severely damaged the republic's economy, while Greece's economic woes have had a knock-on effect on Cyprus, which had large sums invested there. The continuing stalemate over the de facto division of the island, aggravated by disagreements over drilling rights, does neither side any favours as regards inward investment. Add all this to the effects of the global financial crisis, with Cypriot private and public debt spiralling, and something had to give. In June 2012 Cyprus became the fifth EU member to request a **bail-out**. That said, Cyprus's debt is small change compared to bigger European players such as Spain. And Cyprus might also have a hand-winning card up its sleeve – **Russian money** is beginning to flood in to the country, both in the form of big-spending tourists and expats atttracted by a warm climate and the relative familiarity of the Orthodox Church. There seems no doubt about the Cypriot determination to overcome their economic problems: in February 2013 they elected the right wing, pro-austerity Nicos Anastasiades as their new president.

1964	1974	1983	1996
The Kokkina Incident almost leads to all-out war; Green Line across the capital established	Turkish invasion leads to conquest of northern Cyprus, de facto division of the island	The "Turkish Republic of North Cyprus" is established	Clashes in the UN Buffer Zone near Deryneia claim the lives of two Greek Cypriots

advanced further inland. By the time hostilities ended – because of international pressure but also because Turkey had got what it wanted – 37 percent of the island had been occupied. Turkey established a border between the north and the south (the **Attila Line**, commonly called the Green Line, since it was an extension of the one drawn initially in 1964). In order to prevent further incidents, a United Nations "**Buffer Zone**" was set up, with block-houses, barbed wire, and regular patrols. By this stage around 200,000 Greek Cypriots had been forced out of the northeastern occupied zone, and 50,000 Turkish Cypriots moved into it. In 1975 the occupied zone declared itself the "Turkish Federated State of Cyprus" and finally, in 1983, the "Turkish Republic of Northern Cyprus".

Solving "the Cyprus Question"

Today many Cypriots have no memory of a united island. Since the invasion there have been numerous **UN resolutions** condemning the illegal regime in the north, all of which have been ignored. According to one British diplomat, the intractable nature of the problem was that "no Turkish Cypriot could ever forget the period between 1963–74, and no Greek Cypriot could remember it". Though a flippant remark it goes some way to summing up the impasse in which the minority Turkish Cypriots fear Greek domination while Greek Cypriots will never forget or forgive the invasion of 1974 (for the Cypriot government position see Ⓦmfa.gov.cy and the Turkish see Ⓦmfa.gov.tr).

There have, however, been some signs of movement on the "**Cyprus Question**". In April 2003 restrictions on crossing into north Cyprus imposed by the Turkish Cypriot regime were suddenly relaxed, allowing thousands of Greek Cypriots from the south to visit the homes and villages from which they'd been expelled. On May 1, 2004 the Republic of Cyprus became a member of the **European Union**, leading to a bizarre situation where a part of the EU is being occupied by a foreign power.

Pressure on and in north Cyprus has been growing. Turkish Cypriots in the north have become irate at being treated increasingly as a province of Turkey, and have taken exception to the large number of immigrants coming in from the Turkish mainland. Faced with increasingly open discontent, the Turkish Cypriot regime cracked down hard on dissidents, starting with the arrest of the editor of an opposition newspaper in July 2000. Faced with increasing discontent with unemployment and living standards in the north, the Turkish Cypriot leader **Rauf Denktaş** (see box, p.206), poured scorn on the idea that there could be a united, federal state of Cyprus. In 2003 he claimed that there were Turks who lived in Cyprus and Greeks who lived in Cyprus – "the only true Cypriots are its donkeys".

The most recent attempt at lasting solution was the **Annan Plan** of 2004 which proposed a "United Republic of Cyprus" as a federation of two states. In a **referendum** on the plan, in the north two to one were in favour, despite Denktaş's opposition; in the south three to one were against. Negotiations continued in 2008 between the north's **Mehmet Ali Talat** and the republic's **Demetris Christofias**. However, the election of conservative president **Nicos Anastasiades** in 2013 indicated that reunification had slipped down the political agenda, with Anastasiades stating "the most urgent task is to face the financial crisis". Turkey's long-held ambitions to join the EU may prove the catalyst for new talks between the two sides.

2003	**2004**	**2008**	**2012**
First crossing point on the Green Line established, followed by six more up to the present	Republic of Cyprus joins the European Union	Cyprus adopts the euro while the north persists with the Turkish lira	In London, Pavlos Kontides wins Cyprus's first ever Olympic medal – a silver in the Laser sailing event

Geology and wildlife

Whether you're walking across the sands of Fig Tree Bay, trekking in the Troodos Mountains, driving through the vineyards of Lemesos or Pafos districts or exploring a spectacular Crusader castle you can't help but be aware of Cyprus's varied geology and its influence on the landscape. Likewise the island's diverse flora and flora has been influenced primarily by Cyprus's geographical position between Europe, Asia and Africa.

Geology

Cyprus in its present form has its origins in the collision of the African and Eurasian tectonic plates about ten million years ago – the same geological pile-up that created the Alps. For millennia Cyprus consisted of **two islands** – one centred on the Troodos Massif, the other on the Kyrenia Mountains, separated by the primordial Athalas Sea. Slowly the two islands were joined as the floor of the Athalas Sea rose and progressively silted up, creating the Mesaorian Plain. Over time the relatively soft, water-soluble **limestone** of the Kyrenia Massif to the north became weathered into their present spectacularly tortured shapes, while the more extensive and higher Troodos Mountains to the southwest lost their limestone covering to erosion, revealing the much harder and older **igneous rock** beneath. This was not only far more impervious to erosion (hence the rounded shape of the mountains) but also contained a wealth of minerals, particularly **copper**. The significance of the region's geology was further emphasized in the late 1960s when undisturbed samples of **ophiolite** – oceanic crust and its underlying mantle – were identified, proving that the Troodos Massif was created by the sea-floor spreading and the collision of the African and European tectonic plates.

Human geography and environmental concerns

The people of Cyprus have long adapted to the geology and topography of their environment. In fertile Mesaoria, and to a lesser extent elsewhere on the coastal plain, the principal activity is **arable farming**, supplemented or in some places replaced by fishing. The southern foothills of the Troodos Massif are carpeted in **vineyards** and dotted with wineries, the higher hills and mountains of both Troodos and Kyrenia ranges the haunt of sheep and goats. Copper and asbestos were until recently widely extracted from the Troodos range. The western end of the Mesaorian Plain, around Guzelyurt, is dominated by the production of **soft fruit**, particularly oranges and lemons. In most parts of the island olive trees are a source of fruit and oil.

The expansion of the tourist industry, especially in parts of the republic but also increasingly in the north, has provided a much needed additional source of income but has thrown up a number of **environmental conerns**, particularly on the otherwise pristine peninsulas of Akamas and Karpaz. Historically, the greatest cause of natural disasters has been earthquakes, as witnessed by the histories of virtually every town and city on the island. Increasingly, though, water shortages, industrial pollution and the incursion of salt water into freshwater supplies have become common. Since the devastating explosion at the island's principal power station in 2011, a shortage of electricity has also been a problem.

Wildlife

The range of flora and fauna to be found in Cyprus is wide, partly because it is an island with **endemic species** that have evolved in isolation, and partly because its geographical position between Europe, Asia and Africa has made it a major intersection for **migrating birds**.

Plants

Cyprus in the past was heavily forested, but its stock of trees became severely depleted as man cut timber for fuel, to build ships and to make charcoal for copper smelting. Reafforestation proceeded apace from the British occupation onwards – mostly in the Troodos and Kyrenia mountains, and in the great **forest of Tiliria** – and woodland covers about seventeen percent of the island. Upland forests contain **Aleppo** and **Black pine**, the charmingly named "stinking juniper", cedar and many more, with much of the rest of non-agricultural land having a dense covering of scrub or "**maquis**" consisting largely of Phoenician juniper, rock rose, lentisk, terebinth, myrtle, storax and golden oaks. **Cypress trees** and fig trees also abound. Along the coastal plain numerous imported species flourish, among them palm trees, eucalyptus, mimosa and **bourgainvillea**, and cacti such as prickly pear. Cyprus also has a wide enough variety of flowering plants to keep a botanist happy for a few lifetimes – around 1800 different species, of which about seven percent are endemic. For **wild flowers**, the best time to visit is in spring, when a carpet of multicoloured blooms make their brief but glorious appearance – crocus, vetch, buttercup, marigold, tulip, poppy, fennel, gladioli and many more. Autumn too has its glories as the first post-summer rains bring narcissus, and hyacinth varieties into bloom, followed by cyclamen, anemone and crocus. Most famously, Cyprus has a wealth of **orchids**, especially around Larnaka's Salt Lake, the Akamas Peninsula and the Kyrenia mountains.

Animals

Cyprus has a relative paucity of **mammals**, compensated for by a huge range of reptiles and amphibians. As the fossil records show, it was once home to dwarf elephant and hippopotamuses, spared the need to grow to intimidating size by the lack of natural predators. The largest mammal on the island today is the **Cypriot mouflon** (Ovis orientalis ophion) or wild horned sheep – your best chance of seeing these shy creatures is in the special enclosure attached to the Stavros tis Psokas forest station in Tiliria. Also of interest are the island's fourteen or so species of **bat**, among them the Egyptian fruit bat (Cyprus being its only European habitat). Despite their protected status bats are often considered pests and shot in rural areas.

As might be expected in such a hot and rocky country, Cyprus has a large range of **reptiles** (25) including nine species of snake, of which three are venomous (though only the rare blunt-nosed viper is really dangerous). The island's most popular reptiles, though, are its two types of **sea turtle** (green and loggerhead) which come ashore to lay eggs on certain beaches on the west and north coast, and on the Karpaz Peninsula. Of the many **lizard** species, the largest is the starred agama, resembling a diminutive dinosaur, the most common are the little sand lizard and gecko, and the most interesting is the chameleon. Amphibians include the tree frog, the marsh frog and the green toad.

Of more specialist interest are the numerous species of **insects** – butterflies, moths, spiders, scorpions, centipedes – and the teeming **marine life** which you can observe while snorkelling or diving, through the glass bottom of a tour boat, or on the quayside when fishermen bring in their catch.

Birds

Given the island's position between Europe and Africa, up to 250 million birds visit Cyprus on their way south in autumn and north in spring. In total **370 bird species** have been spotted here, of which two are endemic (the Cyprus pied wheatear and the Cyprus warbler); four more are endemic subspecies. Because of this the island can be an ornithological paradise. The best times to see birds on the island are March to May for the north-bound migration and August to October for the reverse flow to the south. Significant species include the **griffon-vulture** with its 2.5m wingspan, numerous owls and raptors including Bonelli's Eagle, found particularly in the Kyrenia Mountains, **flamingos**, which visit the salt lakes of Larnaka and Akrotiri between October and March and the bee-eaters, **golden orioles** and strikingly multicoloured **hoopoes** that you might see between April and September. For more information contact BirdLife Cyprus (☎2245 5072, ⓦbirdlifecyprus.org), and the North Cyprus Society for the Protection of Birds (Kuskor; ⓦkibrisbirds.net).

Sadly, many Cypriots regard birds either as a threat (so farmers often shoot or poison birds of prey) or, far more destructively, as a resource to be exploited. Small songbirds like blackcaps, thrushes and robins, grilled, pickled or boiled and eaten whole are regarded as a great delicacy, and the appetite for this "**ambelopoulia**" leads to millions of songbirds being captured and killed. The birds are attracted by tape lures (recordings of birds), trapped in mist nets or on birdlime-covered sticks hidden among the trees, then killed, often by a toothpick to the throat. The practice has been illegal in the republic since 1974, but enforcement has been at best patchy, and many restaurants still openly have *ambelopoulia* on their menus. Those who oppose the practice – the Committee Against Bird Slaughter (CABS) for example (ⓦkomitee.de/en/homepage) – are regarded by many locals as interfering outsiders, trying to stop a traditional practice that has gone on for centuries throughout the Mediterranean. Campaigners point out that the practice is cruel and indiscriminate – many endangered or inedible migratory species die in the nets or on the birdlime, as well as so-called "indigenous" birds. It is estimated that trapping kills around 2.5 million birds a year in Cyprus.

Books

Given its size and relative obscurity there is a vast range of literature devoted to Cyprus. Before reading anything about the island, the following should be borne in mind. The politics of the "Cyprus Question" are so labyrinthine, the feelings provoked by it so extreme and the vested interests so extensive that personal beliefs, cultural background and political allegiance inevitably colour any writing on the island whether its politics, travel, history, food and wine, music or any other aspect of life. This could be said of most places of course, but it is particularly acute on an island literally divided along religious and nationalistic lines.

What follows is a personal selection of some of the books which might be usefully read in preparation for such a visit, and which the author has found useful in researching this book. This is not an academic reading list, and therefore only the more accessible volumes are included.

It's worth remembering that places of interest, churches, monasteries, museums and ancient sites in the republic have printed, and often handsomely illustrated, guides on sale. In particular, look out for the excellent editions published by the **Bank of Cyprus Cultural Foundation**. In north Cyprus, guides where they exist are often useful but brief – perhaps a single sepia sheet of A4 with a plan of the site on one side and notes on the other. The best private source of maps and historic books on Cyprus is the **Sylvia Ioannou Foundation** which provides downloadable extracts at ⑩ sylviaioannoufoundation.org.

TRAVEL/MEMOIRS

Lawrence Durrell *Bitter Lemons of Cyprus.* Memoir by the great novelist of his settling in Cyprus in the early 1950s – buying and renovating a house in Bellapais, working part time in Nicosia, and interacting with locals who he paints vividly (if sometimes a little patronizingly) with his pen.

Lorenzo Warriner Pease *Diaries 1834–1839.* A fascinating look into the past from an American missionary posted to Cyprus (see p.52), though perhaps one for aficionados (it costs £150 on Amazon).

★ **Colin Thubron** *Journey into Cyprus.* Account by one of Britain's top travel writers of his six-hundred-mile walk through Cyprus in 1972, providing an erudite and beautifully written snapshot of the island on the eve of the Turkish invasion.

RECENT HISTORY

Brendan O'Malley and Ian Craig *The Cyprus Conspiracy: America, Espionage and the Turkish Invasion.* Written by two British journalists, this book persuasively puts forward the theory that, far from being a failure on the part of US foreign policy as Kissinger claimed, the events of 1974 and the division of Cyprus were exactly what the Americans wanted. It is particularly good on the influence of the Cold War and Cyprus's geographical position and strategic importance.

★ **William Mallinson** *Cyprus: A Modern History.* Published in 2008 and concentrating heavily on events from the mid-twentieth century onwards, this is not a brief survey for the casual reader but a fascinating and illuminating analysis of the complicated realpolitik affecting Cyprus. Few of the participants, in particular the great powers, can take any pride in the part they played – the chapter headings say it all: "The Poker Table", "The Poker Players" and "Keeping the fingers in the pie".

Dr Stavros Panteli *The Making of Modern Cyprus: From obscurity to statehood.* Excellent account of Cypriot history, concentrating on the British occupation, the early years of independence and the Turkish invasion of 1974 (though with brief chapters on the previous 10,000 years). Published in 1990, it takes the story only up to the late 1980s.

★ **Yiannis Papadakis** *Echoes from the Dead Zone: Across the Cyprus Divide.* Personal and impressively impartial account by a Greek Cypriot of his growing acceptance that both communities in Cyprus have responsibility for intercommunal breakdown, and that only a change of heart will heal the wounds.

GENERAL HISTORY AND CULTURE

Timothy Boatswain *A Traveller's History of Cyprus*. Coverage of the history of the island, north and south, in the *Traveller's History* series. Useful Chronology of Events and Gazeteer.

Eileen Davy *Northern Cyprus: A Traveller's Guide*. A useful description of northern Cypriot archeological and historical sites dealt with chronologically rather than in regions, in chapters covering the main historic (and prehistoric) periods. Published in 1994 and therefore in parts a little outdated, it's still a very useful treatment.

Professor A. Bernard Knapp *The Archaeology of Cyprus*. Detailed coverage of the archeology of the island by the prestigious Cambridge World Archaeology series. Bang up to date (published 2013), it covers the story of Cyprus from the earliest times to the end of the Bronze Age, and places the island's development in its Levantine and Aegean context.

★ **Andreas and Judith Stylianou** *The Painted Churches of Cyprus*. Something of a special interest title and now out of print. But there's an excellent PDF available to download from ⓦ images.icon-art.info (the link is at ⓦ tinyurl.com/unescochurches). Put together by husband-and-wife team Andreas and Judith A. Stylianou, this title is invaluable to anybody who wishes to explore the exquisite painted churches of the island, particularly in the Troodos Mountains.

FOOD

There are numerous books about Greek food, but not so many about specifically Cypriot cuisine.

Melek Cella *Cypriot Barbecue Delights and Side Dishes*. A cheap but useful little book of recipes written by a Turkish Cypriot. Given the title, the emphasis is on kebabs, but there are also chapters on pulses, salads and dips. Not a glossy coffee-table book but none the worse for that.

Jan Cutler and Rena Salaman *The Illustrated Food and Cooking of Greece* and *The Complete Book of Greek Cooking*. Clear, practical guides to Greek (not specifically Cypriot) cooking by experienced food writers, one of whom is Greek.

Tessa Kiros *Food from Many Greek Kitchens*. A relatively comprehensive introduction to Greek cooking from an author whose background includes a Greek Cypriot father. The recipes are good, but there are lots of largely irrelevant photographs and the pale blue print is difficult to read.

Helen Tsanos Sheinman *Love, Laughter and Lunch: the Evocative Memories of a Cypriot Family's Journey*. Written by a London-born Greek Cypriot, and more a memoir and cultural outline than a cookbook, but includes lots of her family's recipes. Not cheap, but can be found at a discount online.

WALKING

Brian and Eileen Anderson *North Cyprus Walk and Eat*. Lots of general advice and information on north Cyprus as well as eleven walks with recommended restaurants.

Geoff Daniel *Cyprus Car Tours and Walks*. One of the *Sunflower Landscape* series, this includes seven driving tours and thirty walks, all in the south. The book is somewhat unnecessarily bulked out by bus and service taxi timetables, and is an updated version of a much older book.

Rolf Goetz and Gill Round *Cyprus South and North*. Useful addition to the *Rother Walking Guide series*, and covers both sides of the Green Line – not always the case. However, there are some problems arising from the fact that it's translated from the German.

Greek and Turkish

Neither Greek nor Turkish is a particularly easy language to learn. There are pronunciation pitfalls with both, while Greek also involves an unfamiliar alphabet. Further challenges can arise from the fact that, in Cyprus each language has developed separately from its mainland roots, bringing in divergent dialects and accents. Not only can the visitor struggle with the vernacular they're likely to encounter, but Cypriots speak with machine-gun speed and staccato delivery which can make it difficult to follow. Add to this the fact that most Cypriots speak good English, and it might be thought that only the naturally gifted or preternaturally enthusiastic linguist would make the effort to converse in Greek or Turkish. This would be a mistake. Both Greek and Turkish Cypriots are proud of their history, traditions and language, and will react with delight to any attempt on the part of visitors, however ham-fisted, to at least make an effort. And certainly knowledge of alphabet and pronunciation, together with a few well-chosen words and phrases, will go a long way to helping you to navigate your way from A to B, chat with shopkeepers and restaurant owners, and generally enjoy your visit to the island. We've included the basics in this section but for a wider range of words and phrases and an extensive menu reader check out the relevant Rough Guide phrasebook (see below).

Language courses and phrasebooks

Alison Kakoura and Karen Rich *Talk Greek* (book and 2 CDs). Probably the best product for beginners' essentials in print, and for developing the confidence to try them.

BBC *Greek Language and People*. Not a formal language course, but a good basic introduction to conversational Greek.

Asuman Çelen Pollard & David Pollard *Teach Yourself*

Turkish. The usual Teach Yourself course – well structured and relatively cheap, but the quality of the course book could be improved upon.

Rough Guide Greek/Turkish phrasebooks Current, accurate and pocket-sized, with phrases that you'll actually need and useful two-way glossaries. Free audio samples available at ⓦ roughguides.com.

Greek

Bear in mind that the pronunciation given below is approximate – all you can do is use it as a starting point, then try to copy the locals. Cypriot pronunciation is different from that of mainland Greece. So, for example, the Greeks would pronounce the word for "tea" exactly as it is spelt ("tsai"), whereas the Cypriots would say "chai". But if you pronounce it the Greek way, you'll still be understood (probably with a smile – if a Cypriot pronounced it "tsai", whey would be accused of putting on airs).

Greek alphabet

Α/α alpha (a as in cart)

Β/β beta (v as in very)

Γ/γ gama (somewhere between y as in yacht and g as in grow)

Δ/δ delta (th as in they)

Ε/ε epsilon (e as in sherry)

Ζ/ζ zeta (z as in zebra)

Θ/θ theta (th as in thumb)

H/η eta (ee as in tree)
I/ι yiota (ee as in tree)
K/κ καπα (k as in book)
Λ/λ lamda (l as in bog)
M/μ mi (m as in mat)
N/ν ni (n as in not)
Ξ/ξ ksi (x as in fax)
O/ο omikro (o as in fox)
Π/π pi (somewhere between p as in pot and b as in box)

P/ρ ro (r as in right, but with the r rolled slightly)
Σ/σ/ς sigma (s as in say)
T/t tav (somewhere between t as in tap and d as in dog)
Y/υ ipsilo (ee as in tree)
Φ/φ phi (ph as in photograph)
X/χ hi (ch as in lock, but slightly further forward on the palate)
Ψ/ψ psi (ps as in dipstick)
Ω/ω omega (o as in fox)

Combinations

The pronunciation of some letters can be different if they're combined with others, or according to where they come in the word. Therefore:

AI/αι e as in fey
AY/αυ av or af, depending on what consonant follows them
EI/ει ee as in tree
EY/ευ ev/ef depending on what consonant follows them
OI/οι ee as in tree
OY/ου ou as in tourist

ΓΓ/γγ ng as in bangle
ΜΠ/μπ b as in boat at the start of a word, mb as in Cumbria elsewhere in the word
NT/nt d as in dam at the beginning of the word, nd as in pandemonium elsewhere in the word
ΣΙ/σι sh as in shambles
ΤΣ/τσ ch as in char
ΤΖ/tz ts as in cats

BASIC WORDS AND PHRASES

Hello	Yiassou/yiassas (plural)	How are you?	Ti kanis?
Good morning	Kalimera	My name is…	Me lene….
Good evening	Kalispera	I'm English	Imeh Anglos/Anglitha (m/f)
Good night	Kalinihta		
Today	Simera	Scottish	Skotsezos/Skotseza (m/f)
Tomorrow	Avrio	Irish	Irlanthos/Irlantheza (m/f)
Please	Parakalo	American	Amerikanikos/Amerikana (m/f)
Thank you	Evharisto		
Yes	Nai (ai pronounced as e sound as in egg)	Australian	Afstralos/Afstraleza (m/f)
		I don't speak Greek	Then milao elinika
No	Ohi	Slowly	Siga siga
OK	OK/entaxi	Water	Nero
Excuse me	Signomi (to get past) meh sinkhoriteh (to say sorry)	Car	Aftokinito
		Petrol	Venzini/ bezina (local dialect)
Road	Dromos (d pronounced as th sound)		
		Mechanic	Mihanikos
Left	Aristera	Telephone	Tilefono
Right	Dexia	Doctor	Yiatros
Straight on	efthia	Police	Astinomia
Where is?	Pou ine?	Pharmacy	Farmakio

ACCOMMODATION

Hotel	Xenodohio	One night	Mia nihta
Single room	Mono domatio	Two nights	Dio nihtes
Double room	Diplo domatio	Five nights	Pente nihtes
First floor	Proto patoma	Where is the lift?	Pou ine to asanser?
Second floor	Deftero patoma	Do you have wi-fi?	Ekheteh wi-fi?
Ground floor	Isoyio	What time is breakfast served?	Ti ora ine to proyevma?
I have a reservation	Eho kratisi		

POPULAR DISHES

Moussaka layers of minced lamb and aubergine, with a béchamel sauce.
Souvlakia cubes of lamb, pork or chicken cooked on a charcoal grill.
Stifado rabbit (or sometimes lamb) stew with onions, steeped in wine or vinegar, cooked in a sealed container.
Kleftiko lamb or goat dish cooked in an outdoor oven.
Sheftalia minced pork or lamb with onions, stuffed into the lining of a lamb or pig's stomach, and grilled over charcoal.
Keftedes meatballs.
Goubes minced meat and onions encased in cracked wheat and deep fried.
Koupepia minced meat and rice wrapped in young vine leaves.

Bar	Mbar	**Television**	Tileorasi
Toilet	Toualet	**Key**	Klidi
Air-conditioning	Klimatismos	**Pool**	Pisina
Shower	Ndous		

EATING AND DRINKING

Restaurant	Estiatorio	**please**	parakalo
Café	kafeteria, kafenio	**Knife**	Maheri
Can I have the menu?	Mporo na eho to menou?	**Fork**	Pirouni
What do you recommend?	Ti mou protinede?	**Spoon**	Koutali
Lunch	Mesimeriano	**Waiter**	Servitore
Dinner	Vradino	**Salt**	Alati
White wine	Aspro krasi	**Pepper**	Piperi
Red wine	Kokkino krasi	**Table for two**	Trapezi yia dio
Beer	Mbira	**I don't eat meat**	Then troo kreas
Milk	To gala	**Can I have a coffee please?**	Ena kafe parakalo
Bread	Psomi		
Can I order please?	Mporo na parakalo?	**Coffee types**	Kafe gliko (sweet), medrio (medium), sketo (no sugar)
Chicken	Kotopoulo		
Beef	Vodino		
Lamb	Arni	**Tea**	Tsai
Pork	Hirino kreas	**Dessert**	Gliko
Godopoulo	Chicken	**The food was lovely**	To fayito itane poli oreo
Fish	Psari	**What time do you close?**	Ti ora klinete?
Salad	Salada	**The bill, please**	To logariasmo parakalo
More bread please	Ligo psomi parakalo	**I would like to pay with a credit/debit card**	Thelo na pliroso me karta
A bottle of water/wine	Ena boukali nero/krasi		

NUMBERS

1	Ena	13	Dhekatrís
2	Dio	20	Íkossi
3	Tria	21	Íkossi ena
4	Tessera	30	Trianda
5	Pente	40	Saranda
6	Exi	50	Peninda
7	Epta	60	Exínda
8	Ohto	70	Evdhominda
9	Enea	80	Ogdhonda
10	Deka	90	Eneninda
11	Endheka	100	Ekato
12	Dhodheka		

DAYS AND MONTHS

Monday	Dheftera	April	Aprílis
Tuesday	Tríti	May	Maios
Wednesday	Tetarti	June	Iounios
Thursday	Pempti	July	Ioulios
Friday	Paraskeví	August	Avgoustos
Saturday	Savato	September	Septemvris
Sunday	Kyriakí	October	Oktovris
January	Yennaris	November	Normvris
February	Fleváris	December	Dhekrmvris
March	Martis		

Turkish

Turkish is based on the Roman alphabet and most letters are pronounced as in English. There is no "q", "w" or "x" in Turkish and there are some additional characters. The stress usually falls on the first syllable in the word. In the pronounciation given below we have tried to find the nearest approximation to the Turkish sounds which are easy for English-speakers to pronounce while still enabling you to be understood.

Turkish characters

A/a a cross between a long and short "a" somewhere between the "a" in "man" and the "a" sound in "are".

C/c pronounced as a j as in am

Ç/ç pronounced ch as in church

E/e a short sound as in egg

G/g is a hard g as in go

Ğ/ğ this character is silent but elongates the vowel to either side of it

I/ı pronounced like the er in number

İ/i a short sound as in ink

O/o pronounced as in off

Ö/ö pronounced as in the "or" sound (with a silent "r") in word

S/s is a hissing sound as in seven

Ş/ş pronounced sh as in shut

U/u pronounced as in the oo in cool

Ü/ü pronounced as in the u sound in fuse

Y/y is generally used to separate vowels and creates some slightly different sounds in combination as follows: ay pronounced eye; ey pronounced as in they; iy pronounced ee

BASIC WORDS AND PHRASES

Hello	Merhaba	I don't speak Turkish	Anlamadım/Türkçe anlamıyoru
Good morning	Günaydın		
Good afternoon	İyi günler	My name is ...	Ismim...
Good evening	İyi akşamlar	I'm English/Scottish	İngilizim/Iskoçyalım/
Good night	İyi geceler	Irish/American	Irlandalıyım/Amerikalı/
Please	Lütfen	Australian	Avustralyalım
Thank you	Teşekkür ederim	I want	İstiyorum
Yes	Evet	When?	Ne zaman?
No	Hayır	Today	Bugun
How are you?	Nasılsınız? nasılsın?	Tomorrow	Yarın
Excuse me	Pardon (to get past) Özür dilerim (to say sorry)	Where?	Nerede?
		Be careful!	dikkat!
I'm fine	İyiyim	Pharmacy	Eczane

AT THE HOTEL

Hotel	Otel	Do you have a double room?	Bir/iki/üç gecelik çift?
Pension, inn	Pansiyon		
Campsite	Kamping	for one/two/three nights	yataklı odanızvar mı
Do you have a room?	Boş odanız var mı?	for one/two weeks	bir/iki haftalık
Single/double/triple	Tek/çift/üç kişilik	with an extra bed	ilâve yataklı

with a double bed	fransiz yataklı	Can I see it?	Bakabilirmiyim?
with a shower	duşlu	I have a booking	Reservasyonum var
Hot water	Sıcak su	Do you have wi-fi?	Kablosuz var?
Cold water	Soğuk su	Toilet	Tuvalet

AT THE RESTAURANT

Restaurant	Lokanta, restoran	Spoon	Kaşık
Café	kafeh, pastane	Bill	Hesap
Lunch	To yevma	Service charge	Servis ücreti
Dinner	To thipno	Spicy kebab	Adana kebap
Water	Su	Minced kebab	Beyti
Milk	Sut	Rotisseried kebab	Döner kebap
Beer	Bira	Shish kebab	Şiş kebap
Wine	Şarap	Meatballs	Köfte
Tea	Çay	Lamb	Kuzu
Coffee	Kahve	Beef	Sığır
Glass	Bardak	Fish	Balık
Another...	Başka bir...	Squid	Kalamar
Plate	Tabak	Swordfish	Kılıç
Knife	Bıçak	Tuna	Orkinos
Fork	Çatal	Honey and nut pie	Baklava

NUMBERS

1	Bir (beer)	12	On iki
2	Iki (icky)	13	On üç
3	Uç (ooch)	20	Yirmi
4	Dört (dirt)	30	Otuz
5	Beş (besh)	40	Kırk
6	Altı (al-ter)	50	Elli
7	Yedi (yea-dee)	60	Altmış
8	Sekiz (seck-is)	70	Yetmiş
9	Dokuz (dock-uz)	80	Seksen
10	On (on)	90	Doksan
11	On bir	100	Yüz

DAYS AND MONTHS

Monday	Pazartesi	April	Nisan
Tuesday	Salı	May	Mayıs
Wednesday	Çarşamba	June	Haziran
Thursday	Perşembe	July	Temmuz
Friday	Cuma	August	Ağustos
Saturday	Cumartesi	September	Eylül
Sunday	Pazar	October	Ekim
January	Ocak	November	Kasım
February	Subat	December	Aralk
March	Mart		

Glossary

Acropolis Ancient hilltop, usually fortified.

Aga Minor Ottoman rank, commonly used as a term of respect. Comes after the name.

Agora Central market area of a town.

Amphorae Storage containers with large handles and a pointed base, usually made of clay. Smaller than *pitharia* which they complemented.

Apse Curved recess at the eastern end of a church.

Agios/Agia/Agii Saint – masculine, feminine and plural. Widely used in iconography and place names.

Basilica Colonnaded hall-type church based on earlier Roman types, common in Cyprus.

Bedestan Covered market.

Bey Like Aga, a minor Ottoman title.

Cami(i) Mosque

Classical period In Cyprus, 480–323 BC.

Conch Shell-like half-dome above the apse, often decorated with frescoes.

CTO Cyprus Tourist Organization.

Domatia Rooms (especially for rent).

Dragoman Interpreter or guide under the Ottoman empire.

Dromos Street, or the ramp leading down into a subterranean tomb.

Drum Cylindrical vertical section supporting the dome of a church, often with windows. Also one of the sections from which columns were constructed.

EOKA Ethnikí Orgánosis Kipriakoú Agónos (National Organization of Cypriot Struggle) associated with the fight for independence from Britain. **EOKA-B**, a later incarnation, which fought mainly against Turkish Cypriots.

Forum Market and meeting place in a Roman town – equivalent to the Greek Agora.

Frieze Sculpted figures around a temple.

Hamam Turkish Bath.

Han/Hani (sometimes Khan) Hostel for travellers.

Hypocaust Underfloor heating system.

Iconoclasm Eighth-and ninth-century Byzantine movement which declared icons to be idolatrous. Led to the destruction of many.

Ikonostasis Ornate screen between nave and altar of an Orthodox church, upon which are hung (at least three) icons.

Imam Prayer leader in a mosque.

Kafenio Café or coffee house, often centre of a community, patronized mainly by men.

Kale Castle.

Kastro Castle or fortified hill.

Katholicon Monastery church.

Kato Lower, used as prefix for town or village.

Kilise Church.

Krater Large, often two-handed and ornate, drinking vessel.

Lusignan Dynasty Rule by the heirs of Guy de Lusignan 1192–1489 AD.

Medrese School for Islamic religious instruction.

Mihrab Niche within a mosque indicating the direction of Mecca.

Mimbar Pulpit in a mosque.

Mitropolis Orthodox Cathedral of a large town or city.

Moni Monastery or convent.

Mukhtar Village headman.

Narthex Entrance hall or vestibule, often added after a church was built. If there are more than one, the outermost is the exonarthex.

Nave The main body of a church.

Necropolis Literally "city of the dead", made up of above-ground tombs outside the city limits.

Neos/Nea/Neo New (masculine/feminine/neuter) Often used in names of towns or villages.

Nymphaeum Rear wall of a formal fountain, often with statues.

Odeion Small Greek or Roman theatre.

Paleos/Palea/Paleo Greek for "Old" (masculine/ feminine/neuter).

Panagia Virgin Mary.

Pandokrator Figure of Christ with a bible in one hand and the fingers of the other extended in blessing.

Paşa (sometimes pasha) Honorary Ottoman title, follows the name.

Pitharia Large earthenware jars used to store wine or olive oil.

Platia Square in a town or village.

Rhyton Drinking vessel, often in the shape of a horn.

Sadirvan (ablution fountain).

Stele Ancient inscribed tombstone.

Stoa Colonnaded walkway around the edge of the Agora or Forum.

Sufi Followers of an ascetic Sufi Muslim order, of which the best known is that of the dervishes.

Tavli Backgammon, commonly played in coffee houses.

Tekke Sufi gathering place or shrine.

Tesserae Cubes of different coloured stone or glass used in the making of mosaics.

TMT Türk Mukavemet Teşkilatı (Turkish Resistance Organization).

TRNC Turkish Republic of North Cyprus (also called the KKTC).

Small print and index

A ROUGH GUIDE TO ROUGH GUIDES

Published in 1982, the first Rough Guide – to Greece – was a student scheme that became a publishing phenomenon. Mark Ellingham, a recent graduate in English from Bristol University, had been travelling in Greece the previous summer and couldn't find the right guidebook. With a small group of friends he wrote his own guide, combining a highly contemporary, journalistic style with a thoroughly practical approach to travellers' needs.

The immediate success of the book spawned a series that rapidly covered dozens of destinations. And, in addition to impecunious backpackers, Rough Guides soon acquired a much broader readership that relished the guides' wit and inquisitiveness as much as their enthusiastic, critical approach and value-for-money ethos.

These days, Rough Guides include recommendations from budget to luxury and cover more than 200 destinations around the globe, as well as producing an ever-growing range of eBooks and apps.

Visit **roughguides.com** to see our latest publications.

Rough Guide credits

Editor: Andy Turner
Layout: Anita Singh
Cartography: Lokamata Sahu
Picture editor: Mark Thomas
Proofreader: Susanne Hillen
Managing editors: Keith Drew, Monica Woods
Assistant editor: Dipika Dasgupta
Production: Charlotte Cade
Cover design: Nicole Newman, Anita Singh

Editorial assistant: Olivia Rawes
Senior pre-press designer: Dan May
Design director: Scott Stickland
Travel publisher: Joanna Kirby
Digital travel publisher: Peter Buckley
Operations coordinator: Helen Blount
Publishing director (Travel): Clare Currie
Commercial manager: Gino Magnotta
Managing director: John Duhigg

Publishing information

This first edition published June 2013 by
Rough Guides Ltd,
80 Strand, London WC2R 0RL
11, Community Centre, Panchsheel Park,
New Delhi 110017, India
Distributed by the Penguin Group
Penguin Books Ltd,
80 Strand, London WC2R 0RL
Penguin Group (USA)
375 Hudson Street, NY 10014, USA
Penguin Group (Australia)
250 Camberwell Road, Camberwell,
Victoria 3124, Australia
Penguin Group (NZ)
67 Apollo Drive, Mairangi Bay, Auckland 1310,
New Zealand
Penguin Group (South Africa)
Block D, Rosebank Office Park, 181 Jan Smuts Avenue,
Parktown North, Gauteng, South Africa 2193
Rough Guides is represented in Canada by Tourmaline
Editions Inc. 662 King Street West, Suite 304, Toronto,
Ontario M5V 1M7
Printed in Malaysia by Vivar Printing Sdn Bhd

© Jos Simon, 2013
Maps © Rough Guides
No part of this book may be reproduced in any form
without permission from the publisher except for the
quotation of brief passages in reviews.
280pp includes index
A catalogue record for this book is available from the
British Library
ISBN: 978-1-40538-965-5

Help us update

We've gone to a lot of effort to ensure that the first edition
of **The Rough Guide to Cyprus** is accurate and up-to-date.
However, things change – places get "discovered", opening
hours are notoriously fickle, restaurants and rooms raise
prices or lower standards. If you feel we've got it wrong
or left something out, we'd like to know, and if you can
remember the address, the price, the hours, the phone
number, so much the better.

Please send your comments with the subject line
"**Rough Guide Cyprus Update**" to ✉ mail@uk.roughguides
.com. We'll credit all contributions and send a copy of the
next edition (or any other Rough Guide if you prefer) for
the very best emails.

Find more travel information, connect with fellow
travellers and book your trip at ⊕ roughguides.com

ABOUT THE AUTHOR

Welshman **Jos Simon** first fell in love with Cyprus after travelling across Europe in a battered old van as a student. Now, some thirty years later, he has a Cypriot wife and makes regular trips to the island, particularly his wife's home village of Nissou, south of Lefkosia. He's at his happiest walking in the Troodos and Kyrenia mountains or relaxing over a frappe (or occasional *zivania*) at a harbourside café. Jos has written widely about other Mediterranean destinations and is also the author of the *Rough Guide to Yorkshire*.

Acknowledgements

Jos Simon As well as the countless individuals across the island, who helped in the research of this book, sincere and heartfelt thanks are due to the following: Keith Drew and the rest of the Rough Guide team and in particular, Andy Turner for sympathetic and long-suffering editing. Lillian Panayi of the Cyprus Tourism Organisation, June Field of Three Sixty Degrees, Jill Guest of Wave Media Partners and the North Cyprus Tourism Centre for information, advice, letters of introduction, help in accessing a range of attractions, assistance with the language section and

practical support in a whole host of other ways. Sarah Belcher and Anthony Sebastian of Travel PR and their client Sunvil for providing invaluable help with accommodation. As ever, to my wife Doulla for help with the research trips, to the rest of my family (Catherine, Matt, Lazaros, Eliza, Arianwen, Daniel and Chris) for forbearance and support, and to my Kakoulli and Dafnis in-laws for information and insight, in particular Anna and Lazaros Kakoulli, not only for their many years of friendship, but also for putting me up and putting up with me.

Photo credits

All photos © Rough Guides except the following:
(Key: t-top; c-centre; b-bottom; l-left; r-right)

p.1 4Corners: Spila Riccardo
p.2 Getty Images: Hugh Sitton
p.4 Alamy: Jon Arnold
p.6 Alamy: Jack Sullivan
p.7 Alamy: David Robertson
p.8 4Corners: Huber Johanna
p.12 Alamy: LOOK Die Bildagentur der Fotografen GmbH
p.13 Alamy: Plamen Peev (tl). Chris Christoforou (tr). Axiom Photographic Agency/Axiom Photo Agency (c). SuperStock: Travel Library Limited (b)
p.14 Axiom Photographic Agency (t). imagebroker: Rawdon Wyatt (c). Alamy: Prisma Bildagentur AG (b).
p.15 Getty Images: De Agostini Picture Library (tl). Axiom Photographic Agency (tr). Alamy: MARKA (br).
p.17 Getty Images: Michael Breuer (t). SuperStock: Norbert Probst (c)
p.18 Chris Christoforou (t). Alamy: LOOK Die Bildagentur der Fotografen GmbH (c). Nagele Stock (b).
p.19 Alamy: Danita Delimont (t). David Robertson (b)
p.20 Alamy: James Schutte
p.42 Alamy: World Pictures
p.45 Alamy: JoeFox Cyprus
p.63 Alamy: LOOK Die Bildagentur der Fotografen GmbH (t). Jack Sullivan (b)
p.71 Alamy: JoeFox Cyprus

p.80 Alamy: LOOK Die Bildagentur der Fotografen GmbH
p.91 Alamy: JoeFox Cyprus
p.105 Alamy: Danita Delimon (bl)
p.108 Alamy: Xenia Demetriou
p.111 Corbis: Nathan Benn
p.127 Getty Images: Hugh Sitton (t). Nicholas Pitt (b)
p.144 Getty Images: Travel Ink
p.147 Alamy: Patrick E Ford
p.153 SuperStock: Stefan Auth
p.168 Alamy: Iconotec
p.171 Alamy: LOOK Die Bildagentur der Fotografen GmbH
p.183 Chris Christoforou (t, bl, br)
p.194 Alamy: LatitudeStock
p.197 Chris Christoforou
p.209 Alamy: imagebroker (t). Alamy: Life File Photo Library Ltd (b).
p.237 Getty Images: Laura Boushnak
p.248 The Sylvia Ioannou Foundation

Front cover Konnos Bay, Protaras © imagebroker: SuperStock
Back cover Nissi Beach © imagebroker: Alamy (t). Panagia Chrysopolitissa near Pafos (bl). Walking in the Akamas (br) © Axiom Photographic Agency

Index

Maps are marked in grey